The Moral Life
and the Ethical Life

Cursed is every man that has hope in man.

JER. 17 : 5

No one can suffice to himself either for beginning or for completing any good work.

ST. AUGUSTINE

ELISEO VIVAS

The Moral Life
and the Ethical Life

THE UNIVERSITY OF CHICAGO PRESS

The University of Chicago Press, Chicago 37
Cambridge University Press, London, N.W. 1, England
The University of Toronto Press, Toronto 5, Canada

Gift - Publisher

99348

AUG 3 1 1960

BJ
1011
V 85

50-10775
9-19-60

For
DOROTHY

PREFACE

WHAT name shall I give the doctrine propounded in this essay on moral philosophy? Had not the name been pre-empted by a distinguished school of philosophy I would have liked to call my central affiliation "personalistic," since one of the cardinal ideas of this essay is that "person" is an axiological and not a "scientific" category, in the positivistic sense of the term "science." But personalists in the United States stem from a tradition to which I am somewhat alien. I have learned a great deal from them, for which I am deeply grateful; but I do not have the right to enlist under their banner without giving them the chance to pass on my credentials and to reject me if they see fit.

I would have liked also to call myself an "empiricist." I have tried to keep my eyes on the facts of the moral life, and when my own experience seemed limited, I did not hesitate to go not only to the moralists but even to the theologians and to the poets. I believe that experience is the plasma of relevant, meaningful thinking. However, the term "empiricist" would be even more misleading than the term "personalist." I would use it in a homely, nontechnical way, but it has been pre-empted by men given to method-olatrous, a priori lucubrations about the possibility of extending the methods of the positive sciences to all fields of human interest. The result is a positivistic scientificism which seems to me to be inimical to the humanistic liberality of mind which I believe we have the right to demand of students of philosophy.

I would like to call myself an "existentialist" in the sense in which Kierkegaard used the term, because I share his distrust of academic systems. But today the term designates, in the mind of the educated public, a philosophy which is imported from Paris and which is supposed to be gloomy and must, therefore, be false. In fairness to this philosophy and to myself, I would not want to be identified with it. I do not object to its alleged gloominess, since I have nothing but the deepest contempt for the shallow, Philistine optimism of our world; but I object to Sartre's atheism and his total lack of Christian love. All I would mean by the term "ex-

istentialism" is the refusal to allow the content of human experience
to be sacrificed to any purely intellectual ideal, even that of clarity.
Clarity or any other intellectual ideal is a desirable quality of
thought, but the clarity which is today the ideal of postivistic
philosophy seems to me nothing but thinness of content.

I am forced, however, to call myself something, because a man
who does not insist on a label of his own invention—any kind of
label, so long as it is of his own choosing—is merely inviting those
with whom he disagrees to break his bones with the names they
will choose for him. Let me therefore call myself an "axiological
realist"—the term is vague enough not to cramp my growth if
there is any in store for me, and yet damaging enough in the eyes of
those with whom I disagree to meet their needs for an epithet
should they want one. I believe that the moral man *discovers* the
values he espouses, in the same way in which the scientist or the
logician discovers the laws of his science. There is a difference, of
course, between the laws of nature and laws of morality and of
logic, but the difference does not concern us here. Values are real
and antecedent to our discovery of them; this is what I mean when
I say that they have "ontic status." They are a peculiar kind of fact,
since they possess "requiredness" to which we respond, and it is
this aspect of value that is the source of the moral imperative.
Human beings are animals, but they are also endowed with personality; and it is their possession of personality that marks the
radical distinction between them and the other animals. By "person" I do not mean what is meant by the term in the dawning science of "personality," in which psychologists and social scientists
are beginning to be interested. In my terminology the only aspect
of man that positive science can study is the "self." The human
self is a valuing animal, but that he ought to value this rather than
that is something which positive science cannot tell him. A "person" is constituted by the values which the self espouses and which
he is able to espouse because the spirit which inheres in him is
capable of objectivity, whereas the selves of the lower animals are
not.

I do not know whether I have borrowed some of these ideas and
the way in which they have been elaborated; perhaps I have borrowed all of them. My concern is not with being original but with
doing justice to essential facts of the moral life which naturalistic

philosophers, as I try to show in Part I, misconceive or ignore.

Some ten or twelve years ago I began to see that the philosophy which until then I had uncritically accepted and which I thought of as the "new naturalism" could not give an adequate account of certain dimensions of human experience which circumstances suddenly thrust within my purview. For a few years after I began to suspect the inadequacy of naturalism, I continued to think of myself as a naturalist; I could not see the validity of any alternative and vainly hoped that the leaders of the naturalistic movement would acknowledge the need to broaden their vision. I took seriously what the founders of contemporary naturalism have said about the need for the progressive correction of empirical truth. I therefore expected that the social crisis which came to a head with the holocaust of World War II would lead to a rebirth of philosophy; and I hoped that the limited insights of the American philosophies (the idealisms no less than the naturalisms) which developed in the age of the "Robber Barons," with their shallow vitalistic optimism, would be enlarged in the light of the tragic experience of our own days. It is natural that until our day American philosophy should have neglected the tragic dimension of experience; neither a man nor a people can take tragedy seriously in the optimistic flush of youthful expansion. But since 1932, or at least since the last years of the thirties, we cannot plead, as an excuse for juvenile innocence, the limitations of our happy experience. Hitler, Franco, Stalin, and our own physicists and bacteriologists have forced us to look at the reality behind the optimistic mask of our history.

My hope that naturalism would broaden its horizons was vain. What at last led me to take the difficult step of giving up my old intellectual loyalties and losing many loved friends—for I knew that they would not forgive me my defection—was the conviction which slowly gripped me that the limitations of naturalism spring from a peculiar anesthesia from which naturalists suffer, which is shared in greater or lesser degree today by all those men who refuse, as they put it, to lose their nerve and who have no radical quarrel with the secularistic direction of the Zeitgeist. It was not merely a question of insensibility to the tragic dimension of existence; it was something deeper and more extensive, although more vague. My quarrel with the naturalists, I came clearly to see, is the quarrel of a man radically opposed to the present drift of historical events and therefore unsympathetic with those who employ their talent in the manufacture of an apologetic for the direction of contemporary history. I would not for a minute pretend solidarity with men who do not realize that one of the essential marks of decency today is to be ashamed of being a man of the twentieth century. No one can, of course, advocate turning back toward the Middle Ages. So far as students of philosophy are concerned, all I advocate is that they do not play yes men to the age but that they assume the role of critics of it, since this is the ineluctable duty of anyone who takes his thinking seriously.

Once I clearly perceived that at the heart of naturalism is to be found an inability to grasp the meaning of certain essential aspects of human experience, I began to search for a better philosophy. I searched in books that I had until then more or less consciously neglected and in authors whom I had arrogantly spurned or whom, if I had read, I had misunderstood. Ravenously hungry, I swallowed fast and greedily; and, because I was reading against time and for the sake of something infinitely more important to me than my "scholarship" and because the last thing that I then had in mind was the preparation of a book, I do not now remember how much I borrowed from each of the books I then read. There must be many writers whom I have more or less forgotten and from whom I must have helped myself generously. But there are some to whom I feel that my debt is so large that I cannot help being constantly aware of it. Bergson, whose *Two Sources* I did not seriously read until 1940, was the first to show me the basic importance of the distinction between what I now call "the moral life" and "the ethical life." In so far as I had grasped it in my naturalistic days, in the form of the Kantian disjunction between the hypothetical and categorical imperatives, I had done my best to deny the validity of the distinction. The problems to which Bergson's dichotomy gave rise led me back to Kant's moral philosophy, for which I had always had a grudging admiration in my naturalistic days. Kierkegaard, whom I began to read passionately in the late thirties, pointed out to me the importance of the concept of the "crisis" for the completion of human experience. Dostoevski showed me that the inward reality of faith is compatible with an absolutely clear grasp of the problem of evil. Berdyaev and Francisco Romero taught me the importance of the category "person," and Scheler and Hartmann helped me to rid myself of the naturalistic prejudice that denies ontic status to value. Professor Brand Blanshard's powerful dialectic ripped off what remained of my dogmatic behaviorism. From Kafka I learned the limitations of positivistic empiricism for those who take one of the essential tasks of philosophy to be, as I do, the definition of the destiny of man. Bernanos first, and St. Augustine afterward, helped me to recollect what constitutes the inwardness of the religious experience, with which, as an adolescent, I had been intimately acquainted but toward which, as I came close to my twenties, I became hardened and indifferent. From a historian—because I must confess that I am as little ashamed to learn from historians about my problems as I am from storytellers and poets—I learned what the most serious and urgent task of philosophy is; it was not until I read Cochrane's *Christianity and Classical Culture* that the relation which I had always vaguely believed to hold between history and philosophy became fully clear to me. And from Urban first, and from Cassirer afterward, I learned the limitations of positivistic semiotics.

But to consider influences and debts and to make acknowledgments to writers whose books have helped me is to tell half the story. I have learned as much from direct contact with my honest teachers or with my colleagues and friends—including those of my students who have honored me by demanding my best from me—as I have from books. Thus in my graduate days I learned to envisage the moral problem in terms of the relation between morality and brute force from my beloved teachers, E. B. McGilvary and the late F. C. Sharp. The three years that I spent at the University of Chicago, teaching in the College and in the Department of Philosophy, turned out to be the most fruitful years of my life of study. Close intercourse with a brilliant group of colleagues in the Department of Philosophy and in the College was vitally stimulating, and I owe them a debt of gratitude that I intend not to forget. Frequent conversations with my friends Professors Ruth and William O'Meara and with younger men and with students—Earl Edgar, Saul Bellow, Martin Gardner, John Meyer, Frederick Camper, Gertrude Jaeger, William Earle, and others—and, during my last year at Chicago, with the brilliant poet-philosopher, Henry Rago, helped me along the road to clarity. But it is not in Chicago alone that I have been fortunate to find friends and students from whom I have been able to learn. Wherever I have chanced to be, I have found them, and their names would fill one or more pages, were I to cite them in this Preface.

To my wife, Dorothy Gant Vivas, I would not attempt to express the fulness of my debt. Not only did she maintain the home conditions essential to the student and help me unsparingly with the merely mechanical labors of composition, but she encouraged me daily and with her perspicuous criticism helped me avoid serious philosophic blunders and forced me to improve on statements that were not adequate to my intentions and on ideas that were inchoate. To many of my colleagues at the Ohio State University I am also deeply indebted. Professors M. O. Percival, Harold R. Walley, and John Harold Wilson, of the Department of English, and Dr. Marvin Fox, of the Department of Philosophy, discussed with me my ideas and helped me envisage more clearly their implications. They also read the manuscript and offered many useful suggestions for its philosophic improvement. Professor Wilson labored selflessly over Parts II and III of the manuscript and helped me to dispel the verbal fog that made them impenetrable in places. Through the vital interest of Dean Frederic W. Heimberger, of the College of Arts and Sciences, and of Professor James F. Fullington, chairman of the English Department, I was able to secure the invaluable and expert editorial assistance of Mrs. Marshall Dasher, whose meticulous and intelligent criticism of the manuscript greatly improved it. They also provided me with the help of Mrs. H. M. Stevens, who typed the final manuscript. Professor Fullington generously relieved me from my teaching duties in the Department of English for the fall quarter of 1949, thus permitting me to complete the manuscript. My friends in the Philosophy Department gave me encouragement, and Professor Albert Avey, its chairman, also put at my disposal the services of the secretary of the department, Mrs. H. Donald Blair, who typed an earlier version of the essay. If this essay has value, I know how much I owe those who have generously helped. Its faults and shortcomings arise from the limitations of the writer.

ELISEO VIVAS

DEPARTMENTS OF PHILOSOPHY AND OF ENGLISH
THE OHIO STATE UNIVERSITY
April 13, 1950

ACKNOWLEDGMENTS

FOR permission to quote from the book or books mentioned in parentheses immediately after their names, the author wishes to thank the following publishing companies: Cambridge University Press (*Principia Ethica*, by George Edward Moore); Columbia University Press (*Naturalism and the Human Spirit*, edited by Yervant H. Krikorian); J. M. Dent and Sons, Ltd. (*Letters from the Underworld*, by Feodor Dostoevski); Doubleday, Doran and Company, Inc. (*Lord Jim*, by Joseph Conrad); Garden City Publishing Company (*A General Introduction to Psychoanalysis*, by Sigmund Freud); Harper and Brothers (*Touchstone for Ethics*, by T. H. Huxley and Julian Huxley; *Personality*, by Gardner Murphy); Harvard University Press (*Philosophy in a New Key*, by Susanne K. Langer; *General Theory of Value*, by Ralph Barton Perry); Henry Holt and Company (*Ethics*, by John Dewey and James H. Tufts [1925 ed.]; *Ethics*, by John Dewey and James H. Tufts [rev. ed.]); Alfred A. Knopf (*Man and His Works*, by Melville J. Herskovits); Longmans, Green and Company (*The Will To Believe*, by William James; *Conscience and Its Problems*, by Kenneth E. Kirk); the Macmillan Company (*Philosophy for the Future*, edited by Roy Wood Sellars, V. J. McGill, and Marvin Farber); W. W. Norton and Company, Inc. (*The Psychoanalytic Theory of Neurosis*, by Otto Fenichel; *New Introductory Lectures on Psychoanalysis*, by Sigmund Freud); Oxford University Press (*Moby-Dick*, by Herman Melville; *The Foundations of Ethics*, by W. David Ross); Prentice-Hall, Inc. (*Problems of Ethics*, by Moritz Schlick); Princeton University Press (*The Sickness unto Death*, by S. Kierkegaard); Charles Scribner's Sons (*The American Scene*, by Henry James; *The Last Puritan*, by George Santayana); University of Buffalo Publications in Philosophy (*Philosophic Thought in France and the United States*, edited by Marvin Farber); University of Chicago Press (*Theory of Valuation*, by John Dewey); University of North Carolina Press (*A Scientific Theory of Culture and Other Essays*, by Bronislaw Malinowski); Yale University Press (*Ethics and Language*, by Charles Stevenson).

I am indebted to *Commentary* for permission to quote from John Dewey's article, "Philosophy's Future in Our Scientific Age," in Volume VIII (1949); to *Ethics* for permission to quote from Charner Perry's articles, "Sound Ethics and Confused Language," in Volume LV (1945), and "The Arbitrary as Basis for Rational Morality," in Volume XLIII (1933); and to the *Philosophical Review* for permission to quote from D. W. Gotshalk's article, "Causality and Emergence," in Volume LI (1949), and D. C. Williams' article, "Ethics as Pure Postulate," in Volume XLII (1933).

I also wish to thank the editor of *Ethics* for permission to use material from my article, "Animadversions on Naturalistic Ethics" (April, 1946), and from "Julian Huxley's Evolutionary Ethics" (July, 1948); the editor of the *Philosophy of Science* for permission to use material from my article, "Value and Fact" (October, 1939); the editor of *Sewanee Review* for permission to use material from my articles, "Two Notes on the New Naturalism" (July, 1948) and "Philosophy for 1984" (summer, 1950); and the editor of *Western Review* for permission to use material from my articles, "Don Alonzo to the Road Again" (winter, 1947) and "The Objective Basis of Criticism" (summer, 1948).

TABLE OF CONTENTS

xv

PART II

THE MORAL LIFE

PART III

THE ETHICAL LIFE

NOTES

INDEX

INTRODUCTION: MORAL PHILOSOPHY
IS A "PRACTICAL SCIENCE"

A MAN faced with the need to make a practical decision may ask himself, "What ought I to do; what is the right thing for me to do?" Ordinarily this question is asked in face of a specific perplexity and within the context of more or less accepted notions of the right and of the good. The situation in which he finds himself may be perplexing because the soul is divided between incompatible goods or because he cannot clearly foresee the consequences of the alternatives which suggest themselves to him. He would know well enough how to choose, could he be certain of the remoter consequences of the various alternatives; but there are times when a man does not know which of two alternatives is the one that ought to be followed. He is baffled not because he cannot foresee the consequences of the alternatives but because he does not know which he ought to choose. Such experiences are fortunately rare, but the student of moral philosophy must consider them. Even in cultures which, compared with ours, move in deeply cut grooves of custom, situations arise in which men cannot decide by facile rule of thumb what they ought to do. At every turn of the road, every day, men are forced to ask themselves what they ought to do. The question always calls for a modicum of reflection. It may demand only enough reflection to decide which of two well-established rules has the more urgent claim; the question as to whether the rule itself is adequate or valid may not arise. But in any case the decision, when it is finally arrived at, falls within the scope of moral reflection.

The context within which the perplexity arises sometimes forces a man to challenge the validity of rules by which he has customarily guided himself in similar situations. The rule may have lost its power over him because social changes have occurred, creating urgent needs which were not foreseen when the rules first came into existence, or because he has somehow come to believe that they were instituted, or at least are now used, to justify and maintain iniquities which, without the reverence with which custom invests

1

them, would not dare argue their claims.When this happens, a man is torn by a deeper conflict than usual, one much more difficult to resolve than were those mentioned above. But the question that he must answer is no different, at least formally, from the others, since he still asks himself, "What ought I to do?" In respect of content it is somewhat different, since new rules must now be found by which to judge the validity of the customary rules that are challenged; but the question, although perhaps involving more factors and calling for more prudence in order to resolve it satisfactorily, is nevertheless just as practical as the first. It is true that, in order to arrive at a practical decision, this latter question involves one in a more sustained theoretical effort than did the former; but the difference is one of degree, since the questions maintain their predominantly practical orientation and come to fruition in a decision to act.

It is possible, however, to engage in another kind of moral reflection which we must consider more thoroughly than the previous one—the kind in which we shall be engaged in this essay. We shall ask the same questions, at least initially, that we have just considered. But we shall not be satisfied merely to inquire what we ought to do or whether the rules ought or ought not to apply in a given concrete situation. Now another interest takes control of the direction of the inquiry: a theoretical need, a desire to know more thoroughly and abstractly and extensively than was known before what the presuppositions and principles are which govern the ways in which moral perplexities are resolved; what the source of our moral decisions is, and what the rules that govern them are; what the nature of these rules is, and how they are justified.

Why men engage in this kind of reflection is not a question to which I have been able to find a satisfactory answer. Certainly no practical situation by itself, in terms of its own intrinsic demands, need ever give rise to the generalized speculative activity which is called "philosophy." It is a safe guess to assume that moral philosophy is initiated, in part at least, by interest in moral questions of an immediate, intimate—one may even say subjective—nature. But why in the majority of men do practical difficulties lead to their resolution, whereas they lead at least some men in some cultures further and further into purely abstract questions, in regard to which the practical man contemptuously says that they "cut no ice"—this is a question that awaits a satisfactory answer. None of the answers that my reading has suggested seem to go beyond what is, after all, but the well-known historical and sociological fact, namely, that some cultures make of pure speculation a dominant interest. But why do they? Is it a matter of race, climate, geography, or social organization? Or is it the merest cultural accident? Here is a question on which the sociology of knowledge could profitably busy itself as soon as it is done clearing its philosophical presuppositions and developing in an a priori way its empirical method. Perhaps the best answer to our question is the simplest and oldest—that men by nature desire to know. But if they do, it should be remembered that most cultures—whether by art or nature, I do not know—manage to suppress man's desire for philosophy.

Whatever the reason that he sets out on such an inquiry, the man asking the second kind of question or, rather, asking moral questions in this second way not only desires to know, at the philosophic level, but also desires to know about moral matters, which is to say that he has also an intrinsic and living interest in the morally correct resolution of the practical problems which constitute the subject matter of moral philosophy. He is not "a pure knower," but he is a knower and not merely a practical man bent on resolving practical perplexities. And it is his business to balance somehow both interests, either of which, allowed to gain primacy, would totally exclude the other. I see no safe way in which one can legislate in an a priori manner the degree of immediacy or of intrinsic interest which the moral philosopher must retain toward practical problems in order to insure correct results. But that his theoretical and his practical interest must share his energies I am certain.

The reason for the preceding observations will not escape those acquainted with our present philosophical situation and with two serious diseases with which philosophy is at present afflicted: "practicalism," as I shall call one, denies the validity and importance of theoretical inquiries that go beyond the most immediate practical interest; and "purism," as I shall call the other, attempts to insulate philosophy from all practical interests and to make of it a pure cognitive activity. With practicalism we need not concern ourselves seriously. As philosophy becomes academic and tends to repudiate its responsibility to the culture in which it flourishes, the layman in need of wisdom and vision turns to evangelistic practicalists, who confirm him in his myopic prejudice that the exclusive end of moral philosophy is actually to direct social activity toward the concrete and immediate improvement of social conditions. But, since there is no way of knowing except by arduous philosophical criticism whether the ends to which a reformer would lead us represent genuine improvement, the practicalist's impatience with theory is at best hasty. Shallow practicalism—and the expression is pleonastic—can be vicious in its consequences, since the evangelist appeals in the name of philosophy to men who are incapable of envisaging the relationship between the work of the mind and the complex activities which constitute a civilization. Often instinct with the hidden hatred of sustained intellectual effort, he encourages those who happen to listen to him in the name of reasonableness to dispense with reason.

The practicalist, often dubbing himself a "pragmatist," calls on James and on Dewey for sanction; but anyone who has read the works of the founding fathers of pragmatism would never make the blunder of supposing that practicalists are genuine pragmatists. Neither James nor Dewey actually sanctions the shallowness and vulgarity of the practicalistic evangelist. The energy and passion which James, Dewey, and the other founders of pragmatism put into abstruse theoretical work is sufficient proof of this. Pragmatism is a *theory* whose basic category is "action"; it is a *metaphysic* which elucidates and justifies the secular orientation of a culture during a certain period of its historical development. It does this by elevating what are only ephemeral and accidental historical traits into a generic description of universal man and of his destiny. It gives a false picture of man because it abstracts from the culture in which it has flourished certain obvious features and tendencies and universalizes them, ignoring the historical evidence about the nature of man. I intend in the following pages to animadvert strongly upon it; but to charge it with the lack of vision of the practicalist is not fair. Had the founders of pragmatism felt about speculation as some of those who dub themselves pragmatists do, they would never have founded a philosophic school. In the pragmatic movement, this hatred of theory marks the triumph of the epigones.[1]

The harm which the practicalist does is done to the world at large, by depriving it of the benefit of a thorough analysis of the implications and presuppositions of its activity; but the harm which the purist does is done to the philosophy which he pretends to serve. There is a sense, however, in which it is not fair to charge philosophers with sins which, being part of a social organism much larger than themselves, they cannot hope effectively to control. Purism in philosophy does no more than express the specialization which shapes our institutions as our society becomes more and more complex. The effect of specialization on philosophy is to turn it into an autotelic activity and, if I may borrow for my purposes a barbarism of the sociologist, to "bureaucratize" the philosopher. The process of bureaucratization begins when philosophers are given professional status and economic independence. This loosens their ties to their society and weakens their sense of responsibility for their culture. For the pride of socially useful accomplishment the philosophic bureaucrat substitutes pride of craftsmanship for its own sake. The result in philosophy is called "academicism." When the tendency toward academicism is as strong as it is today, it achieves a more or less complete break between the autotelic activity of the academic philosopher and the social world, to meet whose needs the discipline was originally developed. The professional philosopher develops his own outlook, and by degrees his professional and private vision becomes effectively insulated so that he can use it to build his own world. His preoccupations, his practical commitments, his ambitions, are not those of the ordinary citizen. No doubt the isolation sharpens the critical faculty of the philosopher toward his own pure discipline, but it blunts his interest in other disciplines and in broader social needs. Techniques initially in the service of vision and wisdom now become themselves the full and exhaustive content of vision and wisdom, and the initial need for a socially defined wisdom and vision tends to be dismissed as something that only the ignorant layman can ask for. The process does not stop here, for soon the technical skills and procedures that make possible the high professional competence somehow lose their connection with the subject matter which they were devised to elaborate. The skills and procedures become a special kind of pure virtuosity, extremely complex and demanding the highest talent, developing its own intrinsic and absorbing interest. Not long ago I was fascinated by the rhythmic, embryonic dance which was performed by a shoeshine boy at his work: the way he snapped the polishing cloth, threw the brush from one hand to the other, moved rhythmically as he smeared the polish on the shoe. Each act seemed to be immensely enjoyed for the sake of the superb skill with which it was done. The boy taught me a useful lesson as a student of philosophy, but I could not see that the high aesthetic overlay on the technique of handling the tools, in which the boy obviously delighted, led him to do a better job, if the latter was defined by my needs as the owner of the shoes.

The shrinking of the specialist's horizon in turn leads to the recruiting of talent possessed of the proper myopia necessary to carry out the pure specialized activity without being consumed by a sense of futility or triviality. Since the process takes place gradually but, what is more important still, since what "life" is taken to be always depends on conceptual elaborations of the primary matter of experience, it is not easy for the specialist to see that his subject matter has radically changed and that vitality and relevance, as measured by a broad humanistic standard, have been lost. That loss escapes notice because for human relevance and vitality have been substituted the obsessive interest in the skilful solution of professional problems for their own sake, and exacting methodological conditions of rigor and clarity are made to take precedence over relevance and truth. When this stage of development is reached, philosophy has become academic, an illness endemic in the schools which confines the patient to the hothouse atmosphere of the classroom and turns his human reverence for truth into superstitious methodolatry. Condemn this activity as trivial, and the professional philosopher will dismiss the criticism by appealing to the criterion of excellence which obtains within the field and to the fact that technical questions cannot be passed on by an outsider who simply does not understand what is going on.

Academicism in philosophy consists of at least three co-operating factors: autonomy wrongly defined as freedom from social responsibility, substitution of exclusive concern with method for the subject matter proper to the discipline, and the consequent loss of wisdom and its replacement by logomachy. In short, it consists of a prodigious increase in technical competence to a point where the subject matter of philosophy—human experience—is abandoned. Men have dreamed in vain of a perpetual-motion machine. In philosophic academicism they have achieved something that comes close to it: an engine that produces the fuel which it consumes and the raw material which it elaborates.

But, since the specialization that takes place in philosophy is also at the same time occurring in all the other social activities and, while the professional philosopher is becoming a better philosopher and a worse human being, the doctor, the engineer, the artist, the minister, the tool-maker, the bridge-builder, and the tailor are also busy doing the same thing, no one notices that the break between philosophy and the rest of society has done away with its relevance and its utility. Were philosophies able to retain their social relevance in a world teeming with autonomous specialized activities, they would be as welcome as is a Civil Liberties lawyer to a lynching mob. And thus you have, on the one hand, the spectacle—tragic, pathetic, or comic, depending on the angle from which you choose to view it—of philosophers who truculently boast that philosophy has nothing to do with life and, on the other, of the layman who retains his illusions about the connection between philosophy and wisdom and is puzzled and wounded because he cannot find any relevance in philosophy and suspects that philosophy is somehow letting him down. Could we pursue the topic further, it would be possible to show in detail that the loss incurred by this development is mutual.

This is not intended to belittle the fact that specialization leads to the development of a high degree of professional competence which might not have been possible before insulation and freedom from immediate practical concerns were introduced. Nor do I desire to convey the impression that the criticism applies to all professional philosophers indiscriminately merely because they enjoy a degree of social autonomy or because they are specialists. Philosophy, to do its job, must remain an abstruse, specialized activity. Nevertheless, the great Western philosophers have never been irresponsible cultivators of pure philosophy, and the largest number of those who today guide the course of philosophy have, I take it, almost invariably accepted explicitly, or at least always implicitly, their social responsibility. Above all, it is not the high degree of abstruseness or the esoteric language or the specialized interest in special problems in itself that is indicative of social irresponsibility. Responsibility is defined by the ultimate social utility of the final product, which may be many stages removed from the solution of a minor and special problem in which a philosophic specialist may now engage. Nor should it be overlooked that the only social service that a philosopher can perform *as philosopher* is not through his political or economic activity but through philosophy itself. It is a waste of the energies of philosophy and of the not too abundant means with which society provides it in comparison with science to demand work of it for which others are better fitted.

The threat of sterile academicism is one which all philosophers face but which the moral philosopher ought to be much more worried about than anyone else. If he loses his primary intrinsic interest in moral problems and substitutes for it interest in how to elaborate his subject matter to meet extrinsic standards of rigor and clarity borrowed from logic and mathematics, his activity becomes a game in which (as Dewey puts it in a phrase that I shall have occasion to use again in this essay) "a dialectic of concepts has taken the place of examination of actual empirical facts."[2] This is what the self-styled "analytic" school of philosophy is after—a dialectic of concepts severed from their complex referential ties with the murky actualities of the moral life. I call it "self-styled" because philosophy has always been analytic and no school has the right to appropriate the term to itself. But philosophy has also been synthetic and synoptic, and toward these functions the analytic philosopher shows deep distrust. He takes "clarity" to be the exclusive goal of thought and, without regard to consequences, undertakes to pay for it in terms of relevance to the actual human problems that thought ought to deal with. I say this not so much in order to attack a school of philosophy of whose aims I disapprove radically but to warn the reader lest he waste more time than necessary on this essay. If what he seeks is the "clarity" of the analytic philosophy, I earnestly entreat him to close this book without delay; for its writer is primarily concerned with the data of the moral life, the actions and choices and judgments of men, and how these bring men face to face with the truth about their evil selves and, through self-knowledge, point to their ethical salvation. Philosophic theories have come within the purview of the writer because they have helped him to interpret the data with which he is concerned and, in the case of naturalistic theories, because in his opinion they misinterpret it radically. The author is, in short, in a contemporary French phrase, "committed," "engaged," and he would not, for all the rewards the world has to offer, choose to be a levitated, pure intelligence, looking on the human drama as the bacteriologist looks on his cultures. The game of a dialectic of concepts is hopeless, since the concepts of the moral philosopher, even when manipulated by a clever linguistic analyst, are inherently and ineradicably vague and it is always possible for a mind with even mediocre linguistic cleverness to make two meanings grow where one grew before. But, more to the point, how could a man with a sense of the urgency of the human problem and a vision of the role philosophy has played in history dare to take time for such a game?

Attention to the complexities of the problem, however, must not lead us to overlook the fact that academicism cultivates virtues—rigor, systematic elegance, freedom from confusion—which should be prudently emulated by all who are engaged in philosophic activity; but prudence will keep the interest within reasonable limits, allowing the moral philosopher to bend his energies to problems worthy of attention, when worth is defined in terms of human relevance. *The subject matter of moral philosophy is not language, nor is its exclusive end clarity.* Its end is practical wisdom and its subject matter human experience. But wisdom is not reached without a modicum of clarity, and human experience cannot be clarified and ordered independently of language.

The science of morals is, then, a distinct discipline, but it possesses no more social autonomy than any other activity within a society. Its objectives are theoretical, but not purely so. Aristotelian terminology is helpful in bringing out its nature and proper function. Moral philosophy is a "practical science" whose objective is to grasp "truth in agreement with right desire."[3] Its end is not to send people to join so-called "progressive" movements or radical or liberal parties; its end is primarily to elicit and define the principles of right action and good choice. This task is so exacting that a self-respecting student who would avoid charlatanism has little time to rake the leaves in his front yard, let alone carry on political activities. The value of philosophy need not be discussed; for, while men who happen to live in simple, static societies no doubt can carry on without its aid and reach heaven, in a world like ours the mediate, roundabout action of philosophic thought on practice is one of the factors that mitigate our barbarism.

In order to give the notion of "practical science" specific content and thus further to specify the nature of moral inquiry, it is desirable to contrast it with the position whose errors it seeks to avoid. The contrast will therefore be invidious, but I see no way in which I can avoid that and do justice to my subject. It is not easy to expose the errors of moral philosophers who conceive that the end of their discipline is, as Schlick would have it, nothing but knowledge,[4] since the arguments they use to defend their position are technical and back of them is a desire that one can readily sympathize with: to emulate the physical sciences, which, by remaining virginal, have miraculously become prolific in practical benefits (as they are indiscriminately called) and without a doubt reach something that can be called "the truth" far more convincingly than philosophers could ever claim to have reached it.

There is one general argument against the possibility of social science and therefore of a "pure" science of morals which I propose to consider hastily before turning to the question of a science of morals as usually proposed by positivists today. It is this: the positive physical sciences are theoretical structures expressing in propositions the invariant relations that hold between empirical phenomena. But the phenomena themselves are not altered by the predictions which the formulations of the invariant relations enable us to make. The object of physics may be interpreted by a realistic epistemology or by a phenomenalistic one; it may be conceived as existing prior to the inquiry that defines it or as constituted in part by that inquiry; in any case no physical process expressed in a law is influenced by its expression. In the social sciences the case is different. Let us take a simple illustration. Knowledge of the laws of economics and how they affect the stock market, if accepted, would become one of the factors affecting the volume of stock sales. This argument could be disqualified by the assumption of an ideal point of view or level of discourse—the scientific—as distinct from the practical; but this ideal condition does not, in fact, obtain in regard to the society within which social science develops, and it therefore remains a question whether the social sciences are possible in that society. And were our world to become fully unified and were Western patterns to retain hegemony, the social sciences could be cultivated only by animals from other planets. At this point it is no longer possible to reply with aplomb that the difficulty is "purely practical," for the final unification of the universe would leave the cultivation of the social sciences to a metacosmic being. However, so long as the results of the investigation can be practically kept from influencing the relations which they express, a pure science of morals is quite possible.

A pure science of morals would canvass what is called "good" or what actions are called "right" in a given demographic area, defined explicitly, and would formulate inductively the rules or standards immanent in judgments and practical decisions for that area. By a series of progressive abstractions, it would arrive at a formal statement of the traits distinguishing anything whatever which anyone whosoever called "good" and any action called "right." Not only would it make explicit the truly operative implicit principles of conduct, but it would also state the manner in which these actually differ from the ostensible moral codes, and it would try to formulate the factors and directions of change of both real and ostensible codes.

Empiricists in value theory today seem to be interested in two main tasks: in demonstrating in the abstract that empiricism can be applied successfully to value theory and in analyzing logically the fundamental moral categories. But the actual application of the empirical methods of inquiry to problems of fact they do not seem to attempt. This inquiry, when successfully completed, will help us "guesstimate" (if I may use a coinage of the Luce publications) the moral judgments and practical decisions of our fellows. As I have said elsewhere in a context which I now largely repudiate, empirical light on the actual processes of valuation is needed because "in a modern civilized community the systems of value in which individuals partake well nigh defy the human power of analysis. The complexity and conflicts of modern society are reflected in the individual, and his values must perforce remain inconsistent and vague, and it is often practically impossible, therefore, to discover the criteria which govern them. Were not the social scene split by conflicts of all sorts, our values would be somewhat more congruous, and a closer agreement between our judgments would be the result. But we are split and fractured into small groups, some of which have and some of which lack material loci; we share criss-crossing traditions; different religious, cultural, and political loyalties claim us; we are members of different economic classes, and these are in rapid flux; and within the same nation we are divided by regional differences. Our judgments are chaotic because they are made by men whose interests are vague and confused, inconsistent and unstable. The first and most elementary task in defining the criteria of value must therefore be the practical task of defining the groups or classes to which the individual belongs. The second would be that of finding out the particular criteria which are unconsciously used in each system, and if possible the laws of their change. This is an empirical job. . . . I do not know of any work on this field that begins to tackle the questions here raised."[5]

Value empiricists have not yet given us much, even by way of hypotheses that could be tested, as to the actual empirical laws of valuation. In order to investigate these, we could borrow from anthropology and from political theory the organistic and the materialistic hypotheses and from psychology the hypothesis which C. W. Morris has been investigating of late.[6] Each of these has its obvious defects, however, and they appear far from being comprehensive enough, even if they are valid as far as they go. But these are questions to be decided "in the laboratory," so to speak; and the important point for us in this context lies elsewhere. For, in spite of all the propaganda that has been carried on by naturalistic moral philosophers about the empirical method, if one wanted today information of an empirical nature on the problems of value, one would have to start almost from scratch, and one would have to borrow from sociology and anthropology and psychology the hypotheses available within these domains. Empiricists in value theory have been so interested in a priori demonstration of the validity of their position that they have almost entirely neglected to practice their principles. These questions are at least as important for the empiricist as is the purely logical and semiotic analysis in which he prefers for the most part to engage.

Nor can we leave out of account, if we are to be fully empirical, the important question of the autonomy of morality—the problem, that is, of its relation to a structure of sustaining religious beliefs. In the seventeenth century, men like Spinoza and Bayle fought hard and successfully to gain acceptance for the idea of the autonomy of moral systems, of their independence of all religious sanctions. By the eighteenth century the autonomy of morality had become so thoroughly accepted by secularist philosophers like Hume that it was not even argued. Groethuysen has shown in detail how the transformation took place in the France of the eighteenth century.[7] Today it seems necessary to reopen the question and ask whether a purely secular system of morality can perform its function adequately. The problem is a difficult one, but, in spite of its difficulty, it must be broached. And not, on the one hand, in order to advocate the incorporation of morals into some dominant religious scheme or some existing orthodoxy or, on the other, to argue in a partisan temper for its total independence from all religious energies but in order to discover, in an attitude as objective as we can muster, the kind of life that a purely secular civilization makes possible for man. On these questions we do not have factual information; all we have is propaganda for and against the positions taken and the faiths of philosophers passed off as actuality. What would society be like if it became completely secularized—that is, if it utterly and thoroughly lost all traces of the rich religious tradition on which it now lives? What kind of man would the purely secular man be, brought up from the cradle without the benefit of a rich heritage of religious values and living in a purely secular society? This is an empirical question on which neither history nor sociology at present can give us an answer, since neither the historian nor the sociologist has ever had the opportunity to observe such phenomena. I know of two societies run on moral schemes which are entirely autonomous, utterly humanistic, completely free from religious sanctions—and both are nightmares: Aldous Huxley's *Brave New World* and George Orwell's *Nineteen Eighty-four*.

The sketchy account I have given of the problems of an empirical science of morals is not complete or very thorough; but for our purposes it is good enough, since what I wanted was to give content to the distinction between an empirical science of morals which is purely scientific and a "practical science." When a man asks a moral question because he is morally baffled and does not know what to do, he does not ask, How do men behave under these circumstances? What he wants to know is how one—he, they—*ought* to behave. The pure science would answer the first of these questions, the purely descriptive one, while a practical science seeks to answer the second, the normative. The moral philosopher does not merely define what is considered or thought or said to be right. He claims to tell us what *ought* to be done, what *is in truth* right or good.

From certain remarks made by Hume in the Introduction to *A Treatise of Human Nature* and, even more specifically, from the last three paragraphs of Section I of *An Enquiry concerning the Principles of Morals*,[8] it is possible to gather that what he had in mind was to make a contribution to what we have called a "pure science" and that he thought that the method of experience, which had been so successfully applied in natural philosophy, could with equal success be applied in moral disquisitions. This is how Santayana interprets him: "Hume's own treatises on morals, it need hardly be said, are pure psychology."[9] But did he really have in mind a "pure science"? A discussion of this question suggests itself as a desirable means of making certain distinctions which seem essential to the correct elucidation of the nature and function of moral philosophy. For Hume was an empiricist not only in the sense that he traced knowledge to impressions but in the contemporary sense, since he distinguished between the then still relatively new method of "natural philosophy"—the positive natural sciences—and the methods of the metaphysicians, to which, by indirection, reference is made in Section IV, Part I, of the *Treatise*. Here Hume counsels the true philosopher to restrain "the intemperate desire of searching into causes" beyond those which can be established by a sufficient number of experiments, to rest content "when he sees a further examination would lead him into obscure and uncertain speculations." Yet, although an empiricist, Hume, as I read him, undertook to make a contribution to what has here been called "a practical science" and not a pure science. Let us see why.

As he finally stated it in *An Enquiry concerning the Principles of Morals*, Hume's moral philosophy has a classical simplicity which is genuinely admirable and is probably the reason that his influence is still powerfully operative in contemporary moral philosophy. The source of the moral judgment he found in benevolence; the criterion he discovered inductively and took to be utility; and the definition of virtue (it should be noted that Hume did not draw a distinction between the terms "good" and "right"), which he gives in a footnote at the beginning of Section VIII of the *Enquiry* and again in Appendix I, can be compressed into the formula: "The good is that which we approve impersonally." Errors in judgments in this system arise from misconceptions about the utility of objects of approval caused by undue influence on our discrimination: public opinion, prejudice, and ignorance tend to make us believe that there is utility where none exists. But Hume was convinced that "the sentiments which arise from humanity, are not only the same in all human creatures, and produce the same approbation or censure; but they also comprehend all human creatures."[10] This assumption enabled him to arrive at an inductive statement of the source and criterion of the moral judgment, but the method by which he elicited it was speciously inductive or at any rate very cavalierly employed. With its aid, nevertheless, he was able to make a show of reason for brushing aside the diversity of conflicting judgments in order to reach their common form: the principle of utility arising from universal benevolence. Since behind the apparent diversity and conflict of judgments a universal principle actually operated, the problem of the moral philosopher was identical with that of the physicist, once the source of error had been indicated, since the immanent principles of judgment were in fact obeyed. To ask, therefore, whether they ought to be obeyed was to ask as superfluous a question as to ask whether a stone which one lets slip from one's hand *ought* to fall. The answer is, "My dear fellow, it does." The parallel is more exact than may appear at first glance, since the sources of error of moral judgment correspond to the multiple determinants altering the actual course of an otherwise unalterable or invariant event. Hume's theory is *descriptive*, but it describes how a man *ought* to act in the sense that it tells him how, were he free from error, he would act. Hume would have agreed with Schlick that "even as a normative science, a science can do no more than *explain;* it can never set up or establish a norm. . . . It is never able to do more than to discover the rules of the judgment, to read them from the facts before it; the origin of norms always lies outside and before science and knowledge."[11] But Hume would not have maintained that ethics "seeks nothing but knowledge." For Hume it seeks correct moral knowledge; it attempts to tell not what men do—always after the fact, since the norm lies beyond and before it—but what they *ought* to do, since it discovers that there is nothing else they do, when free of error, than what they *ought* to do.

Hume's moral philosophy is therefore more than, or, if it be preferred, different from, the pure science of human norms which Schlick holds moral philosophy to be. For Schlick, moral philosophy is psychology concerned with the laws of choice and approval. This also it is for Hume. But for the latter it is, besides, a science to which one can go for light on what one *ought* to do.

Why then don't we go to Hume for our moral philosophy? The answer is that we cannot accept his assumption about the universality of the human sentiments and the consequent uniformity of objects of approval and censure. We know too much anthropology, and our knowledge leads us to emphasize the heterogeneity of moral judgments. But doesn't that mean that, in view of the "varieties of moral experience," morality is relative to the culture that produces it? Here at last we have a scientific hypothesis, backed up by the social sciences, which enables us to dispense without qualms with the lucubrations of philosophers.

The sociological theory or, as we shall call it in the next chapter, "the theory of cultural relativism," is a "naturalistic" theory. Before beginning our examination of it and of other theories of value influential today, it is advisable to have some notion of what the writer means by "naturalism." In this country and perhaps to a lesser extent in England, the word is in common use. If Sidney Hook is right, it means "the wholehearted acceptance of scientific method as the only reliable way of reaching truths about the world of nature, society, and man."[12] This is what the contributors to *Naturalism and the Human Spirit* meant by it. In this volume Dewey says: "The naturalist is one who has respect for the conclusion of natural science."[13] By this he does not mean that a naturalist accepts the results of scientific inquiry, which of course he does, but that he looks forward to and helps in the enlargement of the domain of natural science. However, while the term is clear, the area to which it applies is not easy to delimit. In its generic sense it includes, besides instrumentalists of various degrees of purity of strain, the now moribund epistemological realisms which flourished in this country for three decades; a number of "materialists" of several varieties, generally of Stalinoidal tendencies (who often exhibit an animus against Dewey and against positivists); and, in so far as these are distinct from the other two, a group of positivistically inclined philosophers, a number of whom have lately found a name and call themselves "analytic" philosophers.[14]

The question that must be examined first is whether, as Sidney Hook maintains, what distinguishes naturalism is wholehearted acceptance of scientific method. Let us see first what that acceptance includes by quoting the whole paragraph from Hook:

"A few preliminary remarks are necessary in order to indicate in what sense the term 'naturalism' is to be understood. Despite the variety of specific doctrines which naturalists have professed from Democritus to Dewey, what unites them all is the wholehearted acceptance of scientific method as the only reliable way of reaching truths about the world of nature, society, and man. The differences between naturalists in the history of thought can easily be explained in terms of (1) varying historical conceptions of what fields and problems are amenable to scientific treatment and (2) progressive refinements in the methods of inquiry themselves. All their differences can in principle be resolved by appealing to the *method* to which they give common allegiance, except for those temperamental differences of emphasis and selective bias which no naturalist claims to be an avenue to truth. The least common denominator of all historic naturalisms, therefore, is not so much a set of specific doctrines as the method of scientific or rational empiricism."[15]

Hook's statement assumes the existence throughout Western history, from the days of Democritus until our own day, of a single coherent and continuously developing "method" of arriving at knowledge, which can be called "scientific." But a look at the history of philosophy will reveal that the concept of scientific method accepted by Hook is drawn from modern physical science, which dates from the sixteenth or at most the fifteenth century. One could argue with some plausibility that the explicit formulation of the method of modern physical science, as today understood by the naturalists, did not come until considerably later than its birth. One could even argue that whatever identity of techniques and of actual procedures may be found in the practice of laboratory men today, as to what their method is or whether they use one or many, *philosophers* do not seem to be in agreement. The criticisms that the pragmatists and positivists make of men like Russell and White-head (whose knowledge of science cannot be belittled) seem sufficient to indicate this. Be all this as it may, only a complete disregard of historical facts permits one to speak of a "scientific method," in our sense of the term, as existing prior to the Renaissance. Before that time "science" was a term which covered all the intellectual disciplines which claimed to seek for truth, however conducted. Pythagoras and his followers must have known and Aristotle certainly knew something about scientific method in Hook's sense of the word. But they were not naturalists. Probably men like Eudoxus, Archimedes, Aristarchos of Samos, and Hipparchos of Nicaea employed scientific method with great success. But whether one is willing to extend its application to all inquiries or restrict it only to some is of the essence of the argument. If a man who employs the method of rational empiricism (assuming that anything definite can be put under such a label), no matter in how restricted an area, is a naturalist, then Plato, Aristotle, Pythagoras, and the others were naturalists—and where, then, would we go to find nonnaturalists? The assumption which might justify Hook's definition of naturalism seems to be that, once you commit yourself to the method of "rational empiricism," it is only your morally erroneous lack of logical courage that prevents you from extending it to all areas of inquiry; hence "in principle" you are a naturalist. But this is an incredibly naïve assumption, involving an egregious begging of the issue; for men who do not allow the universal application of the method of "rational empiricism" often place their limitation on very carefully considered philosophical grounds.

This is said although the writer is not ignorant of the fact that, in another sense of this ambiguous term, "empiricism" has had a long history in the ancient world, going as far back as the skeptical medical tradition that closes with Sextus Empiricus. But this empiricism was a "philosophic" empiricism, not a scientific one, in our sense of "science." It cannot help Hook's contention, since we find it allied throughout its career with a skepticism that was decidedly antiscientific; for it was calculated to justify medicine as a practical art by puncturing its claims as a science, while on the constructive side it consisted of an appeal to common sense rather than to systematic knowledge, the validity of which it rejected. There is, indeed, a vague connection between ancient empirical skepticism and contemporary naturalism, but this connection is a negative one: it is established through their skepticism rather than through their empiricism, for in regard to the validity of experience for knowledge they disagree. By these references I do not intend to settle in a few lines an immensely complex historical problem but, on the contrary, to show that a simplistic division of the history of philosophy cannot stand up even against the most shallow look at historical reality. Defined as Hook defines it, contemporary naturalism is an essentially rootless phenomenon whose intellectual ancestry is to be found in the nineteenth century, and it is hardly a philosophic doctrine but rather an antiphilosophic attitude. To connect it with the naturalisms of the Western tradition through its methodolatry is false, since they have always had a distinctively *philosophic* doctrine, whereas what contemporary naturalism chiefly consists of is scientifistic enthusiasm. By "scientifism" I mean the propagandistic fervor which is the subject of this discussion, the unempirical faith that science can give us a complete philosophy for all our human needs.[16]

Naturalism, then, cannot be defined in the scientifistic way in which Hook defines it. We must seek another definition. For the purposes of this essay it is necessary only to distinguish between "naturalism," as G. E. Moore defines it, and the classical naturalism which I shall call the "cosmological." Moore's naturalism can be called "methodological," but not in Hook's sense. Moore writes: "I have thus appropriated the name Naturalism to a particular method of approaching Ethics. . . . This method consists in substituting for 'good' some one property of a natural object or of a collection of objects; and in thus replacing Ethics by some one of the natural sciences."[17] When Moore comes to tell us what he means by the term "nature" in the next paragraph, he writes: "By 'nature,' then, I do mean and have meant that which is the subject-matter of the natural sciences and also of psychology. It may be said to include all that has existed, does exist, or will exist in time."

The difference between this statement and Hook's is, of course, that the prestige of history is not invoked for a movement which is ahistorical. The latter statement is more fair, since its claims are more modest. This methodological naturalism is the one which is most popular in the United States at present. The "cosmological naturalism" is older and broader, since its emphasis is not on the method used to define the subject matter of inquiry but on whether or not nature as a whole can be conceived as self-sufficient. To say that nature is self-sufficient is to say that there is no need in our scheme of thought for a God in some sense distinct from His creatures. It will be found that methodological naturalism implies the cosmological position as to the self-sufficiency of nature, on the more or less explicit assumption that, since all that we can know is what is known by the given method, that is all there can be said, or can be *meaningfully* said, to exist. But not all cosmological naturalisms are scientifically methodological, since a philosopher could be an atheist and yet conceive of nature in diverse ways. He could, for instance, place the creative principle of nature within it, as the early Stoics did. Or he could conceive of nature as composed of levels of reality, some of which are not in time. Nicolai Hartmann seems to be an atheist who believes in the a priori status of value. Beyond this point it does not seem useful to carry on the analysis of what the term "naturalism" means, because what it refers to is exceedingly complex and fluidly indistinct. The best way to specify it is therefore by exhibiting it ostensibly; and it is hoped that the reader will gain a more or less clear notion of how the writer uses the term from the philosophies upon which he animadverts in the following chapters. Neither in its cosmological nor in its methodological meaning does "naturalism" apply, as "materialism" and "idealism" do, to systems or well-defined schools of philosophy. What it refers to is a body of attitudes which underlies certain diverse philosophic systems and gives them their direction. It refers to something we could call "philosophic atheism" and which goes considerably deeper than the methodological problem which arises when we try to define ethical terms by reference to properties of spatiotemporal things.

The double use of the word "naturalism" and of its derivatives seldom causes radical trouble for a man in his capacity as moral philosopher, since the problems which the ambiguity generates are beyond his range. But there are times when the difficulties to which it gives rise are of some magnitude. Thus W. D. Ross, who is today one of the most distinguished of antinaturalistic writers on moral philosophy, does not seem at all concerned, so far as I can see, with the question as to whether or not the values intuited by educated, mature men are aspects of a self-sufficient universe which precludes the possibility of a transcendent Creator. And whether a man like Charner Perry is a naturalist or not is a question that the reader may find as difficult to decide as the writer does on the basis of an examination of Perry's work. Perry once informed me that he considers himself a naturalist, and in chapter v (p. 91) I have stated my reasons for accepting his own characterization of himself.

Now criticism of a philosophical doctrine can be launched from a contrasting point of view which pretends to avoid the errors which it exposes, or from no point of view at all, in the absence of a developed philosophy. The latter approach is sometimes disparaged, but I take it to constitute an important activity both theoretically and practically. The critic may not be capable of clearing the rubble which he makes, let alone of rearing another edifice in place of that which he has destroyed, but he can often excite a creative mind to do what must be done. The animadversions recorded in the following chapters are made, I trust, from a constructive point of view, since in Parts II and III of this essay I have attempted to draw the outlines of a moral philosophy which claims to avoid the errors of naturalism. But, in Part I, I have tried to confine myself exclusively to negative criticism, except in so far as it has seemed absolutely necessary to present positive ideas in order to make the negative criticism intelligible. In spite of this adverse criticism, I have not been blind to the excellences which the moral philosophies animadverted upon contain, and in Parts II and III I have tried to absorb those excellences into my own views whenever I was able to do so. I hope those whom I have thus treated will agree with me that this is the highest praise a thinker can be paid.

The theories that I have selected for criticism express certain social trends which are actually at work in the modern world and which I consider evil. Contemporary naturalism, particularly as formulated by American philosophers, tends toward what I call "moral vitalism," and it thus disregards important factors without which it is not possible to formulate an adequate moral philosophy capable of doing justice to the complexities of human nature and to the moral forces which would regulate it. The term "moral vitalism" is intended to replace the term "ethical vitalism," used in several published essays of mine, and the change is made in the interest of verbal consistency. By "moral vitalism" I mean the fallacious theory which holds that value is constituted by, or conferred on, an object through the act of satisfaction or fulfilment of a nonvalue term or factor, either biological or psychological (more usually the latter), which is designated by a variety of names, depending on the scientific preferences of the philosopher doing the labeling. Among the names used, the most common are perhaps "desire," "interest," "appetition," "need," "drive," and "impulse." This list is not exhaustive. From this "biologistic" or "psychologistic" reductionism, the "moral vitalist" goes on to argue that if one value is conferred on an object through the presence of a desire toward or an interest in it, it follows, of course, that two values are conferred by two desires and the more desires or interests that we seek to fulfil, the more value we shall realize. This is a rationalization of the vicious secularistic "romanticism" of our day, which is addressed to unlimited expansion of life-forces.

PART I

ANIMADVERSIONS UPON NATURALISTIC
MORAL PHILOSOPHIES

CHAPTER I

MORES AND MORALS

IN ORDER to keep close to the empirical subject matter of moral philosophy, instead of beginning with a definition of what is the "good" or what is meant by it or what is, or is meant by, the "right," let us begin by considering morality as broadly as we can, as it is found actually guiding human intercourse, in the street, the shop or business office, the home, the church. Viewed thus broadly, "morality" is a term that refers, so to speak, to the traffic rules of a society, the rules that govern more or less explicitly and more or less successfully the lives of the members of a community—the "do's" and "don't's" by which people live. Such established forms of behavior can be empirically observed.[1]

Considered as broadly as that, morality is no more than what Protagoras, in Plato's dialogue by that name, sought at first to maintain that it was. Morality is custom, and the moral philosopher must remain content to extract the rule of right conduct by inductive methods from the more or less explicit, more or less consistent, patterns of behavior that are actually to be found structuring human activity at the social level. The right is what is recognized as right; the good what is considered good; and both are more or less clearly known and proved, in a pragmatic way, in the actual process of daily living. The jurisdiction of morality is not well delimited. What is good or right may be extremely difficult or even impossible to formulate satisfactorily in given instances and in certain areas of behavior; but it may be relatively easy to determine practically what is right in a given context, since much is left not to explicit formulas but to the tact and sensibility of those involved in the specific situation, which practice and example inculcate in the members of a group.

In Plato's *Protagoras* the older philosopher was right, conceiving morality as he did and dedicated as he was to the practical task of education, in feeling impatient with Socrates, whose interests, although more profoundly practical than those of Protagoras, must have seemed the expression of an oversubtle, a purely logomachous mind. Virtue, said Protagoras, can be taught, and a hasty glance at the social scene is all that is needed to reveal how manifold are the agencies which teach it daily and everywhere and in all sorts of ways; nor can it be learned without this enormous effort to which the whole of society bends its energies unceasingly. What, then, is morality but the mores of a community, its rules of traffic, its accepted ways of behavior, what it considers proper and approves of, and what it considers improper and disapproves of? If we should later on in our inquiry discover that the moral life involves more than custom and its principles, we shall have to bear in mind that from custom it derives its basic meaning and that, however much we may have to enlarge and to refine and to add to the concept as living becomes more complex and new needs appear, the truth of Protagoras' theory can never be totally rejected. For custom, itself the fundamental expression of the energies of a people, not only channels their efforts but gives them the forms through which their more or less clear conceptions of excellence are expressed. Were customary rules always effectively obeyed, were there always customs at hand to cover all contingencies, were these rules in harmony with one another, and were men so simply constituted that an appeal to their sense of what is proper would be sufficient inducement to keep them in the safe grooves of custom, the problem of the moral philosopher would be relatively simple. Were this the case, his problem could not extend beyond the exigencies and demands of the sociologist's discovery, by inductive means, of the structural principles immanent in a relatively definite and fairly objective subject matter. His task would consist in explicitly formulating the rules of a given society, since, at the level of custom, they are seldom found explicitly stated with the nicety that a scientist would demand. In stating them, he would discover and make explicit to himself the contradictions and inconsistencies found operative in the society under study and whatever frustration and conflicts these lead to.

But, to admit that the custom theory has an irreducible modicum of truth is not to say that it can answer all the questions to which the moral philosopher desires answers. And yet, in spite of the devastating criticism to which it has been subjected, contemporary sociology largely sticks by the Protagorean doctrine, now called, of course, by many different names. We find it in an older form in Sumner, spoken of as "folkways." We find it in a brilliant, modernized version in Malinowski's *Crime and Custom in Savage Society*. We find it in Linton, in Margaret Mead, and in Ruth Benedict—indeed, in the majority of American anthropologists with whose work I am acquainted. The most recent and one of the most careful formulations that has come to my notice is that of Melville Herskovits, to whose exposition of it we turn. Herskovits believes that scientific evidence can be offered for the theory which he calls "cultural relativism." He finds the evidence in the "critical and fundamental" experiments of M. Sherif, from which he quotes the following paragraph:

"The psychological basis of the established social norms, such as stereotypes, fashions, conventions, customs, and values, is the formation of common frames of reference as a product of the contact of individuals. Once such frames of reference are established and incorporated in the individual they enter as important factors to determine or modify his reactions to the situations he will face later—social and even non-social at times, especially if the stimulus field is not well structured."[2]

The point of view which Sherif's experiments are claimed to support is formulated by Herskovits, in italics, in the following manner: "*Judgments are based on experience, and experience is interpreted by each individual in terms of his own enculturation.*"[3]

Sociologists, it will be remembered, love grating neologisms which they think turn their discipline into an exact science; but the difficulties which beset the "enculturation" hypothesis when applied to moral judgments do not wait long to make themselves felt, in spite of the formidable terminology with which Herskovits protects the theory. One of these difficulties sociologists could not resolve, even if they were aware of it, for the psychological determinants of value to which Sherif points may be interpreted either as the means of discovering values or as some of the factors which constitute them; and which of these interpretations is acceptable is a question for philosophers. Another difficulty arises when we consider a society beset by the problems which violent changes generate. Consider the following quotation from Herskovits: "Each people, having standards, not only inculcate them in the young so that each generation is enculturated to the value-systems of its predecessors, but they see to it that transgressions of accepted codes are punished. . . . Yet every culture knows the rebel, which means that man's experience encompasses cultural change as well as cultural stability."[4]

This statement may be satisfactory to the sociologist, but the moral philosopher discovers in it a nest of difficult problems centering about the question of what custom one falls back on in societies in the midst of changes. However the question be answered, the moral problem appears to transcend "enculturation." Although, as compared with Western civilization, some societies seem to be utterly static, one can safely assert that changes arise in all human societies as a result of emergent energies or changing natural conditions or the exigencies of increasing or diminishing population or the stern demands of political calamities. In view of these changes, one asks: How do individuals improvise moral solutions to problems not encountered before? Just such a condition of affairs existed in Greece at the time of the famous disputation between Protagoras and Socrates. The great Sophist argued that virtue could be taught, since, for him, morality was custom. But what is one to do when custom breaks down, or how is one to decide morally in situations which are not provided for by custom? There will be not only situations in regard to which custom does not guide us but others in which we will be embarrassed by too many rules supplied by too many customs. Is it enough for a man like Protagoras to say that society is the teacher of morality? What morality did custom actually teach in a world and at a time like the one in which Protagoras lived? In Rome do as the Romans. But which Romans? The poor, the middle class, the rich, the clergy? The Catholics, the Communists? On what principle does one choose between conflicting social principles? It is situations such as these, in which custom provides us with no rules or in which the rules with which it provides us have broken down or are in conflict, that expose the glaring inadequacies of cultural relativism when taken as more than a point of departure from which to tackle the problem of moral

judgments. This is the point at which Socrates and Plato recovered
the moral problem after Protagoras had fumbled it and the point at
which we moderns have encountered it since Hobbes's day.

Now the cultural relativist, sensitive to the charge that his views
end in utter moral nihilism, argues that his theory, in Herskovits'
words, does not deny the validity of "the force of the codes that
prevail at a given time in a given culture. Everywhere, man seemingly always sets up goals for himself, and ideals towards which he
strives. Because these are subject to change, or differ from people
to people, does not make them any the less effective within a particular society during the period they prevail."[5]

But the problem is not whether or not men set up goals for them
selves but how to choose from among those goals that offer themselves to them as beckoning alternatives. And in the absence of a
criterion by means of which to choose the correct one from among
those actually found, the individual who repudiates all the prevail-
ing codes and adopts his own cannot be corrected. Thrasymachus
had the virtue of lucidity and of consistency: he saw that from his
point of view the ground of moral obligation was to be found where
Santayana, in our day, finds it and where relativists and positivists
who think the problem through from their point of view are finally
bound to find it—in the will that chooses this way or that. But,
unlike Santayana and the others, Thrasymachus saw clearly what
the doctrine implied. What does the will choose but its own interest, its own gratification? However, the matter is not quite so
simple, for we still want to know what we shall choose when the
will is divided or when it is opposed by another will that we love.
For Thrasymachus the conclusion is obvious: justice is clearly the
interest of the stronger. But at least two questions remain: Who is
the stronger when our will is opposed to another will, even though
weaker, that we love? and What is the stronger's interest in cases
when his interests are not clear or are in conflict? To seek for the
source of morality in the will is to seek for it in the nature of man,
so that perhaps Alexander Grant is not altogether correct when he
says that it was Plato who first sought to ground ethics in psychology.[6] The Sophists, whom his master opposed, had already done so.
Be that as it may, it is not difficult to see that the theory of Thrasymachus does not advance the problem—and not because there is

something prima facie wrong about the notion that right is defined by might but because might does not tell us how to choose, because it cannot be a rule of conduct.

Might could be a rule of conduct if the will were consistent with itself throughout the career of a man from his birth to his death; if he wanted one thing and one only and if he wanted it always and steadily. But when his wants are many and mutually incompatible and their incompatibility forces him to reflect fleetingly on the alternative he must choose, might must be supplemented by reason to the degree that one of the impulses afoot is the desire to live more than a haphazard and ephemeral existence. For, even if one chooses as his principle of conduct that in case of conflicts he should yield to that impulse which at the moment appears to be the strongest, irrespective of consequences, he has done more than act on the basis of merely blind might; might has been enlightened or, if the term should appear objectionable, supplemented by something which we may here call "reason." This is the case even if the choice is to a great extent unconscious and the hesitation of the individual before mutually incompatible impulses does not reach the level of fully lucid, fully conscious reflection. Even then, might has been enlightened or supplemented, although I would be impatient to add that the enlightenment or supplementation which it has received is miserably inadequate. When a man's needs are many and mutually incompatible and it is practically impossible for him to decide, as it often is, which of his impulses is the strongest or which is the one which he will continue to want in the future and when among his wants is to be found the need for the affection and companionship of fellows whose wants frustrate, if satisfied, some of his own or who would be alienated by his inconsiderate satisfaction of his own interests, the "might" theory presents us with the same formal difficulties that we have just encountered in the case of custom; indeed, it is but the custom theory individualized. But the defect of this theory, at least at this point, does not consist in the fact that it searches for the ground of morality in human nature but in the way in which it conceives human nature, naïvely and simplistically, and thus fails to see that the will cannot help entangling itself. This, at any rate, must have been what Plato felt, for it is also in human nature that he sought for the solution of the problem of morality. But, to be sure that he did not miss it, he sought for it in human nature writ large, set in its proper context, viewed in its relations to the cosmos, and conceived, finally, in a deeply religious way. And Aristotle agreed with his teacher, too, in respect of the manner of resolving it, although he disagreed with Plato about the conception of man and of the world and the method of knowledge that should guide the inquiry. Aristotle thought that man's psyche could be investigated independently of other sciences and that morals or politics could be investigated in terms of its own first principles. It is not an unfair generalization to make that, since the days of Plato and Aristotle, philosophers who have investigated the problem of morality at all seriously have sought to find its basis in human nature and that the radical differences center on the question of how man's humanity is to be conceived. This, I take it, is true even of Aquinas, who recognized the validity of the natural law. And this is no less true today than it has been historically. And it is true even of the transcendentalist, whose quarrel with the naturalist arises from the latter's narrow and incomplete notion of human nature.

There are two corollaries of Herskovits' version of cultural relativism which I cannot accept. The first holds that the validity of the moral judgment depends on concrete values in regard to which the judge makes choices and preferential judgments. This denies the ontic reality of the formal aspect of the judgment. The error of this assumption will become obvious when we discuss the way in which moral perplexities are resolved. The second corollary, very widely accepted among cultural anthropologists, holds that since values are relative to the culture in which they function, moral judgments are culturally relative, in the sense that the criteria of validity by which we accept them or reject them are immanent in the culture and are in no sense to be derived from any other source than the culture in which the values themselves function. This was the position that the writer defended in several articles on value written prior to 1942. In the article already quoted in the Introduction I put the matter in the following way:

"If a system actually obtains it is possible to find by empirical means 'the rule' which governs the judgments made within it. *Objectivity is defined in terms of this rule.* For the rule can be stated and verified; and by means of it the single concrete judgment within the system can in turn be verified and corrected. The procedure of verification consists in finding out whether the judgment in question obeys the rule of the system in terms of which it claims validity. Thus when I say that something is good, and I do not mean merely that I like it, in other words when the judgment does not refer to a value in isolation arising out of an idiosyncratic preference, I mean not only that it will satisfy an isolated interest, but that it will not interfere with the other interests which make up my system, but will rather aid or foster them. But I also mean that other members of the social system with which I identify myself will concur with this judgment. More concisely stated, I mean that in terms of a certain implicit system of values this object will be found good. Such verifications, rough though they must remain in practice, are often made by us, and are implicit in all our social relations."[7]

Now it is perfectly true that, in one sense, values are relative to the culture in which they function. But exactly in what does their relativism consist? The anthropologist in his own professional capacity has no means of deciding whether the values that are such an important constituent factor of culture are discovered or created by the culture. This is a difficult philosophical question—and one which we shall try to answer by disposing of naturalistic value theory. Nevertheless, it is true, at least at the purely descriptive (as contrasted with the normative) level, that the values which in a given culture constitute the human person are normally controlled effectively by the culture. The process of "enculturation" opens certain values to the members of a culture and seeks to elicit their interest in these values and to secure it by institutional means. And it also shuts out other values by actual negative conditioning or mere indifference. It is not likely that Andaman islanders will discover, as things now are for them, the values of abstract speculative thought or the values of impersonality essential to the development of science. A head-hunter in the eastern forests of Bolivia will not discover the values of universal love that elevate the Christian above other men, and tolerance for the religious convictions of other human beings could not reasonably have been expected of the Puritans or of the Spaniards of Charles V's and Philip II's days.

Cultural relativism also seems to hold that it is impossible to make comparative judgments of value of cultures as a whole and to place cultures in an order of rank. "Evaluations," Herskovits tells us, "are *relative* to the cultural background out of which they arise," and elsewhere he says: "The assumption that the cultures of non-literate peoples are inferior to our own is the end-product of a long series of developments in our intellectual history. . . .

"It was the controls provided by science and the machine technology that gave Europe and America the final word in debates about cultural superiority. 'He who makes the gunpowder wields the power,' runs a Dahomean proverb. . . .

"With the possible exception of technological aspects of life, the proposition that one way of thought or action is better than another is exceedingly difficult to establish on the grounds of any universally acceptable criteria."[8]

There is no doubt that the first paragraph of this quotation is factually correct: a long series of developments in our intellectual history are preconditions of all the judgments we make, including those we make about the hierarchical validity of our judgments. But to dismiss the truth of a statement on the grounds of the conditions of its origin is to commit the genetic fallacy. How we come by our judgments is irrelevant to the truth which they may contain. The question that needs be tested is whether the judgment is correct or not. Suppose I were to assert that genetic factors are pertinent to our determination of truth: to establish this proposition, I could obviously not fall back on genetic considerations. There must be at least one proposition, therefore, the truth of which cannot be established on genetic grounds, namely, the proposition that genetic grounds are pertinent to the validation of propositions. But if there is one, why can we not use the criteria employed to establish that one in the establishment of other propositions?

Again the cultural superiority which we claim and to which Herskovits refers in the second paragraph of the quotations does not depend, as he seems to believe, on our science and our machine technology alone, nor does it depend on whether or not we have subjugated the people over whom we claim cultural superiority. The problem is a purely intellectual one and can be settled only in terms of the superiority of the arguments adduced on one side or the other. Since the discussion is being carried on by men like Herskovits and his critics in technical journals and books, we can be almost certain that neither nonliterate people nor the imperialists are acquainted with it or could decide as to its merits. Again, Herskovits tentatively accepts the superiority of one technology over another but does not inquire whether this may not entail superiority in other aspects of life—certainly, it entails scientific superiority; and whether scientific superiority does not entail superiority in other respects is a pertinent problem which ought to receive careful consideration but which Herskovits ignores.

Let us consider, finally, Herskovits' contention that since there are no universally acceptable criteria, the proposition that one way of thought or action is better than another is exceedingly difficult to establish. Several observations must be advanced. The first is that the degree of difficulty is indeed great, and it may be added that, when the difficulties have been overcome, the results are very poor indeed as compared with the results obtained by the physicist when he overcomes his difficulties. We cannot prove with the clarity and certainty with which propositions are proved in the laboratory that one culture is superior to another and that one set of values is superior to another. At best, the results will be infected with vagueness and ambiguity. But all this is irrelevant if the possibility is admitted of arriving at some sort of decision containing some degree of validity, however small. We must therefore consider whether it is at all possible to establish the superiority of one way of thought and action over another.

In order to do so, we must first make explicit two possible meanings in Herskovits' statement; for, as it stands, it may be taken to deny the metacultural validity of truth as well as the metacultural validity of moral judgments. Another ambiguity must be made explicit, for Herskovits may mean that *in fact* there are no universally accepted criteria of truth and of moral judgments or that there are no normative criteria which are universally valid, which is to say, *which ought to be accepted universally.* Let us first take up the question of truth, which is the easier of the two. It is the case that probably there have never been, and it is certainly true that there are not at present, any universally accepted criteria of truth. There may never be. This is a question of fact which can be easily ascertained. But the normative validity of the criteria of truth does not depend on being actually accepted, and we may be certain that idiots and insane men will never accept the criteria of truth, however defined. Take any true statement whatever, *TS*, defined in any way whatever. Its truth will depend on its criterion, *c*, and *TS* will be true irrespective of whether *c* is accepted by one tribe or one nation or, indeed, by any number of people at any time in any place, however these are defined.

But Herskovits may not mean to assert that the validity of truth depends on whether the criteria that define it are or are not actually accepted. He may mean that *there are no criteria of truth that ought to be accepted universally* because truth is culturally determined by culturally varying factors. It is not likely that this is what he means, since Herskovits is a social scientist and hence intends his statements to hold universally. Thus, when he tells us that, with the possible exception of technological aspects, the proposition that one way of thought is better than another is exceedingly difficult to establish, he does not mean that this statement is valid only for his own culture, but he means it universally and would claim that its truth holds for all people, although only those will accept it who are capable of understanding what is intended by it. But if this is what he means, namely, that science is valid only intraculturally and not metaculturally, he will have to establish it universally and objectively, if he expects his readers to agree with him and not merely to chalk it up under the heading of Herskovits' interesting idiosyncrasies; that is to say, he would have to establish it in a way that transcends all cultural determinations of its truth, and this would be self-contradictory. Suppose, however, that he retorts that he has some means of avoiding Epimenides' trap—whether by means of the theory of classes or in some other way. If he makes that claim, he is clearly appealing to techniques of argument which, to be applicable, must be assumed to transcend cultural determinations (for reasons which we need not investigate here and which themselves transcend cultural determinations). It still remains true, nevertheless, that convincing certain primitives of the validity of science,

given their prejudices, is exceedingly difficult and perhaps in some
cases utterly impossible.

We may now address ourselves to that part of Herskovits' statement which refers to the difficulty of establishing the moral superiority of one way of action or thought over another. As in the
former case, what we must inquire is whether it is possible to establish it. But in the cultural relativist's doctrines we must distinguish
two kinds of questions, only one of which is of primary interest to
the moral philosopher as moral philosopher. This is the question as
to whether the validity of a moral judgment can be established only
by reference to criteria inductively gathered from the culture to
which the individual making the judgment belongs. If the moral
judgment is relative to the culture within which it is made, it is not
possible for a democratic man to condemn a Nazi or for a Soviet
Russian to condemn an American or vice versa. Hence it is not possible to resolve in a moral manner radical conflicts arising across
cultures. The second question is whether we can pass judgment on
the relative excellences of cultures taken as wholes, with the end in
view of arranging them in a hierarchical order.

The first of these questions is one which the moral philosopher
must somehow answer, and the answer which the writer offers is
to be found in Part II of this essay. To say at this point any more
than this is merely to open myself to misunderstandings in a field in
which, when all precautions are taken against misinterpretation,
one is still bound to leave room for it. I hold—and, in Part II, I give
my reasons for so doing—that the techniques involved in the moral
resolution of conflicts within cultures are operative across cultural
boundaries, although value patterns are in some sense culturally determined. If this is the case, cross-cultural judgments may be
passed, and the moral techniques employed in the resolution of
moral conflicts within cultures can be used to correct them.

The second question is not one with which the moral philosopher
needs concern himself and is one which, although it is possible to
answer, is indeed, as Herskovits indicates, exceedingly difficult to
answer with accuracy or hope of wide consensus. The reason is, of
course, that the data which must be kept in mind with a modicum of
clarity are so complex that it is impossible to give them the detailed

and focused attention which they deserve. Among the great civilizations of the world it is not at all easy to tell which was the greatest
or best. This is also true of nations within a cultural area. Is French
nineteenth-century culture higher than English? The question cannot be fairly answered. Was the culture of the Middle Ages greater
than the Greco-Roman? I would say that it was and would offer as
reason that the medievals cultivated all the values for which we
honor the Romans and the Greeks, but they added other values
which never managed to lodge themselves in the heart of the Greco-
Roman world. But how good is the opinion of an ignoramus on such
matters? A Rostovtzeff, in amicable discussion with a Gibbon and
a Toynbee, at which a Socrates and a Pericles, an Augustine and a
Thomas or a Dante, were allowed full hearing, might arrive at a
valid decision. In addition to their learning, of course, we must demand of these historians an impartiality and a wisdom which we
could not expect of a Gibbon.

But, while it may be well-nigh impossible to list the great civilizations of history in an order of rank, the distinctions which we
commonly make between barbarians and civilized men and between
these and savages or primitives do not seem to me impossible to
defend with a modicum of success. Let us look into Mr. Fortune's
Dobuans.[9] On his record, the life of the Dobuans is infected by
paranoid traits and crippling practices and beliefs that to a critical
outsider seem clearly to stunt them as human beings. Their intellectual interests are narrow and shallow—if they have any at all;
their technological skills are undeveloped, and their accomplishments are minor when compared with those of a civilized man. In
the activities and virtues which they cultivate, civilized men surpass
them, but civilized men also excel in virtues that they have not discovered. The cultural relativist will argue that the grounds on
which I condemn the Dobuans are not grounds which they will accept, for they do not recognize as such the values which I claim they
lack. But the normative validity of a criterion does not depend on its
being recognized, or there would be no normative criteria at all,
since there would be as many as there are acts of valuation. The
question is not whether Dobuans recognize the value of philosophy
or science or of a humane, sweet life, but whether a rational man
does.

Dobuans are human beings, and the question is whether some-how it is not possible to arrive at a notion of what human be-ings *ought to be*. Where would we derive such a notion from? I suggest that we derive it from the general excellences of which human beings have shown themselves capable. But the notion of what man ought to be cannot be derived inductively from concrete and specific instances of excellences already achieved, for that would close the door to future excellences which men have not yet achieved. What is required is an analytic approach to the nature of virtue or excellence which would seek to grasp its essence, in order that it might serve as a criterion by which to judge virtues of which we do not yet dream, no less than those with which we are fa-miliar from our studies of the great civilizations. The definition of excellence thus arrived at will be extremely vague, but it will not be so vague and useless as it may seem, since all human beings exhibit in their living the tension which is created by the discrepancy be-tween what they are and what they ought to be, between value as absent and value as actualized. If the notion of excellence can be validly applied to a cultural area, as Herskovits believes that it can, there is no reason why it cannot be applied to the whole human species, although, perhaps, the results will be extremely inaccurate.

If it is argued that there will be numerous instances in which sharp differences of opinion will arise between cultures as to what excellence is, because what is considered an excellence in one coun-try is not considered one in another, we must reply that this will no doubt be the case. But such cases are identical with those in which differences of opinion arise as to judgments of value across cultures, and these are resolved by the techniques analyzed in Part II of this essay. Nothing in the procedure involves a denial of the concrete uniqueness of the Dobuan, even as compared with the cultures of the neighboring islands; nor need we neglect the pervasive fact of diffusion and cultural assimilation, to assert the possibility of com-paring the Dobuan with other human beings. To deny the possibility is tantamount to denying the Dobuan his humanity—a formal trait, not a concrete quality, which the Dobuan shares with other men in other cultures in the islands that constitute his archipelago and with men elsewhere in Africa, America, Europe, and Asia. It is in terms of this humanity, vague as the notion is, that the judgment against

the quality of the life he lives is passed. And what the judge is saying is that in developing and institutionalizing his kind of life the
Dobuan may have succeeded as Dobuan but he has failed, in part at
least, as a human being. All this is very vague, of course, but at
least it does not exclude facts which are relevant to the problem on
grounds which, when looked into, turn out to be quite fallacious.
Cultural relativism, in short, denies the human community which
underlies the varieties of culture in the world and which makes a
Dobuan no less human for all his gnarled paranoia than any other
human being on the face of the earth.

Thus the critical observer of Dobu culture knows of men whose
lives have, by comparison, an internal sweetness and freedom from
narrowing practices and beliefs which enable them more fully to
realize themselves along moral lines than Fortune's islanders. Comparatively, Dobuan life seems to be a sordid hell. Of course, it need
not be concealed that the judgment is based on a vague criterion of
what human life ought to be; but this is not a descriptive, but a
normative, notion. The cultural relativist argues that practically to
expect the Dobuan to prefer a life of sweetness is merely to decree
destruction of his moral identity, and this the Dobuans, who know
inwardly the reality of their own life, would never consent to do.
This argument is irrelevant unless one assumes that "it is best for
a people to be that which they in fact are and want to continue to
be"; but this assumption is itself a normative criterion. Now the
question becomes which of two normative criteria applicable universally to all cultures is to be preferred. In order to answer this
question, we must leave the position of the cultural relativist behind. Let us look at this point with some care.

Let us ask the Dobuans why they reject alien forms of life and
prefer their own. Is it merely a matter of their preference, which is
the result of social conditioning? If this is their answer and by it is
intended that the process of conditioning is not one susceptible of
rational criticism, they utterly stultify themselves. For, by descend-
ing from the plane of reason, they abandon the means by which to
criticize those members of their own culture on whom Dobu training did not for any reason whatever take. Criticism is a rational
activity which goes beyond the brute assertion of arbitrary preference. The latter may be asserted and the causes for espousing one

value may be given. But causes are not reasons, and the members of the culture whose values are disapproved also had causes which led them to choose their values. If a culture is content to accept values on causal, nonrational determinations, it cannot expect the individual to do otherwise. And that turns all choice of value into mere arbitrariness. The same will also be true in respect to the values espoused by a man at one period of his life as against another and in respect to one value within his consciousness and another with which the former may be in conflict. The upshot is, thus, pure solipsism of atomistic values. The argument against such an extreme position is that it contradicts the patent facts of the moral conscience, for we are, indeed, often able to correct our value judgments and within society such corrections are constantly taking place.

Dobuans could answer, however, not that they prefer their own values but that their values are better for themselves. This is not the same as maintaining that they hold their values because they do, and that no reason can be offered. Reasons are now offered for preferring their values, since it is argued that a people's values *ought* to be preferred by them. The question is now open to criticism, for the implied criterion on the basis of which it is said that a people's values are better for themselves can be criticized and its ground can be inquired into. In other words, to make the claim and intend it as a rational claim, that their values are better for themselves, opens them to giving and receiving reasons for holding their opinion. They must then put their claim through the gauntlet of criticism, and thus it turns out that the claim to validity which they offered for their criterion is other than they said it was: it is no longer that it is theirs, as they started by arguing, but that it is rationally defensible.

The assumption under these observations is that the perception or apprehension of value is an immediate affair, in the same sense that the apprehension of any other character of the world is. That this is the case I need not establish here, since it is a fact; and the interpretations that deny it will be taken up when we examine R. B. Perry's version of the interest theory. This is indeed "intuition," but "intuition" in the sense of "perception." I am not saying that we always intuit or perceive values correctly. I do not make that

claim in respect to primary or secondary qualities, and it is likely
that I am much more fallible as regards tertiary qualities than I am
as regards the other two. All I need to say is that we perceive
values and that perceived values can be discussed and perception
can be corrected. If I am asked, How do you correct it? I answer
that I correct it in the same way in which I correct any statement
about objective traits. The results are less certain, and agreement is
more rare, but this is a question of degree, not of kind. If, then, I
can perceive a value anywhere and can perceive an increment in
that value, I can judge whether civilized culture is higher than savage, difficult as I may find it to decide whether two savage cultures
or two civilized peoples are on the same plane or not. Shall anyone
deny who has directly grasped the specific quality of Aztec culture
that it was, with its essential unmitigated core of barbarism and in
spite of its high refinements along aesthetic lines and in the daily
relations among men at the family level, lower in its moral achievement than the civilization of Europe in the Middle Ages? One runs
into sentimental, Mexicanized gringos who refuse to see in the
Mexican masses anything but perfection. Many virtues the Mexi-
cans indeed have. But to miss what D. H. Lawrence saw is to look
with romantic lenses. Anyone in search of objectivity should read
Bernal Díaz and then, with open eyes, visit contemporary Mexico,
where so much of the pre-Columbian barbarism is still to be seen.
Whether Dobuan or Zuñi cultures are superior to Kwakiutl, I cannot tell, for my knowledge of them is too superficial. But it seems to
me nonsense to assert that we cannot compare Dobu or Kwakiutl or
Zuñi with our culture and decide which of them has expressed more
of the potentialities of man.

It is very possible that the examples that I have chosen do not
prove my point. I may be wrong about the Aztecs and the Dobuans
and the Zuñi. These peoples may have achieved a greater civilization than the French in the thirteenth century or the Romans in the
days of the Antonines. I base my judgment about the barbarism of
the Aztecs on something essentially harsh that I discovered in their
art, during a short stay in Mexico, and on what I read about their
human sacrifices in Bernal Díaz. But my knowledge is neither extensive nor deep, and it may be easy for a Vaillant or someone else
to correct me.[10] But if I am corrected, my point holds—for my point

is not that my judgment is infallible. My point is that cultures can be compared and judgments about them corrected.

Many years ago I heard Ralph Linton argue that we cannot prove that one culture is better than another, because in all cultures we find men intelligently employing the means within their reach to achieve their objectives. I do not know whether he still holds this view, but it is one frequently encountered in anthropological circles. But again the argument misses the point, namely, that in building a St. Sophia's or a St. Peter's or a Chartres Western man has expressed greater needs and, in expressing them, has created greater means to do so, and for many reasons—among which one, no doubt, is luck—he has reached greater achievement in this activity than the savage did who built the best clubhouse in Melanesia. Nor does this argument imply, above all, that the builders of St. Sophia's were, on some biopsychological criterion, more intelligent than the Dobuans. One of the most sacred dogmas of American sociology asserts the intellectual equality of the peoples of the world, and I yield second place to no one in my respect for the thirty-nine articles of social science.

The upshot of this discussion can be easily formulated: the Protagorean theory of morals as mores and its corollaries give us an imperfect account of moral phenomena. Can other forms of naturalistic moral theory solve the moral problem? In the remaining chapters of this part we turn to an examination of six naturalistic theories which exert great influence today.

CHAPTER II

THE INTEREST THEORY. I

IN SANTAYANA'S first book, *The Sense of Beauty* (1896), and almost by the way, in a few pages, he offered a sketch of a theory of value which since then has become one of the three or four most important conceptions of value held by contemporary American naturalists. Santayana presented the theory again in 1905 in *The Life of Reason* in a more fully developed form and used it as a foundation on which to erect a philosophy of history. He returned to it in *The Winds of Doctrine*.[1] The success of the interest theory of value is not to be credited merely to Santayana; it is also to be attributed to the rigorously systematic elaboration given it by Ralph Barton Perry.[2] Santayana himself gives credit for the theory to Spinoza, although the latter could have found it in Hobbes or in Aristotle, since it is one of the definitions of "good" found in the *Rhetoric*.[3] Santayana makes no reference to the contemporary value writers from whom he may have derived inspiration; but, whatever one may say of his originality, there need be no doubt about the importance of Santayana's contribution to the development of the theory.

Stripped to its fighting weight (to borrow one of Santayana's own happy phrases), the interest theory amounts to this: Man's desires or interests create his values. His "reason" organizes them; its function is not merely to contemplate their more or less perfect embodiment in the temporal contingencies of the flux. Man is able to increase value through the power of reason to observe past consequences and to foresee the course of future events. This is rational planning, which seeks to maximize satisfaction. The life of reason, or the moral economy, is a life dedicated to this end.

If we conceive the life of reason as Santayana did, as a philosophy of history, we find that it manifests itself wherever human progress has taken place, wherever human beings have succeeded in expressing their energies toward a satisfactory, harmonious life; this they have done in society, religion, art, and science. But the life of reason fails to come to flower among peoples who have never tried it and among those who have tried it and have found it wanting. The former are barbarians and are characterized by romanticism; the latter are postrational moralists and are characterized by other-worldliness, asceticism, and world-weariness.

Santayana has said repeatedly that his teachers were "the Greeks," and he has said many harsh things about his teacher and colleague, William James; but it is clear to any reader of Santayana that his historical connections are much wider than these references would suggest and that his debt to William James, even if only by way of passionate negative reaction (and it goes much further), is very profound. Now in his moral theory William James was even more of an impressionistic and unsystematic thinker than his younger colleague. The most sustained and systematic exposition of his moral thought with which I am acquainted is to be found in the essay entitled *The Moral Philosopher and the Moral Life*.[4] In this essay, concealed as a hearty approval of progress and as a yea-saying in a void universe, is latent the brutality of Darwinism, which was so attractive at the turn of the century. For James the moral life is the result of the stabilities and harmonies achieved by desires struggling with one another for satisfaction; order is the result of the elimination of the weaker and less insistent desires:

". . . as our present laws and customs have fought and con-quered other past ones, so they will in their turn be overthrown by any newly discovered order which will hush up the complaints that they still give rise to, without producing others louder still.

". . . Pent in under every system of moral rules are innumerable persons whom it weighs upon, and goods which it represses; and these are always rumbling and grumbling in the background, and ready for any issue by which they may get free."[5]

I have elsewhere argued that this is a straight might-makes-right theory of morals, although I am not ignorant of the facts that can be used to prove that James was a liberal and humane man.[6] Of James's admirable character there need be no doubt, nor is it in question. But in the only systematic expression that he left us of his moral theory, what he did was to translate into the field of morality the conception of the struggle for existence which was one of the articles of faith of his day. The flagrant inconsistency between his essay on moral philosophy and his other opinions and actions; between the Darwinism of his ethical views, on the one hand, and, on the other, his interest in the halt, the blind, and the meek; his opposition to aggressive war; and his enlightened views on political and social matters—these are not relevant here, although it is not difficult to see that they are of interest to the historian of ideas and to the sociologist of knowledge, since they illustrate the basic confusions of liberalism.

The temperamental differences between James and Santayana cannot escape those acquainted with both minds. James was rationalizing and celebrating in his philosophy the national energies at the beginning of their triumphal world expansion. Santayana was alien to that activity. James speaks of "the perfection of rottenness" of Santayana's philosophy, of his "Spanish tradition," and of his "Latinity." These phrases say very little about Santayana, but they do point to the deep-rooted temperamental differences between the two men. What for William James was life teeming with energy and the promise of growth was for Santayana waste of energy, since it produced nothing but ugliness and the blundering and meaninglessness of industrial chaos, with its teen-age gawkiness and its cracking voice. Santayana asks whether current civilization is a good and whether the horrors of a materialistic democracy are susceptible of mitigation. And it is not difficult to see that the questions arise from his dissatisfaction with his immediate environment, although in 1905, instead of speaking out directly, he speaks of "current civilization" and of "industrial democracy."[7] His criticisms irritated the sanguine founder of pragmatism, although Santayana's criticisms of the land in which he lived were very similar to those which William James's brother made in his travel notes on the land of his birth. Let us remember, from the many passages that one could recall, the well-known page on the commercial travelers, of whom Henry James asks:

"Whom were they constructed, such specimens, to talk with, to talk over, or to talk under, and what form of address or of intercourse, what uttered, what intelligible terms of introduction, of

persuasion, of menace, what developed, what specific human process of any sort, was it possible to impute to them?

"What women did they live with, what women, living with
them, could yet leave them as they were? . . . How, when people
were like that, did any one trust any one enough to begin or understand any one enough to go on, or keep the peace with any one
enough to survive?"[8]

William James, however, is not troubled by the drummer and
what his ubiquitous presence signifies; he is seemingly undisturbed
by what to his brother and to his younger colleague are the unspeakable vulgarity and spiritual aridity of the scene. He welcomes
his world. The criticisms he has to make of it are minor, compared
with the repudiation involved in the attitudes of the other two. And
he declares smugly that the barbarians were "in the line of mental
growth." How little he understood Santayana comes out clearly in
his remarks on *Interpretations of Poetry and Religion*, where he sets
"those who insist that the ideal and the real are dynamically continuous" in opposition to Santayana, who expresses in a splendidly
impertinent manner "the other view." This is said by a teacher and
colleague about Santayana, the man who told his readers on every
permissible occasion that every natural situation is capable of an
ideal development and every ideal must have a natural basis. It is
true, however, that Santayana deliberately sought refuge in what,
for James, was a profoundly alienating and unsympathetic tone—
precious, snobbish, and supercilious. In place of the rushing energy,
the noise and the bustle of the age of the Robber Barons, Santayana
put the ideal of a carefully planned life in which emergent energies
were guided by traditional achievements and the objectives of a
man or a people were defined and controlled, metaphorically speaking, by the "dramatic unities, the laws of versification"—to which
James rudely said "Bah!"[9]

It is an interesting fact that, although temperamentally Ralph
Barton Perry was more in sympathy with James than with Santayana, in respect to moral *doctrine* Perry, as we can see in *The
Moral Economy* more clearly than in *General Theory*, has a closer
affiliation with Santayana's orientation than with James's Darwinian
romanticism. Without intending to press the question of actual in-

fluence, it can be maintained that Perry's work constitutes a clarification of Santayana's conception of the life of reason. The spirit of Perry's work is totally different, but in method and in formal results there is close similarity. Perry's study is exhaustive, scientific, objective, and, by comparison with Santayana's, it is unimaginative and academically constipated; but they both advocate the same value theory, and their formulation of the moral problem is the same. It consists in defining the manner in which interests can be integrated into as broadly comprehensive and stable a pattern as possible with the material at hand. Unlike Santayana, who does not scruple to tell what the life of reason is, Perry in *General Theory* studiously maintains the objectivity of the scientist and refrains from advocating a particular moral ideal in preference to others. What he tries to do is to elucidate in as scrupulously neutral and rigorous a manner as possible how interests are actually organized. The general principles which are immanent in the organization indicate the direction in which moral judgments can be corrected. But the upshot of all his neutrality and of all this scientifically disciplined aloofness is identical with that proposed in his own *The Moral Economy* and quite congruous in method with Santayana's more impressionistic moral views. In vain, as it seems to me, does Perry attempt to retain his scientific neutrality; for the results are not objective or neutral, since his own preferences have been included in his assumptions, as I hope to show below when I examine "moral vitalism."[10]

Not only is the result of his investigations similar to Santayana's, but the assumptions are also similar. For the "interests" (a term that Santayana uses interchangeably with "desire") which must be ordered, while they are said to differ in their various dimensions, have each taken for itself as much claim to a place in the resultant pattern as the rest, and the agency of integration is, for both Perry and Santayana, "reason" similarly conceived. The problem of integration, Perry tells us in a section entitled "The Rationalization or Justification of Interests," is inevitable.[11] It consists in removing the disunion from which interests may suffer, in order that they may achieve one of the various modes of integration possible without those modes of nonintegration which disunion conditions; in short, "the central problem of integration is to achieve *harmony* in

place of *conflict*."[12] Integration is achieved through "mediation"—
which is the use of reason in order to introduce integration where
it did not exist before.[13] This is clearly but a technical analytic
statement of conceptions stated more generally and in a less
rigorous fashion in *The Moral Economy*.[14] And since it is what
James had in mind when he defined the moral problem as that of
finding "the more and more inclusive order" of ideals,[15] we can put
James in the same group with his younger colleagues. They all conceive the problem as that of organizing into some kind of ordered
pattern units of psychological force, desires, interests, each of
which envisages only the object that will satisfy it. They are
mechanists, since they analyze the phenomenon under investigation
down to its atomic components and then show the ways in which,
without reference to a whole to which they are thought of as existentially and logically prior, the components are integrated into
systems by means of connective forces external to the units they
connect. Because of these shared aspects, we are justified in examining them under the same heading. However, some of the criticisms here offered apply to Santayana and Perry exclusively, because I am at a loss to discover what James's views on the subject
under discussion were.

In the writer's opinion the most serious objection to the interest
theory of value consists in the myopic and oversimplified conception of the human personality on which it bases its analysis. The
criticism can be stated succinctly: The theory fails to realize that
a man is more than a bundle of integrated interests and an intelligence or reason that organizes them. If human beings were nothing more than bundles of interests, moral philosophy would not be
able to discover any solid ground on which to attribute to them a
higher value than it finds in the brutes. That higher value is intrinsic
to them and is related to their status as "persons"—a term which is
an axiological category. Even if we accept the validity of the exclusively psychological approach to the person, the inadequacy of the
picture of the self which the interest theory offers us can easily be
discovered. All we need do, in order to perceive it, is to confront
its account with those psychological components of the self which
the theory ignores and which we can easily discover by observa-

tion. Before turning to the substantiation of this criticism, however, it is desirable to indicate that the inadequacies of the conception of the person from which the interest theory suffers are the sources of the prejudiced analysis of "conscience" which Santayana offers in *The Life of Reason* and of the many contradictions and confusions which can be discerned in this work, particularly the radical contradiction between a purely descriptive, relativistic moral theory and the normative conception of moral theory on which, at the same time, Santayana insists. These questions will not be taken up here; they have been studied by the author in his contribution to the Santayana volume of "The Library of Living Philosophers."[16]

It is also desirable, before turning to an analysis of the conception of the self put forward by the interest theory, to lay down certain stipulations as to the terminology which will be employed in this essay. The term "self," as Bradley pointed out,[17] has many usages, but these are all, I take it, variant interpretations of data of an exclusively psychological nature. Even when men like A. E. Taylor discuss the self,[18] they confine themselves almost entirely to questions of psychology. For this reason I have decided to use the term to signify psychic phenomena exclusively, thus keeping in harmony with writers as diverse as William James, Bradley, Bosanquet, Taylor, and others.[19] But I shall hold below that the category "person" is not psychological but axiological. Here all that is necessary is to state that the reality which constitutes the person rests upon and, so far as we know empirically, depends on the psychological self. Nor is this reality open to exploration by the techniques and restrictive methods of the scientific psychologist. The concrete human being, the man of flesh and bones, as Unamuno was fond of calling him, is an animal—something the biologist studies. But he is also a psyche or self, which classical psychologists used to study (for whether the psyche or self is still studied by contemporary psychology is a question I find difficulty in answering). Above the self or psyche man is a spiritual person. The possession of "spirit" distinguishes him from the other animals, gives him a worth that no other creature has, and enables him to become a person. Perry seems to use the two terms "person" and "self" synonymously, but what he means by them is what I call "the self."

In criticizing the interest theory's notion of personality or self, we shall analyze Perry's doctrines, for they are much more systematically and lucidly stated than are Santayana's. Indeed, so little does the concept of "self" or "person" (in the purely psychological meaning of this latter term) seem to concern Santayana that neither in Munitz' study nor in Howgate's do the words "self" and "person" appear in the Index, and in the 698 pages of the Schilpp volume there are only five references to the word "self" and two to the word "personality."[20] For Perry, "a person is an organization not among the objects of mind, but among its *acts*,—of cognition or of interest." A person consists of an "intra-organic integration" most simply represented by habit and memory.[21] But Perry is interested in one case of intraorganic integration which he considers "of central importance," the integration of interests. The conception is clearly stated in the last paragraph of his discussion of "Personality as Intermediation of Interests":

"We conclude, therefore, that personality and its prerogatives are peculiar to organic individuals of the human species, or to units of life having the peculiar structural and functional organization characteristic of organisms endowed with a highly developed central nervous system. Personality consists in a type of integration or interdependence of interests such as occurs when the interests in question are dispositions or activities of one concentric and integumented organism. It is a peculiar autonomous system, or field of control, such as in the physical man is conditioned by one continuous nervous tract having a continuous history."[22]

In fairness to Perry it should be pointed out that he does not simplistically consider the personality to be an additive affair made up by adding interests to emotions, to pleasure-pain capacity, etc. Accepting a distinction drawn by Russell and Broad between composition and addition, he affirms that the personality consists of the composition of interests. But the point relevant for us is that Perry seeks to define the personality and to explain its development in terms of the integration of interests.[23]

But let us look into the defects of this theory. According to it, the units that are organized into a moral economy should be capable of manifesting themselves clearly and distinctly to introspection, at least under ideal conditions. This is an essential assumption of the theory; for, unless there is the possibility of knowing our multiple desires or interests in their various strengths and directions, no less than in their prospective consequences, we cannot organize them. Interests are organized, Perry tells us, according to four "notions"—correctness, intensity, preference, and inclusiveness.[24] But, unless the various interests are individually distinct and easily available for inspection at the moment of moral reflection, these principles could not be applied to their organization. Consider the example that Perry offers in his discussion of "Personality as Intermediation of Interests," and you will see that he deals with interests as if these were always fully apparent above the level of consciousness and available for inspection when conflicts arise or when one of them demands peremptory satisfaction.[25] Perry holds that the composition of interests is endowed with a capacity for emotional excitement, whose function is to facilitate "supreme exertion" by concentrating and augmenting available energies and by protecting the organism against the effects of strain and injury, and a capacity for pleasure and pain.[26] This, we are asked to believe, is all that is necessary in order to give an account of the human personality. If we fail to recognize in this blueprint what makes each of us what he is, so much the worse for us. The integration or pattern of desires or interests is, it is concluded, an a posteriori affair—the product of forces which, I take it, are organized into the ideal man by lucid and conscious foresight. The pattern thus organized constitutes the moral unity, man, with whom moral philosophers have to deal.

A moment's notice reveals to us, however, that the human beings whom we know—Peter, Paul, and John—bear only the most superficial resemblance to these ingenious and shallow robots whose behavioristic minds are built on the blueprint of a computing machine, but neither whose voices nor whose manners succeed in deceiving us. In Perry's conception the self and its constituent interests lack depth. This can be seen throughout, but it can be conveniently illustrated by examining Perry's treatment of moral control. The question refers to the process by which a given interest is modified, which is essentially the same process as that "by which a capacity for interest, whether specific or general, is realized."[27]

There are, we are told, four methods of control. But since I fear that a summary could not do justice to the flavor of Perry's words or to the quality of his vision, I shall resort to a long quotation:

"Viewing our topic under the aspect of control, let us take any normal individual and ask what influences affect him, or can be brought to bear upon him, in such wise as to beget in him a state of interest which he did not have before. To make the hypothetical case both simple and specific let us ask how he can be brought to desire the apple which I hold in my hand. There are four methods of appeal or inducement of which all may be jointly effective, or of which some may succeed where others fail.

"The simplest method is to present the apple to the subject's sensory experience, so that he may feel and smell it, and thus receive effective stimuli to an interested response for which he is already predisposed. I present the apple in such wise as to excite an appetite and at the same time direct the appetite upon this particular object. I may use less rudimentary methods. . . .

"A second method is to manifest or stimulate an interest in the apple on my own part. I may gloat over it, express pleasure in it, or taste it, with unmistakable symptoms of satisfaction. In this case, I seek to arouse the interest not simply by affording it a suitable occasion, but by exhibiting the interest itself.

"Should these methods fail I may resort to starvation. I may, assuming a control of the circumstances, see to it that the appetite which I hope to excite is deprived of eligible objects other than that which I have to offer. I may remove the apple to a distance, or threaten to throw it away, or describe a prospective dearth of apples. . . .

"Finally, should my subject still manifest indifference, I may seek to gain my end indirectly through dealing with his other interests. . . . Through satisfying, or thwarting, or deadening his other interests by any of the first three methods, I may so affect his general state as to render him more susceptible to the interest which I am seeking to implant.

"All of these methods are employed in everyday life—in the way of a man with a maid or of a maid with a man, in parental exhortation, in religious edification, in efforts to extend personal influence, to obtain public support, or to create a public demand.

In all of these cases the accepted maxims are the same: 'Give the people what they want,' that is, present your case so that it will appeal to the object's existing interests; 'Show that you mean it,' that is, manifest in your own person the interest which you desire to awaken in another; 'People value only what they have to work for,' therefore, hold the object at a distance, so that an effort is necessary in order to obtain it; 'See him just after dinner,' in other words, cultivate or seize upon a receptive mood when the subject is favorably inclined either through his general well-being, or through the absence of more attractive alternatives.''[28]

There can be no objection in principle to the discussion of complex subject matter through the use of simple and specific illustrations, if these clarify without vulgarizing it and giving an impression that the problem they seek to clarify is as simple as they are. But I submit that if all that the reader knew about the problem of moral control was what he learned from Perry's discussion of its methods, he would be left extremely perplexed by the fact that so simple a problem is so persistently and tragically bungled in practice and that men so seldom succeed in achieving adequate moral control. I have not overlooked, I trust, the ambiguity of the illustration, which would delight a student of Empson with a dash or two of orthodox Freudianism in his mental veins, since the subtle coupling of apples and the ways of a man with a maid and of a maid with a man point to the ambiguity so clearly that even a mole could see it. But is control so easy to achieve? Perhaps it is in the case of desire for apples, if these are literal apples. But not in the case of symbolic apples or of other objects; and there are at least two reasons for the difficulty.

The first is that interests are not atomic, separate components of our volitional life. At the common-sense level, we usually speak of them as if they were, and, for practical purposes, there is no harm in conceiving of them in this manner. But the moral philosopher needs to go beyond the rough-hewn differentiations of common sense in order to be able to criticize its vague and contradictory insights successfully. Interests are not separate, self-existing vectors, like arrows, which can be taken out of their quiver and shot from a bow, and their identity does not change in the handling. To speak of a man's interests—in his career, his home, his church, his financial holdings—in this manner injects an initial falsification into the discussion which is probably one of the sources of the overconfidence that the interest theory displays in the capacity of reason to correct the integrations of interests. A man's interest in his career, let us say, does not possess its peculiar and unique specificity of drive and affective tone by itself. Its identity depends on intricate relationships with the interests in conjunction with which it forms a complex, more or less harmonious, integration. It probably waxes and wanes as it is helped or hindered by the whole ambient set, which, in subtle and not easily describable ways, modifies it, draining it or charging it with energy, modifying its affective tonality, and thus varying its essential nature, even though leaving its direction unchanged. But, above all, it has a steady, intrinsic specificity, since it is now identified with a task on hand, now with others' opinions of one's talent or ability, now with one's desire for betterment or for admission into an honorary society or some sort of recognition not entirely dependent on one's efforts.

What is a career—the career, let us say, of a surgeon or a teacher? Does the career of a teacher refer to the activities in the classroom and his research alone? And interest in it—does it include interest in the activity in the classroom *and* in the student? Or does it include interest in the well-being of other teachers? And, if so, does it extend to a man's loyalty to his institution or his department? Does it include his partiality for universities in general as compared to the social worker's partiality for neighborhood centers? Alter to some extent any of the elements which constitute the complex of interrelated circumstances, both objective and subjective, in which a man finds himself, and to some extent you are also likely to alter his interest in his career. But to what extent and in what direction cannot be too exactly determined in advance, so that the comparison of interests is not like the matching of a piece of fabric with a spool of thread or a tie with a suit and shirt. Interests in isolation and in system are different things; and the reason is that they are not related to a system mechanically but in the manner of components of the organic wholes which they compose. When we take this into consideration, it casts doubt on, if it does not altogether force us to abandon, the belief that interests can be controlled as the desire for an apple could be if we had unlimited power over the individual in whom we wished to create the desire and no scruples about what means we adopted to modify him in accordance with our will.

But the discussion has been carried on as if reflection upon our manifest interests were all that is required in order to achieve a successful integration. And we must now ask whether this is indeed the case. We must remember that the purpose of the integration is to achieve a pattern productive of satisfaction without conflict or frustration—productive, in a word, of happiness. And the question which we must ask is whether the result aimed at can be achieved by the rational manipulation of interests. I have no doubt that it could if interests were what Perry conceives them to be, if they merely floated on the surface of consciousness. We know, however, that what is normally revealed at the conscious level is only a part— and not a wholly representative part—of the constitution of the mind or self. Interests have roots in the mud of the id—for it is to aspects of the mind to which Freud has called attention that I am referring and for which, therefore, a convenient terminology lies ready at hand—deep beyond the reach of the prying eye of intro- spective awareness. They are manifestations of energies which we cannot directly envisage. This is, in Freud's terms, "the obscure inaccessible part of our personality," and he continues:

"We can come nearer to the id with images, and call it a chaos, a cauldron of seething excitement. We suppose that it is somewhere in direct contact with somatic processes, and takes over from them instinctual needs and gives them mental expression, but we cannot say in what substratum this contact is made. These instincts fill it with energy, but it has no organization and no unified will, only an impulsion to obtain satisfaction for the instinctual needs, in accord- ance with the pleasure-principle."[29]

From this source, in interplay between the demands of the ex- ternal world and the instinctual demands of the inaccessible part of the mind, the interests somehow develop. But, since we remain for the most part ignorant of their interconnections under the surface, it is not so easy as the philosophers of the life of reason assume to tell what exactly are the effects of their satisfaction or their denial.

The harmony that obtains at the level of consciousness is no guar-
anty of genuine harmony, of genuine fulfilment of the whole self.
I do not mean merely that we may fail to achieve harmony because
of the factors described by Perry under the heading of "Specious
Integrations."[30] For Perry the solution of the whole nest of problems to which the data of deep analysis give rise, consists "in the
creation of comprehensive purposes, which enjoy the support of
their constituent interests because they make the most liberal
possible provision for them all."[31]

But the question to which we need an answer is: How do we
know that the provision that we have made is the most liberal? A
man plans with the best will and with the finest intelligence, he
tries to make the most liberal provision, he meets the social demands made upon him, and he studies earnestly to discover what it
is that he really wants. Let us assume that he is one of the lucky
few among mankind who can go after what they want unrestricted
by financial or class obstructions or by race prejudice and the like;
let us assume that Fortune loves him and is faithful to him; and let
us further assume that he is physically well endowed. We have him
launched on the road to happiness. But in the midst of his activity,
in the most unexpected fashion, he gradually finds himself baffled by
a sense of futility, corroded by a profound dissatisfaction. He refuses at first to give in to it. But the essential sense of urgency that
buoyed him up cannot be recaptured, and, almost without knowing
it, he loses faith.

Men usually do not lie down on the side of the road, drop their
pack, and let the army march on. Even if they wanted to, circumstances do not allow them to. There are commitments to the family,
to the institution, to the job; there are the habits of a lifetime, which
cannot easily be broken. Men carry on, against all obstacles and
even against the worst one of them, the death of that inside them
that pushed them on and imparted quiet joy to their work. But their
hearts are dead, and the farce they try desperately to play ceases to
deceive them and those around them. Look around you in your profession, and you will notice that the throng of the successful failures
is larger than one has reason to suspect. You have to peer beyond
appearances, past circumstances that seem propitious and conditions that seem to favor them rather than to obstruct them. When

you do, you find that they are dead. Why? It is not easy to tell, except in the most general terms. Perhaps because some deep need, deeply repressed and therefore never suspected, ends by killing their faith, or because the satisfaction of the needs they have favored ends up by weakening the whole structure. We do not really know. But the evidence of the conditions cannot be denied or gainsaid. We can see them if we but look around us, respectable men who do not successfully conceal the quiet desperation that possesses them or the cynicism that dooms them. To what extent could the conditions have been controlled by them, had they had a wisdom and a luck that we cannot expect human beings normally to have? This is a question for which we do not have a ready answer. I suspect—and psychoanalysis confirms my hunch—that the psychoses from which the mass of men suffer are only to a very limited extent corrigible by their individual efforts; and for that reason, if I believed that happiness was the end which moral philosophy sought to achieve, I would long ago have abandoned its study as an illusion on which it is not worth spending our efforts.

Fenichel tells us, what in any case we know from other sources, that "different societies, stressing different values and applying different educational measures, create different anomalies."[32] Be that as it may, the belief that the integration of the prima facie interests which we can discover in ourselves can guarantee a successful satisfaction seems to be unwarrantedly optimistic. As Fenichel observes, only by delving into the "universe of unconscious drives and their irrational manifestations" can we hope to understand that not merely "unusual and suddenly erupting mental states" but also ordinary or normal ones are "dependent on unconscious conditions; and that ordinary volition is determined just as are disorders of the will."[33] The interests that emerge in consciousness cannot be taken at their face value. Their faces have been plain enough, and they all claim to carry their papers with them in good order. We think, therefore, that we can tell that this is a good one and ought to be favored and that that is an evil one and should be discouraged or repressed. But Dostoevski, Freud, and Gide (to mention no others) wrote in vain if we are so readily satisfied. One has to remember that interests are all suspicious characters and that we cannot tell from merely looking at them whether they truly are what they look like or something quite different. Since the interests emerge from, and are determined in their nature and direction by, the inaccessible volitional mass, no successful organization of them can be achieved without reference to their source. As Fenichel puts it: "It is obvious that an apparatus whose function is to organize, to direct and if necessary to suppress cannot be understood without a knowledge of what is organized, directed, or suppressed."[34]

This is the reason why an organization achieved in terms of phenomena which appear above the level of consciousness, taken only at this level and merely in terms of repugnances and compatibilities which can be discovered by simple introspection, is singularly shallow and incomplete. If what is desired is an adjustment of the largest number of desires possible in terms of *correctness*, *intensity*, *preference*, and *inclusiveness*, it becomes necessary to know considerably more than the conception of the person presupposed by the interest theory of value allows us to know. Hidden needs, unknown hungers, ambivalent attitudes, and dark ambiguous preferences have to be considered, for these have the power to reverse and frustrate the shallow, lucid plans of the conscious self. When these factors which the interest theory leaves out of account are reckoned, the theory's notion of what constitutes an ideal organization and by what means it is possible to achieve it must be radically altered, so radically, indeed, that the result is more likely to deserve the name of the "life of unreason" than the name that Santayana gave it.

If, after all that has been said, it is still possible to define the person in terms of interests, emotions, pleasures, and intelligence, we should at least distinguish clearly between the normal, conscious interests which make for their object in a simple and directly observable way and these subterranean denizens which, no less than the respectable interests, make up the distraught and pathetic creature which is man. Sadism, masochism, the Polycrates complex, vague fears and pervasive anxieties, aggressive tendencies, concealed hatred directed against ourselves, covert envy, malice tied to love—all these factors and innumerably more, which have always baffled the poet and cannot be ignored by the moral philosopher, modify the behavior of the individual beyond the level of direct rational control. They are factors determining our conduct in-

dependently of, and often in opposition to, the consciously discriminable interests which, according to Perry, make up the moral
economy.

Once the awareness of these factors enters the picture, it forces
us to recognize that the self, or the integration of effective constellations which for the interest theory define it, so far as knowledge goes today, is only one, and an indeterminate, element in the
achievement of the moral economy. Disruption of the economy
does not result merely from frustration of surface interests or from
manifest conflicts but from the manner—about which we are as yet
almost entirely in the dark—in which the hidden factors of the self
enter into the selection of values through the inhibition or encouragement of interests. The value of life as lived, which is distinct
from the values acknowledged by the person or even those he
espouses, seems to a very small extent to depend on cognitive preferences dictated by what Santayana and Perry call "reason." And
even less does it seem to depend on whether a large or small number
of interests decided on by the four notions of Perry are satisfied or
not. The preferences operate below, as well as above, consciousness, and denial of interests is no less necessary than satisfactions to
secure the tension and tone without which life as it is lived loses its
value. Thus the belief controlling the conception of the moral economy into which the interest theory of value issues is not necessarily
true, either for the person or for the interests considered abstractly.
Perry asserts that when two constituent interests are opposed, "a
state of things in which these identical interests were harmonious
. . . would be better than the given state of conflict."[35] I shall refer
to this conception of the moral life as "vitalistic" because it assumes that life is good and the more life, the better. Perry's statement, of course, must be taken in its context, where we find that its
truth depends on the hypothetical application of the standard of
"inclusiveness" which has been defined earlier. But the point of
these remarks is that, even when thus taken, it leaves out of account the fact that the tension and sometimes the anxiety generated
by a conflict may be essential factors in producing the tone and
value of life as it is lived.

To the moral vitalist this view seems morally perverse and theoretically false. To the writer the absence of awareness of the phe-

nomena to which attention has been called makes moral vitalism a superficial doctrine, a pathetically false picture of the moral life. Of course, it is in no way denied by these remarks that important components of the moral life with which we have to deal are interests conceivable as vectorial forces which must be integrated. It is intended merely to assert that a moral theory cannot be considered adequate without a conception of the total personality and that such a conception must include more than the vectorial unit forces which seek satisfaction and the foresight or reason which organizes them; for man, the actual actor of the moral drama, as we have come to know him through the efforts of poets and sages, is a complex, burdened, pitiful, and wonderful creature. He may be the paragon of animals, of noble reason and of infinite faculty; in action he may be like an angel and in apprehension like a god; but he is also a petulant thinking reed and a hopeless mess. He is in love with life but also hates it deeply and subtly. He is capable of crime and sin but also has a tyrannical and whimsical conscience that tortures him for trivial misdemeanors as brutally as it punishes him for unpardonable sins. Narcissistic, he hates himself; full of insufferable vanity, he seeks to humiliate himself; the victim of systematic self-deception, he is capable of unsparing self-knowledge. But, above all, in what he wants he is hopelessly confused, vague, self-deceived, inconsistent, and divided. Nothing, I suspect, would give him a worse sense of misery and of guilt than letting him have all that he wants. In any case it would take an Augustine, a Freud, a Dostoevski, a Kierkegaard, and a Shakespeare, aided by a Boas and a Machiavelli, pooling their several talents and techniques, to split open the secret heart of this contemptible lump of living clay and extract its wonderful essence. Santayana and Perry are very able philosophers, but we cannot take too seriously the conception of man that they give us as adequate for an account of the moral economy.

CHAPTER III

THE INTEREST THEORY. II

FOLLOWING Santayana and Ralph Barton Perry, naturalistic value theory in the United States has sedulously eschewed value realism of the types defended by men like Laird and by Hartmann and Scheler. The possibility of value realism is rejected by an epistemology which draws a sharp distinction between primary and secondary qualities, on the one hand, and tertiary, on the other. Our immediate task, therefore, is to examine the reasons for this distinction. Since the distinction has been most carefully drawn and most rigorously defended by Ralph Barton Perry, his formulations will be examined.

Before entering into our task, let us note that Perry criticizes Santayana because the latter does not unambiguously defend the interest theory and suggests in some of his statements a distinction between the interest, which projects the value, and the value itself, as an objective character. Perry holds that Santayana errs in making this distinction; but he believes that Santayana is on the right side, in spite of the comfort which his inaccurate statements give men like Moore and Laird, for Santayana does, after all, believe that value consists in the response by which a state of the subject is imputed to the object.[1]

In defense of the distinction which Perry draws between primary and secondary qualities, on the one hand, and tertiary, on the other, he begins with an analysis of the view of Moore and Laird, which he formulates as follows: "the term 'good' is employed as a predicative adjective interchangeably with such adjectives as 'green' and 'yellow.' "[2] This view, Perry observes, is based on the pan-objectivist's failure to find any difference between primary and secondary qualities, on the one hand, and tertiary, on the other, which would compel us to assign to the latter a different status. But if there is no difference, Perry urges, one should be able to find "a distinct *quale* which appears in that region which our value-terms roughly indicate, and which is different from the object's shape and size, from the interrelation of its parts, from its relation to other objects, or to a subject; and from all other factors which belong to the same context, but are designated by words other than 'good.' The present writer, for one, finds no such a residuum."[3]

I will argue that the proper discrimination of the data will reveal the prima facie objectivity of value characters or of values, which is required by Perry. In passing, let us note that all our evidence must be merely "seeming," or phenomenal, since we are discussing whether or not *characters in perceptual appearance* are indeed objective. And I hope to show that the prima facie objectivity of values is not confined to aesthetic values alone but applies to ethical values also. The phenomenal objectivity thus established is enough for the value student, since the ontic status of value, the fact that value is more than mere phenomenon, follows from the denial of the assumption that the reality which is disclosed by physics is more truly real than that which is disclosed by ordinary perception. But perhaps it is advisable to clarify this statement somewhat. Before doing so, I beg leave to introduce a parenthetical observation. It will be important to remember later, in the constructive parts of this essay, Parts II and III, the basis on which values will be said to have ontic status. The validity of the notion of the ontic status of values will not be assumed suddenly as proved without proof. The first step in the argument will be developed in this chapter in some detail, and it will consist of showing the phenomenal objectivity of value character which Perry takes a good deal of trouble to deny.

But how can I show that value is independent of the experience through which it is apprehended? For the phenomenal objectivity of value does not imply its ontic objectivity, as perspective realists and objective relativists will point out. I would not undertake to prove that value *exists* independently of the perception or knowledge of it because the word "exist," whether as a verb, "to exist," or as a substantive, "existence," can become at times a great troublemaker. What I believe can be done is to show that value has ontic status or is ontically objective. And, having established the phenomenal objectivity of value, the second step is to point out the fallacy in those theories that accept the bifurcation of nature into two classes of objects: on the one hand, into independent objects, existing in the objective world, known by positive science, and possessed only of spatiotemporal characters or primary qualities and, on the other, into subjective experience, which as a class includes among its members "value experiences." The second step is taken by showing that the objects introduced by the bifurcation have a methodological status and not an ontological one, as both Galileo and Descartes led men erroneously to believe.

On the face of it, it would seem that values are phenomenally objective, in the sense that *they are discovered to be qualities that reside in objects and can themselves be objects of attention*. When I say that a certain primitive people are hospitable, I speak of a value which characterizes the culture and which is discernible as resident *in* certain customs of these people, entangled somehow in the manner in which they treat their guests. The linguistic difficulty I am having, evident in the inadequate expression "somehow entangled," cannot be construed as evidence against the fact that it is the tribe that is hospitable and that this value does not depend on anyone's noticing it. The tribe may never have been studied, and its members may themselves be unconscious of this value. Values are somehow entangled in physical objects, and the proposition holds for *all* values, whether moral, aesthetic, or any other kind you choose to mention. On the face of it, they are objective because they reside *in* the object which they qualify or characterize and *in* which we perceive them.

Let us take a number of random samples as they suggest themselves spontaneously. A man says "Jane is beautiful" and means to point to a quality which belongs to Jane in the same way that the fragrance belongs to a rose and sweetness to ice cream. Of course, he may be mistaken about Jane's beauty; the beauty may not be Jane's own but lent to her by the artist who dressed her before she came to the party; again, men all too frequently confuse sexual attractiveness with beauty. Confusions of this sort are extremely difficult to clarify; but, since the practical consequences to which they lead are trivial or at least the very confusion prevents us from taking them seriously, the effort required to reduce them is seldom spent. No less an objective statement is made when we say, "the storm is sublime," or "John is generous," or "Achilles is brave," or "Mary's walk is more graceful than a panther's," or "Francis of Assisi is a saint or has a saintly character." This last value judgment makes a good illustration, for Francis' saintliness has been carefully checked by the experts whose business it is to pass on his canonization. The value was correlated with numerous and complex facts which "subtend" it (as I shall call it);[4] and, while the value character must be apprehended directly or immediately, its presence is verified by pointing to the facts in which it resides. A Mohammedan theologian may conceive "saintliness" in a different way from the College of Cardinals at Rome; but, if he does, the discussion that will ensue between him and the cardinals will be carried on in objective terms. In like manner a man's honesty or his generosity is an objective value residing *in* the men who are honest or generous, somehow entangled in certain modes that they have of behaving toward their fellows.

Value belongs objectively, also, to such distinctly subjective experiences as "effort," "struggle," and "aspiration,"[5] and by this statement I do not mean anything paradoxical. The effort is made by someone, by you or by myself, and in that sense it is something intimately subjective, as subjective as a toothache or a deep attack of anxiety. But the value of the effort is one thing, the effort is another. Physical effort is not so intrinsically valuable as moral effort, and the effort involved in winning a place on an Olympic team or in a beauty contest seems to this writer less valuable than the effort which carried Lincoln or Roosevelt through their jobs or the courage that carried Socrates through his trial and his rejection of Crito's offer. The value of the effort is a complex value and is distinct from the effort; for the physical effort involved in defending one's home may be intrinsically the same as that required to rob it, but the efforts seem to have different values. When it is said of someone's effort that it is valuable, the statement refers to an objective character of his effort, although the effort is a subjective experience. You reply, "No, really it was wasted or futile because it was misdirected." Now, leaving aside the question as to who is right, it should be noticed that we can discuss the value of effort, but when we do, we consider it to be an objective character. It was praiseworthy, I said, but you replied that it was worthless. You speak in the same way of the toothache: It is very bad, you tell me, and I believe you to have a bad toothache; I have plausible evidence. But I also believe that your toothache is not so bad as the one Fred had last week, and the reason is that he could not work, although he wanted to, and was distracted by the pain, whereas you went to the office and—with diminished efficiency, it is true—managed to do a day's work. The objectivity of Jane's beauty is public; something which you and I and everybody else who looks at her can perceive. The badness of your toothache is utterly private. In this sense it is subjective, since it belongs to a toothache which itself is private, and therefore the only evidence I can have of it is circumstantial and indirect. There are consummate artists among malingerers, whom it is difficult to show up. But such values—the beauty of Jane, the badness of the pain, and the worth of the effort—are, in the same sense, objective. For the objective-subjective polarity is ambiguous. Values can be objective in the sense that they are external to us as perceivers, that they are somehow outside or beyond our bodies; but this is a trivial sense. And they can be objective in the sense that they are objects of perception and are distinct from the psychological processes in the perceiver by means of which or, if you prefer, in which or through which they are perceived; and this is the important sense for our theory of knowledge about them. What I mean is that they are no more objective when they are perceived by our organs of external perception than when they are perceived by our internal organs of perception, our capacity for reflection. The sad beauty of the full moon, shining quietly in a cool summer night, is an objective value, and so also is the value of the beauty of Jane as I think of her now with my mind's eye—as we so properly say—and bring her loveliness to my memory. You, who never saw her, will never possess that value, but that is definitely your loss. I can remember her and now recall her vividly and enjoy in memory her beauty, though she died long ago. The value of the gratification which I get when I reflect upon the full, physically satisfied condition of the body, the pleasure I enjoy after a good dinner as I sit by the fire and deliberately delay the lighting of the cigar—this, too, is objective, although its seat is internal, inside the body, and it could be only inferred by my dinner companions in a very rough way, nor will they ever know exactly how I feel at the moment.

The important prima facie objectivity of value consists in the fact that values are objects of apprehension, even when their locus is intracutaneous. The actual physical locus of a value does not matter: the valuable effort of my friend is in his will and in the activity to which it leads; but I can indirectly infer this value, although in some respects my inference is more liable to error than his immediate experience of the value is likely to be. For him the value of his effort as object of perception is as objective as it is for me; as to its locus, it is somewhere inside his body. The disvalue of my toothache is inside my mouth; the beauty of Jane outside my body and in her face.

Because certain thinkers seem to have a great deal of difficulty in grasping what is meant by the epistemic objectivity of value at the phenomenal level, I beg the reader to bear with me for a little longer while I go over what I have already said from a slightly different point of view, in the hope of making my meaning clearer. Experience is polar, and the experience through which value is apprehended involves the same polarity as any other kind of experience. This is as true of perception directed inward upon events of the body, of what Locke called "reflection" (in which the mind perceives purely mental objects), as it is of experience of external objects. Experience is polar even in those relatively infrequent cases where attention focuses exclusively on pleasure and pain. This means that we can distinguish perfectly clearly and distinctly an object of perception (which itself may not be a clear and distinct object) or, as I prefer to say, of apprehension. Normally, however, we are intent upon the object and give little or no heed to the affective processes in the self which take place when the object is grasped. But affective processes—either pleasure or pain—usually accompany the grasping or apprehending. There are two ways of expressing the phenomena to which I am referring, depending on whether we view the phenomenon from the inside outward, so to speak, or from the outside inward. Viewed from the inside outward, we can say that pleasure colors the object—or we can use a more or less similar expression; viewed from the other end, we can say the object arouses and defines the character of the pleasure. There is nothing in the phenomenon that denies the objectivity of the objects of experience. This is the reason why both parties are right in the quarrel as to whether there are several kinds of pleasure or one only. Pleasure qua pleasure is always the same; but, since the sources of pleasure vary from experience to experience and define it, pleasure as apprehended varies with them.

The upshot of this discussion is that the epistemic object can always be distinguished, although seldom can it be separated from the apprehending subject. Hence the phenomenal objectivity of value. Perhaps this is an exaggeration, since in experiences in which the degree of consciousness is low or in certain types of purely sensory experiences, as Whitehead somewhere points out, it must be admitted that it is almost impossible to distinguish the object from the subject experiencing it. This qualification does not impair the truth of my observation, however, since in experiences of value we have to deal with a relatively high degree of discriminating awareness. A Cuban who knows about such matters once told me that a tobacco-taster or appraiser (I do not know the technical term by which this skill is known) will close his eyes and concentrate on the aroma of the cigar as the smoke is wafted gently to his nose, in order to discriminate its quality. I dare say that if he concentrated on the pleasure which the cigar smoke gave him, he would lose his high capacity to discriminate its aroma. The liquor-taster, I am told, rolls the liquor in his mouth and spits it out, in order to discriminate the bouquet. Words like "aroma" and "bouquet" refer to the specific, discriminable quality of cigars and of liquor, qualities which are utterly distinct both from the physical properties which subtend them in the objects in which they are discovered and from the psychological processes necessary to apprehend them. In normal experience the smoker who is not an excessive smoker or the drinker who is not a drunkard enjoys both the quality of the object—the aroma of the cigar or the bouquet of the wine—and, at the same time and without discriminating it from the former, the pleasure that the object produces. But if it is the pleasure of the wine or the cigar that he is exclusively after, the effort to make the fine discriminations in which the lover of fine wines or of good cigars indulges would tend to get in his way. The glutton "wolfs" the food, the drunkard gulps the drink, and thus they put up with stuff of dubious quality. The result is ironic, and even paradoxical; the man intent on pleasure is a poor sensualist and is likely to enjoy less of it than the man disinterested enough in pleasure to be able to discriminate the objective qualities of the objects of apprehension.

I am not trying to suggest that the subjectivist has reached the extreme position of the glutton or the drunkard; what I am saying is that in his theory he places emphasis on the state of the body, on the experience of pleasure, rather than on the experience of objects. His own actual experience may be quite different from his theory; it may be the very opposite of his theory. Indeed, some theoretical subjectivists of my intimate acquaintance are not at all subjectivistic in their actual living. They insist on the finest discrimination of objective characters, irrespective of the pleasure that these characters give the experiencer.

Let me reiterate that the referent of any value term is vague at best. Consider the word "beauty" as used by a hedonist. For him it does not seem to point to the prima facie objective quality of a perceptual object, let us say Jane, but to the feelings which that quality produces in him. When Casanova says Jane is beautiful, it is doubtful whether he means to refer exclusively to the objective quality of Jane which we said resides somehow *in* her face. What he has in mind is the fact that, as I believe it was Stendhal who put it, Jane is a "promise of pleasure." But Casanova is an expert on pleasure, and the way in which he judges the sources of his pleasure and the order of rank in which he arranges them are possible because he perceives the value of each source objectively. He is able to discriminate among objects of pleasure and to decide which is capable of producing a greater and which a lesser pleasure. But I am doing Casanova an undeserved injustice, since he is also a cultivated judge of beauty and, on occasion, looks at the beauty of women objectively, in the same way as he does when he says of a statue that it is beautiful; he means to speak of the statue, although perhaps not in an exclusively objective way, for he may mean the statue-as-giving-pleasure. If he means the latter, he may be called a halfway objectivist, whose criterion of beauty is hedonic. I once heard a man say that he could find no experiential difference between looking at the painting of a nude and looking at a naked woman. Men like that are sensualists, they are pathetic subjectivists, in that as regards nudes, whether on canvas or in the flesh, they center attention on their own sensual reactions to the nude and not on the aesthetic values of the objects of perception. But as regards the value of their reactions, if they can ever be brought to attend to them, they would be objectivistic; for, however we refer to those values, whether in terms of intensity or exquisiteness or in some other way, these characters which variously distinguish their subjective reactions are objective characters of the reactions, in the very sense that the badness of the pain of a toothache, shared by no one but felt exclusively by him who suffers it, is an objective character of the ache.

Let me support my contention by invoking the aid of C.I. Lewis' great authority. Lewis admits the prima facie objectivity of value, although for reasons that are not pertinent here, he goes on to deny the ontic objectivity of value and maintains that belief in its ontic objectivity is based on verbal misunderstandings.[6] Lewis distinguishes the class of values which he calls "inherent" and contrasts it with those which he calls "instrumental." He defines "inherent" values as those values "which are resident in objects," so that they can be (in my terminology, not his) apprehended or discovered in experience when the object possessing them is presented to apprehension. Inherent values constitute a subdivision of extrinsic values, and the latter are values which, as he puts it, are "for the sake of something else," of something intrinsically valuable. But, for him, only actual or possible experience can be intrinsically valuable.[7] I can call on Lewis only to support my contention that values are inherent in objects phenomenally, for Lewis will have none of ontic objectivity. Ontically, objects do not reside in things independently of perception, he tells us, except as "potentialities" for experience of values.

Here we witness the injection into value discussion, in a veiled manner, of a notion which is very similar, from the point of view of the function that it accomplishes, to "emergence." In any case, the fact that, phenomenally, value is objective—a value which Lewis terms "inherent"—is the fact that I have tried to assert. It is a fact of experience discoverable through experience. Lewis gives the impression that inherent values are all aesthetic values. He writes: "Thus the conception of aesthetic or inherent value as constituted by the quality of the particular experience, in the presence of the object. . . ."[8] If Lewis means (as he seems to, judging by his examples) that the only inherent values to be found in things are aesthetic values, I would certainly disagree with him very radically. But to grant as much as Lewis does when he recognizes the inherence of aesthetic values, if only at the phenomenal level, is already to concede a great deal, and I am glad to cite the distinguished Carus Lecturer as defending, in contrast to Perry, the phenomenal objectivity of values.

The prima facie character of the objectivity of values may be granted, but it may still be argued that it is the effect whose efficient cause is an interest and that therefore no value can conceivably exist unless somehow created by an interest. I hold that this is far from being the case.

Many values can be brought under this theory only by an *ad hoc* elaboration of it, which makes it extremely implausible. Let us take a class of values which, for convenience, we shall call "gratuitous values." I mean those which come to me unsought for, unexpectedly, and are the objects of apprehension, although they cannot be said to have been created by a pre-existing interest, but of which it would be more true to say that, when they obtrude into awareness persistently, end by creating interest in them. Some of these values are fleeting and are barely able to sustain attention, and then only so long as they are present. These values are, in the economy of values, relatively trivial; they are usually hedonic values, and the gratification to which they lead seems ephemeral. But neither of these facts is relevant to the question of their relation to interest. Among them are to be found simple values of sight, touch, taste, and the values discovered through our response to certain thermic conditions. Unexpectedly, as I go by the flower-shop on my way to work, the florist opens the door, and the fragrance of a bunch of lilacs he has in his hands strikes me. Quickly I become aware of it, so quickly, indeed, that it is almost in retrospect that I notice it, because an instant before the door opened I saw my bus rounding the corner and I quickened my step. The value perceived in the fragrance of the lilacs is a very trivial value indeed, since it will not have any perceptible consequences for the rest of my life. I will never recollect it, and it will not affect in any detectable manner my actions. But in its own ephemeral way it is real and positive and as objective as the goodness of the dessert which I heard my wife say she intended to serve for supper and in which my interest is considerable because it is my favorite. In no sense of the word "interest" can I recognize an interest as creating the value I perceived in the fragrance of the lilacs, although, had not the bus appeared around the corner or had I missed it before I smelled the lilacs, it is quite possible that the value felt could have created an interest which, in turn, could have had the consequence of making me loiter a few minutes that I might more fully enjoy the value of the lilac's fragrance.

We could save the interest theory by saying that the physical smell created the interest, which in turn projected the value on the lilacs, and that all of this happened with tremendous rapidity. But a theory that can be patched up every time that it springs a leak is not a theory that can be sunk, and an unsinkable theory is not empirical. By the invention of *ad hoc* hypotheses every time a difficulty occurs, we can keep the most worthless theory going against all criticism and against all evidence. An empiricist who is serious about his method scorns to use *ad hoc* patches.

There is another class of values which exist for the individual and are "recognized" as existing prior to the existence of an interest through which they may be espoused, and which, indeed, depend on this recognition (among other factors) to create the interest which we may later develop in them, in order to turn them into "espoused" values. This, by the way, fixes the meaning in which the terms "recognized value" and "espoused value" will be used in this essay. To the class of recognized values belong all those which a man or a people consider values and which he or they do not directly and actively espouse. Espoused values are positively held as a result of the presence of an interest in us toward them that maintains them as our values. To the class of recognized values belong those values not directly and immediately discovered by innate interest but which, nevertheless, must somehow be known to be values before they are espoused, since the interest must be created in us (often through activities requiring rigorous and prolonged discipline) before we can espouse them. The class of recognized values seems to be a larger—and it certainly is a more important—class of values than those that we have called "gratuitous." To it belong, among others, all cultural values whatsoever. I would include in it the values put by men on ritual and ceremony which complicate physiological processes, such as the refinements introduced by all cultures into courtship, no less than the values of the arts and sciences. These values cannot be "reduced" to physiological determinants, nor can they be explained in terms of instinctive drives introduced *ad hoc* to account for the creation of culture. One has to recognize the value of music or of painting before one can develop interest in it, unless we assume that for every value a man recognizes there exists a hidden starved instinct that leads to its recognition. But the assumption of hidden instincts would lead the naturalist to utterly devastating consequences, since not only would it open him to the criticism of contemporary behavioristic psychology but it would commit him to a telic structure to account for the instinct. These values, which are the distinctive values of culture, must have been discovered and their recognition as valuable must have preceded the disciplined educational effort required to create the interest which led to their being sustained through incorporation in cultural institutions. As first discovered, probably, they were only vaguely and rudimentarily perceived, and their importance (their place in the scale of values for a human being) was probably not fully grasped. In order to grasp it fully, the creation of an interest in them was required, which, in turn, led to a fuller or a more complete grasp of their nature and importance until, with favorable historical conditions, they came to be fully realized and deeply appreciated. But some modicum of recognition, however small, had to precede the interest.[9]

It could be argued with some plausibility that one recognizes only values which are already espoused by someone or that are acknowledged collectively. This might explain the effort which a man puts into developing an interest when he decides to espouse a value which carries prestige in his society. I remember a man who, years ago, tortured himself pitilessly by trying to learn to appreciate modern music. The effort led finally to the breakup of his home, but, at long last, I believe, learn he did. Why did he do it? For a number of reasons undoubtedly, the most important of which could well have been the desire to enjoy a value that some men had shown they were capable of enjoying. This is the reason why youngsters learn to smoke: to emulate their elders and feel like men.

And I am prepared to believe that this is the way in which much cultural activity requiring discipline is transmitted from one generation to another. In short, a prior interest starts the process of recognition and espousal. But the plausibility of this interpretation, if it is intended to account exhaustively for the phenomena of valuation, disappears when we look at the actual data. For a man emulates others in respect to some of their values, which involve difficult disciplinary training, but not in respect to others of their values, interest in which he could more easily develop in himself. He does not accidentally hit upon them, nor does he attempt the impossible task of becoming a faded carbon copy of his teacher. "Identification" is indeed, as Freud points out, a very primitive phenomenon in human life, but, as we shall see in a subsequent chapter, it does not dispense with the fact that the discriminative process involved in identification implies selective recognition of some values to be emulated.[10]

It is true that the pre-existing interest in the older man leads the boy to discover the valuableness of the older man's values. But why does he discover the worth of some of the hero's values and not of others? The naturalist, as already indicated, cannot assume pre-existing innate interests if he is going to stay within the framework of a purely naturalistic explanation, because the psychologists whom he accepts will not allow him to do so. Nor can he assume a chance selection, for this assumption fails utterly to do justice to the nice discrimination involved, the quick way in which the boy will focus on some of his hero's virtues and ignore his weaknesses, not totally ignoring but merely disregarding valuable qualities in the hero that may be even more valuable than those which are selected because they are obvious. The process is, at the very least, as satisfactorily explained on the hypothesis that values are real and are discoverable prior to the existence of interest in them. To explain this process, the interest theory has to violate its own naturalistic assumptions and load the organism with a machinery of instincts for which there is no room within its own presuppositions.

But, even if we ignore these arguments—and I do not see how they can be ignored—there is the phenomenon of the selection of heroes which involves analogous problems but which is not the identical question discussed in the last paragraph. The boy, we say, emulates the older man, makes a hero of him, and imitates him. But note that just as he does not imitate the values of his hero indiscriminately, neither does he pick his hero indiscriminately. It is possible that obscure physiological factors determine him tropistically toward the object of his choice, as they probably determine him also, later, in the choice of a sexual partner. We know little (so far as I can find out) about the physiological determinants, if any, of our human preferences and repulsions. But even if we allow an argument based on ignorance, this does not preclude the fact that the boy does make a selection among a number of possible heroes based on discriminations which he makes of the quality of the personalities of those from whom he chooses.

I conclude that a man chooses among values, although perhaps in a somewhat vague and not fully conscious manner, on the basis of their objective importance, which in turn entails a recognition of them as valuable prior to the arousal of the interest that enables him to espouse them. In other words, one does not tacitly take another man's espoused values at that man's estimate of them, nor does one altogether uncritically accept the collective recognition of values. One chooses among them in terms of what appears to one to be their valuableness or worth. Were it merely a desire for gratification or emulation dictated by desire for social prestige or hero-worship, there would remain the problem of explaining how, without recognition of the value traits of objects as valuable, a man could come to want to actualize them in himself and how he could choose among them the ones he decides to actualize.[11]

The doctrine that it is interest that creates value ought to explain also those instances in which a man gifted with creative powers sets himself off against all the interests with which education has endowed him and repudiates the values of his community in favor of an ideal for which no interest existed prior to his discovery of the value which aroused it. The doctrine should also explain how the ideal, once stated, frequently becomes contagious and, against all extant and sturdily implanted "interests," engages the sympathies of men who, before they came into contact with it, had no suspicion that they would be called to the service of a cause. The phrase "to be called to the service of a cause," which applies to men who serve ideals but not to those who use ideals in their own service, quite naturally expresses their relations to their ideals by saying that it is they that are called. In all these cases the *recognition* of the value is prior historically and logically to its *espousal* and is a condition of the creation of the interest in it that is necessary to sustain the value in actuality against the call of other values and the competition of other interests.

But, even if we were to allow that the recognition of a value on the part of a man is possible through the indirect activity of an interest for some other value, it could still be argued that the discovery of value must have preceded its espousal when the value first dawned on man. This would not be true of values which could readily be connected with innate instincts and drives—the value of sex, of food, of rest; such values could have been created by pristine interests. But the values which might be supposed to be created by pure biological needs are elaborated in culture beyond the degree required for the satisfaction of the biological need. In simpler terms, higher cultural values cannot be reduced to simple biological factors. We simply do not know, since we have no records, how these higher values were discovered. But that they were discovered prior to their integration in human cultures we can be certain, since they were not created by pre-existing needs but rather they created the interests that sustained them after their recognition.

When the theory of evolution was extended from biology into the social sciences, its truth was accepted in these fields without inductive proof. Darwin and his followers presented conclusive evidence of the fact that species vary and are related, thus establishing evolution as an acceptable hypothesis. Evolutionary biology won against its scientific, philosophical, and religious opponents, and the Darwinians totally defeated the anti-evolutionists. The victory in the field of biological evolution enabled the evolutionists to occupy without contest far more territory than they had conquered through the force of their logical arms. As a result, until Boas discouraged the evolutionary approach in cultural anthropology, "proof" in the field of social phenomena consisted in the *ad hoc* selection of facts and the exclamatory conjuration to the effect that only this theory could account for the facts. But even in the great days of social evolutionism no one could have claimed legitimately that the interests that sustain the higher values preceded historically or logically their discovery and created them. The discovery of the value—which for the evolutionist had to be a survival value—must therefore be assumed to have preceded its espousal and its institutionalization. Cultural evolution is today, fortunately, long dead and decently buried, except among Marxists. But a naturalist holding onto the interest theory in order to account for the inception of the higher values in culture would have to fall back on the embarrassing assumption we have already discussed: the instinctive presence of the interest needed to create the value.

When Perry demands that *quale* other than secondary and primary traits be pointed out to him *in* the region which the value term roughly indicates, he demands that his interlocutor destroy the tertiary character of the value and turn it into either a primary or a secondary quality by giving it a distinct spatial locus. But when I say that I find the value of generosity *in* an action or that beauty resides *in* Jane's face, the "in" of my statement is a relational "in" and not a spatial one. Jane's beauty is not in her face like the blue of the Atlantic in a map, whose area is said to be to the right of the coast line; nor is the generosity in the action as the coin is in the pocket. Jane's beauty hovers, as it were, above the freshness of the skin, the sparkle of her eyes, the impudent mouth, the dimple of the chin—hovers over these merely physical and, as merely physical, value-free, qualities of Jane's face. This is true of the value of generosity. I saw Paul help Peter when the latter was in need and the former had no obligation to do so. The value of Paul's generosity was not *in* the money given Peter, nor *in* the act of giving it, nor *in* giving it to Peter simply because Peter was in need, nor *in* Paul's giving it, but "in" the complex character, relationally understood, as an added character other than the describable fact that Paul gave Peter help and Peter accepted help from Paul. If I know that Paul is giving it to Peter in the hope that Peter, who is a drunkard, will go on a big binge which will lead (or so Paul hopes) to his being fired, the same "giving" loses the character of generosity and takes on another character—the character of a mean act. The meanness is *in* the act, as a tertiary character relating to the whole act, but not *in*, in the way in which the money is first in Paul's hand and later in the bartender's till. To ask that it be shown to be "in" some region in the sense that the money is in the hand or the green is in the dollar bill is, to repeat, to ask that it cease to be tertiary and that it become secondary or primary.

Another argument by which Perry seems to set some store, judging by the space assigned to it, reads as follows: In respect to values, "the more closely these are examined the more clearly do they appear to be either modes of attitude or impulse, and thus motor; or sensory *quale* which are localizable in the body. They rapidly lose all semblance of that inherence in the object which becomes increasingly clear and unmistakable in the case of color. In short, the attentive effort at localization, whereas it unites the 'secondary' qualities with the object, dissociates the alleged 'tertiary' qualities, and tends to unite them with the sentient. It becomes less and less tolerable to speak of a red or yellow organism, as it becomes more and more plausible to speak of one that is covetous, bored, tired, hopeful, enticed or delighted."[12]

Now I do not find this to be the case; I find it to be the case only when I disregard the distinction between a character and the subjective conditions which reveal it. Here, in the failure to distinguish clearly between a value trait and the psychological conditions necessary to discover it, seems to me to lie the source of the fundamental error of the interest theory. We saw this in Perry's criticism of Santayana, whom he finds hesitating between the interest view, the view that value is an objective trait, and the view that value is "the transformation of an element of sensation into the quality of a thing." We see it, beyond the shadow of a doubt, in the following statement: "We have thus been led to define value as the peculiar relation between any interest and its object; or that special character of an object which consists in the fact that interest is taken in it."[13] If it is the relation, it cannot be the relational character, since the two are different aspects of a relational complex. If it is the character of an object which consists in the fact that interest is taken in it, we are not through, because we still want to know why interest is shown in it; and if to this is answered, "Because it promises to satisfy the interest," then there is something prior to the interest and related causally to it. And if it is answered, "We do not know," I submit that I do, namely, because it has a character capable of arousing and normally satisfying interest.

To discover aesthetic traits, two distinct sets of conditions are necessary: first, physical conditions *in* the object. If Jane's face were pockmarked, her eyes were crossed, her nose were longer than it is and bulbous, like W. C. Fields's or J. P. Morgan's, and if she did not have a dimple, I would not say Jane was beautiful. So with Paul's generosity; let us beg a difficult problem of moral philosophy and assume that Paul's intentions are part of the necessary objective conditions of the generosity of his acts; if, then, his intention was not to help but to destroy Peter, the generosity would become (as we say inaccurately) meanness.

In addition to physical conditions in the object, there are, second, conditions in the subject—powers and aptitudes which determine the capacity of the subject to discover values. To discover the beauty of music, certain sensibilities, some of a purely physiological nature, it would seem, and others considerably higher, are required. To discover the aesthetic value of art, one condition is trained capacity which can be developed only through disciplined effort; only thus equipped are we able to perceive *in* the object the aesthetic intention governing its construction and, *pari passu*, its value. However this is achieved, this capacity does not create the value—the value was created by the artist through the manipulation of the material. (It would, however, be more exact, even though less idiomatic, to say the value was "actualized"—or some such term—by the artist.)

These conditions obtain for any act of perception of any quality—tertiary, secondary, or primary. Certain subjective conditions, as well as others of an objective nature, determine my apprehension of those traits which, as apprehended, are called "the length" and "the specific gravity" of an object. So it is with color. When these conditions obtain, tertiary qualities possess as much self-evident objectivity as the secondary and primary qualities can possibly claim. And if the existence of these conditions makes the tertiary "subjective," then Berkeley's argument holds for the others no less. Perry says that the fact that a tertiary quality "does not possess the

self-evidence of yellow argues that it is not an empirical quality."[14]
But Jane is self-evidently beautiful: I found her so when I first
looked at her; so did the jury who elected her County Fair Queen
and the talent scout who took her to Hollywood. Since then she has
proved to be self-evidently beautiful to millions of admiring fans
who crowd to her pictures. Similar reasoning will do as an answer
to Perry's argument that primary and secondary traits are worn "in
public" by things and "any passer may note them." But I find—and
what I have already said of Jane confirms it—that Jane (who knows
it is her beauty and is accustomed to have men recognize it) not
only wears her beauty in public but rather looks for opportunities
to exhibit it in public places. Perhaps Professor Perry was thinking
of the beauty of veiled Mohammedan women? This is true not only
of aesthetic qualities but of many moral values: Achilles and Hector
—we may gather—wore their courage for all men to see. Their
thirst for their due meed of glory called for ostentation of their
courage. Generosity, when genuine, tends to conceal itself but
never succeeds completely, while envy does, too, and succeeds
more often.

Perry's last argument consists in pointing to what he takes to be
"the most serious defect" of this type of theory, namely, "its failure
to provide any systematic principle whatsoever. There are as many
indefinable values as there are feeling attitudes, and since these are
to be regarded as objective qualities rather than as modes of feeling,
there is nothing to unite them, not even the principle of feeling."[15]
But this charge is inadmissible for the following reasons: (1) The
philosopher should not be expected to invent systematic principles
where none are to be found. (2) It would seem to be a sufficient systematic principle to offer a definition of values as objective traits.
(3) One could systematize them either, as Perry does, in terms of
the interests that actualize them or in terms of the kinds of physical
conditions which subtend them or in terms of the order of rank that
is found to obtain among them, as Nicolai Hartmann has tried to do.
The fact that some writers have not given us their systematic connections does not prove that values cannot be systematically ordered, until the task is tried and shown to be impossible.

CHAPTER IV

THE INTEREST THEORY. III

WE ARE now in a position to inquire how the value conceptions of the interest theory are elaborated into a moral philosophy. As stated in chapter ii, the interest theory is vitalistic.
According to it, a rational man will naturally aim at the "maximum
of satisfaction eventually possible." Santayana tells us that if the
"moral ideal" is to have jurisdiction over the desires or interests
that seek satisfaction, its authority must emerge from the need to
control their admission into the organization. It has such authority
"because the ideal is the object of a more profound and voluminous
desire and embodies the good which they [the disruptive desires]
blindly and perhaps deviously pursue."[1] Santayana's secularistic
humanism, with its persistent and lucid rejection of indiscriminate
satisfaction and its frequent and severe strictures on barbarian
morality, should not be allowed to obscure the vitalistic basis of his
moral doctrine; for, if Santayana rejects the satisfaction of any impulse, he does so with regret and only on prudential grounds. It was
not until long after the publication of *The Life of Reason*—until the
period which, for convenience, may be marked roughly as beginning with the appearance of the second edition of this work—that he
veered away from moral vitalism toward what, in 1904, he called a
"post-rational morality."[2]

Somewhat similar remarks apply to Ralph Barton Perry's version
of the moral economy. It must be owned that the vitalistic bias is
not explicit in *General Theory of Value*, but it controls the discussion
in certain important passages in which Perry analyzes the problems
which arise from the need to compose and adjust group interests.
Where it is sufficiently explicit, so that all one needs to do is to
point to it, is in his earlier and more popular book, *The Moral
Economy*.[3] Like Santayana, Perry strictly qualifies his moral vitalism by prudential considerations and veils its true nature, but these

qualifications are not dictated by awareness of any factor in the moral situation which contradicts the vitalist principle. If desires or interests are to be inhibited or repressed, this is to be done because they are incompatible with the extant organization and somehow threaten its durability and its massiveness.

There are many later versions of moral vitalism, but I am not acquainted with any one which is inspired with a wisdom as liberal and sympathies as catholic as those that guided Santayana in his exposition of the life of reason or which was elaborated with the nice regard for technical precision which characterizes Perry's *General Theory of Value* and even the more popular exposition of his views in *The Moral Economy*.[4]

The question which we must examine is whether Perry and Santayana have validated the logical transition which they make from fact to value. A complete answer involves two independent arguments, each, as it seems to me, decisive: (1) a purely logical argument, applicable to all naturalistic value theory which contends that value can be deduced from, or exhaustively defined in terms of, physiological or psychological facts and (2) a purely material argument, addressed specifically to the vitalistic theory of our authors.

The logical arguments need not detain us long. Even if we should grant the alleged facts on which the moral vitalist rests his doctrine, we must, nevertheless, object to it on the ground that no norm declaring that the facts ought to be as they are can be logically *deduced* from the facts considered as facts—considered, that is, in the way in which the naturalist asks us to consider them, as value-free. Grant what will be shown below to be false—that men actually prefer to satisfy a greater number of appetencies to a less—it does not necessarily follow that they ought to do so. It may be right to do so, but it may not be. And if it is right, it is not because it follows logically from the fact that that is what men naturally choose to do. To establish a deductive relationship between fact and norm or, perhaps better expressed, to elevate the fact to the status of norm, a naturalist would have to interpose between the value-free fact and the deduced norm the question-begging assumption that what men actually prefer is what is right. The naturalist may have adequate grounds for this assumption, but these grounds are certainly not to be found in the alleged fact that men prefer abundance of life to its opposite. The naturalist may, of course, introduce the assumption into the argument and declare it to be an unjustified, because unjustifiable, postulate or hypothesis, or he can bring it into the argument under the guise of a definition. But that amounts to instituting value by fiat and turns his theory into a more or less impure form of the theory to be examined later under the name of "postulational morality."

Logically fallacious, the doctrine of the moral vitalist also grossly oversimplifies the facts of human experience. The strength of the theory is said by some of its advocates to derive from the fact that it has the backing of biology and psychology.[5] Yet it is open to the criticism that it is not sufficiently empirical or scientific, for it ignores an important block of relevant facts. It is simply not true that men "naturally aspire to abundance of life, fullness of being," in the expansive and romantic sense assumed, implicitly or explicitly, by the moral vitalist. We need not call into question here the hoary assumption to which a large number of philosophers still seem to be inclined, to the effect that all men do, in fact, desire happiness. The assumption is true but useless if it defines happiness as that which any man wants; it is false if it defines happiness more restrictively. In either case it is irrelevant here. The point in which we are interested is whether what men universally mean by the "good life" is the abundant life, that is to say, a life involving a maximum of satisfaction of desires. Even a cursory examination of the facts will reveal that the opposite has been the rule.

There are two sets of considerations which flatly contradict the moral vitalist's cheerful assumption: one is more easily discernible at the social level, the other at the level of individual experience. Both, however, seem to be human traits.

At the level of culture, among the obvious and distinctive facts is man's natural exclusiveness, his natural tendency to trim and constrain and mold and check his natural impulses. If we judge men by the variety of their cultures and the circumstances to which cultures severally force them to adjust, we must conclude that man gives evidence of a plasticity greater perhaps than that of the Norwegian rat. But when we look at him in culture, we must also con-

clude that men choose a small number from the rich, open possibilities which, it would seem, natural resources offer them, considered
abstractly. From this point of view their plasticity is extremely
limited. But this is not all, since the impulses required to realize
these values are pared and whittled and are thus provided with restricted means of expression. The realized values are ordered in the
form of more or less organic patterns whose principles of exclusion
and inclusion are utterly a posteriori. This, of course, is a manner of
speaking, for the process is not and never can be fully conscious,
and it would be truer to say that the needs and desires which finally
become components of a social value pattern organize themselves.
Be that as it may, a tremendous sacrifice of gratification which cannot be explained on purely prudential grounds seems to be involved.
But this is a "sacrifice" only in terms of the external and abstract
vitalistic assumption that men naturally prefer the largest possible
number of satisfactions. From this standpoint, the inhibitions and
taboos which are a universal feature of culture seem to put a tremendously irrational burden on the members of the culture. If we
view the same process from the inside, however, the restrictions,
checks, and constraints involved do not necessarily appear as sacrifices at all, since the possibilities rejected are blandly ignored or excluded more or less scornfully; and those included are used as raw
material that must be *in-formed*, that must be more or less ruthlessly
molded into a pattern. We can go further and argue that selectivity,
inhibition, and constraint are part of the means by which men give
life worth, charge it with quality and tension, and thus make it
human.[6] A gratification which to an outsider seems utterly innocent
and capable of adding to the charm or delight or freedom of living or
that may seem capable of making for a more rounded type of individual is neglected or fiercely resisted, when it could be easily enjoyed. And the moral vitalist, confronted with such patent obduracy, can do nothing but bewail the stupidity or mulishness of
men who seem impervious to "rational" appeal. What he fails to
see is that such an appeal, instead of being rational, is a violation of
the essential rationality of the other man's being.

Meager as the knowledge is which social scientists have about
the formation of cultures, it would seem, then, as if some kind of
inward "syntax," so to speak, controlled their temporal develop-

ment, giving them their specific genius or distinctive quality not through inclusion but chiefly through exclusion. We are faced here with obscure facts which make one feel that the naturalist's effort to eschew all teleological suggestions disqualifies him for dealing with the phenomena of value at the social and individual level. Of course, perhaps even in the most static and isolated societies, invention and diffusion go on constantly, modifying, expanding, and limiting the interests and drives that select the values of the culture. And, no doubt, purely accidental factors contribute to the process of constant transformation. But anthropologists have fully recognized what they call "ethnocentrism," which Linton speaks of as the "reluctance to accept new elements of culture" which "slows down their rate of spread even when it does not completely inhibit their diffusion in certain directions."[7]

Reiteration of this point is advisable because it is cardinal; restrictions and inhibitions are not, per se, evil, although on occasion they may become so; nor are they always the result of prudential forethought and hence to be done away with as soon as possible. Some of them no doubt are, but many are not—and the latter, no less than the former, seem to be essential factors in the constitution of value. Or if it is held that interests are not constitutive of value, as I have argued, restrictions and inhibitions must then be considered essential to the discovery or selection of those values that are espoused by men and societies. There is no doubt that poverty of resources and the exigencies of the traffic, so to speak, counsel the inhibition and control of impulses. These, however, are not the only sources of inhibition; and to disregard the others is not only to oversimplify the complexity of man's psychic nature, prettifying the reality into a shallow Pelagian picture of man, but also to miss the relation between impulses and value. Satisfaction of appetency or interest is not by itself sufficient to confer value on objects, at least not considered abstractly at the purely biological level. We do not merely want "food" but a certain kind of food; and taboos and institutionalized preferences soon play havoc with our needs, considered biologically. Unrestricted gratifications of uninformed drives result, to the degree to which they are possible, in trivial or worthless satisfactions, whereas the gratification of informed drives or interests results in fulfilment, in worth, in purposive and more or less massive value. Between mere satisfaction and fulfilment there is a difference not only of degree but of kind. Another way of saying this is that, when interests are constitutive of value or, in the realistic theory, when they point to values, they are interests in objects which either actually or potentially can function in the complex of activities which constitute a society, with the qualification, of course, that a society transcends the criteria with which a utilitarian or hedonistic or vitalistic rationalism seeks to measure it.

These facts, together with the consideration that a naturalistic philosophy cannot, without inconsistency with its own assumptions, introduce a genuinely teleological notion of man, make it impossible for the interest theory to elaborate, as both Santayana and Perry have done, a philosophy of history. Yet *The Life of Reason*, as we pointed out in chapter ii, is not only a moral philosophy but a philosophy of history; and Perry believes also that the philosopher is able to state the principles of "what might fairly be regarded as a philosophy of history. . . ."[8] For Perry as for Santayana, the criterion is "progress," and, in the former's words, "strictly speaking, there is only one internal principle of progress, namely, *rationality*."[9]

However, if the good is constituted by desire or interest, we can speak of goods only where there are interests or desires, whether actually present or latent. This is seen by Perry in his "outline" of a philosophy of history, when he tells us that a society can be said to be internally progressive when it can "provide more fully for its constituent interests and develop its latent possibilities."[10] But no evidence is offered that in those cultures called "primitive" there are "latent possibilities" such as have become actualized in civilized cultures, and that in all civilized cultures the same latent possibilities are to be discovered. But, if there are not, we have found our way back to cultural relativism. This is a position to which both Santayana and Perry are logically committed and which Santayana explicitly espouses, as I showed in my contribution to the Santayana volume in "The Library of Living Philosophers."[11] The question here is not, of course, whether Santayana and Perry do or do not have a philosophy of history—for both of them have, and both claim to have one—but whether, with their interest theory of value and with their naturalistic conception of man, they can have one.

One of the contradictions in Santayana to which reference was made in chapter ii springs from the two conflicting theories of man between which he shuttles, one mechanistic and the other Aristotelian.[12] The naturalist cannot condemn a man or a people because he or it fails to live up to what the so-called "great" peoples of history have achieved, until he shows that they had latent aptitudes that they failed to realize. In the absence of this evidence, all he can do is record their actual achievements. An Aristotle, however, can, for he has a notion of human nature which involves a telic aspect, and it is in view of what men potentially are that he judges what they actually can be.

At the individual level the facts again contradict the moral vitalist, for appetitions are not simple affairs, pointed like arrows unambiguously toward their object. Frequently, they present themselves accompanied by an opposite and inhibitory tendency. This may not be true of all tendencies and impulses; nor does it seem to be true in the same degree of all men, considered as members of the same social group; nor is it perhaps the same for all ages of man. But in varying degrees it does seem to be true of at least some impulses, among which are to be found the sexual, the impulse toward power, and even the very will to live, which play such dominant roles in the creation of culture.[13] Impulses are not always naturally free to go toward their objects unimpeded. That is not their nature. They are often ambivalent, inwardly self-contradictory, and in some of them, at least, the anticipation of fulfilment is restrained by an accompanying tendency to deny the impulse free rein. This tendency may be distinguished, but does not seem to be separable, from the positive aspect of the impulse. Drives, even when externally free to arrive at their object, often seem to be internally complicated and entangled. One both wants and at the same time and in the same sense does not want something; pleasure is streaked with pain, ecstasy with despair.

Another point which the moral vitalist seems to ignore is that anxiety and a more or less obscure tendency toward self-destruction, inhibition, and dread frequently stalk desire, robbing satisfaction of the pure quality of delight which, in theory, it apparently should have. The evidence that these phenomena are universally to be found stalking desire is irrefragable and is not hidden in esoteric studies of obscure philosophers. The need to deny the value of the unburdened life runs its steady course through the history of thought even in our optimistic West. It goes back of the *Phaedo* and back of Koheleth, and it has run steadily since then until the twentieth century, in spite of the fact that it has been excluded from the attention of most ethicists by superficial factors in the cultural ethos. Schopenhauer, in an optimistic century, put it at the base of a comprehensive philosophic synthesis. Nietzsche recognized it and honored it by making it the object of his furious, lifelong attack. Kierkegaard and Kafka took it to be central to the constitution of the human spirit. It is discoverable in the Dostoevskian ideal of the good man; J. W. Krutch emphasizes it in his study of Samuel Johnson; and it frequently shows its head in Shakespeare. And in our own day Freud, starting with a radically hedonistic conception of the mind, had finally to take it into account. Indeed, if the testimony of men be at all pertinent, it would seem that it is the moral vitalist who has no ground to stand on. The evidence against his shallow assumption is overwhelming.

Nor can this inhibitory tendency be called, in any legitimate sense, "moral." It is something which lies below the level of morality, though it is an all-important factor in the formation of the moral life. That we are dealing here with a nonmoral phenomenon can be gathered from the fact that it frequently shows itself accompanying impulses which are not particularly involved in any serious way in our normal moral activity. Freudian terminology, if we can extend it beyond the context for which it was designed, enables us to say the same thing more simply and somewhat more clearly: men are not exclusively moved by the pleasure principle. "The goal of all life," writes Freud, not without a touch of melodrama, "is death."[14] There is more to the facts than the moral vitalist recognizes, namely, the complications brought in by the presence of the death instinct. Freud spoke of these two factors of the psyche—the pleasure principle and the death instinct—as if they were separate mechanisms independent of each other, springing from different sources and addressed, therefore, to different objects; he traced their source to vague cosmic tendencies and frankly admitted that much of what he said about them was purely speculative; what is more, his whole description of the mind, as I believe his critics have not been slow to observe, seems to be closely patterned after a mechanical model. But, when the worst has been said of the Freudian theory, there is no doubt that Freud, as I have already stated, increased considerably our knowledge of the mind. For our purposes we need attend only to the fact that what he called "the death instinct" (as well as the phenomena of repression and masochism) "may be," as he puts it, "primary"; that anxiety and, as Kierkegaard puts it, "the dread which immediacy experiences in the face of its own good fortune" are inherent in the human personality.

"Just as the physician might say that there lives perhaps not one single man who is in perfect health, so one might say perhaps that there lives not one single man who after all is not to some extent in despair, in whose inmost parts there does not dwell a disquietude, a perturbation, a discord, an anxious dread of an unknown something, or of a something he does not even dare to make acquaintance with, dread of a possibility of life. . . ."[15]

Thus, whatever we choose to call it and however we may seek to analyze and explain it, there seems to be an obscure inhibitory factor which retards, if it does not altogether prevent, the satisfaction of desire and which precludes the facile simplifications about human nature which are at the basis of moral vitalism. Let me repeat that the terms by which we designate this phenomenon are not important, for it is not our interest here to analyze it. All we need do is discern more or less clearly the fact itself. Nor does the reference to Freud and to Kierkegaard—incongruous bedfellows, at best— imply acceptance of their doctrines. Such varied references merely signify the acceptance of the common insight which they acknowledge, namely, that men do not naturally seek abundance of life. Neither did we need Freud and Kierkegaard to point this out to us. A sympathetic consideration of the meaning of asceticism and of the universal tendency toward otherworldliness present in every culture, although acknowledged and institutionalized in only a few of them, as well as some attention to the presence of taboo in all cultures would have revealed the facts ignored by the moral vitalist.

It will be of no avail to reply to the foregoing criticism that the tendency in question, in so far as it is indeed present, bespeaks a pathological condition either in the individual or in his culture. The categories of "health" and "disease" may be used at the physiological or psychological level in a purely descriptive, utterly neutral, way to distinguish some conditions or processes or states from others; but for the moral vitalist these categories do not function *descriptively* but *evaluatively* and hence beg the issue.

CHAPTER V

THE POSTULATIONAL THEORY
OF MORALITY

THE most obvious defect of vitalist moral theory consists in its fallacious attempt to derive value from fact. It is natural that a philosopher who seeks to avoid this error and yet wishes to avoid moral skepticism, which might seem to be its alternative, should be led to propose the view that norms themselves cannot be justified, since the attempt necessarily involves one in an infinite regress. The essays which will be considered next—Charner Perry's "The Arbitrary as Basis for Rational Morality" and "Principles of Value and the Problems of Ethics" and D. C. Williams' "Ethics as Pure Postulate"—develop this view forcefully.[1] The works of these two philosophers exhibit some important differences in respect to the matter presented, the way in which it is handled, and the various implications and interests which apparently control the course of the analysis; but for our purposes these differences, radical as they intrinsically are, can be neglected. Attention is focused almost exclusively on Charner Perry's essays because he seeks to lay bare the baffling psychological reality which confronts the moral philosopher and to analyze the logical structure of the moral judgment, whereas Williams is concerned simply with the logical problem. Nevertheless, since Perry does not label his own view, I shall refer to it for the sake of convenience, borrowing the term from Williams, as "the postulational view." The term is not adequate, but it must do in the absence of a better.

It is perhaps desirable to note that, although, so far as I know, the postulational view is not defended by a large number of philosophers in its pure form, in a hybrid form it is one of the most popular stopgaps of naturalistic moral theory. For instance, Sidney Hook, one of Dewey's disciples, champions a hybrid postulational and instrumentalist theory of value in an article in which he attempts to defend democracy from a naturalistic point of view. Another instance of a hybridized postulational view is found in the same volume in which Hook's essay appears, in an essay by Edel.[2]

Before beginning the discussion of the postulational theory, we must somehow settle the question of whether Charner Perry is a naturalist. It could be argued that he is a realist as to value, in the sense in which we call Laird and Hartmann realists, and hence in G. E. Moore's sense of the term not a "naturalist." The opening sentence of "Principles" reads as follows: "Values, perhaps, are here, there and everywhere. It may be that they are scattered through the world like plums in a pudding or fish in the sea."[3] In the article he is concerned, initially, with the question as to how to apprehend, or get at, the principles by reference to which the judgment's objectivity can be validated. These, he argues, are apprehended by abstracting what is general and necessary from the content of actual judgments. Very similar statements are made in a long review that appeared in *Ethics* of Ewing's *The Definition of the Good*.[4] If we take these statements in conjunction with Perry's criticism of Stevenson's *Ethics and Language*, a fairly clear case could be made for Perry's value realism, since one important reason for this attack was Stevenson's nominalism.[5] It is admitted, of course, that ethical realism cannot be naturalistic in Moore's and Ross's definition, since it makes values irreducible and gives them ontic status. But, in an older and perhaps more classical use of the term "naturalism," Perry can legitimately be called a "naturalist." According to this older usage, a naturalist is one who believes that the whole content of experience and experience itself and its objects are "natural," in the sense that neither experience nor its objects require a supernatural agency for their explanation. A world which in an ontic sense is not value-free is one which contemporary positivistic naturalists reject as bitterly as they reject a world which is God-created.

The basic fact that Perry underlines and from which he starts is the hopelessness of the quest of traditional philosophers for principles of valuation which should be universally acceptable to reasonable beings. But, while he is willing to abandon the traditional quest, he insists that the alternative is not skepticism. Nor are value judgments purely descriptive, for they express the need *"to make a selection among possible courses of action."*[6] Hence the problem of value consists in discovering the grounds for choice. Now it is clear that there are no self-evident principles on which we can depend to guide our choices. It is not difficult to see that a "pure" intellect, exploring the comparative desirability of two alternatives unaided by inclination, could never reach a decision. How, then, are choices made? The answer is that "a commitment," which is to say, an "arbitrary" act of the will—determined by principles and purposes previously established—nips the reflective process off and forces a decision. This act is "arbitrary" in the sense that one cannot offer *logical* grounds for the preferences expressed, since the preferences themselves constitute the ground for the valuation. But, though "arbitrary," the act is not "irrational," because reflection has preceded it and furnished it with relatively clarified alternatives and because the will is determined by "beliefs, ideals, principles, and the result of previous reflective decisions."[7]

At this point Perry's second essay contributes greatly toward the clarification of the doctrine, by disclosing more carefully than did the first what is involved in the commitment which determines choice. A commitment is expressed in a judgment, of course, and is followed by a decision. Now we can distinguish by abstraction the general principles from the specific matter of our judgments.[8] Should we want to justify the reasonableness and objectivity of a decision, we attempt to show that the general principles which guided it "apply to any similar choice" and furnish the abstract "schema within which reasons for choice are found."[9] Since the general principles are presupposed by all choices of the same type, what actually determines a specific choice cannot be these principles but a "force, a restless urge, which we may call vitality or the will to live" and to which interests and desires are "attached." It is this vital force that determines, through successive commitments, the operative principles of action and types of obligations and values actually acknowledged by an individual: in other words, it is the vital force that defines the individual's recognized field of ethical activity.[10] The upshot of this analysis is the recognition of a dialectic, of a "discrepancy between the principles of value which as necessary general conditions are presupposed in all choice and the ethical rules or principles which determine the individual's specific obligations to himself and to others."[11] This is true for social choices no less than for individual ones. The resolution of social conflicts is possible on shared commitments, prior to which or in the absence of which no question of justice can arise. In the resolution of conflicts "there is always the possibility of a failure on the part of groups or individuals to find a basis for agreement. When this occurs, the ensuing procedure is outside the scope of morality. There may be resort to force or passive resistance."[12] But this, Perry is careful to point out, is not the same as saying that "might makes right." What is intended is that in the absence of agreement there is simply no principle of right which will give a determinate solution to the problem. I believe that this theory is open to two very serious objections.

The first is best expressed by calling attention to the divorce which the postulational moralist is forced to make between the objectivity of the judgment and the ethical character of the decision. The objectivity or reasonableness, we just saw, is validated by an appeal to inert general principles or norms governing choices. But the ethical character of the action at the individual level depends on private principles and norms distinct from the general, though also implicit in the structure of the individual self or, at the social level, in the contracts and agreements accepted by the individuals who constitute a society. The divorce, however, allows us utterly to neglect the general principles, since they play no significant role in the testing of the moral quality of actions. Nor could they conceivably do so, for they are either abstracted from all judgments—and then they, of course, apply equally well to right and to wrong ones—or they are abstracted only from valid or adequate or right ones; and that presupposes the possession of the very criterion which the act of abstraction is intended to elicit. On this theory, therefore, Perry is fully justified in divorcing the objectivity from the morality of judgments. And the divorce furnishes the reason, Perry lucidly argues, why genuine conflicts between ethical judgments do occur. When they do, no "theoretical" solution—which, of course, is to say no "moral" solution—is possible, and to resolve them we must fall back on force.[13]

The same helplessness before conflicts is involved in Williams' treatment of the subject, for he takes seriously the analogy between a logical and a moral system. Whether the analogy holds is the first question we must ask Williams. Mathematics is a *pure* deductive system, and the question as to the origin of the relations and operations denoted by the symbols is utterly irrelevant to the validity of the conclusions; whereas morality, if it is a deductive system at all, is a material system, nor can we claim for it the structural organization that a mathematical system has, since it is neither closed nor static nor rigorous. Its terms are not exactly arbitrary symbols, since they refer to existential subject matter—refer, at least, to the values which men discover in their phenomenal experience. Moreover, the existential subject matter is in dynamic process, and its boundaries are defined only in the vaguest of ways. The analogy, therefore, seems most superficial and irrelevant. But, worse, it is morally misleading, since, from it, it follows that the postulation on which any one system rests cannot preclude other postulations giving rise to other systems which will be mutually incompatible among themselves. The practical upshot is the justification of mutually warring systems, each internally self-justified and each enthroning as ultimate authority the unchallengeable autocracy of the domineering will that makes the commitment or lays down the postulation. This may not be what the theory is designed to achieve, and, so far as Perry goes—in the second essay explicitly and in the first implicitly—the theory is expected to do the very opposite, for his theory is offered as an answer to subjectivism.[14] In practice, however, it amounts to the same thing as subjectivism, since an appeal beyond the personal principles or norms which determine the ethical field is said to be not only theoretically fallacious but expressive of a "futile desire for a superior moral justification."[15]

But how does the individual judge the moral adequacy of his own judgment? He can do it in terms of his commitments, which are expressive of "habits, ideals, and purposes which constitute the self."[16] Inconsistency with these is moral error. But if a man is consistent in his actions, he is invulnerable to moral challenge, no matter what his fellows may think of him and of his principles. This, then, is what the postulational theory says to a man or to a society whose judgments are challenged by another: "At the private level it is only you, and at the social level only those who agree with you, who can judge the ethical adequacy of your decisions, nor can that be done in terms of any other principles than your own." Now this aspect of the theory is glorified in warm language by Williams, who tells us:

"A man's morals are his real rock-bottom axioms, and like the axioms which lie at the root of a purely logical system they are unarguable because they are at once apparently self-evident and apparently undemonstrable."

And again:

"It becomes increasingly persuasive, as one contemplates the affair, that ethics possesses the same kind of self-evident certitude, and the same utter provinciality, as are possessed for instance by Euclidean geometry, and that it possesses them because it is a system of resolves rooted logically in certain fundamental resolves which are postulates, and which may be *pure* postulates in the sense that, although there may be *causes* of them, there literally is no *reason* for them. They are what happens, with the blank indemonstrability and the blank irrefutability of a natural event."[17]

To call a moral judgment "provincial" seems doubtful praise, but to call it "self-evident" does not merely seem, but flatly is, utterly erroneous; for, if genuine ethical reflection is anything, it is, above all, radically burdened by perplexity, obsessed with the problem of its own validity, instinct with reflexive distrust of its deepest motivations. Consider its tendency to escape decision and eschew the world of action. The ethical man will suffer evil rather than inflict it; he will uproot desire rather than risk wronging others by satisfying it. If he is at last forced to decide a radical ethical conflict, as sooner or later he will be, he does so with a heavy heart; for he knows that by his decision, as A. E. Taylor somewhere has said, he takes his soul in his hands. How different, then, is his attitude from that of the postulational moralist, who boasts of his insularity and monadic impermeability. With all theories which insist that there is an inviolably private element in the ethical judgment, the postulational doctrine is in danger of encouraging dogmatism. If the postulational system is not a completely closed system, this at least is true of it: that the voice of an alien moral plea cannot be heard from within it. Imagine an intelligent and more or less self-conscious, but nevertheless hardened and consistent, criminal. How can we, on this theory, condemn him? We may, of course, shoot it out with him, but for that no elaborate philosophic machinery is needed. But a significant moral judgment on his actions we cannot pass. Nor can we expect him to condemn himself. Our condemnation is adequately parried by him with the rejoinder that, in acting according to his commitments, purposes, and ideals—and, of course, he will call his objectives his "ideals"—he is acting morally. And the seed of self-condemnation which we might wish to plant in him or that in some way might miraculously arise in his soul would be successfully dug up by the same thought. This holds, of course, for a Nazi who, instead of defending his objections to non-Aryans on the pseudo-science of race, should call them his real, rock-bottom axioms or arbitrary commitments. His appeal to his science of race is open to challenge; his axioms are undemonstrable and irrefutable. And this shows that, by ruling out the "theoretical" validity of disapproval—either reflexive or transitive—the theory disclaims interest in one of the central facts that make up the phenomena of morality.

Moreover, this theory cannot offer an acceptable explanation of the universal phenomenon of self-condemnation or remorse. If disapproval is expressed against specific acts, the theory would say that it is an expression of a schizophrenic nature, the result of an inward division. A part of the self judges by calling the other part to the bar of its own commitments or rock-bottom postulates. Such an explanation leaves out of account the fact that men not only condemn some of their actions some of the time but not infrequently condemn themselves, their ideals, their habits, their whole life, what they have so far stood for and passionately sought—condemn themselves absolutely and *in toto*.

The advocate of the theory could answer, and not without some specious plausibility, that no one really condemns himself thoroughly, since a man who attempts to do so does not condemn that in him whence his self-disapproval arises. What must be meant, then, by a "thorough self-condemnation" is that somehow a new self has arisen which turns on the old. But is it not precisely this obscure phenomenon of rebirth, in which a new self emerges, and emerges seemingly undetermined by the dominant structure, by the rock-bottom axioms and ultimate commitments of the extant personality—is not this the phenomenon that requires explanation? If anything determines the self, it should be its rock-bottom axioms, its basic commitments; but here we are confronted with the fact that radical moral reflection somehow leads to the repudiation of these basic commitments and rock-bottom axioms while they are still constitutive of the self. We are told that it "is difficult to understand why anyone should need a recommendation or justification to himself."[18] And we must retort that on the assumptions of the postulational moralist it no doubt is.

I see no way in which the postulational moralist will be able to account for the phenomena of remorse, repentance, and conversion in their moral, not in their purely psychological, aspect. When he faces the problem, we shall see him, I dare say, thoroughly reconstruct the notion of postulational morality or of moral commitments beyond which it is impossible to appeal, in order to recognize that sometimes men do, in fact, appeal to something beyond their commitments and rock-bottom axioms. In any case this seems certain, that the obscure process through which a new ethical self is born cannot be understood on the assumptions of the postulational doctrine and must therefore be brushed aside as a futile effort to gain a superior moral justification. But, whether the postulational philosopher or anyone can or cannot explain these obscure phenomena, the facts of self-condemnation and rebirth are too important to be brushed aside as futile because they do not fit the theory.

Nor is this all that the postulational doctrine neglects; for, in denying the possibility of a theoretical resolution of truly radical conflicts, it betrays the most important function of morality. To my mind this is the most serious objection that can be brought against it. It is not when superficial disagreements occur which are underlain by deeper agreements but when all agreements have failed or when no agreements have ever existed that men have most urgent need of morality to save themselves from the brutality of their autocratic commitments and their provincial rock-bottom axioms. It is then that the most urgent need arises for a living faith in the possibility of an ethical mediation which transcends the shrewd arrangements of expedience and the dictates of worldly wisdom and which has the authority to condemn our arbitrary commitments and our rock-bottom axioms, thus condemning us, too, absolutely.

It must not be concealed but must be allowed in the freest possible way that that living faith is seldom on hand when we are most urgently in need of it. Men prefer, more often than not, to stand by their commitments and rock-bottom axioms, and even to die for them, rather than bring them to the bar of conscience. And I suspect that the reason is that the latter does not allow the expression of our autocratic wills. But sometimes the living faith in the primacy of the ethical does come to the rescue. And that it does, though indeed rarely, can be seen by anyone who reflects on human experience.

On one version of history the claim that morality transcends expedience seems fantastic, so clearly does the process of human development seem to be constituted by the brutal warfare of radically conflicting ideas.[19] Homer and Thucydides seem to have seen nothing else, and who would dare say that their eyes were dim? But a shift of standpoint will reveal the inadequacy of that reading and the paradoxical power of the ethical. When the historian records a noteworthy victory of conquest, the growth of an empire, or the expansion of a culture—and what else does he record? what he puts down is the triumph of provincial axioms and the success of arbitrary commitments that have been strong enough not to permit others to obstruct them. But it is the business of the moral philosopher to look beyond these facts, however numerous or obvious they may be. And when he does look, he cannot fail to see the way in which the ethical appeal sometimes penetrates the armor of the conqueror, robbing him of his sleep and bruising the nerve of his arrogance. This does not happen often; but it does happen. And it is a fact that the moral philosopher cannot afford to ignore or to dispose of by condemning it in the name of his own theory. To the postulational moralist men's need to justify their principles seems futile. One has to reply that there is something terrifying about an age whose philosophers accept a moral theory which vaunts its provinciality, when the most urgent human need has always been, and in our day more than ever is, to break down that provinciality, since neither channels nor oceans nor a great navy nor nuclear energy will protect men from their provincial axioms if they live, as they do, in one world.

But it is not because the postulational doctrine is dangerous that we cannot accept it. Doubtless it is; but, if it were true, we would have to accept it and change our ideas of the meaning of the moral life. The objection to it, here made, is that it falls short of the truth; for the need for a superior moral justification survives the philosopher's theoretical condemnation, as one of the most universal and obsessive traits of the human being. Men, if psychologists are to be trusted, have discovered most ingenious ways of evading their own self-condemnations; but seldom do these elaborate and ingenious techniques of rationalization work efficiently. The existence of the need for rationalization reveals, however, the important role that the tendency to condemn ourselves plays in the development of the human personality and, through it, in the determination of the ethical problem. The phenomenon of self-justification must, then, be subject matter for the moral philosopher which he must seek to understand and integrate in his doctrine. I do not mean that because the need exists it ought to be capable of being satisfied. That is an a posteriori question. I mean merely that it cannot be dismissed as the postulational moralist dismisses it.

CHAPTER VI

THE INSTRUMENTALIST MORAL
THEORY. I

SINCE the moral problem, as we saw, cannot be formulated in terms of the interest theory of value and since the postulational theory leads to a narrow, hard-shelled insularism which brooks no correction from the outside, we must ask whether it can be formulated, as Dewey attempts to formulate it, as the problem of discovering the "desirable" by means of the intelligence, conceived, of course, in the specific instrumentalist way in which Dewey presents it.

My answer, I would like to suggest in advance of its detailed presentation, is that Dewey turns out to be as disappointing as the moral vitalists and the postulational moralists, and for essentially the same reason—because Dewey, as I shall try to show, has no adequate theory of the person. It is not merely, as has been argued as regards Santayana's and Perry's theory of the person, that Dewey's conception of man is oversimplistic, that it fails to do justice to human complexity; it is also that a naturalistic theory of man fallaciously reduces the distinctive subject matter of morality and must needs leave out factors essential to a comprehension of the moral process. The factors that it leaves out, whose omission makes the error one of kind and not one of degree, will not be exhibited at this point but must wait for the expositions of the subject to be found in Parts II and III of this essay. However, the problem of Dewey's philosophy is not a purely technical one. Dewey himself would not have us take him as a professional philosopher whose interest is confined to the problems of philosophers; as he conceives the function of philosophy, it is to deal with the problems of men. The influence that Dewey exercises reaches far beyond the confines of the philosophical profession. A criticism of the import of his views in their practical implications is therefore as pertinent—indeed, as urgent—as is the analysis of the technical adequacy of his philosophic speculations. Our examination, therefore, will move from chapters vi and vii, in which the reader will find a technical criticism, to chapter viii, where he will find a criticism of some of the broader aspects of instrumentalism.

The problems of morals must have obsessed men since they achieved human status. It could not have been otherwise, since the kind of man you are and the actions which you perform must be my concern and the man I am and what I do must necessarily interest you, in so far as the areas of our respective powers and activities overlap. Whether I oppose you or agree with you, co-operate with you or attempt to block your plans, is something to which you cannot be indifferent. Allow a man the capacity to think, without which we cannot call him a man, and matter for moral reflection will never be wanting if he is living in a world inhabited by other men and moved by powers which help him or oppose him. The world in which he lives, if he thinks at all, will give him a great deal to think about. Nor will his thought be called forth only when he has to settle some practical difficulty, overcome some immediate obstacle; wonder is native to man, and the child is no less innately curious than his pup, but he is also—and in this he seems to be radically different from his pup—given to reflection about what arouses his curiosity.

If the objective world had given man nothing to think about, moral subject matter would not have been lacking; his anger, his fear, his failure to satisfy the hungers of his body, mind, and spirit, the harsh response when a tender or comforting word was needed, the indifference of those about him to his needs, the fearful threat— all sorts of experiences must have forced him to reflect about his relations to his fellows. He could not have been so pressed by the need to keep himself fed, to keep comfortable and safe, that he lacked a few minutes, now and then, in which to live over his anger, his fear, his shame, his defeat, to wish that he had acted differently, or to enjoy again the success he had achieved. And, in so far as he surveyed his actions in tranquillity and in his memory reacted toward them, he had begun the moral trek, a march that would ome day transform him from a moral into an ethical agent.

How these feelings and attitudes which constitute man's moral reactions were first implanted in him we do not know, nor do we have any way of finding out; but, as soon as he found himself estranged from himself by shame or resentment or embittered by anger or paralyzed by fear, he must have begun to have another experience—the experience of reliving his feelings and wondering about the objects and persons that caused those feelings. When this complex type of experience first took place, even at the most rudimentary level, man became a moral being.

The manner in which he faced his moral perplexities, of course, could not have been very systematic at first, nor could his reflection have gone very far. It may have been, at its beginning, merely subjective, merely justificatory or dramatic; it may not have consisted of anything more than the reliving of an experience in imagination, in order to improve upon reality or to enjoy in anticipation the fruit of future exploits. Or it may have consisted only of the effort to straighten out events that had been tangled by a world never sufficiently plastic, in order to cash in imaginatively on rewards not really earned or to deflect shame or to justify resentment or to improve somehow on the act to be performed. All a man needs is a very small amount of imagination and a short hour in which to recollect his actions, in order to be faced, and not always pleasantly, with their consequences and with the more or less articulated feeling that if they had been different they would have been preferable. The moment such adjectives enter into the imaginative rehearsal of experience, we have the wonder of a man who has begun his moral career. At that moment the animal becomes the man.

To that new modality of experience man brings varied aptitudes and a rich capital of feelings, attitudes, expectations, emotions, habits, and channeled satisfactions. He lives in a group, uses some rudimentary tools, communicates through language, has achieved some mastery over his environment, and has begun to feel within himself, by his dominion and his dependence, the inchoate mass of affective-ideational experience that to his own inward light constitutes the nucleus of his individual self and of his person. He is a person because he is capable of passing moral judgment on his own actions and on those of others. Awareness, as it appears and becomes reflexive, reveals an "I" and "a world," or at least the rudimentary nodulations out of which they will grow. These appear set over against each other in terms of oppositions and agreements, which later, when man has become more philosophical, he will in a fully critical sense call "the moral." They are not yet clear and distinct representations, but they are increasingly distinct nuclei in the undifferentiated totality of experience within which the "I" and the "non-I" arise. They are nodules in the stream of representations. There is as yet no definite boundary to them, nor are they capable of subtending a claim to self-identity for long after they appear, because they dissolve easily. They are no less precarious than they are indistinct.

To speak of a self is to speak of self-awareness and is, at the same time and in some degree, to speak of a *moral* self. If it could be proved that one seldom achieves it or that one does so only late in human history, then it would also be proved that moral experience is seldom present and that it is only late in man's history that it makes its appearance. But I do not see how this could be proved, and the theory of the late development of the self rests on an assumption and a definition which do not seem admissible.

The theory of the late development of the self once had strong backing from anthropology and seems to have been widely shared, but fortunately we are in a position to show that it has no valid basis in fact. It holds that when men ceased to be brutes and began their climb up the evolutionary ladder toward full human development, the social organization that emerged was tightly bound by rigid custom accepted by them in a mechanical way and not on any rational ground. In one particularly influential formulation, that of Dewey and Tufts, the assumption involves a level prior to the level of custom in which conduct arises out of instinct and fundamental needs.[1] This conduct, according to them, is more or less "rational," since it is instituted to satisfy these needs and may therefore be in accordance with fundamental laws, but it is not consciously directed by moral judgments. As evolutionary development takes place, instinctive conduct is followed by conduct regulated by the standards of society, for ends involving the social welfare. The essential characteristic of this second stage in the evolutionary process is to be found in the way in which members of a group accept unreflectively the mores and the moral standard that is involved in them: "The group morality with its agencies of custom set up a standard, but one that was corporate rather than personal. It approved and disapproved, that is it had an idea of good, but this did not mean a good that was personally valued. It enlisted its members, but it was by drill, by pleasure and pain, and by habit, rather than by fully voluntary action."[2]

The breakup of this stage, the story goes, is brought about by both sociological and psychological agencies, which, when they make for moral progress, lead to a reconstruction of social and individual forms of behavior involving the capacity to accept responsibility and voluntarily to choose wider aims and ideals than were chosen by a member of a custom-bound society. In short, it would seem that the difference lies primarily in the way in which standards and objectives are accepted, and only secondarily in the scope of these standards and aims. The alleged reason for this would seem to be that reflection is a necessary condition of the discovery of a higher law.[3]

The assumption of a break between customary and individual morality is qualified by the authors of our story in two ways: first, as we have seen, they distinguish three, not two, levels of morality —the instinctive, the customary, and the individualistic; and, second, they point out that at the customary level men may have occasionally reflected, while at the individualistic level men still tend to act customarily. The distinction is not intended to be interpreted sharply; but, in spite of the qualification, Dewey and Tufts offer the reader an extensive and fairly detailed description of a custom-ridden society in which the reflective process, without which human actions do not exhibit a moral dimension, is in abeyance. It seems to me that both the assumption and the definition controlling this interpretation of morality must be rejected.

The notion of a "custom-ridden" society has been brilliantly disposed of by Malinowski for at least "primitive peoples" as we know them today from field studies—if the evidence and hypotheses built on observation of Melanesian peoples are extensible with the proper alterations, as I take them to be, to other primitive peoples living today.[4] About this no more need be said beyond referring the reader to Malinowski's book. Whether there ever was a time in the remote past when the condition existed of which Dewey and Tufts write is not a question the discussion of which is likely to be very profitable. Nor is the assumption that there was such a time necessary for our correct understanding of what morality is. Of the structure of society and of the psyche of the animals that constituted, at the prehuman level, our ancestors, we know absolutely nothing or so very little as to amount to nothing. The earliest records that we have on which we can base any speculation at all about prehistorical man indicate—in so far as they indicate anything at all—that these men were fully human; and the evidence here consists precisely in the fact that they left us these records. What sort of moral development was achieved by the men who left us the paintings of Altamira and of the caves of southern France? How much did they reflect about their values? I cannot tell nor can anyone else positively, but my guess would be that men who were capable of the fine aesthetic expression of which these men gave evidence were fully human and could not have been very different from us. That does not mean, of course, that they pursued the identical values and were capable of the same theoretical sophistication of which we are capable; it merely means that they probably had the same degree of moral sensibility, though perhaps focused toward different objects than those toward which we, the men of contemporary technological society, focus ours. But whether the difference between them and us was greater or less than that between Mongolians and Patagonians or between Brazilians and Englishmen, we cannot tell. And if anyone should want to argue the contradictory thesis, how could we test his belief? The burden of proof, however, should be assumed by him.

Nor is it necessary that we be able to settle this question. If we conceive the human as consisting of certain intellectual, moral, and spiritual minima and if what we are after is to understand the generic structure of the moral experience, then the distinctions between the systems of values which obtain in various societies do not have a decisive importance. If these minima are lacking, the animal is not human, and, for our purposes, we can leave him out of account, unless we are interested in a speculative description of the genetic process by which we could trace his development from his premoral phase to his moral one. But in regard to this phase we have just said that no evidence is available. Hence the primitives, in the historical sense, will not help us understand the genesis of morality. If they are human, they are moral; and if they are not moral, they are not human—and this by definition.

The distinction, then, between custom and reflective activity does not mark two stages in moral evolution. The validity of the distinction could be defended, however, on the grounds that it is a heuristic device to enable us to perceive the essential factors involved in the constitution of morality. On this interpretation we will find in moral phenomena a customary component and a reflective component; and what makes activity moral is the presence of the latter component. To this defense we must reply that it involves a reading of Dewey and Tufts that neither the words nor the general intention of the text sanctions. After all, the first edition of Dewey and Tufts's *Ethics* was published in 1908, at a time when cultural evolutionism had not yet been swept away. Dewey and Tufts still took their social evolutionism seriously, and the revised edition of the *Ethics* (1932) was not sufficiently rewritten to erase that impression. But we can confirm the interpretation of the analysis of custom as a heuristic device from Dewey's *Theory of Valuation*, where, however, custom is not attacked and the object of criticism is blindly impulsive action or mechanical routine. The shift of emphasis, of course, is an expression of the fact that the polemical situation has changed and Dewey is now chiefly concerned to defend "the possibility of genuine propositions about the direction of human affairs."[5]

The doctrine of the *Theory of Valuation*, succinctly stated, is this: The active sense designated by the verb "to value" is primary, and the noun "value" is derivative. The problem of value theory, therefore, is what constitutes "an evaluation," an act of valuing. The answer is that an evaluation always involves the discovery of means to ends, both modified by reflection. Valuation propositions can themselves be evaluated, and these evaluations constitute distinctive kinds of propositions, since they refer to the future and involve activity. But the problem to which they give rise concerns "whether they express only custom, convention, tradition, or are capable of stating relations between things as means and other things as consequences, which relations are themselves grounded in empirically ascertained and tested existential relations such as are usually termed those of cause and effect."[6] They are distinctive, in other words, because they are about a different kind of fact than merely factual propositions: the fact as to whether the outcome attained, as a result of the activity instituted by the valuation, shows the fitness of the means employed by comparison with the result intended. The logic involved in the validation of valuations is thus the same as that involved in validating any proposition. Desires by themselves are not good or evil. The difference "between reasonable and unreasonable desires and interests is precisely the difference between those which arise casually and are not reconstituted through consideration of the conditions that will actually decide the outcome and those which are formed on the basis of existing liabilities and potential resources."[7] The difference consists in the fact that, in reasonable action, *desires are reconstituted through reflection.* This, then, is what makes the distinction between good and evil. The idea is repeated a few pages later on in terms of the distinction between the desired and the desirable:

"Every person in the degree in which he is capable of learning from experience draws a distinction between what is desired and what is desirable whenever he engages in formation and choice of competing desires and interests. There is nothing far-fetched or 'moralistic' in this statement. The contrast referred to is simply that between the object of a desire as it first presents itself (because of the existing mechanism of impulses and habits) and the object of desire which emerges as a revision of the first-appearing impulse, after the latter is critically judged in reference to the conditions which will decide the actual result. The 'desirable,' or the object which *should* be desired (valued), does not descend out of the a priori blue nor descend as an imperative from a moral Mount Sinai. It presents itself because past experience has shown that hasty action upon uncriticised desire leads to defeat and possibly to catastrophe. The 'desirable' as distinct from the 'desired' does not then designate something at large or a priori. It points to the difference between the operation and consequences of unexamined impulses and those of desires and interests that are the product of investigation of conditions and consequences. Social conditions and pressures are part of the conditions that affect the execution of desires. Hence they have to be taken into account in framing ends in terms of available means. But the distinction between the 'is' in the sense of the object of a casually emerging desire and the 'should be' of a desire framed in relation to actual conditions is a distinction which in any case is bound to offer itself as human beings grow in maturity and part with the childish disposition to 'indulge' every impulse as it arises."[8]

Back of this doctrine is the naturalistic assumption that values arise from value-free situations, or, as Dewey would put it, values arise "only when it is necessary to bring something into existence which is lacking or to conserve in existence something which is menaced by outside conditions."[9] The lack makes its presence felt by the existence of a desire. And the resolution of the moral problem consists in the successful satisfaction of desires. Situations or objects which, on reflection, are believed to meet this condition are called "good"; and those that, on reflection, are believed to maintain the perplexity or to frustrate or increase the tension of desire are called "evil." But, since desires or interests cannot be satisfied in isolation but must be satisfied in "definite existential contexts . . . , and since these contexts are situations within the life-activity of a person or group, interests are so linked with one another that the valuation-capacity of any one is a function of the set to which it belongs."[10] This means, I take it, that the satisfaction of a given interest or desire, to be morally adequate, must be adequate to the set to which the interest belongs and that what can be meant by "good" is the character of an object capable of satisfying desire in the context of linked interests to which that desire belongs. A number of questions remain, however. Is the total set of satisfied desires itself a good set? What turns desire that is capable of continued satisfaction into good desire? Does the goodness of the good desire emerge in the process of continued satisfaction? Or is it given to it by the intellectual process that transformed the original urge which sought satisfaction, and transformed the world along with it, so that the result is "satisfied desire in a situation that permits satisfaction"? If so, where did intelligence get the goodness with which it endowed the original desire? And if a desire, without the need of being transformed by thought, can, by a happy accident, meet with continued satisfaction, shall we not call it "good," or, in other words, must all desire be transformed by intelligence before we can call it "good"?

The question that confronts the moral man is not whether a desire and a situation can be so reconstructed that the result is a continuous satisfaction of the reconstructed desire in the reconstructed situation. What he wants to know is whether both the reconstructed desire and the reconstructed situation will be morally good or right. One has not observed a man in a moral situation if one has not grasped that what a man wants to know is not "How can I satisfy my desires?" but "How can I satisfy my desires within the frame of the moral law?" He may not know what he means by "good," but he knows that he does not merely mean "reconstructed desire satisfied in a reconstructed situation." For if a desire is good merely because it links successfully with other desires, then what the theory boils down to is that by "good" is meant what succeeds, and by "bad" what fails. But in a society of sadists what would succeed would be what is ruthless and heartless and inhuman. Nor is it admissible to appeal to "growth in maturity," for, as this phrase is usually used, in a eulogistic sense, it means growth in the ways of *good* maturity and not in the ways of *evil* maturity. But, if what we mean is growth in good maturity, the question we have asked has not been answered. What we need to know is how we can be assured that, when intelligence reconstructs desire in terms of consequences and available means, it reconstructs it in such a manner that its satisfaction will be really good. Two alternatives are possible: either Dewey assumes implicitly that intelligence is instinctively or naturally inclined toward the good, or he means to offer us a definition. But the first alternative is easily disproved by facts, and the second is a definition some of the consequences of which contradict what Dewey generally stands for. A pure intelligence—which is to say an amoral one—can tell us that the satisfactions of a reconstructed desire are good only if it somehow possesses a criterion of goodness which is distinct from its own operations.

It is true that in the first edition of Dewey and Tufts there seems to be a recognition of this fact. In a passage already referred to, the authors say:

"While, then, the general movement is on the whole a movement of individualism, it demands just as necessarily, if there is to be moral progress, a *reconstructed individual*—a person who is individual in choice, in feeling, in responsibility, and at the same time social in what he regards as good, in his sympathies, and in his purposes. Otherwise individualism means progress towards the immoral."[11]

It is not clear in the first edition whether what is added to the developing individual—social consciousness—is a *moral* dimension which he achieves in the process of natural growth or a nonmoral dimension, whose functioning constitutes the morality of the new stage. In the revised edition the whole of Part II has been rewritten more in line with Dewey's own later views and shifted polemical orientation. It seems to me that we are justified in concluding that the doctrine presented in *Theory of Valuation* is the clearest conception and the one we should examine.

If on the basis of this doctrine we were to point out that Dewey is committed to the belief that what is good is what is successful and that a strong and clever man, not too heavily burdened with human sympathy, can therefore get by morally with actions which in the average man must be reckoned as crimes, Dewey would retort that we are wilfully misunderstanding him. Social conditions and pressures, he would point out, make themselves felt on the strong and clever no less than on the average. Dewey would also point to the reference to growth in maturity to be found in the passage quoted. But if "good" is defined by the reconstitution of the desired, brought about by reflection, one could still argue that a clever man can get by with what would constitute a crime for an average one, since growth in maturity for the former consists in learning precisely how to avoid the unpleasant consequences that the average man cannot escape. Either "growth" means a natural condition which is perfectly free of value, or it means a growth in *moral* apprehension and sensibility. If it means the latter, our clever and strong man would naturally refuse to accept the new notion. He would retort that we have now introduced a new kind of term into our account, a moral term, which arises not from his reflection but from ours. And no wonder that it does, he adds haughtily, since it is clear that we lack the strength and cleverness with which he is endowed and are given to worrying a good deal about the effects of our actions on others, something over which a strong and fearlessly masculine consciousness never loses sleep. According to this doctrine, Hitler may have been "unreasonable" or unscientific because he did not reconstitute his overambitious ends in the light of the inadequate means at hand; or, if he merely made a miscalculation as to the means, he was not evil but mistaken about a question in respect to which he was not scientifically well enough informed; but he was not evil. Had his diplomacy been more astute and had he succeeded in driving us to a break with the Russians, or had he remained content with the Munich victory and proceeded to exterminate the Jews within his own borders, he could have reckoned successfully with the social pressures, and one could not have accused him of being morally wrong.

Just as James disapproved of American imperialism while formulating a Darwinian theory of morality, so Dewey disapproves of Hitlerism, Stalinism, and of the use of the intelligence for certain ends. Why, then, does he not see where his theory leads him? The only plausible explanation that occurs to me is that he tacitly takes for granted the existence of *a good will* as operative in the deliberations of valuational intelligence. Reflection alone cannot reconstitute the desired into the *morally* desirable. We can discover what will satisfy a need, if that need is only a physical one, by the use of the intelligence; but, when the need is a *moral* one and when the situation involves the conflicts of the actual, complex, moral nature that one runs into in real living situations, unless the intelligence is lighted by love and self-distrust of its own motives and by a quiet capacity for abnegation it is not likely to succeed in arriving at a moral decision. This is to say that the intelligence must be a *moral* intelligence, the intelligence of a moral man.

When something more than the intelligence is brought into the picture, the error of the belief that the moral problem can be analyzed in terms of the purely psychological categories of "desire," "satisfaction," and "reflection" becomes evident; and one can easily see that the question of the satisfaction of desire and whether that satisfaction is broad or narrow is only a small part—and not the most important part either—of the moral problem.

It is agreed that reflection must precede the resolution of a perplexity for it to be moral, since good done accidentally may be good to the recipient but is not good for which the doer can claim moral credit; but reflection is not necessary to constitute an act valuable—in this respect the first edition of Dewey and Tufts was closer to the truth. Many automatic, purely habitual acts which I perform are valuable. In South America a good man without much thought gives centavos to beggars, who bless him in the name of the saints, and in the Bowery the same good man refuses nickels for cups of coffee to bums who curse him secularly. Both actions can be habitual, and within its frame each is "good." Nor is reflection, as we have seen, enough to endow an act with *moral* quality. The resolution will have to be arrived at by *moral* reflection—the reflection of a moral person—to be moral. Moral reflection is moral as well as reflective, which means that it will call forth not only our intellectual resources but also those of our good will, and both on the same plane. If "intelligence" is lacking, all the good will in the world will not help us resolve our perplexity satisfactorily. However, an action done by a stupid person with good will may be more moral than a merely intelligent action of a man who does not have good will. Again, the intelligence can and does work toward conservative as well as toward progressive ends, and the two words "conservative" and "progressive" do not necessarily indicate a better or worse morality but, rather, two nonmoral, antagonistic forces in the social process, both essential to the constitution of human societies. There are times when one wins over the other and represses it or inhibits it, but not for long. And I suspect that one would find them immanent in a relatively static society, no less than we find them in ours. In any case it indicates either an exceedingly naïve or exceedingly partisan mind to assume that "progressive" and "conservative" necessarily indicate a better and a worse morality, respectively. The Nazis were progressive—*from* democracy they sought to progress *toward* their own goals. The powers that fought them, or at least some of the Western powers that fought them, namely, England and the United States, were conservative, while some others, like Brazil, were deeply antidemocratic and, from *that* point of view, reactionary. And among the things that the conservative powers sought to conserve were not only their own empires but the ways of life and the values of their cultures. Yet, it seems to me, in this case the conservatives were right and the progressives were wrong. This is often the case in spite of the prejudices of the Deweyian "progressive."

We conclude, therefore, by returning to our contention: the moral resolution of moral situations involves something more than intelligence—it involves, if it is to be moral, a *sui generis moral* factor which cannot be reduced without residuum to nonmoral factors.

Another radical defect of instrumentalism is its conception of man. Dewey does not think of man as do the interest-theory mechanists, but with his categories, as already indicated, he is no more competent to grapple with the complexity of human experience than R. B. Perry and Santayana were. Like them, Dewey also considers in his account of moral experience only acts of reflection and choice which are carried on entirely above the level of consciousness and involve distinctively appreciable factors. Since he considers only an abstract and shallow human being, devoid of psychological depth and complexity, it is very easy for Dewey to reduce ethical and religious phenomena to their purely secularistic moral components. This is the notorious "scientific humanism" of which propagandists for instrumentalism speak. This philosophy reduces man to a size that can be easily measured by "humanistic" standards, since anything for which scientific humanism has no room it considers a perversion or a failure of nerve or vestigial or superfluous.

My criticism of Dewey's scientific concept of human nature, then, is that it is not scientific enough; that it does not envisage the full complexity of the human personality; that it needs to be enlarged to include factors, powers, and phenomena of the self that it ignores. But it must be remembered that while Dewey's theory can be corrected from a scientific point of view, this does not mean that an adequate scientific psychology could give us what Dewey fails to give, a normative moral philosophy. Freud's grasp of the complexities of the mind is deep, while Dewey's is shallow; but, for all Freud's depth, as we shall see in a later chapter, he cannot solve the problem of the moral philosopher. Such a philosopher needs the best information available on how behavioral phenomena, observable under laboratory conditions, can be explained in terms of their causes; and he needs the insights of depth psychology. But such knowledge is ancillary for him. What he strives for as moral philosopher is an accurate account of the structure and content of the moral life as *moral*. This involves knowledge of valuation as a normative process, knowledge of the way in which the normative moral criteria control the correct value judgment, and hence knowledge of the source of moral authority. And such knowledge is autonomous. Dewey's theory, we have seen, does not account for the moral factor in morality. But what I am trying to suggest here in passing is not that his moral theory is defective but that his science is shallow.

Dewey's emphatic rejection of introspection and his expressed attitude toward psychoanalysis will not let a true Deweyian inquire into these fields. Again, if the work which C. W. Morris has done on the basis of Sheldon's theories is at all valid, the psychology of *Human Nature and Conduct*, on which Dewey grounds his moral faith, is inadequate; and, if the speculations of men like Fromm have any validity, certain basic Deweyian values like "self-reliance"— involved in his appeal to the individual to use his intelligence— must be re-examined.[12] These points I do not consider it necessary to elucidate because, with only some superficial changes, the criticisms I made of Ralph Barton Perry's and Santayana's notion of man apply to the instrumentalist theory of man.

CHAPTER VII

THE INSTRUMENTALIST MORAL
THEORY. II

DEWEY'S central effort in the analysis of moral theory, no less than in the analysis of the purely scientific act of reflection, has been addressed to elucidating the manner in which "inquiry" or thought brings about an "*existential* transformation and reconstruction of the material with which it deals."[1] Through this analysis, Dewey is able to indicate how all the terms of a situation on which reflection plays are modified as a result of its activity. In a genuinely reflective act no term is exempted from this process of transformation. In morals this reconstruction includes not only what Dewey calls the "ends-in-view" of prospective action, which must be reshaped to meet available means and avoid remote untoward consequences, but also the initial presuppositions, commitments, and needs, to satisfy which these ends were projected. Thus reflection, by forcing clarification and redefinition of our ends-in-view, modifies our ideals, our basic orientations, and our commitments and makes possible intelligent reconstruction of the objective situation. Moral reflection arrives at its goal when the end is tested by its capacity to satisfy not the needs that initiated the reflective process but the needs which reflection clarified and refined. Read the analysis of ends-in-view, from which moral reflection starts, as contrasted with "concrete ends in their terminal nature" or "aims attained." Follow Dewey's discussion of "propositions about valuations" as contrasted with "valuation proposition." You will no doubt conclude, in the light of the whole tenor of his conception of the process of thought, that, in one respect, Dewey furnishes us with a more adequate picture of the moral life than is supplied by the postulational theory, because moral reflection is, in the literal sense, *reflexive*, and the full implication of this aspect of it the postulational theory virtually denies.[2]

In self-defense Charner Perry could point to those passages in his essay in which he shows clear awareness of the fact that value reflection involves the formation, as well as the expression, of personality. For instance: "Though it frequently happens that reflection has the task of reconciling two or more conflicting interests, the crucial and significant situation is that in which the person concerned is perplexed as to what his interests are, and *surveys the world and himself in order to determine what to be interested in.*" Or: "Reflection or deliberation plays a part in the formation of the personality or self."[3] There would still remain, however, those passages referring to conflict; and these are crucial, because they give clear indication that Perry holds that moral decisions are arrived at by forcing the situation to measure itself against our own Procrustean principles, which are the expression of the "take-it-or-leave-it" attitude of our demands. Take this important statement:

"If there are people whose actions and principles obstruct the following of our own moral principles and purposes, then doubtless we shall do what we can to remove, overrule, or hamper the obstructing persons; but the conviction that our own moral principles are finally and really right is either a rendering of the fact that after all our own moral principles are all that we have or else it expresses a futile desire for a superior moral justification."[4]

But this advantage of the instrumentalist theory over the postulational theory of morals is not enough to save it. The argument that follows will seek to show that the errors into which the instrumentalist falls are the very opposite of those which, as I have argued, afflict the postulational theory; for the instrumentalist gives up on principle all truly regulative principles and thus leaves himself without protection from the wiles of expedience and the pressure of opportunistic rationalization.

One cannot miss in Dewey's writings on valuation and on ethics his clear awareness of the evils inherent in the acceptance of fixed maxims and principles in moral reflection. His objections to such fixities have diverse sources, among which the most prominent are the following: the empiricist's aversion to apriorisms; the reformer's need to respond to the ever new, concrete demands of human beings; and the vivid sense that he has of the way in which principles end by becoming rigid rules which, like sanguinary gods, instead of serving human life, sacrifice it to their own majesty. Principles, he acknowledges, have some binding force on moral situations.[5] Nevertheless, he insists that they cannot be allowed to have the finality of fixed rules, for when they do the "center of moral gravity" has been put outside "the concrete processes of living."[6] To theories appealing to fixed principles of judgment Dewey has opposed as alternative a conception of morality whose method "may be called experimental."[7]

Exactly what is meant by "experimentalism" in moral philosophy? It would seem absurd to assume that one can experiment with men's moral principles and ideals as one can with guinea pigs or with physical objects; yet that is what the instrumentalist actually claims. He cannot mean it in any plain sense, but where has he explained his own esoteric meaning, where pointed out what the difference is between guinea pigs and men's ideals? An interpretation of the experimentalist doctrine that would allow a Nazi to argue that the elimination of the Jews was carried out as an experiment in the interest of the great majority of mankind would be absurd, since it utterly disregards Dewey's well-known humane spirit. But it is, nevertheless, of capital significance, in that it points to an area in which the doctrine of instrumentalism requires precise elucidation. Obviously, not all ideals can be considered as experimental hypotheses, nor can all desiderata be admitted as ideals. How, then, do we distinguish between the sheep and the goats among ideals? A "pure" intelligence, as Charner Perry has so clearly shown, does not help us. Sooner or later we find ourselves driven back upon something which is more than intelligence and which functions as a fixity or an apriorism in respect to the required choice. In the assertion of this insight the postulational theory seems to me to have got hold of something basic to the moral life. What that fixity is, however, is not any old caprice that any Tom, Dick, or Harry chooses to lay down as a commitment or postulation, but one which is capable of resolving moral conflicts and which guarantees the continuation of the moral life. We shall study it in Part III.

Yet Dewey insists that all appeals to principles transcending the claims in conflict are to be grouped under the same rubric of "dogmatism" and all equally condemned: appeal to divine revelations, to divinely ordained rulers, to the so-called "natural law," to private conscience, to the commands of the state, to the constitution, to common consent, to the majority, to conventions, to traditions coming from a hoary past, to the wisdom of ancestors, to precedents. "The common feature" of appeal to these principles, we are told, "is that there is some voice so authoritative as to preclude the need of inquiry." Dewey believes that the logic common to all of them prescribes a closed mind in moral matters.[8]

One looks in vain in this indiscriminate proscription of all appeals to principle as dogmatic for a sympathetic inkling of the fact that men of uncompromising principles possess, in their uprightness, a certain quality of heroism and devotion of which a world pullulating with stooges, easy yes men, and unprincipled back-benders with a taste for boots seems in most urgent need. And one looks in vain for awareness of the fact that appeal to fixed principles may involve a complex and oblique strategy by means of which men seek to defend not their principles but something much more precious—their own integrity, their own ethical essence, their own identity as persons—against the disruptive pressures of outward circumstances and the disintegrative effect of facile compromise. But from the instrumentalist all you will learn is that a man's loyalty to irrevocable commitments is always pathological dogmatism, giving rise to fetishistic idolatry of principles for their own sake.

Back of the instrumentalist's disregard of the value of personal integrity lies Dewey's defective notion of human nature, which explains man under the simple psychological categories of habit and impulse developed in *Human Nature and Conduct*. Let me reiterate that it is impossible with such categories to develop an ethical theory. Professor Allport has incisively pointed out that Dewey has no theory of personality. But note that it is not, for the moral philosopher, merely a question of Dewey's failure to do psychological justice to "the stability of organization in the individual personality."[9] It is this, but it is also a question of the failure to grasp the necessity for moral theory of the concept of "personality" as a normative category. Remember that, for Dewey, men are adequately understood as systems of impulses and desires, regulated by habit and intelligence. Principles and ideals are for him but needs and demands stated in generalized terms. Hence, if a secularly oriented intelligence cannot effectively satisfy its ideals, it is of the essence of its wisdom to modify or abandon its demands. But this conception of human nature is true only of the uprooted denizens of our acquisitive civilization. It is not desires that constitute men but values, organized hierarchically against the disruptive forces of the world; these are our true selves, the innermost core of our moral personality.

Thus, for all his talk of "positive respect for human nature when the latter is associated with scientific knowledge"[10] and of his belief in the dignity of men, the instrumentalist cannot truly value individual integrity. His emphasis on change precludes it. If we view man as a system of impulses whose satisfaction is regulated by habit and intelligence and if we conceive of moral activity as a technique of satisfying desires, why should man elicit respect? From such a standpoint no one desire need be better than another. It may be more urgent, more inclusive, or somehow preferable; and this is all that can be meant by calling one desire "better" than another. The important thing, therefore, is to satisfy our desires, and if this object will not do, then that one will. From this point of view there is no reason why we should not submit ourselves to the demands of things as they are. This is the upshot of Dewey's wisdom. The important thing—but this, of course, cannot be a principle, since none are permitted—is that we frame our principles and rules with regard to "actual conditions."[11]

A moral man cannot lightly risk the disruption of his personality. Somewhere he has to make a stand and hold, whatever the cost, saying to the demands of "actual conditions": "I must be who I am, I can do no other." Such a man distinguishes between the drive of desire, which is from the inside out, so to speak, and that of value, which is from the outside in. You cannot alter your values lightly, not because they are yours but precisely for the opposite reason, *because you are theirs.* Recognition of moral values brings with it a sense (if I may again use, or perhaps misuse, Köhler's term)[12] of "requiredness," which puts one in a condition of servitude toward them. And it is this acceptance of their requiredness that compels us to protect them from corruption and external threat and to distinguish them as ends from the means that are necessary to realize them. This is the basis of the distinction of means and ends which moral men make, according to which means are discontinuous with moral ends: means are not reverenced, nor are merely practical ends. Means and merely practical ends can be continuous; but moral ends are not continuous with their means because they occupy a preferential place in our consciousness, since we are theirs, since they are the source of our moral being, constitutive of it and hence something not merely precious but sacred. Who does not see this has not begun to understand the nature of the moral phenomena which he is called on as moral philosopher to analyze. One is loath to experiment with one's values, for one is loath to risk self-destruction. To create new principles is to create new selves. But a self is not a suit of clothes that can be discarded when fashion decrees a new shoulder line or pleats in the trousers. The idea that "principles exist as hypotheses with which to experiment" and that the business of intelligence under changing objective conditions is "to create new principles"[13] is thus seen, if intended as distinct from sheer opportunism, to be utterly unintelligible. Imagine Socrates, under the well-meant advice of his instrumentalist friend, "creating new principles" to meet his changed situation in respect to the Athenians who had jailed him and in respect to the jail-keeper who was willing for a consideration to look the other way as Socrates sneaked out. In acting with regard to "actual conditions," as his experimentalist friend advised him to do, would he have remained Socrates? A Socrates that betrays his moral integrity is no longer Socrates. Is such a man, who deliberately chooses to perish rather than open himself to the corruption of expedience, a pathological case? Then, by all means, let us have more pathological cases of this kind. Health is not desirable when one achieves it by becoming an evil man.

But, says Dewey's defender, this represents a perverse misunderstanding of instrumentalist doctrine, since Dewey has pointed out in the *Ethics* that "the alternative is not between abdication and acquiescence on one side, and neglect and ignoring on the other; it is between a morals which is effective because related to what is, and a morality which is futile and empty because framed in disre-

gard of actual conditions."[14] To which one must answer that it is
not the business of moral reflection *to affirm what is*. That needs no
affirmation. More often than not what it needs is denial, fierce opposition—and the more robust and uncompromising, the better.
The business of moral reflection is *to affirm what ought to be*. Nor is
"what ought to be" a formulation of our desires—as often as not it
is a stern rejection of all our desires. Only by forcing the actual to
conform to the pattern of the ideal can we morally improve things
as they are. Furthermore, we must still ask the instrumentalist
what he means by "effective." "Effective" for what? And what
"actual conditions" has he in mind? Assume what is belied by the
historical record, that Socrates' quixotic dogmatism was futile and
that he would have been more "effective" had he followed Crito's
opportunistic advice. It is still pertinent to ask whether he would
have remained Socrates; for consider that the "actual conditions" of
his moral personality were threatened by the "actual conditions" of
which Meletus, Anytus, and Lycon were the representatives. Are
we to assume that one set of actual conditions—those constituting
Socrates' personality—was less "actual" than that represented by
his contemptible accusers? But also note that, in turning down
Crito's offer, he was not falling back on rock-bottom postulates.
Socrates did not assert the right of his private voice to sit as judge
on the adequacy of his decisions. His private voice only held him
back. He was willing—nay, eager—to bring the matter before the
bar of reason—not of experiment, but of reason, mind you; for an
"experiment," even a mental one, was utterly impossible. But there
was one actual condition that reason did not allow Socrates to ignore: a sacred contract, even though an implicit one only, between
himself and that which he ought least to wrong, not the Athenian
people but the laws. Rational in his approach; willing, therefore, to
open his principles to the scrutiny of reason and to correct them if
proved wrong, Socrates knew that there was one thing that he could
not do, and that was to experiment with that which was the very
condition of his ethical identity, the laws by which he was bound
and to which he owed all he was.

    The man who gives up regulative principles shuns the responsi-
bility of making genuine moral judgments and assumes, instead, the
job of haggling for each interest against all the others and of

juggling them into a working compromise. As the means of adjudging between demands, the experimentalist arms himself with a universal sympathy for each and every demand and with whatever prudential rules he may have at hand. (But his rules cannot be regulative, since they must be tested by their capacity to adjust claims and must be themselves adjusted to circumstances no less than circumstances to them.) Can he, thus equipped, adjudicate the validity of one demand over the rest? All he can do is to play a more or less shrewd game of bluffing pressures and desires into scaling down their demands and ever so gently but firmly pushing those that can be pushed out of the way, while hiding under the pretense of sympathy for actual conditions the stark nature of compromises dictated by force.

If the only choice one had were between the obvious evils of a "rules-is-rules" morality and the experimentalist's morality, ours would be a hard plight. But it may seem to those who have had a taste of the latter that against the dogmatic will one can always make some sort of appeal, by contrasting the decisions of the dogmatist with his professions of respect for the moral law. And if this appeal fails—as in the majority of cases no doubt it will—at least one knows clearly where the dogmatist stands, and one may be able to put one's self beyond the reach of his power. But the man who dispenses with principles and appeals to the factors in the actual situation, if he has the preponderance of power on his side, has you entirely at his mercy, since seldom are you able to tell exactly how you stand toward him in regard to the situation over which the difference arose.

The instrumentalist will observe that this is not the way in which he proposes to resolve conflicts. "The method of experimental intelligence" calls for discussion of conflicting claims "to be settled in the interest of the widest possible contribution to the interests of all—or at least of the great majority. The method of democracy—in as far as it is that of organized intelligence—is to bring these conflicts out into the open where their special claims can be seen and appraised, where they can be discussed and judged in the light of more inclusive interests than are represented by either of them separately."[15]

Let us note in reply that the appeal to the factors at issue is purely illusory under the conditions of conflict of uneven powers, since facts are dumb and discussion of moral issues soon reveals that the difference arises out of divergent interpretations of the facts. With power on your side, the facts are defined by you; and my failure to accept your interpretation will be construed by you as lack of a desire to co-operate, which, of course, fully justifies you in the use of force. The weak, denied the right to appeal to fixed and well-defined principles binding on the strong no less than on the weak, are left utterly without practical recourse. It is not a question of one party to the conflict being evil and the other not, but of the tendency we all have to interpret facts to our own satisfaction. We do this in spite of our principles, even though we acknowledge their regulative role; but how much easier it is to do it when we are ruled by one principle only, namely, that principles should be shunned.

CHAPTER VIII

THE INSTRUMENTALIST MORAL
THEORY. III

MY DEEPEST opposition to instrumentalism arises from my rejection of its purely secularistic world view. In its conception of moral salvation, all naturalism is committed to secularism, since its essential meaning as a cosmological doctrine is irrevocably atheistic. Naturalism must actively deny, therefore, the nontemporal dimension of man. But in Dewey and his followers secularism becomes militant and intransigent; as evidence, witness Dewey's "Antinaturalism in Extremis," his contribution to the Krikorian volume, and his disciple Sidney Hook's militant warfare against any kind of expression that so much as raises a doubt that the institutions of religion are without intellectual validity.[1] It does not seem improper, therefore, to discuss secularism in connection with Dewey. However, the substance of the remarks contained in this chapter, with appropriate modifications, applies to a great extent to all current naturalisms in contemporary American philosophy.

His followers are correct when they assert that no other American philosopher has so deeply influenced the thought of his generation as Dewey. The impact of his labors not only is measured by his numerous academic disciples but is also discovered in the pages of those who have opposed him: men like Cunningham, Sellars, Warner Fite, and the American positivists testify to the impact of his thought. In so far as a philosopher has a say in the creation of a culture's values by the way he defines them and clarifies them, no thinker can claim so deep an influence in his day on the history of his people as Dewey. But this influence seems to me deeply to be deplored. However, in spite of his radical repudiation of tradition, his philosophy is rooted in the rich soil of German idealism, and therefore it cannot give us so erroneous an account of the moral problem as the interest theory can, with its specious clarity and elegance but with its radical irrelevance.[2] While we must criticize Dewey for the spiritual myopia of his theory, it should not be forgotten that the grasp he has of the moral problem is in some respects much closer to human reality than that found in other types of naturalistic moral theory.

But the reader will want to know why I pass such harsh judgment on the philosophy of instrumentalism. He remembers that it has been identified with what in our day has been thought of as noblest and most urgent: it is "liberal," "democratic," concerned with "human freedom" and "dignity"; it looks to the future and not to the Middle Ages and the auto-da-fé. Isn't to oppose it to give comfort to all the dark and reactionary forces of our day? An argued answer to our question would take us far from our subject, but some sort of answer must be given to it by a writer who asserts that the technical criticism of a philosophy cannot constitute a complete case against it.

Let us first note, then, that in contradiction to a tendency in his thought which breaks up caked conceptual dichotomies in favor of the inherently fluid, dialectical nature of the real, Dewey has encouraged the simple-minded division of men and ideas into "liberal" and "reactionary." On the one side are to be found light, goodness, and truth; on the other, the enemies of man, the friends of darkness and error. The great advantage of this division is not hard to see. All one needs to judge a vision of the world or a man or an idea by is a shibboleth, and shibboleths can be had for the taking any time, anywhere, and by anyone. Do men say the word correctly? Then let them pass. Don't they? Then they are out. In our day there are innumerable shibboleths—"democracy," "freedom," "human dignity," "progressivism," "liberalism," "naturalism"—all of which are monopolies of the right side, which is, of course, the left. But philosophers are not after orthodoxy but after truth. They find as much evil in the hearts of the self-proclaimed lovers of man as in those whom the self-proclaimed lovers denounce, and every day they see believers in the dignity of man that are as ready to crush that dignity as any SS guard or NKVD agent ever was. Not all the light do they find on one side or all the darkness on the other. And thus the philosopher is led to the conclusion that his task is not that of adding to the already hopelessly embittered partisanship of the social and political scene, strengthening the political self-righteousness of men who are just as confused, baffled, weak, pathetic, and misguided as those they condemn because of their confusions, bafflement, weakness, and evil heart. The philosopher's job is another, and one which this partitioning of men into the evil and the good absolutely precludes.

Our question, therefore, is not whether Dewey's philosophy has been on the "right" side; it is whether it does justice to the human situation. If it does not, its liberalism is deceptive. And let us remember that there is not one of the indispensable values the possession of which is not claimed by the other side: freedom, dignity, enlightenment. Each side has its own version of freedom, of dignity, and of enlightenment: there is the freedom of Herbert Hoover, the freedom of the Fascist and of the Stalinist, just as there is the freedom of the liberal John Dewey. But isn't there a fourth, the only real one, out of which these factious, myopic *guerrilleros* tore their own little partial versions and over which they cannot claim exclusive monopoly? We cannot therefore take for granted that because Dewey writes in defense of a value labeled "enlightenment," he is truly on the side of light. I have shown that instrumentalist moral philosophy is technically inadequate, and from this it follows that the enlightenment which it pretends to defend it does not truly defend. But, first, is it enlightenment? The term cannot be defined without reference to a notion of man, and it appears that Dewey's notion of man is egregiously inadequate.

Dewey criticizes medieval philosophy because it hired itself out as the handmaiden of theology. He criticizes Greek philosophy because it systematized at the theoretical level the structure of Greek society with its master-slave relationship, into a distinction between knowing and doing. For Dewey modern philosophy until 1859 or, more exactly perhaps, until 1903, has been singularly devoid of men in possession of the truth. In brief, according to the instrumentalist, the history of thought from Thales to our own day is almost entirely a history of error. But isn't Dewey's philosophy open to the same criticism that he makes of Greek, medieval, and modern philosophy? What Dewey has tried to do is to take philosophy out of the sacristy and hire her out as bottle-washer in the laboratory. But is this new menial job better than dressing saints for the procession? Consider that the maid could, in the sacristy, once in a while steal a drink of the consecration wine, which gave her quite a kick and always led to interesting results. Philosophy under Dewey's management no longer smells of incense and beeswax. But does the smell of hydrogen sulphide that now clings to her make her more attractive? Dewey assigns to philosophy the task of rationalizing and deepening the power and enlarging the jurisdiction of science and of intrenching the secularistic conception of human nature at which our technological culture arrived, thoughtlessly but at least with a divided conscience. Dewey thinks of himself as a critic of his world and its values; but he is doing nothing more than throwing his weight behind some of the most sinister forces that are operative today in the world, those that are leading us toward Orwell's and Huxley's nightmares, since the effect of his philosophy is to thin and trivialize the dignity of men. Considered in respect to the direction of his activities, it turns out that Dewey is not a critic of his day but of the past.

He is thus doing exactly what the Schoolmen did and for the same reason, because he has been driven along with most of his contemporaries by the onrush of his culture and has not been able to stand aside and ask whether the objectives that he served were worth serving. He is what my people call *un alzado*, a man up in arms; Dewey is up in arms against the human tradition, against the precious heritage of our culture. His influence, institutionalized in numerous departments of philosophy and in primary and secondary schools and teachers' colleges, has been profoundly effective in accelerating the process of disintegration. He has, unwittingly, undertaken to soften us up for the Red push. He is the biggest of the big-time promoters of the "brave new world." What he has never seen is that, in his haste to get rid of all the values that the historical process has weakened, he has advocated the destruction of all the values that are basically constitutive of our humanity. The task of the wise philosopher is to help effect the historical change with the minimum of loss. Dewey, the pioneer, has urged us to march West, but to travel lightly; but, in getting rid of all our impedimenta, we somehow threw away some precious bits of ourselves. Dewey has convinced a few men of science and a band of half-educated public-ity agents and some ignorant evangelistic quacks that science is in as much need of championing today as it was when Wilberforce made a monkey of himself by his ill-considered efforts to wrest his humanity from the jaws of Darwin's bulldog; and he has convinced large numbers of gullible readers that we can save democracy or, rather, the bankrupt doctrine of inalienable rights on which democ-racy was erected in the eighteenth century only by rebuilding it upon instrumentalist foundations.

No Deweyian can give one good, radically theoretical reason, one that goes beyond expedience, why he prefers democracy to totalitarianism or why he regards other men as his moral equals. And on his relativistic basis there can be no reason that can stand up under criticism, since for relativism, once a man is adjusted to a system, that system is better for him than an angel's utopia, nor can men, naturalistically described, be anything but what, in fact, they are, unequal. Men are equal ethically and religiously, not factually.

Instrumentalism knows nothing of human beings; it knows the behavioristic robots with which its scientistic methodology fur-nishes it. It is true that Dewey has spent a long and busy life elaborating a philosophy of events, guided by the same method that has given us reliable knowledge of the physical world and designed to serve as a basis for a generous conception of democracy. But, if we look closely at the thought of the instrumentalist, we shall dis-cover that *what he has done is to turn a political theory into a philosophy of human life.* Since for him the social task must come first, the needs and activities of the spirit must be relegated—in fact, if not in so many blunt words—to a distinctly secondary place. This is the reason why instrumentalism remains vague and noncommittal about the operative structure of the moral life and its orienting values. On its own terms, of course, this position is defensible because, as we have seen, Dewey has put the resources of a powerful intellect into disparaging regulative principles and final goals. What the content of a man's life should be, what ends he ought to serve when he has acquired the freedom and the security which he seeks, cannot be defined in terms of a conception of man that does not go beyond the exigencies of social and political behaviorism.

Ultimately, however, no one concerned with moral problems as seriously as Dewey is can successfully avoid the formulation of final ends; and in his philosophy, for all its rejection of them, you will find them too, since it accepts the ethos of our day uncritically. With this the Deweyian must accept the vague corollary that the end of life, when rationally determined, must in some generic sense be aesthetic satisfaction, in both the ordinary and the Kierkegaardi-an sense of this word. On the negative side, his final end excludes, as superstition and as "failure of nerve," such ideals as contempla-tion, inwardness, the mystic's union with God, the renunciation of the world-weary, and the disgust of the man who has stuck his nose too close to the world's moral reality. Sustaining his positive ends, you will find in the instrumentalist an optimism impenetrable by experience and, by implication, a terror of pain and a systematic mutilation of the deeper insights into those aspects of existence that give birth to the Karamazovs, to Gulliver, to Macbeth or Lear, to the visions of Goya, and to the Oedipus sequence.

Dewey's crusade in favor of science reveals the pathetic gap that exists between advocating growth and actually growing. He is still fighting the Wilberforces who obstructed Darwin. He does not realize that the Wilberforces are dead and buried. No one who counts at all opposes science any longer. Even some theologians are falling all over themselves to prove that they accept its conclusions and that they are quite willing to apply its methods themselves. What we need today is not propaganda for science but criticism of the tendency to borrow from science a conception of human destiny which is purely secularistic. The scientists, serious men bent on their own business, never thought of giving us such a notion. They know the limitations of their methods. It is the scientistic philoso-phers, the self-appointed handmaidens of the laboratory, Dewey and his men, who are bent on turning an abstract scientific descrip-tion of biological evolution politically interpreted into a metaphysic of human destiny. And what does this add up to? The pursuit of secular happiness, interpreted practically, turns out to be the pursuit of gadgets.

On such foundations instrumentalism would rear a philosophy of education. But what it can give us is not education but training. Education assumes as final end the information—*in-formation*—of humanity somehow into the animal, or the drawing of the human form somehow from it, by the skills of the spiritual obstetrician. A philosophy that starts by telling us that questions about human destiny, questions about ultimate objectives, make no sense because ends and means are continuous, can have nothing very serious to say about education, however much it may have to say that is worth listening to on training. We have seen that no moralist can avoid final ends. Instrumentalists are not an exception to this rule. Their education is for "modern man,"[3] but it takes no perspicacity to notice that the term is not a philosophic concept but a slogan. On examination it turns out to be old hat: if we could add enough scientificism of the Deweyian-positivist variety to our thinking, the dosage would be certain to bring about the Blessed Age of history. Remember, however, that those who cheer for instrumentalism are doing more than advocating the spread of the effective area of science. What they are advocating is the spreading of "the" philosophy of science; for, just as Deweyians have a corner on democracy, so have they one on science. All it means, in practice, is the spread of antireligious naturalism, which adds up to uncritical worship of scientific method for its own sake and the autocracy of secular values.

Dewey rejected the classical philosophies because they are not fit for our modern age. But is the modern world of science fit for man? This question we have never seen Dewey discuss. He and his disciples take it for granted. Now there have always been philosophers who have made it their business to sell their day to their contemporaries—T. H. Huxley, for instance, or the French philosophers of the Enlightenment, or Bacon—but the business of the genuine philosopher is to correct his age. In general terms, the Deweyian strategy is familiar to us. First, it disparages the past and belittles its achievements. Next, it exaggerates the breach between it and our day, making the Holy Year of 1859 of the Christian Era the first year of the new scientific calendar. Lastly, the Deweyian strategy tries to sell us on an idealized picture of what science could do for us in the social sphere if we but chose to apply it. We reply that there is today no knowledge of society worth the name of "science," since the conclusions of social inquiry have no predictive value, and that what there is can hardly be "applied," since men do not seem to be able to come to agreement on objectives; but we thereby show our obscurantist bias and our ignorance of recent philosophy. In *Logic: The Theory of Inquiry* and in *A Theory of Valuation* we have been shown what is the method of all science, social no less than physical, and with their aid we can, if we want to, resolve our differences about objectives. It should also be remembered that social science is a young science. Give it time, and it will do as well as physics. In fact, of course, social science is older by two thousand years than modern physical science, but what is history to the scientifist?

As against the instrumentalist's aim, I would suggest that a truly humanistic philosophy must needs be opposed to those forces in our world that would completely secularize it. Complete secularization would be a form of barbarism, all the more dangerous since it thinks of itself as the highest flowering of civilization. And this is the reason, as it seems to me, for the ferocity with which instrumentalists and positivists attack a genuinely humanistic education. I know of no teacher worth considering who would like to go back to the Middle Ages or who would not give science ample room in his curriculum; but I do know of many—with whom I am fully in sympathy—who conceive of a liberal, humanistic, general education as issuing forth in men awake to the need to retain in as vital a condition as possible the humanistic values without which men cannot be completely human. For these values the instrumentalists, for all they have to say to the contrary, have no genuine respect.[4]

The instrumentalist's attitude is rooted in the fact that he is narrowly anxious about the specific dangers that, in his view, threaten our political institutions. It is, I fear, his political anxiety that causes him to misconceive the function of education. For instance, Sidney Hook in *Education for Modern Man* defines the fundamental social problem of our culture as that of defending and extending our democratic institutions and providing for the security of men.[5] For him, therefore, the problem of education must be defined by its relation to the political task, which is basic. I would argue that the political, for all its importance, is a secondary task for the teacher and that to make it into the primary bespeaks a lack of historical vision and a parochialism that effectively obfuscates the most radical issues. As the Deweyian defines the fundamental problem of our day, the difference between him and Zhdanov is relative, for underlying their important differences lies their agreement in the primacy of the political. The difference is one of degree of consistency, and in this respect the advantage is all in favor of the Russian.

Let me reiterate that as against belief in the primacy of the political the truly humanist teacher—and properly viewed the teacher must share with the statesman, the priest, and the poet the ultimate responsibility for the success or failure of his people and culture—must conceive the fundamental problem today, yesterday, and always to be the need to stave off the snarling beasts of barbarism that are always and everywhere on the alert to get out of their inward cages into which culture drives them. The teacher's job must be to guide man to grow to his full stature as human. This he does not by enlisting him in a party but by making him the possessor of the sustaining intellectual and moral structures of civilization. Today that need is more pressing than it ever was because two factors, the final liberation of the masses in the powerful industrial states and the triumph of positive science with the resultant speeding-up of the technological revolution, have set us a date with history against which we must race.

Until only recently the so-called "civilized" world got along more or less satisfactorily with a few clerks—a few poets and moralists and a relatively small number of chattering schoolmen. These men tried to soften the hearts of the ironclad men and to awaken in them a yearning for something beyond the exultation of victory in the field. When the warriors gave way to those who ruled the world from behind the money scales, the clerks were there to do what they could and all in all they did their work well enough. The large mass of the population they influenced hardly at all, but it did not seem to matter, for the mass was thought to be effectively excluded from shaping in any direct way the course of history. Only a minority was thought to shape it. And it was these few whom it was necessary to educate. As D. H. Lawrence has somewhere said, your duke could keep the moral end of it up since only he had the thousands per year necessary to do it. The mass could be left in the dark about the ends they served. You have to know at firsthand the peons of our colonial areas—for instance, of our oil and banana colonies on the Caribbean shores—to realize how little human the vast majority of mankind must have been in the great ages of the world; to have some notion, that is, of what the masses must have been like of whom Thucydides and Mariana and Gibbon do not say much.

Today, at least in the powerful states, the mass is effectively reaching for the controls of history. It has wrested from the minority the right to determine its own destiny. (This is not true in Russia, of course, where the revolution was long ago betrayed. Yet it is in the name of the masses and in terms of values quite distinct from the aristocratic that the slaveowners in Russia control the course of events.) Therefore, the most important question that the teacher must ask himself is whether men can be taught that they cannot be eulogistically called "men" if they free themselves from the tyranny of the ideal. If we teachers and clerks cannot make this clear to them, the fate of civilization and of man himself has passed into poor hands. The barbarians from whom the eighteenth century thought itself forever safe are not merely living beside us in the colonial areas or in the slums of our large cities or even next door to us but are teeming within each and every one of us. Inside us lie untamed our own brutality and the natural tendency inherent in each animal to define value in terms of his own interests, which is to say, to view the world in terms of his passions and lusts. When this tendency becomes a philosophy, it turns into the worst barbarism imaginable, a much more subtle and insidious one than that which once threatened so-called "civilized" Europe from beyond its marches. If by now we have not seen this clearly, we have totally missed the lesson of the last two wars and the events that are now taking place.

Those who have grasped the meaning of these events see that it is not merely a question of democracy versus some other form of government—no man with a historical sense would suppose that by means of this or that form of government alone men can live adequately. The political problem is important because democracy seems at the moment to offer the possibility of realizing some essential values to which other forms of government at present bidding for supremacy are indifferent; at any rate what the Russians offer us is only a more naked and a lustier barbarism than our own and a coarser brutality. But much more important to the teacher should be the problem of what man is going to make of himself. Is he going to turn into a man, to humanize himself?

It needs therefore to be said bluntly and without ambiguity that the ends of civilization cannot be conceived as ultimately tied up in any exclusive way with the existence of a highly developed positive science. They never have been. Admirable civilizations have waxed and fallen in which positive science as we know it today was almost totally ignored. The instrumentalist worship of science which Dewey and his disciples so assiduously preach and the contempt for human values which that worship so insidiously fosters are the most barbaric form of idolatry, the most sterile that can be imagined.

This last contention also seems to me to deserve fair consideration, although probably all it will get from the scientifists is contemptuous dismissal as the blind reactionary arguments of a witch-doctor or a voodoo-man in disguise. Grant gladly all that is being said about the practical benefits of science when properly used and of course grant, above all, the beauty and thrill of theoretical knowledge of the physical structure of the world, the fact still remains that science must be "value-free" if it is to be science. If our interest in science, therefore, is not preceded and controlled by an absorbing interest in human perplexities and bafflements, if we do not view the human adventure with a deep tragic sense, we soon turn into positivists—which is to say, men who banish all problems of value into the realm of the emotional on the claim that they are noncognitive and let it go at that. (They are incredible, these scientifists, with their insulated, lucid brains and their blind hearts.) Dewey has opposed this vicious theory vigorously but does not see that it is a natural consequence of scientifist idolatry. For this reason, without values that reach beyond the secular, without some sense of religious piety, without great pity for victims of our daily brutalities and fear of our power for evil, without a tragic and humble sense of the difficulty of the humanist's task, your scientifist turns science into one of the most devastatingly barbarizing forces that man has ever devised. But mind you that I did not say "your scientist," but "your scientifist," for they are totally different persons.

Hence our need to add to science just the things that the anti-humanist denies. But we cannot control science and shall remain at its blind mercy unless we all, scientists no less than the rest of us, gain a full understanding of the values that sustain civilization. This is a moral and religious problem, calling for a conception of man's destiny that transcends a secularistic conception of "happiness." Hence the need for a truly humanistic education, for which Dewey and his disciples would substitute an education for "modern man" which instils in the pupil idolatry toward scientific method and contempt for the achievements of the past, thus fitting him to yield uncritically to the thorough mechanization of his life. (This is the famous instrumentalistic liberation—fitting a man to adapt himself to an inhuman world, liberating him from his humanity.) But where can we go for an education if not to the despised "great books"? Where shall we gain an understanding of the meaning and full range of human life, a sense of the difference between the insensate activity of the instrumentalist beaver—the builder of dams for the joy of building—and the full-grown man in possession of his soul?

We can learn, says Sidney Hook in his book on education, at least as much from "the heroic tragedy" of Warsaw as from the last stand at Thermopylae.[6] And this aptly illustrates Hook's attitude toward the values that give one man, Herodotus, his stature and place him above the Stalinist or anti-Stalinist or above the merely "objective" professional journalist who reported the butchery of Warsaw. Note in passing that, in choosing the stand at Thermopylae, Hook has not chosen the best example that he could have found, for in Thucydides are to be found pages of deeper and more eloquent humanistic value than any you can find in Herodotus. However, we can still meet his challenge in his own terms. Consider, then, the insight into the meaning of the conflict as Herodotus takes pains to make it clear by direct statement and by dramatic means; consider the contrast between the barbarian herd, driven to battle by their captains armed with whips, and the handful of Lacedaemonians whom the spy saw engaged in gymnastic exercises and combing their long hair; consider, in short, the lofty manner in which the conflict was viewed by the ancient historian. The impact of his meaning cannot be gathered from a few pages of Book vii, or even from the whole book, but from the whole *History*, by digesting at leisure the import not only of Herodotus' conception of the struggle between Xerxes and the Greeks but his conception of the relation of men to the gods. So far as Hook is concerned, there is no difference between the qualities that lift one reported fact, the stand at Thermopylae, into an imperishable vision of human heroism and another which, unless it finds its poet, will remain one of the merely sordid minor butcheries of history; and there is none, because Hook does not grasp the grand dramatic sweep of Herodotus. For the instrumentalist an account in the *New York Times* will do as well as Homer, and a story in the *Nation* or the *New Republic* as well as the imperishable visions of human heroism to be found in Herodotus or Thucydides. And for *his* purposes, I am afraid, they perfectly will.

If instrumentalists succeed—and they are working with the drift of our barbaric tendencies, and these are strong—they will leave us no soil which is not covered with the spiritual slag dumps of our technological culture. This is the reason that I take the immediate and most urgent philosophic task of our generation to be to expose the sinister, partial, antihuman goals of naturalism until we loosen its hold on our educational institutions. The second is to supply, instead of these errors, to the best of our ability, a viable truth. But this must wait the development of a philosopher—something which does not happen very often in the life of a people. We are in for a long wait. In the meantime it behooves us to prepare the ground. The job is important and urgent. The United States has emerged, almost overnight, as one of the two powers which will decide the direction of world history for many centuries to come. The peoples of the world look up to it for leadership, but it becomes daily more clear that what they expect is not merely economic, technological, and military aid. That kind of help that the Russian can at least pretend to give the world as well as we can and the promises that he makes on the material side seem more plausible than ours to men whom bourgeois capitalism has long promised all and brutally denied much. Russia promises freedom from ancient burdens and unbearable iniquities. The challenge is real. Deweyism offers them gadgets and a shallow conception of their destiny; it talks to them about dignity and freedom, but, as effectively as any totalitarian philosophy, it denies the basis of both.

The philosophical task is urgent because the United States cannot meet its challenge by peddling secularistic vulgarities, shallow scientistic optimism, or a dwarfish conception of man, which is all that naturalism, particularly instrumentalism, can offer. Contemporary American philosophy has allowed the Deweyites to sell an uninformed public on the idea that pragmatism is the *American philosophy*. A professor of literature at Harvard popularizes the lie, and it is widely accepted at home and abroad. Pragmatism cannot help us meet the responsibilities which history has thrust on this nation. Pragmatism was, even in the days when it was still a growing philosophy, a limited, parochial rationalization of a few of the dominant forces of American society. The instrumentalist version of pragmatism expressed an even more limited number of operative forces than the loose, unsystematic thought of James did. Instrumentalism, the philosophy of growth, has never grown. It was propagated by a man who was a philosopher and has shown an indefatigable energy in the circulation and defense of his ideas. The disciples he has trained in the principles of free inquiry and growth chant back the lesson of the master. I am not aware that the growth and development of this philosophy have carried the initial insights beyond where that first generation of pragmatists left them. With the exception of C. I. Lewis' work on knowledge and value, the thought of James, Dewey, and Mead is applied, not developed.

Pragmatism once met a need. It was a shallow need but a real one. It would have been better if the need had not been met in the way in which it was and, better still perhaps, if the need had not existed. But pragmatism did meet a need. Today it no longer does. It has no vitality; it scorns the new, and it has succeeded in crossfertilizing only with positivism: the result is more of the same thing, with this difference, that the hybrid has absorbed from positivism its lack of practical responsibility.

CHAPTER IX

THE FREUDIAN THEORY OF CONSCIENCE

THE theory to which we turn in this chapter has not yet played an important role in American philosophy. A few scattered writers on value have seen its relevance to their interests. Nearly thirty years ago Edwin B. Holt wrote *The Freudian Wish and Its Place in Ethics.* John R. Reid has some interesting suggestions on the need to view the problem of value in the light of psychiatry. But the full impact on moral philosophy of what used to be called "the new psychology" is yet to be felt by technical philosophers. This is a fact of great interest to the sociologist of knowledge, which is here stated without comment. Sociologists, anthropologists, and psychologists who have not been indifferent to depth psychology have had to do some theorizing on the subject of value; philosophers, for the most part, have not employed the insights of psychoanalysis; and yet the phenomenological description of the person which "Freud" (using the term as a metaphor) contributed is of tremendous importance to them—or, rather, should be, since to date they have not, as a group, noticed it.[1]

We cannot concern ourselves in this chapter with the whole vast and poorly charted problem of the relation of abnormal psychology, psychiatry, and psychoanalysis to moral philosophy.[2] Our interest restricts itself to an examination of the naturalistic account of the genesis of conscience given by Freud. But, since in certain quarters uninformed prejudice against his theories still remains unabated, it is necessary to warn the reader that this writer holds it a high merit that, unlike the moral vitalists and the instrumentalists, Freud takes the conscience seriously and thus, in some respects, comes closer to the empirical data of the moral life than militant empiricists do. Freud's theory begs the moral question at the same point at which all other naturalists beg it; but, whatever criticisms may be brought against him, he cannot be accused, as Dewey accuses the interest theory, of allowing "a dialectic of concepts" to take "the place of an examination of empirical facts." Freud has a deep, if narrow, knowledge of the human mind. He knows what is to be found at its bottom. And if his late-nineteenth-century Weltanschauung puts him on the same plane with the shallow enlightenment-mongers, the contemporary scientifists, who, on the pretext of spreading light, dispense confusion, the depths to which he has dived and what he has seen in those dim waters entitle him to a place, one dares guess, with the small number of Western philosophers who have helped Western man to achieve a knowledge of himself.[3]

In saying this I am not saying that the results he achieved, as we find them formulated in his writings, are valid. With the recession of his strong personality, the doctrinaire zeal with which his words have been held by his followers will no doubt diminish, and the basic formulations which have until now constituted the canonical legacy will suffer the changes which are inherent in all scientific development. Even today, to disagree with the scriptures is to bring down on one's self the analytic wrath of the faithful, who have a tendency to disregard the arguments, since it is easier to psychoanalyze the opposition and thus discredit its claims than to dispose of them logically or to assimilate them. Nevertheless, no matter how far psychoanalysis may deviate from the views of the founder, the historical importance of Freud seems likely to remain.

I propose, first, to present the relevant parts of Freud's theory and next to examine Julian Huxley's formulation of the theory. The procedure involves repetition, but I beg the reader to bear with it because in this manner I hope to be able to make the doctrine more clear than I, a mere unanalyzed heathen without professional training in the mysteries, could otherwise hope to make it. The repetitiousness will not all be in vain, for it will show that the master's ideas, in spite of the verbal changes which they have undergone, remain very much unchanged from their first utterance. Since our interest is in the theory and not in a special version of it, the repetition should enable the reader no less than the writer to focus on what its essential aspects are and to disregard merely verbal differences of statement. And, finally, the multiple presentation will give those readers who are not directly acquainted with the documents a better basis for judging the fairness of the criticism submitted. The

Huxley version of the theory which I shall examine is found in the *Romanes Lecture* for 1943; the reason for the choice is that Huxley addressed himself to the moral problem exclusively, while in Freud the theory of the superego and of the conscience is an outgrowth of his clinical interests. With Huxley's theory, therefore, we are able to look into the way in which Freudianism can be made to function when seriously applied to the resolution of the central problem of moral philosophy.

For our purposes the doctrine of conscience given in *The New Introductory Lectures on Psycho-analysis* is sufficient.[4] Freud tells us that his interest in this topic began when he took cognizance of the phenomena exhibited by those who suffer from delusions of observation. The hallucination that one is being internally observed is, Freud notes, not the same as persecution, "but it is not far removed from it."[5] Attention to these phenomena suggested the question whether "all of us had an observing function in our egos, threatening us with punishment," which in the case of those suffering from the hallucination "had merely become sharply separated from the ego." His clinical observations led him to form "the idea that the separating off of an observing function from the rest of the ego might be a normal feature of the ego's structure," and later investigation confirmed the hypothesis and led to the discovery of the superego. The superego is not the conscience, but an entity which includes as one of its activities the judicial or what we call "conscience."[6] However, Freud tells us on the next page that the superego may be called the conscience, if we do so "in a whisper."

The question which we would like to have light on is: How does the superego emerge? It is not innate, for small children are "notoriously a-moral."[7] One of Freud's objects is to give a naturalistic account of its genesis. And the account reads like this: The superego emerges through the "introjection" first of parental authority and later of the authority of those "persons who have been concerned in the child's upbringing, and whom it has regarded as ideal models."[8]

At this point the exposition of the theory becomes extremely difficult if it is assumed, as I have, that what Freud has undertaken to do is to give us an account of the way in which an amoral animal learns to distinguish between good and evil and to submit himself to the discipline of the former, while eschewing the enticements of the latter. Freud is not difficult to follow when he tells us that "the external restrictions are introjected, so that the super-ego takes the place of the parental function, and thence forward observes, guides and threatens the ego in just the same way as the parents acted to the child before."[9] But now we must ask how does the introjection take place, for, unless it is explained, it merely labels a mystery. The answer is best given in Freud's own words:

"The basis of the process is what is called an identification, that is to say, that one ego becomes like another, one which results in the first ego behaving itself in certain respects in the same way as the second; it imitates it, and as it were takes it into itself. This identification has been not inappropriately compared with the oral cannibalistic incorporation of another person. Identification is a very important kind of relationship with another person, probably the most primitive, and is not to be confused with object-choice. One can express the difference between them in this way: when a boy identifies himself with his father he wants to be *like* his father; when he makes him the object of his choice, he wants to *have* him, to possess him; in the first case his ego is altered on the model of his father, in the second case that is not necessary. Identification and object-choice are broadly speaking independent of each other; but one can identify oneself with a person and alter one's ego accordingly and take the same person as one's sexual object. . . .

". . . The establishment of the super-ego can be described as a successful instance of identification with the parental function. The fact which is decisively in favour of this point of view is that this new creation of a superior function within the ego is extremely closely bound up with the fate of the Oedipus complex, so that the superego appears as the heir of the emotion tie, which is of such importance for childhood. When the Oedipus complex passes away the child must give up the intense object-cathexes which it has formed towards its parents, and to compensate for this loss of object, its identifications with its parents, which have probably long been present, become greatly intensified. Identifications of this kind, which may be looked on as precipitates of abandoned object-cathexes, will recur often enough in the later life of the child; but it is in keeping with the emotional importance of this first instance of such a transformation that its product should occupy a special position in the ego."[10]

Before proceeding, it may not be superfluous 'to observe that the meaning of the technical expression "object-cathexes" may be gathered from the following sentence in *A General Introduction to Psychoanalysis:* "The libido is blocked, as it were, and must seek an escape by which it can find an outlet for its cathexes (charge of energy) in conformity to the demands of the pleasure principle: it must elude, eschew the ego."[11]

Now, according to Freud, the functions of the superego are "self-observation, conscience and the holding up of ideals." For him "the super-ego is the representative of all moral restrictions, the advocate of the impulse towards perfection, in short it is as much as we have been able to apprehend psychologically of what people call the 'higher' things of human life."[12] The superego, however, "is not really built up on the model of the parents, but on that of the parents' super-ego; it takes over the same content, it becomes the vehicle of tradition and of all the age-long values which have been handed down in this way from generation to generation. You may easily guess what great help is afforded by the recognition of the super-ego in understanding the social behavior of man, in grasping the problem of delinquency, for example, and perhaps, too, in providing us with some practical hints about education."[13]

If what was called for was a criticism of Freudian theory in its more general aspects, we would have to go into a more detailed account than that given by Freud in the *New Introductory Lectures.* Such a criticism would inquire whether the explanation of "introjection" by means of "identification" is not one of those verbal explanations which resolve a problem by pasting a label on a mystery. Our concern here, however, is exclusively with understanding the explanation of the genesis of the judicial function of the super-ego.

We can now turn to Huxley. Following Freud, he tells us that the superego—which Huxley prefers to call "the proto-ethical mechanism"—is formed early in the second year of postnatal life and "arises as the result of a special kind of conflict among the chaos of unregulated impulses with which the infant is originally endowed."[14]

The conflicts involved are those arising between love and hatred, as the child begins to draw a distinction between outer reality, represented by the mother, and itself. The mother is identified not only as the source of satisfaction and security but as the power that thwarts some of the impulses the child seeks to gratify. Frustration generates anger (the psychoanalyst's "aggression") toward the mother, who is also loved. Hence "the primal conflict," which "is normally won by love." For this reason "anger and aggression, the accompanying magic fantasies of death-wishes and the like, become branded and tinged with the quality of guilt—in other words—wrongness—and more or less completely banished."[15]

This is enough, I believe, to perceive the inadequacy of Freud's explanation without the need of extended analysis. What he starts with is an amoral child, and what he is explaining is how it develops the faculty or capacity of discriminating between right and wrong actions and attitudes. It does not possess that faculty or power from birth, nor is it latent in him, like the capacity to walk. Now the moral faculty is developed, as we have seen, by introjecting the parental ideals with which the child has identified itself. But this means that it already possesses the capacity to discriminate between ideals and nonideals, which is to say, possesses the judicial power which is called "conscience," whose growth Freud is explaining. This mystery—how a child can possess that which it does not have and how he can have it in order to acquire it—is not made any clearer by Huxley than by Freud. Obvious as this point seems to be, it seems equally obvious that psychoanalytic writers have not seen it. While the fallacy is well enough established by this brief comment, the detailed examination of the assumptions and confusions which prevent the psychoanalyst from seeing the fallacy for what it is, is worth all the effort that it will demand of us. For these assumptions and confusions are inherent in all naturalistic philosophy and manifest themselves in all accounts which reduce the moral faculties of men to mere psychological, amoral data. Let us turn to Huxley's explanation for detailed examination; of clinicians we do not expect a complete moral theory, but of a man writing on moral philosophy and delivering a *Romanes Lecture* we have every right to expect a complete and adequate moral theory.

On the data which Huxley presents, all we have (as in the case of Freud) is a nonmoral conflict in which the victory has gone to one of the parties in it. Through love's victory, anger, aggression, and death wishes have been suppressed; but how "guilt" emerges out of "suppression" is not shown. We have merely the assertion that it does. One suspects that Huxley could have shown that it does only by supplying some other factor, now absent from his account, capable of generating the *moral* character of guilt (or wrongness) in the suppressed impulses. Until the author shows the way in which this distinctively moral factor emerges or arises or is generated, all that has been shown is that the suppressed impulses have been considered obstructive by the victorious ones. But this can be only a purely amoral, a merely physical, attitude on their part. Or does the Freudian claim that all that guilt means is repression? In other words, "defeat" can generate only resentfulness or a sullen attitude, an attitude which might be expressed by the schoolboy's "Wait till I get you!" How does repression become guilt? How does victory make the victors feel that they are not merely stronger but right? For the struggle to move from a merely physical, amoral plane up to a moral one, it would be necessary to show how the stronger are not merely strong and victors but right, and the weak not merely weak but wrong. One suspects that an identification has been introduced, according to which strong or victor equals right, and weak or defeated equals wrong. The suppressed forces must own not merely that they were weaker and defeated but that they had no business existing in a moral sense, no business being there morally. And it is this moral dimension that has been introduced by definitional fiat into the discussion. Or do psychoanalysts claim that it has suddenly "emerged"? Huxley does not make clear the mystery when he tells us that the defeated forces are "branded and tinged by the quality of guilt" and are banished. What this statement does is to bring the phenomenon of morality into being by incantation. Or perhaps it is fairer to Huxley to put the following interpretation on what he had in mind: before "guilt" was branded

THE FREUDIAN THEORY OF CONSCIENCE   145

on the defeated forces, it was—shall we say—"generated," or, perhaps better, it "emerged," as a result of the victory of love over
hatred. But how did the generation or emergence come about? By
the action of what psychic force? Out of what material was it constituted? Did love beget hatred, or have we here a case of partheno-
genesis? What is required at this point, past verbal difficulties, is
careful demonstration of how a nonmoral conflict, resulting in the
victory of one nonmoral force (since that must be the assumption on
a naturalistic plane) and in the defeat and suppression of another,
creates a new phenomenon or quality or entity which we call
"morality." Huxley has to show how the infant mind, siding with
the forces of love, not only says to the suppressed forces "Down!"
but adds, "You are *wrong.*"

Huxley asks us to believe that he has accounted for the fact that
the infant sides with love, but he does not tell us why the infant
does. The difficulty springs from the fact that the infant does not
say to the forces of hatred, "You are in my way, down with you!"
but says to them and means, "You are in the way, and you have no
right to be." In whatever way it is put, a moral term, whose emergence Huxley claims to have explained, has suddenly been introduced into the analysis. Has he introduced the term into his account
because the phenomenon to which it refers has just as suddenly appeared in the actual data? The term points to a totally new phenomenon or quality, which the mind is suddenly more or less clearly
able to discern as an attribute of the defeated forces and as distinct
from the fact that they have been defeated because they interfered
with the victors. Has this quality been invented? How did it get
there? Whence did it come? Is it merely another word for "defeated and suppressed"?

The identification of "suppressed" with "immoral" seems to
account for the Freudian's belief that he has explained the genesis of
conscience, but this merely proves that he does not understand what
a *moral* prohibition is. Not all suppressed and defeated desires are
branded and tinged with the quality of guilt. The mind chooses the
forces which it brands and tinges, just as it discriminates those values and traits of the parents which it introjects. This selectivity is
an extremely complex phenomenon. For instance, the child will feel
guilt when doing something affecting one of the groups to which he

belongs but not another—his companions but perhaps not his parents—but he will reverse the attribution as regards something else affecting the other, the family group. Again, a child will learn what is wrong and what is right in one respect from one person and in another respect from another person, but the attributions will be inconsistent formally and bear no relation to the degree of discoverable love or hatred felt toward the teacher. About the second year, we are told, the child begins to select what it will brand and tinge and to decide how it will brand it, whether burning the word "guilt," so to speak, deep into the skin or merely singeing the hairs. This capacity of his to select would indicate that there is a more plausible explanation of the phenomenon at hand: the maturing mind gradually grasps a quality or attribute of inward and outward phenomena as distinctively moral in kind, just as (later perhaps) it gradually grasps other qualities of phenomena as distinctively aesthetic in kind. The child brands the former qualities thus grasped as "wrong" because he discovers in them something toward which he responds with the feeling of guilt; but, to respond to them in this manner, he has to recognize them as "wrong." And he calls the other group of qualities "beautiful" because he responds toward them aesthetically; but, again, recognition precedes response.

Not all suppressed wishes are or become guilty, nor are all guilty ones suppressed, and those that are merely suppressed—those on which the brand of "wrong" did not "take"—generate resentfulness. But, by itself, resentfulness is no more "guilt" than mere suppression is. The merely suppressed fight back; the guilty somehow recognize—or lead one to recognize—however grudgingly, their moral status. There is a difference between our attitude toward our wrong feelings, on the one hand, and, on the other, our attitude toward those that we suppress but do not consider wrong. And it is this difference the emergence of which has not been accounted for. A merely suppressed force does not admit wrongness, nor does it lead one to admit it; but a wrong force, even when not suppressed, often does. Guilt, it would then seem, does not appear when a value-free force is suppressed by another value-free force, but when a wrong force comes into conflict with a right one. This is missed by Freudians because they fail to recognize that the word "love" is not value-free but already contains a positive value charge. Why should the child side with love?

There is another aspect of the phenomena of the conscience which the Freudians seem utterly to ignore but which the moral philosopher finds worthy of his attention. If it is true that the human animal internalizes or introjects his training and that this process constitutes his conscience, on what ground was the training of the child devised? The trainers, usually the parents, did not train the child merely for the sake of their own comfort, although this factor is no doubt present in the training of most infants the world over. They trained him morally. Where did their morality come from? Training may explain how the child is made into a moral person—I do not believe that it goes very far as an explanation, but let that pass—but it is of no use in explaining how the training was training in *moral* habits. Again, how does it happen that the acceptance of the training involves an increment in his personality, on which he depends to a great extent for his dignity? The scoldings and newspaper spankings that help turn a pup into a well-trained dog, so far as we know, do not give the dog a feeling of dignity. Nor could they. And we can see what happens to a man who has been subjected to threat, punishment, and sheer brutality. Nietzsche in a passage of *The Genealogy of Morals* speaks of the amount of punishment that it takes to create a man who can keep his word. But unjust punishment arouses a feeling of resentment in a man. Just punishment is digested by the conscience, which takes account of it and passes judgment on itself. Fear and threats reduce men in worth and teach them to slink with their tails between their legs. But, as conscience develops, it exalts a man, and even when it condemns him it feeds his self-respect. When you hit a rat a number of times, he will not go into the box that contains the cheese, no matter how attractive the fragrance. Of course, many men do not seem to go beyond the rat. But some do and, taking the injunctions and prohibitions of experience into their discipline through the growth thus achieved, find fulfilment. What requires explanation is not only how a man should defend himself from inhibitions and prescriptions but how, accepting them, he finds the act of acceptance a source of dignity. To explain the complex facts, Freud was forced to add to the pleasure principle a "death wish." In so doing, he enlarged the vision of those of his fellows who have studied his metapsychological speculations. It is interesting to observe, however, how many of his most loyal followers have ignored or belittled the principle of the death wish. A pleasure principle fits easily into a naturalistic conception of the personality; a death wish presupposes the independence of value from experience, which rightly enough is to be feared by naturalists.

The fallacy involved in the account of the genesis of conscience is not one which will create trouble for the therapist within the specialized range of his activities. His fundamental aim is to restore the patient to psychic health, and this forces upon him a value commitment, not only as directive of his therapy but as assumed in the theory which guides it. The terms "health" and "illness" can be used to denote certain neutral, purely factual, conditions; but, in fact, the therapist does not so use them. Health is right or good, illness wrong or bad. For the therapist this is an assumption which he need not make explicit and which in his practice is never challenged, since his patient makes the same assumption when he comes to the physician for help. All this means that Freudian theory does not give us *a theory of the genesis of our capacity to discriminate moral value* but an account, relative to its interests, of the point at which, in the process of maturation, our consciousness becomes capable of discerning moral distinctions. It is quite possible that the Freudians are right in an important sense and that the "beginning of ethics" is somehow to be found in the "primal conflict" between love and hate. All they can legitimately mean by this statement, however, is that the primal conflict marks the point at which the problem becomes philosophically critical, and their clumsy explanation of the appearance of guilt begs the most important problems with which the naturalistic moral philosopher is concerned. Freud was a very great genius, but he was not a universal one. In his analysis—controlled by his own practical objectives—he rode roughshod over many a delicate problem requiring a delicate touch. Hence his disregard of essential distinctions. The capacity to discern moral values must be distinguished from the genetic conditions which make the appearance of such a capacity possible and from the values which that capacity objectively discerns; these factors must, in turn, be distinguished from our tendency to respond to moral values as authoritative, once they are discerned.

Huxley argues that his explanation accounts for "the absolute, categorical, and other-worldly quality of moral obligation, on which moral philosophers lay such stress." This is explained, he believes, by pointing, "in the first instance, to the compulsive all-or-nothing mechanism by which the primitive super-ego operates. It is also due to the fact that . . . the external world first intrudes itself into the baby's magic solipsism in the form of the parents' demands for control over primitive impulses. . . ."[16] Here we run across a popular assumption of naturalistic moral theory, already encountered in Santayana, to the effect that "moral obligation" is synonymous with "compulsion." The two terms cannot be equated, for they are distinct in their normal and in their abnormal—or excessive—manifestations, and the burden of proof that they denote the same thing rests on those who would equate them. They would have to show that the distinctions which we discover existing between them are not real distinctions. Reflection indicates that the sense of moral obligation involves a relationship to values which we feel in some peculiar way to be objective to us, although these values are discernible only as operative within our consciousness. We feel "obliged" toward these values, not because they blindly push us, but because we acknowledge their status in respect to us and can distinguish our mere wishes and drives from our attitudinal relationship to values from which somehow the sense of obligation seems to issue. Compulsiveness, on the other hand, does not involve a peculiar relationship between ourselves and values, objectively discerned and freely acknowledged, but an inward condition of the will utterly indifferent to the value quality of the object or activity toward which it pushed us. If both involve a certain coerciveness, which careless analysis can easily confuse, reflection will discover that the radical difference between the coerciveness of compulsion and that of obligation forbids reducing one to the other. Our attitudes toward acknowledged values with which the feeling of obligation is somehow connected are, or at least are felt to be, autonomous, while the feeling of compulsion is distinctly heteronomous; the one is imposed by one's self acting in regard to values recognized as valuable, while the other is imposed by something obscure in one's self, beyond the reach of intelligent reflection and unresponsive to its pleadings, in whose power we are helpless because it pushes us blindly.

These remarks do not pretend to be an adequate or exhaustive analysis of the difference; they merely point to where the moral philosopher can and should find it. They are introduced to indicate what problems have to be solved by those who would equate moral obligation and compulsiveness or would reduce one to the other, and hence to show scientifically wherein lie the inadequacies of Huxley's account.

Some naturalists would meet the preceding criticism by pointing out that it does not violate their naturalistic presuppositions to assert that conscience "emerges" through natural processes, as, indeed, "mind" and all other observable events and empirical phenomena do. I suggested earlier that this is one of the possible ways in which we could read the psychoanalytic theory. Since the emergence theory is one of the favorite dodges of naturalists, it is necessary to see what it is that the naturalist does by appealing to "emergence."

There are two versions of the theory of emergence to be found in the current naturalistic literature which I believe it is profitable to discuss. I shall refer to them as the "epistemological" and the "metaphysical" versions, respectively. In order to examine the former, I shall turn to a brilliant paper by Paul Henle, to which I refer the reader for an adequate exposition of the matter, for the following discussion is nothing but a hasty rewrite of this paper. The metaphysical version I shall examine as it is presented by D. W. Gotshalk. But between the examination of the Henle paper and that of Gotshalk I shall sandwich a discussion of what I think of as a "crypto-emergence" theory, the theory of levels of integration, as suggested by the editors of *Philosophy for the Future*. This theory avoids the word "emergence" but appeals to the same kind of phenomena that Henle discusses.[17]

As Henle makes clear, "emergence" means that we do not yet know all the conditions necessary to bring about a given phenomenon, or, more exactly, it means that, on a given hypothesis, the appearance of a given quality is not predictable; but predictability is relative to knowledge, and a characteristic, x, is said to be "an emergent" when it cannot be predicted within a given scientific context. Or, as Henle felicitously puts it, "an emergent halts reason in its attempt to map the cosmos." Thus we say that life is an emergent from a complex physical process if we do not know all the physical conditions necessary to be able to predict the appearance of life. (As yet, so far as I know, life seems to remain an emergent; we know many of the physical conditions necessary to maintain it, but not all those that are necessary to bring it about.) What the concept of emergence points to, in other words, is relative paucity of knowledge at a specific stage of scientific development.

Thus far Henle. On the basis of his analysis I believe the following remarks are pertinent: Naturalists use the term "emergence" as a principle of explanation *and that is precisely what it cannot be*. It does not go further than to express hope that future inquiry will reveal all the physical conditions of which we are now ignorant and which must be known in order to assert inductively, in one area of inquiry, the principle of continuity required by naturalism. But, since what is at issue is precisely whether continuity does or does not obtain in respect to two seemingly discontinuous sets of phenomena, as regards whose interconnections we are ignorant, "emergence" not only begs the issue but muddles it. If we could actually create life in the laboratory, life would cease to be an emergent of the process through which we brought it about, and physicalism would have solved one of its major problems. On the other hand, this criticism of "emergence" cannot be the source of much comfort to those who assert without qualification the discontinuity between mind and body or between life and matter, for the same logic that prevents us from asserting continuity prevents us from denying it. The continuity which the naturalist asserts as a "principle" is an open question in regard to which dogmatism ill becomes an inquiring mind. All I need to assert at this point is that, until the reduction between matter and life, life and mind, and mind and spirit is actually accomplished, the concept of "emergence" cannot be more than a begging of the issue. On Henle's interpretation, "emergence" is but a fig leaf with which the naturalist tries desperately to cover his shame. If the theory did not indicate any more than paucity of analysis, those using it would not be open to criticism, since all it would mean was that they were up against it in regard to the phenomenon to which they applied it and had to make do with what they found at hand. Confronted with a discontinuity which has as yet remained stubborn, emergence would acknowledge the plight and would be an earnest of further research. But a fig leaf is not a garment and cannot fully cover the body, and what the naturalist asks us is that we accept it as a fully covering garment.

There seems to be, however, an assumption in Henle's paper that requires passing attention. It is noticeable in the phrase quoted: ". . . an emergent halts reason in its attempt to map the cosmos." I find it in the whole paper, not in anything expressed, but in the way in which the problem is treated. The assumption is that reason is only temporarily halted in its effort to map the cosmos. If I am correct and if the assumption is there, it is necessary to remark that to the faith that reason can map the cosmos, in so far as that faith issues forth in the persistent effort to map it, there can be no objection. If, however, the faith leads, as in fact it does in the case of naturalists generally, to the formulation of a philosophic doctrine to the effect that, given time, the cosmos will be mapped and that the halt marked by an emergent is only temporary, then, of course, it is open to criticism. For whether the cosmos will or will not be mapped by reason is an empirical question in regard to which, so long as emergents remain, there is no sufficient evidence.

The crypto-emergence theory is formulated by its proponents as follows:

"The inorganic pattern of matter is previous to living, minded and purposive organisms, which arise gradually and only as a result of a complex evolutionary development. With the advent of organic life, new, biological laws begin to operate. The principles of physics and chemistry necessarily apply, but are not by themselves sufficient to the biological level. Thus mechanism or the theory that physicochemical explanation is adequate to all levels, is emphatically rejected. If a thing can be explained by physics and chemistry, however, it must be so explained, and there is no justification for adverting to any other level of the organization of matter. The inorganic and the organic constitute distinctive levels, which can be referred to as lower and higher, in the sense that organic material systems are more highly organized and more complex, exhibiting new behavior traits. . . . Organized matter reveals integrative levels of organization characterized by distinctive laws."[18]

It seems obvious that the criticism that Henle makes of the emergence theory applies also to this one, since what this theory really amounts to is the admission that, on a given hypothesis, the appearance of a given quality is not predictable: at the purely physico-chemical level the appearance of life cannot be predicted, since new laws operate at the level of life. The difference between this theory and the emergence theory is, in the first instance, essentially one of terminology. Ultimately there may be another difference, in respect to the effects of this one on the conception of the unity of the laws of science; but this question need not be looked into here. The emphasis in the emergence theory is on the appearance of a new kind of process or new phenomena, while in this theory the emphasis seems to be on new laws which begin to operate with the "advent" of organic life. I cannot see what significant difference would be made by substituting "emergence" for "advent" in the second sentence of the quotation, and I take it that the biological laws which begin to operate with the advent or emergence of organic life are inductive generalizations of the organic processes. It is doubtful whether those who propose the theory—in this case the editors of *Philosophy for the Future*, Messrs. Sellars, McGill, and Farber—really mean to assert as emphatically as they do the distinctness of levels, since such a notion would certainly open them to the charge of blocking inquiry which naturalists like Ernest Nagel make against all such theories. I leave them, however, to Mr. Nagel's mercy, in order to turn to something else: namely, that current theories of evolution explain more or less adequately how some species have perished and what factors enabled others to survive, once the forms of the species had fully evolved, but they do not explain how the organic forms existing at any time came about. This refers to a criticism of evolution quite well understood by now: there are innumerable organic forms which, as they now exist, give the animal or the group an advantage in the struggle for existence; but this advantage belongs to the finished organic form, the form as fully evolved, and not to the component steps which a nonteleological evolutionary theory assumes are necessary to bring about the fully evolved form. Since the authors would have nothing to do with teleology—which they consider a way of thinking inappropriate to our age—what the theory of levels very neatly does is to conceal that point at which science is up against a blank wall.

The metaphysical notion of emergence is defended very ably by D. W. Gotshalk in a paper read at a symposium on "Causality and Cosmic Order" in Indianapolis in 1941. For Gotshalk, emergence is "a new way of calling attention to the underpinning of individuality and causality within which causality always operates."[19] I suggest that we call this the "metaphysical" use of the term, solely for convenience and for lack of a more exact designation. On this definition, emergence not merely manifests itself at certain levels where prediction is not yet possible but is to be found always in every causal relation whatsoever which we are able to observe. The language of the author is so compact and lucid that it is best to let him speak for himself:

"The spectacular cases of emergence have been furnished by chemistry and biology. But the appearance of novel properties in chemical compounds and of mutations in biological agents is merely very vivid evidence of a much more widespread fact. This basic fact I believe to be this, that the members of causal situations *always* possess immanent organization or structure as well as transeunt causal connection or structure. They have individuality and multiple qualities manifesting this individuality, as well as linkage with antecedents and consequents. Moreover, this individuality and quality are with them all the time. They are permanent ingredients. And the sign of their permanence, of their undiminished being through time, is the emergence of the novel. This emergence is testimony that the individual and the qualitative are not eradicated by the operation of causes, but that these factors are as much present after the operation of causes as they plainly were before the operation."[20]

Thus what the advocate of the emergence theory asserts is that qualities are ineradicable through the process of causal explanation and that they must be added to the causal as a principle operative in all situations confronting knowers. It is not difficult to see that the thought back of this argument is closely allied to the speculative demands that make a philosopher like Paul Weiss assert freedom within determinism, spontaneity within causality.[21] This assertion is a necessary corrective of the tendency of the knowing mind to emphasize structure at the cost of the individual events.

By disengaging the two meanings of "emergence," we are able to see with ease that the ontological reductionism of naturalists, whether materialists or not, is illegitimate. When used in its metaphysical meaning, the term invalidates the conclusions of ontological monists, who reduce the universe to "nothing but" this or that—matter, pointer readings, etc. A fortiori it invalidates the reductionism of those who deny the *sui generis* character of moral processes. This, of course, does not solve any problem for us—whether the problem of mind or that of conscience. It merely calls attention to those difficulties which the naturalist disguises and which he has to resolve before he is entitled to his conclusions.

CHAPTER X

A POSTSCRIPT

THERE are two important naturalistic treatises and a fairly popular value theory which the reader doubtless has been surprised to find ignored in these "animadversions." Before turning to the positive task of sketching a moral philosophy, it seems advisable to examine them hastily. I do not stop to examine them with the care devoted to the theories we have already analyzed, for reasons which the following remarks will make clear.

One of the two treatises is *Ethics and Language* by Charles Stevenson.[1] The reason that I have not discussed this book can be stated simply: it is not a book on moral philosophy. It is interesting to observe, however, that, in spite of the author's disclaimer, this book has generally been reviewed as if it were a contribution to moral philosophy; yet we are told in the very first page of the first chapter of the book that the study it undertakes "is related to normative (or 'evaluative') ethics in much the same way that conceptual analysis and scientific method are related to the sciences. . . . One must not expect to find here any conclusions about what conduct is right or wrong. The purpose of an analytic or methodological study, whether of science or of ethics, is always indirect. It hopes to send others to their tasks with clearer heads and less wasteful habits of investigation." And the paragraph concludes: "The present volume has the limited task of sharpening the tools which others employ." I believe that even a hasty survey of what Stevenson actually undertakes will corroborate his own statement that he is not interested in the development of a moral philosophy.

The first task of the moral philosopher is to organize and elucidate the data, the subject matter of the moral life, the stuff of life as it is actually lived at the human plane within which the moral law operates. This calls for as comprehensive a survey of experience as possible, in order to make reasonably certain that whatever theory is devised includes its distinctive, essentially moral features. But, as Charner Perry pointed out in his brilliantly devastating review of *Ethics and Language*, the book exhibits "in a high degree two peculiarly philosophic virtues," in only one of which I am interested at the moment: "the ability to derive from an initial schematism or terminology an apparently comprehensive theory and the somewhat more unusual ability to restate and expand the initial schematism into a book without using any appreciable amount of additional material."[2] I agree fully with Perry. I do not find in the book any consideration of the actual facts of the moral life. Perry contends that the author side-steps explicit inconsistencies and avoids obvious verbal pitfalls. I would, in addition, point out that there are two ways of achieving clarity, the easier of which is by exclusion. This seems to satisfy certain types of mind, which take to positivistic analysis like cattle in the llanos to high land in the rainy season because, confronted with the unmanageable inundations of experience, they dread the danger of drowning in a flood of facts. The irony is most instructive, for it has been the positivists who have gone off to fight the metaphysical windmills, fully panoplied with the new-forged weapons of logic and of methodology, and who have won the highest honors as the crusaders of empiricism. But there is more, prodigiously more, of moral experience to be picked up in one crabbed chapter of the stiff old Prussian apriorist of Königsberg than can be raked up in the whole of *Ethics and Language*. It would seem, then, as if the advantage of being interested in empirical methodology is that it absolves one from concern with subject matter.

Since no searching attention has been paid to the facts of the moral life in *Ethics and Language*, the author has no means of assuring the reader that his definition of "good" or "right" includes the relevant facts: those aspects of moral experience and those features of reality that at the critical, common-sense level fix the usage of the terms for practical men. For in common sense we find confusion and vagueness, but we also find a shrewd, almost instinctive, empiricism that enables mankind, which does not always possess the benefits of the logical therapist, to get on with its work, not altogether unsuccessfully.

According to Stevenson, " 'This is good' means *I approve of this;*

do so as well."[3] Similar definitions are given for "right" and for "ought." Now I do not in the least doubt that what Stevenson takes the terms "good" and "right" to mean is what is often meant by them. How many men actually mean by these terms what Stevenson means I do not know, but it may even be that what he takes them to mean is what in the overwhelming majority of cases they are taken to mean by the overwhelming majority of mankind. But his synonymous translation (which, of course, he does not offer even in the so-called "second pattern" as an exact equivalent of "this is good") is not all that is meant or can be meant by the term "good," as could be found by a genuine empiricist who kept the facts of the moral life steadily under his gaze; and that which the synonymous formula leaves out, no matter how it is interpreted philosophically, seems to me to constitute the most important subject matter for the moral philosopher. Indeed, I would say that what the formula leaves out of account constitutes the only distinctively moral data to which the philosopher has to attend. I would go further and would add that, for reasons which I hope will become gradually clear in Parts II and III of this essay, the man who means by "good" only what Stevenson means by it is a profoundly immoral man. Note, however, parenthetically, that the question is one of theory and not of the philosopher's own operative personal morality, since the most logically consistent of systematic philosophers will be saved from the consequences of his theory by the charming human virtue of schizophrenia. In my actual experience, at any rate, the dichotomy can be illustrated by two extreme cases: one of the kindest, gentlest, and morally most sensitive persons that I have ever known taught with relentless lucidity that might makes right; and one of the most ruthless power maniacs that I have ever had the misfortune to know is an untiring preacher of co-operation and of the supreme dignity of the human individual.

If what I have said holds at least roughly, it appears that Stevenson has inverted what would seem to be the desirable order of inquiry because, until the data of moral philosophy are in and are carefully elaborated by the philosophic worker, one has no way of knowing how adequate Stevenson's schematism is to moral reality. Hence the results of aprioristic analytic inquiries à la Stevenson are likely to make the philosopher content with the empirically clear but thin soup of "patterns of analysis" instead of avid for the nutritive olla-podrida of experience. This is not intended to deny, however, the enviable technical dexterity displayed in *Ethics and Language*. My suffrage is not needed to convince philosophic readers that Stevenson has performed the task he set himself with exemplary skill.

It is not surprising that critics of Stevenson's doctrines have disregarded his own explicit intentions, since in many places in his book Stevenson himself speaks of his theories as if he thought of them as a complete, or at least as a comprehensive, moral philosophy. This is most obvious in chapter xii of Stevenson's book, in which "Some Related Theories" are discussed. For this reason, in order to avoid the charge that I have taken an author's modesty at his own word in order to save myself the trouble of reading his book, I think it is advisable to consider Stevenson's book as analyzing not one possible definition but the "correct" definition of the terms "good" or "right." Thus viewed, I do believe that the skill of the analyst has succeeded in side-stepping the difficulties of a naturalistic approach to moral philosophy. In the review already mentioned, Charner Perry points out that Stevenson's nominalism led him to overlook the fact that the value judgments that he makes involve him in affirmation or acknowledgment of normative principles or ideals which his analysis ignores. On this topic I cannot add anything to Perry's incisive paper or improve on its presentation; the reader is therefore referred to it. In another paper on *Ethics and Language*, W. H. Hay correctly points out that Stevenson's definitional patterns do not provide for definitions which express the meaning of certain ethical statements.[4] To this paper also the reader is referred. In addition, I wish to call attention to three other criticisms to which Stevenson is open; the second and third of these will be indicated briefly, because similar criticisms have been made of other naturalistic systems in this part.

Stevenson does not allow the confusion sometimes made by naïve reductionists between mere morally neutral approval and moral approval; nevertheless, he holds that an adequate distinction between the two can be drawn in terms of introspective psychological data. According to Stevenson, we distinguish one sort of attitude, the moral, from the other, the nonmoral, by specifying the different responses that attend typical stimuli. In his words:

"Suppose that a man morally disapproves of a certain kind of conduct. If he observes this conduct in others he may then feel indignant, mortified, or shocked; and if he finds himself given to it, he may feel guilty or conscience-stricken. But suppose that he dislikes this conduct, as distinct from morally disapproving of it. He may then be simply displeased when he observes it in others, and simply annoyed with himself when he finds that he is given to it. Similarly, if he morally approves of something, he may feel a particularly heightened sense of security when it prospers; where if he merely likes it, he may feel only an ordinary sort of pleasure. These differences in response, given similar stimuli, help to distinguish the attitudes which are moral from those which are not. The full distinction, should the occasion require it, could be made by supplementing these remarks by others of a similar kind."[5]

This passage leaves me utterly bewildered. In spirit it seems to go back in one respect to Hutcheson's "moral sense" because what the author is saying is that, in terms of psychological analysis, there is a perceptible difference between merely approving and morally approving. The difference is drawn in terms of the subject's inward response as discovered by introspection and without reference to its cause or stimulus. The passage therefore raises two capital questions which we may roughly call that of method and that of substance, respectively. It is not difficult to show that the difference between mere approval and moral approval does not consist in what Stevenson says it does, in the heightened sense of security which the morally approved action gives one as compared to the ordinary pleasure which the nonmoral or the merely approved gives. Consider the following examples: If I were utterly broke and in dire need of money for medical attention for a member of my family and were suddenly told that I had won the Irish sweepstakes or that I had been picked in a give-away radio program by chance to be the recipient of a few thousand dollars, I would approve of the happy selection with a particularly strong sense of security and relief. I would do so also if I heard that another, even though I did not know him, who was in distress was thus relieved. On the other hand, I would respond with only a very ordinary sort of pleasure if I heard that some millionaire had paid the surgical expenses of his grammar-school teacher who is now old and in dire poverty. There is a difference, but either it is not what Stevenson takes it to be, or he will have to show that I am a morally corrupted man. The second choice would compel him to make a moral judgment instead of studying moral phenomena.

What, then, is the difference? Stevenson himself makes it clear for us when he discusses the differences between moral and nonmoral disapproval. Nonmoral disapproval, we are correctly told, is accompanied by simple displeasure or annoyance, whereas moral disapproval is accompanied, in respect to an action of the subject, by a feeling of guilt and, in respect to an action of another, by indignation, mortification, or shock. But if what we are trying to do is to explain naturalistically the difference between moral and nonmoral disapproval, we are not advancing a step when we say that, in respect to ourselves, it consists of a feeling of guilt or an uneasy conscience. What we have to show is that this feeling of guilt does not mark a *sui generis* moral reaction but merely refers or is somehow reducible to a nonmoral response. The same thing holds for our reaction toward the actions of others of which we morally disapprove; indignation, mortification, and shock—allowing the three words to stand for what would take many pages to analyze carefully —refer to what seems to be a *sui generis* moral reaction, the first term being most clearly so and the last term least. Such reactions are not to be found in our nonmoral disapproval, which may be physiological or aesthetic or logical. To establish his case, Stevenson would have to show that they can be reduced to nonmoral terms.

In defense of Stevenson it could be urged that he does not intend the expressions "feeling of guilt," "uneasy conscience" (or its equivalents in the quotation), and "indignation," "mortification," and "shock" to be taken as moral terms but simply as psychological terms. This retort involves a reading which strains the passage, but let us accept it for the sake of the argument, although as careful a linguistic analyst as Stevenson does not commit such obvious blunders. The suggested reading, however, does not reach the substance of the argument, since, according to it, what Stevenson has shown is that the feeling of guilt and indignation is not a distinctive kind of feeling. But, if it is not a distinctive kind of feeling, the issue would have been begged, or, rather, it would have involved our author in saying at the same time that there is a difference between moral and nonmoral approval and disapproval and when we call for the difference, that really there is none.

If we ask Stevenson the origin of moral attitudes, he answers that he is not really interested in the question, and he confines his reply to criticizing those who dispose of the problem by saying that it is "simply due to training." This, he believes, is too simple an explanation and covers a complex phenomenon that would be difficult to analyze. It appears that Stevenson inclines to the belief that an explanation of the origin of our moral attitudes would have to give a prominent place not merely to training but to prestige and authority. At this point, however, he tells us that, for his purposes, it is not profitable to push any further the analysis of moral attitudes, since they raise no problems of language or of methodology. It is clear, however, that one hypothesis is inadmissible: that which holds that our moral responses are responses to "values" to which we ought to respond and which are not created by our attitudes but have some sort of ontic status which does not depend on our discovery of them. The hypothesis is inadmissible because, as Charner Perry showed, Stevenson is a radical nominalist; moral principles independent of attitudes and prior to them are variously dismissed as fictions and myths and hypostatizations, but in no case are they ever treated seriously.

The second criticism refers to Stevenson's implicit conception of the nature of man from which his definition of morality in terms of approval arises and which naturally leads him to hold that "the central problem of ethical analysis—one might almost say 'the' problem—is one of showing in detail how beliefs and attitudes are related."[6] As a result of this belief, Stevenson fails to grasp the importance of the problem of self-condemnation or guilt. He discusses what is involved "when an individual disagrees in attitude with himself." If this is intended to cover the phenomenon of self-condemnation, the treatment is inadequate and obfuscates the features of the phenomena that test his theory.[7] Can we say of an individual who knows what he is doing when he acts wrongly that one set of attitudes overcomes another and that the stronger, victorious one is condemned by the weaker? Why, then, do we nevertheless condemn the wrong set when it is defeated? Who or what does the condemning? Attitudes qua attitudes are not capable of condemning anything, and whatever does the condemning condemns victorious attitudes as often as defeated ones. Self-condemnation and the feeling of guilt, then, cannot be analyzed in terms of conflicting attitudes.

I see no harm in calling that in us that does the praising and condemning our "rational faculty." Labeling it does not explain it, but it does identify it. It may be argued that there is no need for inventing a faculty when we can express what we mean by saying that "we approve" of some things and disapprove of others. But this leaves out of account the fact that we discriminate among our attitudes, irrespective of their strength and their success. What factors are actually involved in the resolution of our moral perplexities and in such phenomena as self-condemnation will be analyzed below. At present it is enough to say that the error of the type of approach employed by Stevenson can be traced to the mechanistic habit of mind which fails to go beyond the conception of attitudes as vectors. Attitudes are, in fact, aspects of the total dynamism of consciousness. They can be more or less distinctly discriminated, and sometimes they can be named, but they are not separable factors behaving independently of the rest of our mind. This is a condition which they sometimes achieve in cases of compulsive action, but the anxiety which is created by yielding to a compulsion indicates that, even in such cases, our rational faculty does not abdicate entirely. It is not possible to deal with the complexity of moral phenomena with such simple categories as the mechanistic psychologist puts at our disposal.

The third criticism is that on Stevenson's conceptions of "attitude" and "belief" there is no rational way by which belief can control attitude, and the consequence of this is a veiled might-makes-right doctrine which it is advisable to call to the attention of the imperialistic and totalitarian forces of our age. Stevenson tells us that "ethical disagreement" is not susceptible of scientific resolution:

"I conclude, therefore, that scientific methods cannot be guaranteed the definite role in the so-called 'normative sciences' that they may have in the natural sciences. Apart from a heuristic assumption to the contrary, it is possible that the growth of scientific knowledge may leave many disputes about value permanently unsolved. Should these disputes persist there are non-rational methods for dealing with them, of course, such as impassioned, moving oratory. But the purely intellectual methods of science, and, indeed, *all* methods of reasoning, may be insufficient to settle disputes about values, even though they may greatly help to do so."[8]

If impassioned, moving oratory fails and all methods of reasoning are insufficient, what methods can we use? The Athenian ambassadors to the Island of Melos, who with their fleet in the harbor could afford to have a great contempt for impassioned oratory, answered that question for us long ago. The difference between them and us is that the old methods are now implemented, as they say in "federalese," with new and more efficient instruments for convincing those who, being weak, dare to disagree with us. We must, however, congratulate Stevenson because he is candid and courageous. Like the postulationalist, Stevenson has carried naturalism in moral philosophy to its logical conclusion, whereas other naturalists manage to convince themselves—for they do not fool anyone else—that they can be naturalists and at the same time condemn morally the crimes of Al Capone and of Goering. Having congratulated Stevenson, however, it must be added that this cannot be the end of the matter. We must realize that *to deny the primacy of reason in moral matters is to hand ourselves over to the first demagogue who is capable of arousing our passions.* Stevenson's philosophy is the rationalization on the sophisticated philosophical plane of the attitudes of the crypto-fascist. If he means seriously what he says—and I believe he does—what he is doing is manufacturing the metaphysics of imperialism.

The second treatise that the reader may be surprised to find omitted from these "animadversions" is C. I. Lewis' volume of *Carus Lectures.*[9] The reason why I have decided not to examine this distinguished contribution to naturalistic value theory within this essay can be stated very easily. Within the framework of his assumptions and method I do not find anything in Lewis' views to question radically; there are details to criticize, but central and decisive criticisms do not arise. The sense in which value judgments are verifiable is clearly established, and the useful distinctions that are drawn, for instance, between basic or ultimate value and other types of value, between inherent and instrumental, and between intrinsic and extrinsic values, have already entered into circulation in this country. I cannot accept, however, one of the basic assumptions which control Lewis' analysis, namely, that values are always values in experience, although they are not necessarily in actual experience and much less are they in one individual's personal experience. So far as I can discover, this is an assumption which is justified by what Lewis takes to be the self-evident absurdity of the contradictory. Lewis holds that to talk of a value which is a value for no one, which "by no possibility could any human who should experience it find satisfaction in it or by means of it," is to talk falsely or to talk meaninglessly. "Nothing," he tells us, "is good except relative to some possible felt goodness."[10] Lewis allows, however, "inherent" values which reside in things; but those who have studied him will remember that these are only "potentialities" of value. Otherwise we would be speaking of values that wander outside some substance, like June moths in the dark night, and this is something that values do not do.[11]

Lewis makes a great advance beyond naturalistic moral philosophers who seem to assume that the subject matter of moral philosophy is somehow obsolete and is best taken care of by value theory. He disengages clearly what he refers to as distinctly ethical questions from questions of value and its verification; the former are not empirical, while the latter are. But, since he denies the ontic objectivity of value, it is not even possible to surmise how the problems of obligation and of moral authority will be solved by him. Before we can consider his views, we must wait until he develops, as he seems to promise to do in the last paragraph of his book, the subject which he calls "ethics."

The third theory to which I referred in the first paragraph of this chapter is the subjectivistic theory of value or, as I shall call it in order to distinguish it from the views of C. I. Lewis, the theory of "hedonistic subjectivism."[12] According to this view, value consists of, or is, the positive hedonic experience or hedonic tone of experience, variously characterized as pleasure, satisfaction, gratification, or joy. This view is thus in many respects extremely close to, and in some respects indistinguishable from, C. I. Lewis' doctrine, both in content and in the specific formulation of it to which we shall refer below. From the point of view of the doctrine to be developed in Parts II and III of this essay, both Lewis' theory and hedonistic subjectivism can properly be called "subjectivistic," since they both hold, as we have already seen in respect to Lewis, that ultimate or basic value—the kind of value from which the value of everything else correctly called "valuable" is derivative—is an experience of felt value or, in other words, is a value which at some time or other is actually a value for someone. This felt value is called by Lewis "intrinsic" value. But, while it is the case that both Lewis' and the present theory can be properly called subjectivistic theories, it is necessary to indicate that we find a sharp and important difference between them when we look into exactly what each means by "intrinsic" value. Lewis holds what we may call a "phenomenological objective relativism"; he says that the immediately valuable is "the content of a presentation." The hedonistic subjectivist asserts that the immediately valuable is found in the experience itself. By ignoring the polarity of all experience, he gives evidence of paucity of analysis, and to me this failure seems fatal.

Because Lewis himself wavers between two interpretations of "intrinsic" value and because he interprets hedonistic subjectivism in a manner that makes it appear to be closer to one of his own views than the text warrants, Lewis is not altogether unsympathetic to hedonistic subjectivism. He tells us that value is the content of a presentation and also that it is a mode of presentation; but obviously it cannot be both, since we can clearly distinguish between the object of the experience and the kind of experience through which the object is presented. However, because Lewis occasionally, although not consistently, makes the proper phenomenal discrimination between the object of experience and the kind of experience in which the object functions as such, he is able to speak meaningfully of "inherent" value—by which he means, of course, value in the object considered by itself outside any experience of value. Hedonistic subjectivism must deny the possibility of inherent value in any literal sense and hold that when uncritical common sense attributes values to things, as it does, it does so figuratively, for things outside human experience can be means or instruments to the realization of valuable experiences but cannot contain value in themselves.

If we inquire into the problem of inherent value and ask the hedonistic subjectivist what in external things makes them produce, or leads them to cause or to give rise to the emergence of, intrinsic value, we do not find in his theory the slightest indication that he is at all interested in this problem. Nevertheless, the problem suggests two important questions in which every empiricist ought to be seriously interested, since they are matters of fact. The first is the purely empirical question as to what in an object produces a valuable experience for the subject. There is the possibility that he may find invariant factors susceptible of lawful formulation. The presence in most human cultures of similar classes of values ought to suggest to the empiricist the possibility that this is the case. And if he means what he says when he speaks of production and control, the answer to this question would be indispensable for him. He seems satisfied, however, with a vague statement to the effect that what produces value in the subject is a potentiality in the object. Yet the important question is not asked: "What is involved in saying that the potentiality of value inheres in things?"

Naturalists cannot be sufficiently careful of the concept of "potentiality," which may be the Trojan horse by which ideas of a distinctly teleological nature enter their systems, since, as everybody knows, it is a term deeply imbedded in a conception of what it means to know that includes more than efficient cause in its scheme. It may not be impossible to define "potentiality" as meaning merely the expectancy that a value may be intrinsically enjoyed, given certain physical conditions in the object to which potentiality is attributed, as well as certain environmental conditions, and given certain faculties or aptitudes in the subject of whom we may say that for him an object has potential value. But if we leave out of the concept of "potentiality" the final, the formal, and the material causes, all we can mean by it is a probably invariant relationship between an object in a situation and a subject or between a kind of object and a kind of subject. Thus conceived, what we have is a logical formulation of cultural relativism in which the object in the situation takes the place of values-in-culture and acts causally upon the subject, which is a member of the culture in which the values function.

The term "potency" or "potentiality," or any one of its grammatical derivatives, tends to obfuscate several problems, the most critical of which is the one that the emergence theory pretends to answer but actually begs. Again, if "potential," or any one of its derivatives, is used in a scheme of explanation from which the other three causes are excluded or ignored, another of the problems to which the user should attend is that of proving that the employment of the term does not surreptitiously smuggle in teleological assumptions. If the user can show that, as he employs it, the term does not involve teleology, any reference to any other kind of value whatsoever, except "intrinsic" value, is merely a reference to the efficient cause of intrinsic value. On the other hand, if the only value properly so called is the intrinsic value of pleasure, both the value of truth and the value of beauty lose their essential *sui generis* integrity, and axiological solipsism is the upshot. Our subjectivist can make only one literal judgment of value, "This is intrinsically valuable"—by which he can mean only, whether he is admiring the truth of his own theory or the beauty of his beloved or the moral goodness of a saint, "Oh, what pleasure I am having!" Another interesting consequence of this position is that it leaves no room for anything but insular egoism of the first person singular, as we shall see below.

Some hedonistic subjectivists maintain that we can select the experience of intrinsic value which they declare to be pleasure (variously called) and posit it as the "basic value" on which definitions of the more complex senses of value can be reared. The argument is justified by the contention that the only element of experience by which we can distinguish positive from negative intrinsic value is pleasure. By turning pleasure into a basic value, the hedonistic subjectivist hopes that when the theory is completed it will give us a set of hypotheses in terms of which we can predict and produce value phenomena at will. Since the doctrine is in a programmatic stage, it is not possible as yet to criticize it; but it is not inappropriate to review, in the light of the proposal, the reasons why moral hedonism has been rejected in the past, because a new hedonism will have to dispose of the old arguments.

It is granted without qualification that if the objective of axiology is to furnish us with a purely theoretical, nonprescriptive system, which organizes all known values in a determinate demographic area, with pleasure as the basis of the system, there can be no a priori reason to deny the possibility of such a system. But if axiology is conceived as a pure science, it becomes necessary to recall to the reader's mind what the inherent limitations of such an enterprise are. Let us first observe that before the system can be achieved we need far more knowledge than we have on hand about the actual descriptive laws which govern the grouping of values into social systems. Anyone who has even glanced at what social scientists know about value is bound to feel that a systematic organization cannot be attempted with our present meager scientific knowledge of value and personality.[13] But I do not in the least doubt the possibility in theory of organizing value phenomena with pleasure as basic value. Whether a hedonic system can organize value better than another is an empirical question on which it seems foolish to waste energy until both are presented to us for comparison; in advance of its construction, it is very easy to misunderstand the nature of the accomplishment and to claim more for it than can legitimately be claimed. The scheme thus constructed would have no prescriptive or normative validity and could, at best, predict for us that if the values operative in a given society were organized from a hedonic standpoint, these would be the laws that govern their grouping, these would be the practical consequences of such an organization. To institute the system as a practical affair would require an authority which the system does not itself justify. Until the justification is produced, we need not trouble ourselves, at the philosophic level, with such an approach to value.

The man who conceives of value theory as a practical science, however, finds it pertinent to ask whether from the standpoint of moral philosophy hedonism passes muster. My answer is flatly that it does not. There is no doubt that pleasure is a value and that a modicum of pleasure is an important part of the human economy.

Pleasure is occasionally an intrinsic value. But, unless my reading of human experience is totally false, rarely do men actually look on pleasure as defining their destiny and as exclusively giving value to living.[14] This is not true of positive suffering, whose continued presence may destroy our capacity to espouse any and all values. With the exception of masochism perhaps (which in a loose, non-erotic sense is far more widespread than we are likely to imagine), pain can never be an intrinsic good. At best, then, the normal attitude toward pleasure seems to suggest that men are loath to believe that the content of the good life consists of pleasure when life is at its purest and most perfect.

The fact that mankind does not agree with the hedonistic subjectivist is, of course, no argument for not prescribing its cultivation as end, since a mere fact is value-free; but it does suggest that it may be prudent to ask why pleasure, which is a good valued for its own sake, has not defined human destiny. The reason is that, unless pleasure or joy is "bracketed" off as an object of introspective analysis (if I may raid phenomenology for a term which I will employ for my own purposes), unless, in other words, pleasure is mentally isolated from the object which functions as its cause and is attended to in isolation, it is not a central object of attention in normal practical activity. We are normally content to take our joys and pleasures as marginal aspects of experience, as components of other intrinsic values which we put at the center of our moral life. And the decisive reason for this is that to grant pleasure a central place in the scheme of values appears to normal men to be derogatory of other values espoused for their own sake and which men place higher than pleasure in their hierarchy of values. Interest in pleasure tends to draw attention to our own physical organs, which are the seat of pleasure experiences; and this concern forces us to sacrifice, or at least to demote, all other values to a position which we are loath to assign to them. I am clearly aware of the fact that I am appealing here to consensus, but the appeal is justified in a simple way. Whenever a man sacrifices pleasure to an action to which he may be led by moral outrage, he declares the superiority of another value to pleasure. We often find men making such sacrifices. Indeed, I believe observation will prove that, by and large, pleasure is the most spendable of values. Even your intensely egoistic sensualist cannot be consistent in the primacy that he gives to pleasure, and whenever he is morally outraged he shows that in a crisis he is willing to put other values above pleasure. In short, men find a thoroughgoing hedonism incompatible with the moral exigencies of practical living.

We could, of course, insist again that the appeal here is to fact and that, although men are not hedonists, nevertheless *they ought to be*. But I am afraid that, unless I changed my opinion very radically, I could not recognize the obligation to act exclusively for the sake of my own pleasure or in an unqualified way for the sake of the pleasure of others. To the philosopher proposing the hedonistic imperative I would answer: Such a morality as you propose seems to me repulsive and involves a complete betrayal of what I take to be the import of human destiny. And what we must inquire at this point is by what means a man who starts with a definition of value which leads to such consequences can correct his definition or can argue with me rationally and thus avoid the practical difficulties in which he seems to find himself. I recognize without qualification the categorical obligation to prevent wanton suffering, and, for reasons that I need not enter into here, I hold this to be a universally valid imperative. I also recognize the obligation under certain circumstances to contribute to the pleasure of others. The recognition of this obligation is inconsistent with hedonistic subjectivism, however, since altruism commands me at the cost of pain to myself to contribute in some cases to another man's pleasure, even if I cannot identify my interests with his and even if I hate him. The positive imperative of the hedonistic subjectivist does not seem to me to have any rational force whatever; and, were it to be universally accepted, I believe it would lead to a life unspeakably contemptible in moral quality and one which would revolt us all as deeply as does the life of *Brave New World*.

I am, of course, at this point appealing to what my reader takes to be the order of rank among values. The validity of the appeal presupposes an exposition of a number of topics, some of which will be attempted in Part II. As will be seen there, the appeal is fundamentally to an intuition of an objective order of values having ontic status, and I would neither conceal if I could, nor could I conceal if I wanted to, the intuitionist nature of my views. I do not hold that mankind's basic intuitions of value are beyond the reach of criti-

cism, however. It is also desirable to remember that the postulational and the definitional approaches to value are so obviously
crypto-intuitionist that it is not worth proving it. But, while I readily admit that the positive part of this essay is based on an appeal to
intuition, the appeal I have made at this point is not intended to establish a basic value but to challenge the value selected by the
hedonistic subjectivist as basic. The issue is not "What is the basic
value?" but "Can pleasure be selected as a basic value?" I argue
that it cannot be because it would go against what I take to be the
moral nature of man. The point has been succinctly stated by Kant,
and upon his statement of it I rest my case:

"But that there is any intrinsic worth in the real existence of a
man who merely lives for *enjoyment*, however busy he may be in this
respect, even when in so doing he serves others—all equally with
himself intent only on enjoyment—as an excellent means to that
one end, and does so, moreover, because through sympathy he
shares all their gratifications,—this is a view to which reason will
never let itself be brought round. Only by what a man does heedless
of enjoyment, in complete freedom and independently of what he
can procure passively from the hand of nature, does he give to his
existence, as the real existence of a person, an absolute worth. Happiness, with all its plethora of pleasures, is far from being an uncon-
ditioned good."[15]

The hedonistic subjectivist may reply that I misrepresent his
views because he is not a moral egoist. He does not ignore the
other-regarding values. Indeed, the hedonistic imperative points to
our obligation to increase the pleasure of others. The question
therefore arises, In what sense can the hedonist ask us to concern
ourselves with the pleasure of others, and how far should our concern extend? If the theory lays down that we *ought* to rejoice in
another's pleasure unconditionally, it introduces into the system
surreptitiously another intrinsic value than the experience of pleasure, and this is incompatible with a consistent hedonism. The
hedonistic subjectivist will answer that it is not inconsistent with
his position to prescribe that we *ought* to concern ourselves with the
joy of others if we identify ourselves with their interests. I retort
that, rather than proving the altruistic nature of the system, the re-

ply underlines its egoism by limiting our concern for others to those who, because we identify ourselves with their interests, contribute to our pleasure. It cannot, of course, prescribe with whom we ought to identify our interests, since this would involve the positing of a value as intrinsic which is not necessarily capable of producing an experience of pleasure for the individual positing it.

It should also be observed that the assumption which seems implicit in the position—the assumption that we, in fact, tend to rejoice when those with whom we identify our interests are experiencing pleasure—is a psychologically naïve belief, which is contradicted both by experience and by what we know of the ambivalence of our attitudes toward the members, to express it in sociological lingo, of our "in-group." In order to avoid this criticism if we base the obligation of altruism on our identification of our interests with those of others, we must restate the principle as follows: Reflection indicates that it is desirable to increase the pleasure of others with whom we have identified our interests, when by so doing we increase our own pleasure. For if we do not gain pleasure by our efforts, the advice is inconsistent with the basic assumptions of hedonistic subjectivism. I have no doubt that there are men who act to some extent on such a principle, but I do not doubt either in what contempt they are held by the majority of mankind for doing so.

Hedonistic subjectivism ought to be condemned, then, because it does not give an adequate account of the moral life. It is desirable, nevertheless, to draw out what the doctrine actually involves in practice. What the doctrine does is to justify narrow, parochial practices, extending the benefits of our moral sympathy to our fellow-tribesmen when we rejoice in their pleasure, and leaving the door open for any excess we may wish to put upon the members of the tribe on the other side of the brook. The Hopi Indian, whose term for "good" is "hopi," which is the same term he gives his own tribe, and whose term for "bad" and "stranger" is "non-hopi," may not know anything about philosophy, but, without the benefit of theory, he has reached the same conclusion that the hedonistic subjectivist so scientifically and periphrastically formulates in his doctrine.

My criticism is, of course, irrelevant if moral philosophy is a purely academic, merely theoretical game. But an insular, a paro-chial, a limited, a narrowly tribalistic moral doctrine, as was pointed out in the chapter on postulational morality, has no rational answer to political schemes which call for the liquidation of Jews or Negroes or of kulaks or of Roman Catholics or of the *bourgeoisie* or of any other group of men, because in the tribal mind of the liquida-tor the group stands in the way of progress and social pleasure. No one can call himself a democratic man and pretend concern for lib-eral and humanistic values and at the same time seriously advocate a moral philosophy which tells us that reflection on his activities counsels what in practice would be a narrow tribalistic selfishness disguised as the newest scientific psychology.

In view of these considerations I conclude that, even if the hedonistic subjectivist should be able to achieve a systematic or-ganization of value theory with pleasure as a basic value, I doubt very much whether he would be able to convince many men that his moral scheme meets the demands of a normal moral conscience that takes the moral life seriously. If moral philosophy is viewed as a practical science and not as a purely theoretical game, the quality of the life it would practically enact must be considered in judging it.

CHAPTER XI

SUMMARY

THE examination of the forms of naturalistic moral philosophy which at present dominate our culture has led me to the conclusion that they are infected with radical theoretical errors which lead to frightful practical consequences.

Cultural relativism does not tell us how we can solve morally a practical perplexity for which our society does not provide a customary norm; or, what is the same thing, it does not tell us how we can choose morally beyond custom or transcend it when it becomes obsolete. Nor does it tell us how to choose morally which of two conflicting customs is better in a society in which such conflicts exist. Nor can it explain, in cases in which an individual condemns the customs of his society, how to adjudge the conflict.

The claim made by Santayana and R. B. Perry that values are constituted by interest has been shown to be false. While many values are discovered by pre-existing interests, the greater number of values must be recognized as such before they are espoused; and the fact of recognition, when analyzed, entails phenomena which force the interest theory into *ad hoc* repairs which cannot in fairness be allowed to any theory. The interest theory commits, besides, the vitalistic fallacy. In the case of Santayana's version of the interest theory I have referred the reader to a study of his *The Life of Reason* which appeared in *The Philosophy of George Santayana*, in which other basic confusions of his theory are examined by the writer.

Instrumentalism claims that intelligence is constitutive of the good. Interests or, as it prefers to call them, desires are presupposed by the moral life; but the distinction between the desired and the desirable or good is constituted by the activity of the intelligence in arranging and selecting the desires that can be satisfied and transforming them in view of the context (the problematic situation) in

175

which they seek satisfaction. The error of this theory is that it presupposes a *good* will, which neither desire by itself nor intelligence by itself nor intelligence guiding desire can account for. Again, instrumentalism, because of its distrust of all moral criteria, ends up in sheer expedience. I also argued that, as the dominant philosophy of the United States in the first half of our twentieth century, instrumentalism is dynamically inimical to everything in man that seeks satisfaction beyond a shrunken, purely secularistic conception of human nature. What instrumentalism envisages as the desirable is a Deweyian variant of *Brave New World*.

Postulational morality saves us from pragmatic expedience by insisting on the role played by our basic moral commitments in the rearing of a moral life, but it offers no means for resolving radical moral conflicts.

Freud fails to explain the genesis of the moral conscience.

The first view examined in the last chapter was not considered extensively. The reason for this is that its fatal errors have already been exposed. In addition to them, we may note the failure of the theory to reckon with the relevant facts of the moral life in framing its definition of the good; its failure to distinguish between mere approval and moral approval; its failure to give an adequate account of self-condemnation. It was also pointed out that positivistic moral theory leaves us at the mercy of the next demagogue that happens along and that it constitutes an excellent philosophy for imperialists.

The second view examined in the Postscript was taken up because it has had a revival of late, thus demonstrating how difficult it is to kill error in philosophy. When we look into it, we find that, if we take hedonistic subjectivism as a purely scientific theory and not as practical moral philosophy, we cannot judge a priori the claim made by its proponent that he can organize all values in a system with pleasure as basic. There are, however, reasons to believe that he has not fully considered how much more he needs to know at the purely scientific level than he does at present before his task could succeed. But, even if he succeeded, he could not tell how a man *ought* to act. If we consider hedonistic subjectivism as a practical philosophy, we find that its hedonism belies the capacity that men have for espousing other values than pleasure for their own sake and that what it adds up to is a narrow egoism. Again, its definition of "intrinsic" value fails to distinguish the phenomenally objective character of value from the conditions of its apprehension.

If we view naturalism panoramically, we find that several types of error are endemic in it. The first is the still deeply rooted belief that the data of psychology are logically prior to the definition of value and constitutive of it. This error is clearly present in the interest theory and less clearly so in instrumentalism and in hedonistic subjectivism. If it were true that value theory depended logically on knowledge of psychology—either because value was deducible from the results of psychological analysis or because, for some other reason, such knowledge was logically prior to the recognition of value—knowledge of psychology also would be logically prior to the definition of truth, which is one of the values, and no inquiry could ever get started because some antecedent knowledge of what is the truth is required before we set out on its search. In fact, however, no psychological inquiry can modify the normative criteriology which rules in the field of logic; yet the majority of naturalists, who resent deeply and justifiably the fallacy of psychologism in logic, are likely to be systematic psychologizers in moral philosophy. Psychology is not decisive in value theory, although it may put blinkers on our eyes which prevent us from considering data which ought to enter into our speculation. But no knowledge of the purely psychological processes involved in the apprehension of value can throw any light on the presence of a value at the phenomenal level.[1]

An obvious corollary of this fact is that psychological knowledge of the subjective conditions for the apprehension of value cannot tell us how valuable a value is, as compared to another value, unless we are in possession of a principle of order among values which is independent of our scientific knowledge of the conditions of apprehension but which, nevertheless, may be clarified by the knowledge that the philosopher or psychologist provides us. Once we know how valuable a value is in comparison with other values, scientific knowledge of the conditions of value may enable us to produce it efficiently and maintain it in existence; but neither psychology nor biology nor physics nor philosophy can give us a knowledge of the order of rank among values which is more than an improvement of the common-sense knowledge we bring to it.

If scientists could establish a causal relation between the discriminated value and certain psychological or, better still, physiological phenomena, such that, given one, we could reliably expect the other, to that extent our "scientific" knowledge of value would be advanced. Some naturalists hope that in the future we shall be able to infer from psychological data alone whether a human being is undergoing an experience of value or not. I do not think it is profitable or wise to argue for or against this hope, except to say that it is very unlikely that I shall see it realized in my lifetime. I try to keep in mind that it is necessary to be on the alert lest the dream be passed off on us as an accomplished reality. On the other hand, I also try to keep in mind the fact that science is likely, when the outsider least expects it, to take a sudden successful kangaroo leap into the unknown.

These points should have been clear long ago, and they have been made in this essay. I believe it is desirable to reiterate them because we can still find philosophers classifying value theories as "conative" and "affective" and criticizing theories because they are based on antiquated psychology. This indicates that in the critic's mind the definition of value is taken to be somehow logically dependent on psychological data; but, since the so-called "conative" theories have no more or less logical relation to the results of psychological investigations than the affective theories, to raise the question as to whether the psychology is old or new is not merely gratuitous but confusing. The question that it is profitable to raise is not whether affective or conative psychology or any other kind of psychology, actual or future, is best fitted to offer us a correct definition of value, but whether the naturalist has discriminated the phenomenon of value correctly, and whether his theory accounts for the relevant value data which constitute his primary subject matter.

The word "intuition" may be objected to. We can keep it or substitute for it a term like "apprehension" or "experience" or "knowledge" or "grasp" or "perception." Whatever term we finally choose, it cannot but refer to the more or less vague envisagement of value which is no different from the envisagement of any other datum or object. The same kind of activity is involved in seeing that this is a color or a length or a volume or a time duration as is involved in intuiting it as a good or a beauty or a truth. Analysis will refine the datum and help clarify the criterion by which we give it a place in our value hierarchy. It will reveal the structure of value more clearly and delimit its spread more distinctly. But it cannot help us dispense with the primary intuition. To pretend that it can is to pretend that science can start without the help of the primary sensory discriminations of common sense.

There is another error that pervades practically all the naturalistic theories which we have examined. When we ask for the conception of human nature on which these theories base their moral reflections, we discover that, for all their empiricism, they know only those isolated aspects and factors which are borrowed from a scientific psychology which itself ignores the personality of the moral creature that struggles, sometimes successfully, to resolve his practical perplexities in a moral way. This leads to the further discovery that these self-proclaimed empiricists accept as their data little besides thin scientific abstractions. In their hands empiricism is a technique of paying lip service to facts and carefully screening out practically all the facts which are critically relevant to moral philosophy. What it feels like actually to be confronted with a moral perplexity, to be torn between the knowledge of duty and the drive of desire; what it is to hunger desperately for inward peace, for relief from chaotic passion, or from the compulsion of vice; what it is to be poisoned by malice or hatred or envy and to know it; what it is to say to one's self from the depths of one's heart, "I am despicable" —these are experiences which one would think constitute, in part at least, the empirical data of moral philosophy but of which one finds hardly a spoor in the empiricists' treatises. No wonder they are amused, these scientistic philosophers, by what they take to be the absurd importance that Augustine placed on the childish raid on a fruit orchard. The normal man takes such childish peccadilloes in his stride and much else. The important thing is to out-Stevenson Stevenson in the elegance and rigor of our systems.

How, one asks, could all these men have lived through at least one devastating war, and some of them even through revolution and exile, men who live (to borrow a phrase from my friend Saul Bellow) in a world in which the gases of Auschwitz still circulate in the air, men who must have heard rumors of the police techniques of

the Russians and who must be aware of the iniquities and hypocri-
sies of which we of the Western democracies are capable—how can
such men call themselves empiricists and allow so little of the actual
content of the moral life to find its way into their speculations?
They are self-proclaimed empirical philosophers, these naturalists,
equipped with a formidable panoply of methods, with the most up-
to-date techniques of analysis, whose empiricism consists in an
elaborate ritualistic litany of praise sung to science. It is a strange
empiricism that absolves empiricists from the task of looking into
the actual facts of the moral life.[2]

Before turning to our next task, that of sketching a theory of
moral philosophy which tries to do justice to the facts of the moral
life, I believe that the antipositivist owes it to honesty to admit
unambiguously that, if we accept under the term "knowledge" or
"reason" or "science" more than the experimental scientist accepts,
we open the door to verbalism, confusion, vagueness, the inter-
minable chatter of the schoolmen; we open the door to the weary
critical wrangling of which Part I of this essay is probably an excellent illustration. We must remember, however, that the intellect,
in the narrow form in which the experimental scientist, qua scientist, permits himself to use it, does not have the exclusive and
unqualified primacy over the moral life which the scientist gives it
over his own subject matter. To conceive of knowledge in a broad
sense is thus to gamble on the chance that, along with confusion and
vagueness and error and logomachy, there will stray in some of the
truths that feed man's heart and not alone the lucidity which merely
feeds the few ounces of soft tissue that he calls his brain. I say "to
gamble on the chance" because it is by no means certain that wisdom is the result of nonscientistic speculation; metaphysicians can
be as narrow and dogmatic and spiritually myopic as any positivist
normally is.

This, then, in the last analysis, is the choice before us: on the one
hand, scientism and the primacy of the method of the physicist; on
the other, a speculative, nonscientistic philosophy. The first gives
positive results at the cost of the whole man, and it abandons the

moral life to the unrestricted forces of unreason. The second promises but cannot guarantee to minister to the full needs of man.

These I take to be the results of the analysis that has been carried out in Part I. But, as I hope the reader will see in Parts II and III, they are not the only results arrived at, because our survey of naturalistic moral philosophies equips us with important insights which ought to be incorporated into moral theory and warns us of errors to avoid and problems to be solved. With this in mind we turn to our positive task.

PART II
THE MORAL LIFE

CHAPTER XII

THE RESOLUTION OF A MORAL PERPLEXITY. I

SINCE we are not able to find in current versions of naturalistic moral theory an answer to our question, we are forced to ask again, "How do we resolve a moral perplexity?" Succinctly stated, a moral perplexity is resolved by searching for a solution which sustains and strengthens or at least does not positively threaten, or does not threaten too radically, the values which we take to be constitutive of our personality or moral self. This assertion applies to more or less "normal" moral situations, in which the perplexity which confronts the moral agent does not force a reconstruction of the moral personality. Cases in which the situation forces a repudiation of the extant values, either in part or in entirety, will make us qualify the answer here given.

Whether, normally, the solution strengthens, or at least does not threaten, the person is a question of degree. The ideal would be to arrive at an alternative that not only sustained but reinforced the person's values. If growth and expansion happen to be important values of the moral self, as at certain periods and in certain cultures they tend to be, then the moral resolution seeks to reinforce and sustain these values also; however, to give the values of growth and expansion an unqualified primacy, as some vitalistic philosophies tend to do, is illegitimately to turn into a universal condition one that is only partially or locally valid. Most young men and some nations under certain historical conditions place at the center of their scheme of values the vitalistic ones; but there is repulsive incongruity in an old man behaving like the character from Pola whom Aschenbach sees in the boat in *Death in Venice*, and a wise and ripe civilization rates other values higher than those of mere biological youthful vigor and growth.

It is not possible to determine on a priori grounds the values that make up a person; and even with full knowledge of the social world to which a man belongs it is not possible to predict, except loosely and vaguely, the manner in which his constitutive values are organized. The reason for this brings us back to the doctrine of cultural relativism: societies more or less effectively control the values that their members are allowed to discover and are permitted to espouse; but cultures cannot create, and most cultures do not want, individuals who are exactly like one another. In all societies, unless totally isolated, the process of diffusion gradually integrates new values into the extant system of the culture, and, within varying limits of tolerance, purely idiosyncratic value differences are allowed play. Thus the selection and specific organization of values in each individual are at best only an approximate copy of the loose and vague conception which his society inculcates as the ideal type for him: what a man considers "morally acceptable" in a concrete way depends on his own moral sensibility and on the values that constitute his person. I believe that we have the capacity literally to discover values, and, if this were all that intuitionists like Ross were intent on maintaining, I would apply for admission to their ranks. To the extent to which it is operative, this capacity to discover values is the pivotal point in the moral process, since it enables men to correct what they incline to consider right and good by comparison with what they discover to be right and good. But the grasp of the worth of a value, the apprehension of what the value's rating is in comparison to the other values we espouse, seems to be conditioned more or less effectively by subjective factors from which it is doubtful whether individuals can ever completely liberate themselves.

If this is true, moral philosophers must abandon the notion that they can actually reach an unqualified objectivity in their moral theory; and we must give up the hope, as human beings involved in moral conflicts, of ever achieving apodictic certainty in moral matters. The subjectivity which creeps into all moral valuation accounts for the ubiquity of moral conflicts among members of a society and between societies. This is the irrefragable truth of the relativist that we ought not to lose sight of and that the so-called "absolutist" tends somehow to dissolve or ignore. But it is not the whole truth. If the values that we acknowledge were determined without qualification by culture, the conclusion of the relativist would have to be accepted in the way in which he formulates it; but our apprehension of values is not entirely controlled by cultural factors, and hence there is considerably more to the resolution of moral perplexities than an appeal to extant socially acknowledged values could resolve. For one thing, the phenomena to which the relativist points and which are found within the area of data that in this essay are called "morality" are not exhaustive of the subject matter in which the moral philosopher is interested. There are the phenomena which I call "the ethical." It must, of course, be admitted that what is concretely meant by "right" and "good" by one man in a certain situation and in the context of a given cultural scheme of values is not the same as what can be meant by another in a somewhat similar situation. But we shall see that the "relativism" involved in these varying conceptions of "right" and "good" in concrete terms can be reduced by the process of justifying the decisions reached privately. The process of justification, in effect, tests what we take to be the right against a progressively ascertainable notion of what is truly right. The subjectivism thus involved ceases to be vicious, since it can be, at least in theory, gradually eliminated and since in the definition of the moral process are included two factors or imperatives which cannot be disregarded without becoming immoral: The first duty is the duty of resolving moral perplexities not merely in terms that satisfy our desires but in terms that meet the "requiredness" (as Köhler has called it) which the values have that are involved in the objective situation in which we find ourselves.[1] The second is the duty of keeping the moral process open, of not closing it, of not being the first to appeal to force in the resolution of moral conflicts.

The problem of the moral philosopher, dealing with the data of morality before the ethical developments emerge and force him radically to alter his account, is thus to do justice to two sets of facts which do not seem to be compatible and which make up the moral life: one fact demands of the individual that he preserve his personal integrity and maintain his loyalty to principles to which he owes fealty; the other set demands of the individual that he not become a moral despot, using principles as masks behind which to conceal his arbitrary wilfulness. In terms of the preceding examination of moral doctrines, the problem is to bring together into a genuine philosophical synthesis the important insights of Charner Perry and John Dewey.

Moral perplexities constitute value conflicts complicated by the fact that values are sustained by interests which often successfully pass off their objects as valuable. The moral man is the man who undertakes to adjust these conflicts, not merely satisfactorily to himself (if by "himself" be meant, as we have seen is usually meant by naturalists, a dynamic and hierarchically organized system of interests or desires) but *morally* satisfactorily to himself. The first difficulty which we encounter when we look into this answer is a practical one, namely, that it is not so easy as it is supposed to be by philosophers like Santayana, R. B. Perry, and Dewey actually to know what values do, in fact, constitute our personality. Even in well-established, smoothly running societies, in which each man may be assumed to occupy a well-defined station to which well-defined duties are assigned, it is often difficult to learn what those duties demand in the specific circumstances and how their fulfilment affects others and ourselves. Of course, only a simplistic psychology would assume that a man's personality is defined by his public station and his institutional duties. Men are not social insects. Their personalities have aspects other than the social or public one, other than those defined by the institutional roles they play in their society; their personalities have depths of which neither their societies nor even they themselves can be expected to have knowledge. And there are other reasons why it is impossible to expect a man to know with clarity what his constitutive values are, even in a settled society. The most important of these is that it is only through the resolution of moral perplexities that a man can discover, *by creating*, what he is. (The fact that I take the mind's creative powers literally gives rise to a paradoxical difficulty with which we must deal later on.)

But, even if the elements that make up the personality were as easy to separate as sheep in a flock and even if one could therefore resolve practical perplexities with relative ease, the philosopher would still want to know more than this discussion has so far disclosed as to the ground of moral authority and the kind of validity that pertain to the moral judgment; for, in the compact form in which our conception of the moral act has been stated, the source of moral authority seems to arise out of the individual. If this hypothesis were true, it would be impossible to resolve radical conflicts of interests between individuals in a moral way. By consequence, then, such conflicts could be resolved only by an appeal to force.

The first step in the elucidation of our problem consists in analyzing the nature of the moral self or person. It was not, of course, until recently that psychology could have given much help to the moralist. In Hobbes's day and even later in Hume's, or even in the days of John Stuart Mill, the account of human nature which psychology offered the moralist made it impossible for the latter to come to grips with all the complexities of the moral act. Either moral philosophers disregarded psychology, or they floundered in palpably inadequate accounts of the moral agent. But the rudimentary development of psychology cannot be accepted as an excuse for philosophers. They did not need to put up with the simplistic caricatures they used in their moral speculations: if the psychologists failed them, literature offered them abundant light, the pertinence of which, for their problems, many of them obviously seem to have ignored. I do not mean that literature offers (as John Stuart Mill discovered after the mental crisis which he describes in the famous chapter v of his *Autobiography*) a means for "the cultivation of the feelings." I mean that literature is an actual vehicle of important *knowledge* of the nature of man. But if philosophers until Mill's day had little excuse, much less of an excuse have those later philosophers who have had easily within their reach the psychological researches of the last hundred years and the vast accumulation of studies on the nature of man by such psychological novelists as Dostoevski and such philosophical psychologists as Nietzsche or Kierkegaard. Contemporary philosophers have tended either to ignore this material or to criticize it arrogantly without understanding it.[2]

In his classical study of personality, Allport has given us fifty different usages of the term "persona" and its immediate derivative meanings.[3] Starting with the original, theatrical meaning, he goes on to theological, philosophical, juristic, sociological, biological, and psychological meanings and finally to his own usage. These meanings cover a large number of loosely overlapping data. The variety of definitions or usages now current, however, need not embarrass the moral philosopher; a guiding notion should be functionally useful, and, so long as the moral philosopher does not deny facts to which the other usages point, he can, if he considers them irrelevant for his purpose, simply leave them aside. For him the human personality (man at the moral level) is centrally constituted by a hierarchically organized system of values, some of which the person "espouses" and others of which he merely "recognizes," but not all of which are normally discovered by his reflective consciousness as constitutive of himself. In the absence of a better term, I call the "recognized" and the "espoused" values, when I need to speak of them together, the "acknowledged" values of a man or a culture.

It is only in profound moral crises that perspicacious men find out what values truly constitute them. My experience inclines me to the belief that men in general live their lives through without finding out who or what they really are. We think we are courageous when we are cowards, honest when we are cheats and thieves, truthful and generous when we are liars and pigs, and self-respecting in spite of the high coefficient of pliability of our moral spines. But whether we men are actors or are somehow protected from the mirror that would show us ourselves, this I know: that we fight desperately and bitterly against the knowledge of what we truly are, barring no holds and giving no quarter. It takes a crisis to reveal to us what values we truly espouse, and even that is often not enough, for each of us has his system of jujitsu for disposing quietly of bothersome truths. Captain Marlow, who tells the story of Lord Jim's trial and subsequent adventures, has something to say in this connection worth recalling:

"He discovered at once a desire that I should not confound him with his partners in—in crime, let us call it. He was not one of them; he was altogether of another sort. I gave no sign of dissent. I had no intention, for the sake of barren truth, to rob him of the smallest particle of any saving grace that would come in his way. I didn't know how much of it he believed himself. I didn't know what he was playing up to—if he was playing up to anything at all— and I suspect he did not know either; for it is my belief no man ever understands quite his own artful dodges to escape from the grim shadow of self-knowledge."[4]

There is no question that Captain Marlow is absolutely correct. And two pages later he comments again, referring to the days Jim spent on board the ship that rescued him:

"I did not ask Jim about the nature of his feelings during the ten days he spent on board. From the way he narrated that part I was at liberty to infer he was partly stunned by the discovery he had made—the discovery about himself—and no doubt was at work trying to explain it away to the only man who was capable of appreciating all its tremendous magnitude. You must understand he did not try to minimise its importance. Of that I am sure; and therein lies his distinction. As to what sensations he experienced when he got ashore and heard the unforeseen conclusion of the tale in which he had taken such a pitiful part, he told me nothing of them, and it is difficult to imagine. I wonder whether he felt the ground cut from under his feet? I wonder? But no doubt he managed to get a fresh foothold very soon."

The full picture of a man's iniquity and evil is seldom revealed to himself, and what is shown to us by circumstances is, in any case, never distinct and clear. The inward life is fluid and shadowy, and the stream has tremendous depths. It is not merely that we do not want to see but that there is not enough light.

The organization of the constitutive values is achieved by the psychic powers or faculties of which the animal disposes. The animal, as endowed with these powers or faculties, I call the "self." It is the self that espouses the values that spirit discloses to it, and this creates the person. (About spirit more later.) The self is the subject matter of the psychologist, and therefore I am not using the term "self" in a peculiar or idiosyncratic sense; it is necessary to bear in mind that the term refers to a conceptual isolate. Hume was right, for, in reality, moral man never comes into immediate contact with his "self," although he can reflectively come more or less successfully into contact with his own moral self, which is to say, with his personality or person. I am, of course, distinguishing components of man that cannot actually be separated, and I am also disregarding the fact that analysis cannot exhaustively distinguish the components of an organism as if they were independent parts which additively make up a machine. With these qualifications in mind, we can, for our purposes, conceive of the total man as a biological organism, a mere animal, endowed with a self, which is to say, with psychic aptitudes, and with a personality, which is to say, with a system of values which he recognizes and which makes him what he is, which gives him the uniqueness he possesses as a member of the human race.

The "person" or the "personality" or "the moral self" is, then, a composite of values achieved by means of the self's psychological powers or faculties, based, in turn, on a physiological system. We speak of these faculties as belonging to a "self," and we assume that the self stands toward them in the same relation as that in which substance stands toward its qualities for Locke. But introspection, as Hume pointed out, fails to discover a "self" if by the term is understood, as I wish it understood in these discussions, a psychic totality. The parallel with Locke holds because, according to Locke, we are able to perceive qualities but we do not perceive substance, although somehow we can infer it. Here we come up against a problem that clearly transcends the limits of an essay on moral philosophy and leads off into serious questions of the metaphysic of personality, philosophical anthropology, and the relations between the natural and the normative disciplines. In order to explore this question, we would have to suspend our inquiry and undertake another, even more extensive perhaps than this one. This I do not intend to do, but I do believe that it is incumbent upon me at this point to make explicit the assumptions which underlie my discussion.

I hold that the self is more than a collection of aptitudes or powers of the body and that the person is more than an integration of espoused values. I do not think I am altogether ignorant of the attacks to which the substantialistic approach to philosophical anthropology has been subject since, let us say, William James's day; and I am firmly convinced that the scientist, whether psychologist or sociologist, is incumbering himself with useless impedimenta if he starts his inquiry with a substantialistic hypothesis. For his purposes there is no need of such a hypothesis: like De Laplace, who could not find God in the heavens, neither the psychologist nor the sociologist is likely to find, with the kind of telescopes with which *he* looks, a psychic substance or a substantial person within the depths of man. What he finds, as psychologist, is signs, language, and behavior or Freudian instincts and neurotic complexes or some such similar product of analysis. But he has not earned his conclusion that, because this is all he finds, this is all there is to find. What he finds is limited by his telescope—by what he looks for as controlled by the purposes that set him in his search and the conditions of admissibility of what he finds. Science is not metaphysics and cannot rule on questions of reality. It formulates invariant relations into comprehensive systems for the purposes of prediction. But whether or not the objects of its inquiry, the scientific laws it systematizes, are real, and what is meant by affirming or denying that they are real, and whether or not they are the only real things in the universe—these are questions which the scientist qua scientist cannot answer. If the term "knowledge" can be applied only to the findings of the scientist, then these questions are nonsensical. But whether or not the term "knowledge" can be applied only to the results of scientific inquiry and to nothing else is not a question on which the scientist qua scientist can decide. For this reason and without disrespect or inimical bias against science (although, of course, in frank opposition to scientifistic positivism), I can assert that a moral philosopher has to go beyond events, relations, and qualities or beyond categories reducible to these or beyond signs, language, and behavior if he is going to tackle his own problems with any hope of success.

On grounds which will in part be discussed below, I believe that the self is more than a collection of interrelated powers and aptitudes of the body; they constitute a self in the sense that they are the expressions of a psychic totality. And what I mean is that if we take these powers together in their mutual interdependence and if we view them generically as possessing traits (or a trait) which enable us to classify them as psychical and not physical, we are forced to admit that they have a specific organization and share an identity which is much more than the unity which we may claim for them if we consider them additively together. There is a substantival psychic fact of which all our psychic powers are the expression, which enables us legitimately to speak of the aptitudes and excellences of a *self*, as if they were its possession. I am not unaware of the fact that this statement, standing dogmatically stark and unsupported by lengthy analysis, is hardly admissible, since it is so flatly contradicted by a long and powerful tradition which goes as far back as Hume at least. But I shall leave it unsupported, since its justification, as I have suggested already, would take us too far afield. If the reader desires more information on the arguments which I would advance in order to justify my conviction, I refer him to the careful analysis of Felix Krueger, which, on the whole, I accept and which validates, as it seems to me, the belief in a "psychical totality."[5]

Because these are questions on which one is easily misinterpreted, I will be excused if I reiterate that I have asserted that the "psychic totality"—the "self" in my terminology—is possible, so far as we *positively* know, only because it is sustained by an organic structure which it is the business of the biologist to study. This biological structure is, in turn, anchored on a merely physical structure. The psyche makes possible the organization of values which constitutes the person. This is not, however, exactly true, for between self—the psychic reality—and the fully developed person there lies the spirit, between which and the powers of the psyche, as Scheler argues, there is a chasm which cannot be bridged.[6] For the purposes of moral theory, however, we may (for the moment at least) neglect the spirit. We shall consider the person solely as if it consisted of an organization of acknowledged values.

The person is immersed in a social medium, toward which it bears complex and mutually incompatible relationships of dependence and antagonism, which affect the medium but also in part determine the manner in which the biological organism, the self, and the person each becomes what it is. This, however, as we shall see later on, does not imply a total denial of freedom. The faculties with which the self is endowed or which constitute the self organize not only the moral values which make up the moral person but all other values found in it—cognitive, aesthetic, and religious. And thus we see that the human being—the man of flesh and blood with whom we have to do daily, John or Peter or Paul—is not merely what the biologist says he is, or what the psychologist takes him to be, or what the sociologist tells us he is, although the last comes closer to the real person than the others; he is what we have in front of our eyes, a complex physiologically and psychologically endowed creature, whose prodigious faculties enable him to discover and appropriate to himself through the acts of espousal and recognition an interrelated complex of moral, aesthetic, cognitive, and religious values.

Without a social medium made up of institutions through whose aid the values that a man discovers enter into reliably enduring relations with him, a man could never become *a person*. But we must not expect the sociologist to be able to explain the person, any more than the psychologist does. Presupposing society, the sociologist can legitimately investigate a great many very important social components of the person, just as, presupposing the person, he can explain society. But it is impossible to posit society unless we suppose that it is constituted by "persons," as we have here conceived them, and vice versa. This is so important a point that it is advisable to go into it in some detail, although it will involve us in a long digression.

The functionalist in anthropology pretends to be able to explain the development of culture by assuming an infra-social animal, endowed with biological "basic needs" which create cultural institutions. This is repeatedly asserted by Malinowski in his exposition of his method, *A Scientific Theory of Culture*. For instance, in "The Functional Theory" we read: "The second axiom in the science of culture is that every cultural achievement that implies the use of artifacts and symbolism is an instrumental enhancement of human anatomy, and refers directly or indirectly to the satisfaction of a bodily need."[7] On this "axiom" is based the assertion that belief in immortality is "related perhaps to some deep biological craving of the organism" and that art "might have to refer to directly physical reactions of the organism to rhythm, sound, color, line and form, and to their combinations."[8]

This does not mean, as Malinowski explains, that every institution we know of can be traced to a basic need. Malinowski recognizes only seven basic needs, and these seven are said to create institutions, which, in turn, lead to the development of other derived needs. How? I cannot find an explanation. But, unless I have totally misread the book, its author is satisfied that he does explain the development of culture by reference to his axiomatic needs.

I could ask, With what justification does a scientist who is supposed to keep to empirical subject matter lay down material "axioms"? but I will turn to another question. This can be broached by observing that the functionalist approach implicitly posits an infra-social individual whose organic needs are transformed into cultural necessities and imperatives and that this is tantamount to asserting that they are transformed into the world of values which constitute him a person. But the concept of the infra-social individual is ambiguous, and either of the two meanings which we can distinguish in it offers difficulties which render it useless as an explanatory category. The infra-social individual may be conceived either as (1) an analytic isolate or as (2) an actual atomic component which in combination with other components of the same kind makes up society.

Let us first consider him as an analytic isolate. This is not a meaning which seems to have been in Malinowski's mind when he thought of the human animal which is endowed with basic needs; but it has to be examined, nevertheless, because it is one of the meanings which can be attached to the ambiguous notion of the infra-social individual implicitly assumed by his explanation. Thus conceived, he need not have existed temporally prior to the society of which he is a member; rather is he an a-temporal component of his society. This means that the needs now fulfilled by a society are not traced to a *temporally prior* biological or psychological need actually existing before the constitution of society. Rather, the needs are analogous to the elements isolated in a work of art by a discerning critic who seeks to explain its structure. Prior to their informing the work of art, these elements were not what they became after their informing it, and thus we come to think of them as mere data of experience. The work of art, then, may not be exhaustively accounted for in terms of these elements only, because the genetic process calls for powers and faculties possessed by the artist prior to his creative act and for the creative transformation of the elements in the artist's mind. Were this the way in which the functionalist conceives the infra-social individual, he could say that he finds in society diverse institutions and that, when he looks into them, he finds that the individual is interrelated to these institutions in such a way as to manifest actual needs which the institutions are more or less able to satisfy. As the institutions change, the needs change, and vice versa. But which of the two terms of the relational complex we take as primary is a purely relative matter, and our selection of either cannot prejudge the genetic or historical problem, since the choice depends on the exigencies of analysis. On this interpretation no temporal priority can be asserted. This is too simple, however, since we have to take into account the fact of discrepancy between needs and institutions. When the institutions outlast the need, there is no difficulty, since the fact can be explained, at least to some extent, by reference to the interests which the institution vests in those who serve it: the vested interests of its functionaries keep the institution from dying long after it ceases to be of genuine use in meeting the needs of a society.

The emergence of new institutions within an already constituted society causes a radical difficulty because we cannot recognize the phenomenon and, at the same time, interpret the infra-social individual as an analytic isolate but are now forced to interpret him as an actual atomic component. This seems to be the way in which Malinowski conceives of him sometimes when he discusses the role that needs play in his functionalist approach. But this manner of conceiving the infra-social individual runs into two difficulties, either one of which is fatal. The first objection is that the psychologist would no more recognize the validity of Malinowski's axiomatic needs than he would accept today an attempt to revive the long lists of "instincts" with which psychologists used to endow man a generation or so ago. Thus Malinowski tells us, as we saw, that belief in immortality is related, perhaps, to some deep biological craving of the organism. It may be, but I do not believe that we could find a reputable psychologist who would take seriously such a craving, whether deep or shallow. The second objection is methodological, and it is equally fatal, since the manner of explanation involves the reification of the result as process and its employment as explanatory cause. In short, it is tantamount to explaining the power of opium by its dormitive qualities. A third objection may be added to these two, which naturalistic scientists certainly take very seriously, namely, that it suggests a thoroughly teleological conception of psychology. This is for me no objection but, on the contrary, the only good feature of the functionalist hypothesis, since it strengthens the conviction that it is impossible to attempt a serious explanation of distinctly human phenomena without falling back on concealed teleological assumptions.

The upshot of these considerations is that we are utterly in the dark about the way traversed and the factors used by man in order to become a person. The basis for our belief in social evolution is, then, pure faith. And, if this is the case, our belief in naturalism lacks inductive evidence at the point where it claims to have it and where it most needs it. Men who believe that the only way to obtain knowledge is through scientific method should hold an attitude of rigorous agnosticism in regard to how and when man, as we know him, came about. *Biological evolution*, I have said, I do not put into question here, since what we are talking about is the genesis of those dimensions which transform the infra-social animal into the person. I mention biological evolution only to suggest that the reigning scientific orthodoxy maintains itself by ignoring difficulties. The principle of continuity cannot be invoked at this point, since what is at issue is precisely this principle. If naturalistic philosophers admitted this much, with the candor which their commitment to scientific method demands of them, they would have confessed the breakdown of their faith and would have fallen back on agnosticism, as Ernest Nagel honestly does in respect to the origin of language. But, of course, agnosticism is not compatible with naturalism, and Mr. Nagel should choose one or the other.[9] Mrs. Langer, who is a naturalist with a difference, sees clearly her difficulty, but apparently the difference is not enough to allow her to rid herself of her sustaining faith:

"What causes this tremendous organization of substances [which constitute man] is one of the things the tremendous organisms do not know; but with their organization, suffering and impulse and awareness arise. . . .

"Now this is a mere declaration of faith, preliminary to a confession of heresy. The heresy is this: that I believe there is a primary need in man, which other creatures probably do not have, and which actuates all his apparently unzoological aims, his wistful fancies, his consciousness of value, his utterly impractical enthusiasms, and his awareness of a 'Beyond' filled with holiness."[10]

A heretical naturalism which is frankly a faith and which admits the possibility of discontinuity is hardly kosher and holds off agnosticism by sheer Tertullian assertion: "Darwin, we do believe, help us in our disbelief." Naturalism fails when, on the precise questions on which it pretends to be able to throw scientific light, it tells us that it has no light to throw but that the light is coming.

Man as a moral agent, then, is constituted by the values he acknowledges—which is to say, by a hierarchical organization of values at the base of which are to be found those values that he espouses and, above these, those he recognizes, the whole organized hierarchically into a loose system of acknowledged values. Naturalistic moral philosophies make their first radical error when they conceive man solely in terms of abstract psychic powers, faculties, and endowments. They make their second, no less serious, error when they conceive those powers reductionistically, led by the dogmatic insistence that knowledge can be achieved only through physicalist methods. The first error does not appear to have been much noticed, and, although the second has not passed unperceived, the criticism to which it has been subjected seems to have had little effect in halting the trend among naturalists. The reasons for this failure, I dare say, are not philosophic but sociological. Those committing the first error fail to grasp the fact that an organism endowed with psychic powers is an ideal isolate and only one of the components of the moral animal which is man. Man is *moral-man-in-culture*. He is more, for he is also religious-, and philosophic-, and artistic-, and scientific-man-in-culture, but for the moral philosopher he can be no less than moral-man-in-culture. If the philosopher conceives of man abstractly, he cannot discover the source of moral authority and the ground of moral decisions.

While the values which constitute the personality may be said to be organized into a hierarchical system, the organization is never perfect, the order of rank never well defined, and there are always values of which it is not easy to say whether they belong distinctly to the system or not.[11] A "normal" personality is fairly well unified; but this is a definition, since what is meant by "normal" is precisely the fact that it is fairly well unified. But, since a personality has a temporal dimension and is capable of growth, perhaps through the larger part of its career, the unity that the person can achieve is at best only a dynamic unity; as a result, it can be grasped in the concrete only at a given moment, and one has always the difficult problem of deciding, at least practically, what values constitute it permanently and what are ephemeral accretions. But, even putting this difficulty aside, it seems clear to observation that the unity of the moral personality is purely relative and is discoverable, if at all, only from a macroscopic point of view; close scrutiny reveals cracks separating more or less important subunits which seem to enjoy a certain degree of autonomy. Nor is this all. Another great difficulty in our efforts to grasp the structure of the person arises from the fact that it is not all open to introspection, much less to behavioral observation. How much of the self is submerged and how much is manifest at the level of the conscious, reflectively, and how much expressed in action, I do not believe is precisely known. Today we have to reckon with the "unconscious," nor can we dispose of it on the simplistic methodological or so-called "logical" grounds on which I once heard Morris Cohen in a lecture dispose of it. "The notion of unconscious ideas," he retorted triumphantly to a student's question, "is a contradiction in terms." Nor is it possible to dispose of introspection on the behavioristic grounds of Dewey and his disciples, who argue that what is not amenable to external observation cannot be admitted into science. If the method of positive science cannot acknowledge the category of the unconscious and the data of introspection, so much the worse for positive science.

Another aspect of the personality is what I shall call its "telic aspect." I do not mean the perfectly obvious and undeniable fact that persons are capable of purposive behavior. However it is explained, the fact remains that men are endowed with foresight and consciously project goals into the future toward which they direct their activity. We can take for granted that some of this behavior can be explained mechanistically. I cannot convince myself, however, that purposive behavior at the creative level can be explained mechanistically. Benbow Ritchie, a disciple of Tolman, has given an explanation of artistic creation which needs to be read to realize how superficial such explanations can be, how much they are forced to leave out of account in order to be able to order the data they do accept into some sort of plausible hypothesis. Krikorian has tried to explain the creative activity under the mechanistically conceived notion of "problem-solving." In both these attempts (and in similar ones) the genuine novelty which constitutes the creative addition is virtually denied, and what we have, formally, is an appeal to a sophisticated Hobbesian theory of creativity.[12] What I mean by the "telic aspect" of the person, rather, is that, considered from the vantage point from which we must view the person, we see an incomplete axiological whole which tends to complete itself teleologically. If this is the case, it is advisable, in spite of its inherent difficulty, to face as best we can the problem of teleology.

Taken seriously, the concept of teleology gives rise to two distinct problems, the scientific and the metaphysical. In the sciences the problem arises first at the biological level, for below it there is no question as to the desirability of excluding it. The first difficulty we run into is that the term is usually employed in a shallow sense by those who are opposed to the conception. I recently heard a biologist arguing that "there is no pull from the future." Now with our ordinary conception of time, the idea of a pull from the future is silly, and neither Aristotle nor Driesch ever meant by "entelechy" anything so silly. It should be made clear in passing, however, that there is nothing inconceivable about pulls from the future unless we define "time" in such a manner as to make the notion of a pull from the future inconceivable and contradictory. But it can be argued (although I would not trust myself with the defense of a point that requires encyclopedic knowledge) that Driesch's "vitalism" is not the strongest representative of "teleology" today.

The question of teleology arises when organic "form" makes its appearance. Given the biological organism, a biologist can push his inquiry as far as he wishes exclusively along lines of efficient causality as this category is understood today in the laboratory, and he will not require teleology in his explanation. Nevertheless, the question of the "form" or "type" of the organism arises inevitably when we inquire with thoroughness into the origin of the organism's functions and not into the physicochemical conditions of the organism's activity. Thus the concept of "type" or "form" is the ignored fulcrum of the biologist, which he can safely ignore or leave unanalyzed so long as his interest is in efficient causality, in the conditions of maintenance of living processes. In a practical way he knows what an organism is, in that he has objective criteria which enable him to pick out organisms from a random collection of objects both organic and inorganic. And if his scientific objective is to learn what he can of the conditions which enable the organism to behave organically—to maintain itself, to repair itself, to reproduce itself, and the like—a nonteleological inquiry suffices to give him the answers he seeks. This is all that the biologist may be interested in, but it certainly does not exhaust the problems that the existence of organisms gives rise to. Whether these other problems are "scientific" or "philosophic" is a delicate question; all that needs to be insisted on here is that these other problems are genuine problems.

The notion of organic function presupposes in some sense the concept of "type" or "form" to which the functions of the components of the organism must be referred to explain their specific activity; and the questions which the teleologist claims have not been answered by the Darwinian tradition have to do with the origin of these types or forms and their relation to the components of the organism whose functioning brings them into existence. Succinctly put, as I understand the problem, the teleologist argues that the notion of an "organism" entails functions of its component organs, controlled by the type or form, and that explanations carried on along lines of efficient causality do not preclude or obviate, however far they may be carried, the problems which arise when we ask about the relation of the component organs to the organism. It goes without saying that it is not possible to set a priori limits to analysis in terms of efficient causes alone. Biochemistry tells us what the physical conditions of life are, and knowledge along those lines enables us to predict the course of life's processes. But when we go beyond these questions and ask about the origins of the forms, the way in which the organism arose, the struggle for existence and survival may account for their maintenance, once constituted, but does not account for their genesis. What we are given as answers are such question-begging terms as "emerge" and "levels of integration." But these notions can hardly be called "explanations" of what appears or emerges when life begins; for here is a type or form controlling the activities of organs that presuppose the type in order to function as they do. Evolutionism may in the future solve this problem. All that needs to be argued is that, as yet, the problems of teleology have not been eliminated from a thorough and comprehensive inquiry of the organism.

It is not merely among biologists that one encounters a deep-seated prejudice against teleology. One also encounters it among comparatively objective students of man, who quite candidly are prepared to go to any lengths to avoid being suspected of the employment of teleological habits of thought. For instance, when Kluckhohn and Murray define personality, they admit that it has several "functions";[13] but the authors tell us that, to avoid suspicion of teleologism, they propose to use terms like "need," "drive," or "vectorial force" in the interpretation of the "functions of personality." Have they thus avoided teleologism? What they seem to have done is to have substituted terms in which the notion of final cause is decently concealed but not absent for terms in which it is clearly visible. A "need" or a "drive" is not a blind lack which any object will satisfy but a structured lack addressed toward a *determinate class of objects*. The notion finds its meaning by reference to an ideal whole, made up of the present incomplete state of affairs and of something not present, which, together with the present state, defines the whole. The incomplete state is conceivable only in terms of that class of objects which it lacks. Otherwise the need would be utterly blind and so utterly indeterminate that any object whatsoever could satisfy it. But *that* kind of state is not a need. A grocery bag which can be filled by anything small enough to go into it cannot be said to have a need for what is put into it. Only a certain class of things will complete the incomplete state, and it is only in such cases that we can speak of a "need." If I am hungry, the finding of a fountain pen on my plate will not satisfy the need, although lobster, bananas, oysters, beans, horse meat, snails, or eels will. The search for satisfaction may be planned or random, and the finding of a thing which will satisfy the need may be utterly accidental. What makes a thing capable of satisfying a need is not the manner in which the former comes within the reach of a thing in an incomplete state and is incorporated; rather, it is the manner in which, upon incorporation, the completing thing is able to establish a relationship that gives the incomplete state and the completing thing a determinate and interrelated wholeness. The result is that the newly completed thing is capable of performing activities which were impossible before completion and which cannot be conceived as a merely random new state of affairs. At any stage, then, "need" or "drive" presupposes structure, so that a purely nominalistic empiricism, such as is widely employed today in scientific analysis, finds itself helpless before the phenomena involved in organic processes if one asks for an explanation of them as wholes and not merely of the mechanistically discernible conditions that keep them going.

Whether or not the organic structure, while real, is itself a product of chance, depends again on whether a purely mechanistic analysis can be applied to it to account for its development or whether it requires the same kind of explanation we have just insisted on for "drive" or "need." If the latter is the case, teleology has been pushed back another step. But I do not see how the highly *organized* processes involved at the level of the psyche can be traced back to random activities, when the discovery and recognition of value as value are essential to set them going. Much of the subject matter which Kluckhohn and Murray studied under the heading of "personality" involves activities which are value-oriented and which therefore cannot be conceived as random. The personality is an integration of values, and its growth is a growth in the values which men recognize and from which they select some for espousal. Man, as a person, seeks to complete himself axiologically. The activity by which he seeks to achieve his completion enables the person to add values to himself which are congruous with those which already constitute him. But the activity by which values are added is not mechanical, and "congruence" is not a simple criterion when employed in the choice of those values which will be espoused by the person. Additions are accepted by the person not merely because they "fit" the extant organization but even when they do not apparently fit or when there is no question of fitting at all; they are accepted for some obscure reason because the added value or values obey a telic determination of an ideal of the person which somehow seeks to actualize itself. Reflective consciousness may envisage this ideal in only the vaguest and most incomplete way. The ideal consists of a complex of values which is perhaps never more than partly realized. It need not be fully envisaged and, indeed, at first, like Socrates' voice, often functions merely as an agency of rejection which excludes values which, but for its veto, would seem worthy of incorporation. The denial of this telic aspect commits mechanists to an assumption no less telic in nature, since it forces upon them the presupposition that the goal toward which persons work in their self-development is the projection of pre-existing needs, innate and potential, that constitute the values after some such manner as is assumed by the interest theory.

Of course, I do not mean by the term "telic" anything which can be interpreted mechanistically, in the way in which Pepper interprets it, or in the way in which Hofstadter interprets teleology, following Ralph Barton Perry. I mean that the relevant data demand for their complete explanation the positing of a final, as well as an efficient and a material, cause. Hofstadter's paper represents a noteworthy effort "to find a place for objective teleology within empirical science."[14] He tries to explain conscious purposiveness in an agent as viewed not from within but from without. What I am saying is that, besides that aspect of the agent's growth which can be accounted for by the envisagement of ends toward which the agent consciously addresses his activity, his development is purposive. The person's aversions, predispositions, predilections, inclinations, and attitudes, instinctive no less than acquired and unconscious no less than conscious, taken singly and taken collectively, have a direction toward an ideal completion. The movement toward a goal is subjectively evinced to the person by the discovery, accidental though it may be, of an object of which, verbalizing the relationship, one says, "This, indeed, after all this time, is what I now see I ought to have," or "This is what fulfils." The telic aspect of the person is evinced objectively by phenomena such as conversion, moral self-repudiation, and self-discovery. It is said of Van Gogh that one day, when he was a preacher in the miserable Belgian district of the Borinage, he accidentally began to draw a miner and that the discovery of what he did was a revelation to him of what he was destined for. I believe that I know what it must have been like, suddenly finding himself face to face with what he was. Here was the shape of a personality revealed, and what remained to do was to fulfil it. If we say that this can be explained by appealing to a need or an interest which, until then, lay submerged within Van Gogh, we have, in order to remain good mechanists, gone from one kind of telic explanation to another, since innate potentiality and latent powers are clearly telic in nature.

The facts on which this teleological interpretation is based are acknowledged as facts when one forces attention upon them, but the prejudice against final causes is still so strong and irrational and the misunderstandings as to what teleology involves so pervasive and thoughtless that it is hopeless to bring the question up for serious philosophic discussion among naturalists. In the Foreword to a recent collection of essays on materialism the editors dismiss the concept of teleology in the following manner: "General teleology is therefore excluded. The modern materialist foregoes the comfort, unless it be in poetic reverie, of imagining that the order of nature is attuned to his purposes, or endowed with sensitivity and beneficence. Such longings have yielded myths in all ages, but are scarcely appropriate for a scientific era like our own."[15] Let us note that the materialist does not reject all metaphysical longings, since a few lines below this statement we are assured that "materialism does not doubt the possibility of satisfying man's need for a comprehensive picture of the universe." If the need for a comprehensive picture is valid and ought to be satisfied, more than arrogance is required to show that the need for an explanation of the order of the world is not valid and ought not to be satisfied. At this point a number of queries and objections arise to which the writers do not give us the answer. It is advisable to take some of them up.

Let us first parenthetically observe that a great disservice is done to philosophy by the polemical technique of psychoanalyzing away the opposition. The editors of the book from which I have quoted are serious philosophers, and most of their contributors are also. They should have left the technique of imputing motives to the editors and contributors of *Partisan Review*, who liquidate to their own satisfaction intellectual currents they do not like by psychoanalyzing them away under the imputation of "failure of nerve." To call a serious philosophic conception a "longing" is to suggest that it is a mere subjective and vague demand, as contrasted with the "needs" of mature "scientific" minds, and the editors are thus able to gain an easy victory. But in philosophy, at least, easy victories are not worth winning. At its shabbiest, "teleology" probably represents very little more than a longing for a beneficent universe; but in men like Plato, Aristotle, and Leibniz, whatever purely psychological function it may fulfil, it is also a hypothesis grounded on objective argument and claiming objective truth.

The editors of *Philosophy for the Future*, by their failure to qualify and modulate, give the impression that the teleologist is a kind of philosophic Christian Scientist, asserting the unqualified benevolence of the universe. They probably know some who are; but, since they are professional philosophers, they must also know many who are not—philosophers and scientists ancient, modern, and contemporary, who are hard-boiled thinkers but nevertheless see in what they take to be the rational structure of the universe a philosophical problem of the first magnitude. I imagine the majority of men know that the beneficence of the world is unstable, partial, and always, it would seem, ambivalent; but that the order of nature is indeed in part attuned to man's purposes is neither a "longing" nor a hypothesis but, so to speak, a fact of common sense. And the problem is not to assert this patent fact but to gain some insight into its ground. It is at this point that the split occurs between opponents and defenders of teleology. The former take the order of the universe as they find it and, on diverse philosophic grounds, assert that all they need to do is to plot that order correctly so that they may adapt themselves to it. But they take this position, when they are serious philosophers, on the grounds which they state and which constitute an argument, nor do they dismiss with contumely the alternative view.

Thus, whether or not teleology constitutes a philosophic problem cannot be settled by psychoanalyzing away the opposition. Hume took the problem seriously enough to give it his most concentrated attention, nor can anyone say he found it simple. Again, whether the teleologist gains comfort from his analysis or anguish or despair cannot be deduced from the fact that he "longs" for cosmic order; for an answer to that question we usually lack adequate biographical information. The result of belief in teleology is sometimes the sort of cheap Pelagianism which is such a pervasive feature of our intellectual climate and probably of most historical periods. Or it may lead to Manichaeism, since the universe exhibits both good and evil, or to Kierkegaard's anguish. Whatever the result, there is more to teleology than the comfort which it allegedly brings, and that more is what the serious philosopher has to look into.

It would also seem that the writers of the quotation do a serious disservice to philosophy by rejecting teleology on the criterion that it is scarcely appropriate to our age. Do they mean seriously to maintain that they accept or reject philosophic truths on the basis of their "appropriateness"? But they forgot to inform us how we are to decide whether a view is "appropriate" or not to a notion so vague and incoherent as "our age."

I have argued that we cannot, on a priori grounds, decide how far explanation in terms of efficient cause alone—which is what mechanism boils down to—can be carried. But, on the other hand, neither at the biological nor at the psychological level can the notion of "organism" be accounted for genetically in a mechanistic way. But it should be clear that *the formulations of positive science are not here under attack. Nowhere in this essay are they under attack.* They remain beyond the reach of philosophic criticism, since they are systematic abstractive processes, ontologically unprejudiced, directed to the ends of predictive formulations. They disregard the factors which are part of the situation within which a more comprehensive organization, such as the philosophic, is achieved. What is under attack is the naïve assumption that because, for their purposes, the positive sciences dispense with teleological processes these processes do not form part of the furniture of the universe. Positive science has achieved its triumphs by limiting itself rigorously to the discovery of invariant relations found implicit in the data of experience. In other words, it searches exclusively for efficient causes. But the activity of science is rigorously controlled by its aims and the meaning and scope of its results relative to these aims, and therefore science cannot furnish ground for denying reality to what it disregards. That would be as valid as if a recruiting officer, who is exclusively interested in the military fitness of the volunteer and therefore indifferent to his aesthetic opinions, were to deny that men have aesthetic opinions, since, in his examination of volunteers, he has never come across them. If he did come across them, he would not be minding his job and would be lowering the efficiency of the army.

An adequate understanding of the manifestations of personality involves the grouping of the data, not for predictive purposes, but for the end of comprehending the total process as defined by ideal goals. This does not mean assuming, as we have said, a "pull" from the future; but it does involve some sort of notion like "entelechy," which is to say, a notion of structural preformations inherent in the incomplete thing, such that the thing is endowed at an earlier stage of its development with the power of completion along certain lines which are determinate within limits. "Instincts" do not involve pulls from the future, but they do involve pushes from the past toward specific complex goals. They are genuinely telic, in that any process which is called "instinctive" involves preformations addressed to generically determinate goals not yet present but to be realized. And in this sense life and psyche seem to be, and the moral life is through and through, telic.

I asserted above that life and even psychic processes can, within certain limited ranges, be examined for their invariant relations according to the methods of positive science, which forbid the inclusion of telic terms in their formulations. It must also be pointed out that this way of explanation has not produced any results whatsoever when it is applied to moral philosophy conceived as a practical science; the reason is that morality is nothing unless it is activity addressed to ideal goals which axiologically measure progress made toward them. The word "potential" does not camouflage telic factors well enough. The notion of "potentiality" refers to preformations which, within limits and under determinate circumstances, will develop along determinate lines to complete an organic whole. The acorn is potentially an oak, and reference to an end is involved. If Kluckhohn and Murray do not mean to use the word in some such sense, in what sense do they use it? They do not tell us.

The notion of teleology is thus not precluded by the nontelic inquiry of positive science but involves a different kind of understanding from that in which the positive scientist is interested. Nor does it involve "ends," as sometimes naïvely interpreted, i.e., the end of grass is to be eaten by cattle and of cattle to serve as food for man. Teleology has been redefined by antimechanistic biologists who today use the concept to refer to the fact that organisms have powers of self-maintenance, recuperation, and reproduction which are empirically discoverable. These powers maintain the ordered processes of the organism. Such maintenance involves activities whose fruition from the beginning of the species is measured by the effect that these activities—without which the organism could not have survived at all—have on complex organic wholes. The multiplicity of these activities, the narrow limits within which their success is measured, the way in which success is defined by a whole without which the complex activity could not have come about and which itself presupposes the activity—it is the interrelation of these complex factors that precludes "chance" as an explanation. Given the organism as already functioning, the search for causal processes of a strictly mechanistic nature can be undertaken. But not until a meticulous, purely causal account of organisms, starting with purely physical terms, is actually available (and not merely promised as around the corner) can mechanists argue with any plausibility that in biology the telic notions can utterly be dispensed with. Teleology is not a principle of explanation, if by "explanation" be meant the formulation of invariant relations which the positive scientist seeks, but it is a principle of intelligibility. Whatever we *call* it, it is involved in intellectual activity outside the ranges controlled by the aims and the techniques of positive science.

All sorts of metaphysical abysses open around us at this point: the question, for instance, as to whether the formal structures thus found have ontic status; and as to whether they are best understood as the result of design; and, if so, whether—and how—they are analogous to human productive processes; and perhaps a question which is logically prior to all these, namely, what can be meant by seeking to understand structure altogether. But, obviously, a universe in which there exist structures that exhibit traits which call for notions such as "potentiality" and "telic processes" is not a random universe in any ordinary sense of this word. A German biologist—Bleuler, unless I am mistaken—is said to have calculated that the probability that the internal structure of the eye could have a chance origin is approximately $1:10^{42}$. If we consider the human body and the organs which together co-operate toward its maintenance and self-regulation, the chances are enormously against its being a random product in any usual sense of the term. I do not believe that from such arguments we can get to the "God" of theism, as by a simple and direct route. The teleological argument, by disposing of the possibility of mechanism, merely opens the gate for analogical speculations—for metaphysics, in other words, in one of

its most serious endeavors. "Teleology" is a term which calls attention to the fact that the phenomena under explanation involve structures such that earlier stages of the development refer to later and
become intelligible by reference to those later stages, to whose appearance they contribute as parts to wholes. "Instinct" involves a
teleological process, since activities called "instinctive," although
not conscious, find their completion in later activities, without reference to which they remain unintelligible.

If the argument I have put forth holds, it is impossible for anyone
who has respect for the conventional meanings of words to equate,
without previous careful analytic specification of his decision to use
terms contrary to accepted custom, the terms "need" and "drive"
as synonymous with the term "vectorial force." In the last term,
reference to a predetermined object is out of the question, for a vectorial force is merely a force having a magnitude and a direction and
not involving a determinate class of objects which are its goals or its
need-fulfilling objects.

This discussion indicates the error involved in the effort to define
"personality"—even at the physiopsychological level at which
Kluckhohn and Murray conceive it—without clear acceptance of
its telic nature. When the term is used as it is used in this essay, to
point to an organization of values which function as ideals toward
which the person moves, the impossibility of leaving the telic dimension out of account is much more obvious.

The personality has telic unity, but it also has open connections
with the world, or channels of intake and outlet, and this fact makes
its borders with the world theoretically indeterminate. Human
beings are moral persons, unified integrations of values which inform psychic powers; but even above the physiological level it is
not possible to define, in advance of the specific data in each case,
where the individual begins and where the ambient world ends.

CHAPTER XIII

THE RESOLUTION OF A MORAL
PERPLEXITY. II

AT THE core of the system of acknowledged values constituting a person is to be found a constellation which is sustained by active interests. These I call "espoused" values. From history and from anthropology we know (as we saw in chap. iv) that the values men espouse and even those they recognize are a relatively small number as compared with those from which they could choose. We also know that among the espoused values men tend to include a number which are not subtended by biological needs and which, arranged according to different orders of rank in their various systems, are present in all societies wherever and whenever flourishing. These values, espoused individually by the members of a society, are not necessarily espoused by the society collectively. It is a man's espoused values which define the direction of his moral activity. Among them we usually find friendship, pride, courage, loyalty, security, and those values which can, without trouble, be related to man's biological needs. In the *Nicomachean Ethics*, Aristotle studies friendship, courage, temperance; virtues concerned with money, with honor, and with anger; the virtues of social intercourse and justice; and the intellectual virtues. Each one of these "virtues" involves a value, and, although in the concrete they are interpreted differently by every human group because of the varieties of institutionalized expression they are permitted and although in various cultural patterns they are therefore given different ratings, they are widely recognized human values. The fact that they do not exhaust the human capacity points to the limitations of Aristotle's experience—the Greek world with its splendid pagan virtues and its tremendous shortcomings—but roughly they draw the range of human capacity at the purely temporal level. Contemporary anthropologists would make up what would seem on the surface to be a

212

totally different catalogue. And no doubt there would be additions
to the list and considerable differences in the places which these
values would have in the opinion of those who study them. The
historian of medieval Europe or of India would notice that some values which his data would lead him to place as pre-eminent are con-
spicuously ignored by Aristotle and that modern apostles of scientifistic humanism would place some of the values of medieval
society under the heading of pathology. Nevertheless, when we
make allowance for the limitations of data, the prejudices of the
observers, and the complexity and vagueness of the subject, we are
still left with the remarkable fact that the values men espouse,
formally considered, are less varied than certain relativistic doctrines would lead us to believe.

Among the values which human groups seem to select, as already
suggested, from among the totality of possible values and which
they organize and put at the core of their world, we find compatibilities and clashes which are resolved or mediated in many ways.
These values—which I call "espoused" values—are secured and
maintained through those fantastically elaborate constructions
which are man's institutions. To the values discovered and resting
on specific biological and, if there be any, on psychological needs
must be added others which cannot be traced to any such needs discoverable in the individual considered as a biopsychological organism but which are essential to human societies. It is of capital importance to realize that the fact that men rigorously limit the values
included in a culture makes the use of the category "the universally
human" or "generic man" an extremely vague one. The notion of a
human nature—as ideal—which somehow integrates all values now
found only restrictively embodied in various human societies can
be very misleading. On the other hand, one occasionally encounters
among cultural anthropologists a prejudice against universal categories. If this prejudice were taken seriously, they would have to
desist from their inquiries: if zoölogists can generalize in spite of
the uniqueness of their specimens, it becomes difficult to understand
why anthropologists cannot.

The nineteenth century, with its obsession with biological evolution, tended to believe that the core of espoused values consisted of
those which maintain physical survival, and its moral philosophers

undertook the impossible task of demonstrating that the "higher" values could be explained by an elaboration and "evolution" of these basic ones. But whether or not these higher values can be explained by reference to the biological ones is, for our purposes, a trivial problem. The difference between that scientific abstraction, the human animal, and the basic category of the moral philosopher, the person, is the system of values which the person acknowledges and which constitutes him; and the problem of survival as human is precisely the problem of maintenance, against destructive odds, of a value system; that is, all man's values as constitutive of a hierarchical system have, by definition, a survival function, since their disappearance means his destruction.

Thus viewed, the problem of self-sacrifice, which is so difficult for the naturalists, is no problem at all for us. In preferring death to the surrender of his values, a man is merely asserting the supremacy of that in him which constitutes his essence over that in him—his body—which is a mere means or vehicle which makes possible the temporal continuance of his essence during a historical span. This is not to deny that the core of the espoused value system which constitutes the personality sometimes consists almost exclusively of the values of physical survival, of hedonic gratification, and of mere animal existence. Nor is it to deny that some human animals can only with difficulty and charity be said to achieve the human status. The personality consists of values, but, if the person consisted only of the values he espouses, some personalities would be rather low in the human scale. The topic is best left for Part III, where I shall try to show that man possesses an intrinsic worth beyond what results from the fact that he is a carrier of value, a worth which gives his person an absolute primacy.

The values that are organized into systems by groups of men *seem* to have an intrinsic order of rank which is inherent in them, independently of the varieties of organizations to which men subject them. Thus courage and temperance and the values concerned with honor would seem to be "higher," more worthy, more truly values, than those concerned with money. And justice seems to be above all these. But dogmatism on this subject ill becomes the inquiring philosopher, since the difficulties in his way are insuperable: one can never be sure to what extent one's judgment about the order of rank which seems inherently to organize values hierarchically is prejudiced by one's own espousals—which is to say, by the manner in which the self selects values with the end of constituting the person. A broad human survey, however, leaves one with the conviction—extremely difficult to establish against the skeptic's challenge—that, for instance, the heroism displayed by men in the defense of their values and "Christian" love—to call it by its local name—are higher than those amiable values enthroned by the eighteenth century and which excluded "enthusiasm."

It is to the intrinsic and objective order of rank that men appeal when for any reason they condemn the hierarchy of values acknowledged by the society of which they are members. The structure thus appealed to, against which existing iniquities are measured, is an ideal and need not be fully known. The order of rank is known to some extent, since it is at least known as imperfectly embodied in the acknowledged values, but our knowledge of it can never be perfect. Nevertheless, any human conflict that transcends mere legality is decided, if it is decided morally, by reference to this ranking. This is possible because the search to which the perplexity gives rise leads to an effort to grasp more clearly the objective hierarchy of values as envisaged from the standpoint of circumstances of which the perplexity is part. How actually this is done is something which we shall see more fully below. Here it is enough to say that it is done through the dialectical process by means of which claims are clarified and the root of the conflict brought to light. After that, men must depend on one another's good will. A proposed resolution of a moral perplexity is an effort to formulate more adequately than was done previously the correct order of objective values. Whether the formulation is or is not valid has to be decided dialectically by giving and receiving answers in friendly intercourse. This is a process which is extremely inefficient and which tends to break down with appalling ease; but it is the only one we have. The hierarchy of values, as ideal, subsists independently of its formulation and, like the discovery of the laws of nature, is subject to error. There is, however, this difference, that interests and passions interfere with our grasp of the structure of physical nature considerably less, if at all, than they do with our knowledge of the order of rank among values. The tensions created by the discrepancy between our limited understanding of the intrinsic order of rank which values have and what we take to be that order are of central importance both to the moral philosopher and to the practical man, since it is these tensions that furnish the energy which leads us in our moral searches.

The important thing at this point, however, is to realize that our partial ignorance of the true order of rank among values is no ground for moral cynicism or subjectivistic relativism. All that is required for the possible resolution of conflicts along moral lines is the acceptance of what need be only an assumption at the practical level, namely, that the dialectical effort will disclose a basis of obligation which can be universally apprehended and which is constituted by an objective order of rank among values having ontic status. It is either this or a wilful stepping-down from our human condition. There is no other means. If this is not enough, moral appeals are indeed what positivists so cynically tell us that they are: efforts to dupe us into accepting the arbitrary wilfulness of our fellows and, on our part, efforts to make others accept the irrationality of our will. On the subject of the ontic hierarchy of value, therefore, it is not advisable to detain ourselves any longer. Some philosophers have undertaken to give what they take to be a correct account of the objective order of values. Here I must content myself with positing that, in spite of the difficulties which one encounters when one tries to formulate a hierarchy of values as they exist independently of human actualization, such a hierarchy does, in fact, exist. I believe that the order of rank found among values is not one in which all values can be arranged without confusion but in which classes of values—corresponding to ontological distinctions in the components of man—can be so arranged. Thus we may not be able to say that courage, without qualification and considered by itself, is higher or lower than saintliness, but we are able to say that courage and saintliness and wisdom are higher than the values which a technological civilization pursues, those which contribute to bodily comfort.

This essay would perhaps be a better work if this question were fully aired, but I beg to be allowed to advance an extenuation of my failure to do so. I cannot allege the difficulty of the problem because, if an important problem in a discipline is too difficult for a writer, he should not meddle with that discipline at all; but I can legitimately advance the fact that in this essay the question as to the existence and nature of the objective hierarchy need not be settled in order to resolve the problems which will be discussed. The resolution of a moral perplexity, the ground of moral authority, and the justification of moral judgments are problems for the solution of which we must posit the objectivity of values. But, since we cannot appeal to a hierarchy of value as we appeal to the weights and measures in the Bureau of Standards, since these problems can, in the end, be discussed only dialectically—can be argued only by the Socratic method—the specification of that hierarchy is not needed. This conclusion condemns the results of moral deliberation to remain always tentative. I see no virtue in proposing my own conception of an axiological order of rank which would be disputed by each and every reader and which, if settled at all, can be settled only as respects specific issues in prolonged and laborious discourse. *The order of rank is assumed.* Its discovery is actually the task undertaken when a judgment of value is challenged and defended and a conflict resolved. An order of rank of values independent of their acknowledgment by men-in-culture must exist, but its determination seems to be, at best, a vague enterprise because the values men know are values-in-culture.

The hierarchy which constitutes a man's value system can be formally analyzed into the values one *espouses* and the values one *recognizes.* Unfortunately, the nature of existence is such that espousal of some values involves denial or positive rejection of others, and recognition involves a disregard which is not always free of antagonism toward certain other possible values. *Espoused values* are those actively incorporated, positively pursued, and positively assimilated; these, rather than those one merely recognizes, are constitutive of one's personality. Espoused values make up constellations more or less tightly integrated, and it is to them that one refers when one speaks about the "sense" of one's self, about one's "identity," and, at the moral level, about one's "worth." The self-respect or the worth that one attaches to one's self as a moral being, as a person, arises from the fact not only that one espouses values but that one is aware of the fact that the espousal in itself is a value or has value. *Recognized values* are those which one acknowledges as values but which one does not feel the necessity of actively incorporating into one's self, toward which one does not feel active interest. Both the espoused and the recognized values are *acknowledged values*, and these contrast with those to which one denies the character of value altogether, either because one considers them as disvalues or because one is at a loss as to why other moral beings should consider them as values.

I, as a student, espouse certain values; but, although I do not espouse certain other values, I recognize that they are espoused by other members of my society or of other societies which have come to my notice. However, toward certain values I take an attitude of summary condemnation: these are disvalues. Toward some, which I see others consider as values, I take a puzzled attitude, finding them in no sense to be values either positively or negatively. Reading about the conquest of North America, I readily recognize some of the values espoused by the Five Nations but am horrified by their cannibalism. I realize, however, that the realm of values is vastly greater than those I acknowledge, for not only do I see activities espoused by others in which they claim to find values and in which I do not find any, but even the little history I know dimly reveals to me in the past a vast array of values of which I am in no clear sense aware and which seems to suggest that many values not yet embodied in human activity will be discovered in the future if man survives his own destructiveness.

The values we acknowledge are discovered and appropriated, worked for, realized, or defended strongly or feebly because man is endowed with powers and capacities through which their discovery and realization are possible. These powers and capacities, taken together, constitute, as we have already noticed, his "psyche," the form of the body, that without which the human being could not become human, although by themselves they are not sufficient to turn an animal into a man. Other powers, seemingly lesser in scope, and lesser because of the meaner matter on which they can work to make experience, are enjoyed by the "lower" animals. These animals are properly called "lower" because, lacking our powers, they are forever kept from the discovery and realization of values, and it is their discovery and realization which constitute man's achievement and which define his destiny. The difference, however, is a moral difference and not merely a biological one. At the biological or purely scientific plane, "high" and "low" are purely descriptive, factual terms without the slightest trace of value connotation, and no animal is morally lower or higher than another. A man, then, contrary to what seems to be an old and widespread notion, is not human, not really a man, merely because his psyche is what it is but because the psyche can achieve some things—the discovery and realization of values and, through these, the fulfilment of a destiny.

The powers of the psyche have been analyzed phenomenally with considerable accuracy since the days of Socrates at least, although only recently have certain of its dimensions been brought within the range of close investigation. This change has come about not because men, prior to the end of the nineteenth century, were unaware of the phenomena revealed to us by depth psychology but because "psychology" as a science had until then, seemingly, almost entirely ignored certain of the psyche's dimensions, leaving them in the hands of poets and of priests. Even more recently a whole area of investigation into powers of the psyche which the reigning scientific orthodoxy still tries to ignore or seeks to discount has been opened up. I am not competent to judge the positive results which have already been made by these investigations, but some of the names of the men interested in these phenomena and the experimental techniques employed make it impossible to dismiss the interest as naïve or credulous or superstitious. So far, it would seem, enough has been discovered not to invalidate the results of behavioristic investigations but to point to the need for defining the limitations of the results of orthodox psychological research.[1]

The classic analysis distinguishes three chief functions of the self or psyche: intelligence, will, and feeling. To these is often added a fourth, the merely vegetative; but, since this is shared with all living things, it may be left out of consideration. These three, then, are powers or faculties or distinct capacities of the psyche or self, when we consider the self abstractly as independent of a world from which it cannot be separated without destroying it and when viewed without regard to the matter which these powers elaborate into experience. Because these three powers have been isolated and analyzed since the days of the Greeks, we need not enter into an analysis of them—an analysis which, in any case, could not be expected to do more than repeat what is already well known.[2] The moral philosopher need not deny the value of what psychologists have found out about the psyche, and he cannot but acknowledge that we have today a great deal of knowledge of the ways of the mind which Plato and Aristotle lacked; but not all this information is relevant to the moral inquiry, although some of it already used in these pages does force the moral philosopher to reconsider and correct his speculations.

We generally speak of the powers of the mind as if they could function independently of one another. Particularly in the case of the intelligence, we assume that it can normally function in isolation from the will and the affective processes of the psyche. But the effort to discover what the world is like when it is viewed from a standpoint from which all volitional and affective factors have been excluded involves the employment of complex laboratory techniques and procedures which have reached an adequate degree of perfection only since the days, let us say, of Copernicus and Galileo.[3] Outside the exact sciences, what we call "knowledge" is more or less relative to men of flesh and bones; it is relative to the full human complement of prejudices and values which those who seek it bring with them to their search. Common-sense knowledge is sought in order to be employed in behalf of these prejudices and values, and when we attempt to cut it off from its connections with the interests that gave it birth, all we do to it is to turn it into logomachy—into a dialectic of concepts in which meaningful signs are manipulated as if they had no meanings, no reference to the world in which we live; as if they were counters in a game of pure logic or pure mathematics.

On the other hand, in the exact physical sciences careful laboratory devices, exact measurement, controllable and repeatable processes, and attention to observable phenomena or to phenomena that can ultimately be traced to observable phenomena keep purely idiosyncratic determinants from coloring the results of observation. Nevertheless, the knowledge of the exact scientist is also relative in several senses: it is relative to the purposes that initiate the inquiry; relative to the theoretical framework within which the inquiry is carried on, which is, in turn, only relatively fixed; and, finally, relative to the generic human standpoint in terms of which only the results of the search of the scientist can claim validity. This means that the results are valid for all human beings as such and not merely for Russians or Americans or Patagonians or Communists or capitalists. But the results are bought at a price, and part of the price is the exclusion of vast areas of human experience from exact scientific knowability. Since we must know about these areas, however, if we cannot know them scientifically we naturally settle for less. The result is that outside the exact natural sciences what we call "knowledge" is a pretty messy product. Still, this is no reason for skepticism, since a degree of corrigibility can be achieved even in politics and in theology; but it is reason enough to invalidate without examination any claim to knowledge beyond the reach of rational criticism. All knowledge, whether scientific or not, is corrigible. And if the meaning of human destiny were the achievement of the best knowledge possible, irrespective of the nature and rank of the object known, the reasonable thing to do would be to join the ranks of the positivists. But not only the quality of the knowledge but also the kind of objects known are of importance for the orthodox tradition when it defines man's happiness in terms of knowledge. Positivism, which values exact scientific knowledge and nothing else, ends up by turning men into even worse-lopsided barbarians than they are without its help.

It is not irrelevant, while on this topic, to point out, on the other hand, that the fashion of borrowing the name and prestigious authority of science for cognitive activities that fall short of the precision and clarity and verifiability through controlled prediction of which science is capable is, as we say in Spanish, "counter-producing," which is to say that it produces results opposite to those intended. All it does is add error and dogmatism to the already vast stockpile which we have managed to accumulate through recorded history.

If the exact natural sciences are rigorously controlled by an initial selectivity of subject matter, as we have suggested they are, and if the results are relative to the procedures, categories, and objectives which produced them, the results cannot, of course, be congruous with the whole of "reality." This point has already been made, but I do not believe that it is superfluous to reiterate it again and again and again, since it is disregarded by a scientifism which is well-nigh universal. The objects of exact scientific inquiry are not exclusively constitutive of reality, nor do they constitute the essence of reality. They constitute the reality-for-the-scientist, which is quite different from reality-without-qualification. The exact sciences abstract certain of its features from the subject matter of experience as apprehended by common sense; and if the exact scientist calls these features the real, in an exclusive sense, it is the real for his purposes and nothing more. That the objects of science are real there is no question. That they alone constitute the real is a metaphysical claim which may be valid but which cannot be established by the scientist with his equipment. The exact scientist abstracts from the ordinary objects of phenomenal experience certain features on which he focuses attention in the hope of formulating them in terms of propositions susceptible of verification by prediction. The activity involves ignoring or disregarding other appearances than those selected, and those disregarded often are the most important features of the objects of experience for the purposes of practical activity. In normal, practical activity the intelligence is pervasively guided by the will toward practical objectives, whereas in its scientific activity it is led to function as if it were independent of all other powers of the psyche. In its normal functioning, intelligence is suffused through and through with a feeling that seems to be the necessary condition of the discovery of value, including the discovery even of the "truth," as the term is used in positive science. But why should the ontic status of the objects perceived by the intelligence when it seeks the invariant relations of science be more real than those perceived by the practical intelligence? They *may* be more real, as Plato thought they were; but that they are or are not is not a question which can be settled by the scientist.

The results of an intelligence working without the co-operation of will and feeling reveal what the structure of the universe, including man himself, would be like, were no man the spectator of it. At this point there is a contradiction with which realistic epistemology has endeavored to deal, but without success. Since scientific results are results as viewed from the standpoint of an intelligence which is a human power, the results are a picture of the universe—including man—viewed by man from his own standpoint, only now viewed not by the whole of man but by only a part of him. How to avoid the egocentric predicament would therefore seem, practically, to be a problem which is not susceptible of resolution. Exact positive science gives us the world not as it is "by itself" but as it is when viewed by a generic pure human intelligence. From this statement, however, it cannot be legitimately inferred that there are no data independent of scientific perception. Nor can a disparagement be intended of the value of the picture which science gives us, when in the light of these observations it is pointed out that the results of scientific inquiry are controlled, no less but only much more rigorously so, by the purposes which set it afoot. If this point is grasped, it is not difficult to see the folly of trying to force upon the philosopher, who has other purposes, the ideal of the positive scientist. Nor can the theoretical validity and the practical usefulness of the results of positive science be prejudged by these observations.

What is true of the intelligence seems to be true of the will. A pervasive voluntarism, the complementary error of a pervasive intellectualism, seems to be abroad. According to this belief, the will can function unencumbered by the intelligence. But such a will would be totally blind, and the notion that a blind will can function at all is a complete fiction. A totally blind will is one of the assumptions of those positivistic moral philosophers who separate "attitude" from "belief" and who were criticized in chapter x. We can distinguish "attitude" from "belief"; but only in cases of irresponsible pathological activity do we actually find attitudes controlling men which are not pervasively mixed, saturated through and through, with beliefs that are, in turn, to some extent controlled by the intelligence. This statement does not seem to be true of feeling, which seems capable of functioning unleavened by the intelligence at least, if not by the will. If we look carefully at such pure feeling, however, we seem to see that within rather wide limits it is discriminative and appears to know what it is about. In the normal human being, however, and for its normal business the intelligence acts always propelled by the will, which is suffused with feeling; the will moves, enlightened by intelligence and also charged with emotion, and the emotions do not altogether lack their cognitive value, although for certain purposes that value is negligible. At the moral level, at any rate, as Aristotle put it, reason is desiderative and desire is rational; when either frees itself and claims primacy over the other, we have grounds to suspect a pathological condition. I am not talking about the positive science of morals, the end of which may be purely cognitive in purpose and which was discussed in the Introduction, but of the practical-scientific deliberation in which men engage when confronted by a moral perplexity. Here intelligence and feeling, guided by the will, to the ends of a moral resolution of the perplexity, must co-operate, or the results are monstrous.

Human personality, however, consists of more than the values and powers which analysis can distinguish. The values that constitute it are more or less systematically interrelated into a dynamic whole, capable of growth and contraction, which, so to speak, generates its own inertia, tone, and power of selectivity and rejection. A more important constituent in terms of our inquiry, however, is the undefinable characteristic possessed by the person (probably one of its few unique endowments), namely, its self-consciousness, by which is meant the reflective awareness of itself as an integrated system of values which is itself inherently valuable. Reflection reveals, I believe, that men value themselves. This value includes the self-love which classical psychologists used to discuss; but it goes beyond it. And, while this value—the value of one's person—inheres in the total system of values that one acknowledges, taken collectively, and only derivatively in the dominant values of one's system, taken distributively, it is nevertheless an essential constituent of one's person.

If this is what we mean by "person," we cannot expect to discover it anywhere along the route followed by Hume and his tradition, in some simple atomic fact of reflection on the level with impressions and the relations which obtain between them. Nor do we do it justice if, following the naturalistic road, we seek it in the powers themselves, abstracted from the values which inform them and the peculiar integration which binds them and, above all, from the power of reflective awareness that constitute it both subject and object to itself. Much less do we do it justice when we seek for its essence where, in some sense, it seems to have its locus, in the physical organism in which it resides. "Self," as we have already seen, is the collective term which we apply to the powers distinctly exhibited by the human organism, and "person" is the term by which we refer to those powers when they are informed by a hierarchy of operative values which have been integrated. Powers and values make up a unique and irreducible entity, distinct from the organism which manifests it and from the totality of the powers which the organism manifests. For this reason this entity is, in one legitimate usage of the term, *a substance*, in that it is the subject for which all else that is related to it, including its constituent parts as apprehended by it, stands in the relation of predicate to it. It is this entity, the person, which decides moral perplexities and which in the performance of this, its most important function, is called "conscience."

The integration which the person achieves, the interrelationship between powers and values, is a fact, although, so far as I can find out, no one seems to be able to explain how the integration is achieved and particularly what role, exactly, bodily organs play in its coming about and in its continued existence. I doubt if anyone would question that the relationship is intimate. But it should also be noted that the relationship, like that between organism and powers, is much more complex and obscure than a simplistic physicalism allows. Materialism pretends to explain it by denying one of the terms in the relationship, thus denying the irrefragable fact of experience that awareness and all other powers of the psyche are distinct from the alleged conditions which are said to cause them. Fortunately for us, these mysteries need not block our progress, since we can accept the facts as given to us in experience, content to attribute to the psyche as its cardinal function the task of subtending the integrated system of values which constitutes the person.

CHAPTER XIV

THE RESOLUTION OF A MORAL PERPLEXITY. III

WE ARE now in a position to inquire as to how a moral perplexity is resolved; but let us keep in mind that a perplexity is such for a determinate person in a specific situation arising out of his specific experience. In a genuine moral perplexity a man does not know what is the right thing to do, what he ought to do. When a man knows what he ought to do and for some reason cannot bring himself to do it, he is in a difficult situation, but he is not facing a genuine moral perplexity. The majority of so-called "moral problems" are of this latter sort; therefore, they are not objects of inquiry in this chapter. Of course, moral clarity is a matter of degree: a man may know more or less clearly what he ought to do, or he may be to some extent confused, in which case his inability to act results from the unstable state of his mind. But the type of perplexity to be analyzed in this chapter is that which I have characterized as "genuine" and which will be referred to throughout the chapter as "the normal," in order to distinguish it from an extreme case on which attention will have to be focused later in the chapter and in which an individual, as a result of his deliberation, concludes by condemning himself.

Normally in a moral perplexity the moral qualities of the alternatives which the imagination suggests are not clearly perceived, or, if the moral quality is perceived, the qualities of the various alternatives do not stand out differentially, or they stand out as having negative values. Taken by itself, each of these alternatives, in abstraction from the context within which it would be realized, may appear to be right and may be backed by existing interests. However, when we consider the alternatives in relation to ourselves as moral agents—to the organized system of values which constitutes us—the distinctive quality disappears. An alternative that appears as "right" or as "the best one possible" in a given situation is acceptable to the totality of values which constitutes our person because it seems to strengthen our values or at least not to threaten them, because it appears to go with them, to "fit" into them. If it does not appear to fit and still we are not totally indifferent to it, it is because it constitutes a more or less distinctive threat to our values, because it appears to some extent as potentially disruptive. But since, as we have seen, an individual is perhaps never perfectly integrated, the "person" to which reference is here made may not be the whole person—the total organization of all the acknowledged values of a man—but that part or suborganization which is involved in the perplexity more or less directly and which is prospectively threatened or favored by the various alternatives under scrutiny. If the person were well integrated, all his values, working harmoniously, would make the proper choice among the alternatives. Because a man's values are seldom well integrated, wisdom and prudence, which are the only means on which he depends to avoid moral blunders, often let him down. A moral decision often tends to be in some measure partial, tends to favor aspects of the person which are not truly central at the cost of others now recessive in respect to the perplexity but which may perhaps be more central to the person. After the crisis, when these aspects come forward and make themselves felt, new perplexities arise, which call for new resolutions, which, in turn, will lead to other perplexities. Nor need one be "abnormal" for these suborganizations to function in this manner. I believe psychologists would agree that the integration which we are able to achieve is a matter of degree. Thus Gardner Murphy: "Actually the main dynamics in most cases of double and multiple personality seems to be an exaggeration of a conflict situation which is present in nearly all of us, namely, a conflict between a conforming and a guilty non-conforming trend."[1] The assumption that the nonconforming trends are guilty is worth passing notice, for division within the conscience is thus defined in terms of one clear trend or set of trends to which we conform and of another which would disrupt the socially approved trends. But these conflicts in the person are not only between conforming and nonconforming trends but also between constellations of values, each of which, considered by itself, appears to be acceptable and legitimate.

These conflicts, while they may not be disruptive normally and are usually more or less successfully resolved by the moral agent, must nevertheless be of great interest to the moral philosopher, since, in deciding the right alternative, we must reckon with the fact that what seems right for one of the constellations may not seem right for another. Thus the problem as to which trend is guilty is much more difficult than Murphy, who, it would seem, implicitly accepts cultural relativism, appears to believe.

When in a normal perplexity we are forced into deep, anxious, difficult probing of ourselves before the alternative is chosen, the core of espoused values which comes closest to constituting the essence of the moral personality tends to become decisive in the choice, unless the individual is pathologically split. Even in the latter case the two personalities making up the individual may share values in common which function morally. Readers of Morton Prince's famous study of Miss Beauchamp may have noticed what seems to me to be implicit in the study (although Prince does not himself have occasion to point to it) that, deep as is the opposition between Sally and Miss Beauchamp, there are some values shared by both and by all the other personalities finally discovered. These values, it must be admitted, are of a minimal biological nature; but there seems to be a tone, also, which is shared by the integrated suborganizations which constitute the various persons.[2] I may be wrong about this, because the separation of these two people was very radical. Murphy recognizes the unity of the self and refers to a "deep-level self,"[3] which includes part at least of what I have chosen to call the essence of "the person." It is this "deep-level" moral self or essential person which asserts itself in radical crises, when anxious reflection gives it a chance to come forward to present its claims as against those of the more superficial suborganizations of values which may be urging alternatives to which they are partial. This "deep-level self" or essential person is recognized by the fact that it involves the stronger espousals and is thus felt to be the seat of moral self-identity. When a man feels his integrity threatened, it is this deep-level self that is at stake.

Unless I misread writers on moral philosophy, "character" is the term used to denote what I have been calling here the "moral person": the constellation of acknowledged values (with the habits and

dispositions innate or acquired which sustain them) which constitutes the basis or ground of the moral judgment. I prefer not to use
the term "character" because in a radical moral perplexity it is
wrong to say that it is one's character—the values which our habits
and dispositions have integrated—which does the resolving, unless
one adds in the same sentence that, before the resolution is possible,
one's character must be discovered in the crisis by the search which,
indeed, creates it. There is no perplexity when character functions
unimpeded and no "given" character when one is radically perplexed morally. A perplexity, to the extent to which it is radical,
causes strains and stresses in the suborganizations of values and
tends to dissolve or break them up. When the decision we are called
on to make is truly radical, it involves a choice favorable to our idea
not of our actual moral personality but of our ideal moral personality. This ideal is forged under the impact of the probing that the
perplexity has forced us to engage in. Thus a radical moral decision
is creative in two senses: first, because the discovery of the fitting
solution involves a creative act and, second, because the inward
search for our essential moral personality involves also the creating
of an ideal person toward which we may act as if it were real and as
if we ought to maintain it but which is, indeed, not actual and
which, in our efforts to maintain it, we are really actualizing. The
energy required to arrive at the decision and to actualize it is not
merely deployed outward, upon the manipulation of means to
achieve some definite end, but inward, in the transformation of the
person, in its reconstitution according to the ideal which, through
the decision, is made more nearly possible. The moral agent faces,
so to speak, not merely outward but inward and not merely toward
the past and present but toward the future, seeking to conserve and
salvage through an act of creativity what he truly is, his "deep-
level" values. He thus creates both his destiny and his character.
The experience involves deep anxiety and, when radical, leads one
to turn toward all conceivable sources of help. This fact explains
why the moral experience is so seldom pure and so readily integrates with the religious.

The term "character," as usually understood, is part of a conception of personality which has neither hidden depths nor breaks; if a
man is sincere, his ostensive resolutions, motivations, intentions,

and decisions are what they claim to be. Ivan Karamazov was a respectable man, a man of "good character"; yet he was a murderer, fully as responsible as Dmitri and Smerdyakov for the parricide. But in a two-dimensional psychology which ignores the hidden reality of the personality it is not possible to bring the charge of parricide against him, and from the point of view of such a psychology he is not guilty but innocent. Ivan does not himself know of his responsibility until his interviews with his half-brother during the latter's illness. He begins to suspect it at the end of the second interview, and he does not fully acknowledge it to himself until after the third. In the novel it is the lackey who, for dramatic reasons, is used to bring Ivan face to face with his conscience. The means do not matter; what matters is that, once a man recognizes what is below the surface of normal reflection, he acknowledges it as part of himself as moral agent. If he does not, his morality is rudimentary. The man confronted with a radical moral perplexity must undertake a descent into the depths, a painful inquiry into his actual, as opposed to his ostensible, motivations and values. And to discover his actual values is to create himself, since the formulation is constitutive of an ideal which was not yet fully formed.

How is the ideal created? Out of what materials? And, if it is indeed a case of genuine creation and not merely a shuffling of values already acknowledged, how do we know that it is a good and not a reprehensible ideal that we have created? We have here two basic questions: one purely descriptive and another normative. The first of these is the basic question of this chapter, and the second, subdivided into two—the problem of the ground and source of moral authority and that of the justification of a moral decision—will be discussed in the next two chapters. At present I hope to analyze certain features of the normal moral perplexity that have not yet been investigated. But when, later, we turn to our first question, it will be asked in a different and, I take it, a more critical form. How, it will be asked, is it possible for a man to condemn himself totally and without extenuation? This question involves the problem of the creation of an ideal, but it poses it in a more difficult form. The creation which takes place in the resolution of a normal perplexity consists of an extension of constitutive values already operative; but when we repudiate our constitutive values altogether and forge an entirely new personality, a naked, empty self must do the choosing, and how this process is possible is not at all obvious.

Let us turn back to the normal moral perplexity. In such cases, it was said, the prospective decision which is deemed right is chosen in preference to others when the agent perceives it to be "fitting." This is an irreducible moral term. If right, the chosen alternative *usually* promises satisfaction and security; if wrong, it is *usually* accompanied by a tone of rejection, fear, and discomfort or anxiety. But the "right" is not that which produces pleasure, nor is the wrong that which produces displeasure. At this point and after what has already been said about it and what has been said about it by its numerous critics, it is not necessary again to exhibit the fallacies of moral hedonism. Suffice it to state dogmatically that a right decision may promise a diminution of pleasure or, more strongly, may be productive of considerable displeasure. Kant was probably right in suspecting a decision when it was productive of pleasure. Nor need a decision satisfy any specific standing interest other than that which the requiredness of value arouses. If a man has never had to make a moral decision which involved a sacrifice of deeply rooted, insistent interests, productive of pleasure or prestige or comfort, he has never gone through a moral crisis, and, although he may be a very good man, utterly above moral reproach, what he has to say on the subject of pleasure we may safely ignore. This is, incidentally, one of the points at which psychiatrists and psychoanalysts, with their uncritical eudaemonism, become genuinely corrupting forces in our society. But no less dangerous, although less obviously so, is the shallow sentimentalist who tells you that the "right" decision is always productive of greater satisfaction and greater happiness than the wrong. This optimism is worthy of a Herbert Spencer and is mostly cant. The moral life involves serious, often irreparable, sacrifices, sometimes prolonged and anguished; and not infrequently it demands of an individual that he go through unspeakable torture and at the end give up his life. When a man meets these demands, he is a martyr or a hero. Those looking for happiness, as it is nowadays understood by a culture which worships bodily comfort and gadgets, would do well to go after their happiness where they are likely to find it and not look for it in the

midst of moral reality. They can have their happiness and their respectability and whatever else it is that they want. The only guar-
anty that the moral philosopher can give the moral man is that he
will save his personality from destruction, not that he will be
happy.

Conversely, the wrong decision may promise intense pleasure
because it satisfies an intense craving. Anticipated or accrued pleasure is thus, Herbert Spencer to the contrary notwithstanding, a
most unreliable index of whether a prospective alternative is truly
right or not. An intense craving can cause a temporary disorganiza-
tion of the person and may succeed in making his permanent claims
mute and impotent. But, viewed in a broad, temporal perspective,
the right is usually productive of satisfaction *in the long run;* and, if
satisfaction brings with it pleasure, then the right is usually pleasant
in the long run. But it must be reiterated that it need not satisfy any
specific interest and that a decision to accept the right alternative
may bring with it only a reduction of the anxiety that the prospect
of a wrong decision aroused. This reduction, of course, involves a
modicum of pleasure, to which may be added the pleasure produced
by satisfaction of the interest which the requiredness of value is
able to stimulate. But the decision is right not because of hedonic
consequences but because it maintains the organization of values
which constitutes the person or, at least, because it does not
threaten but, indeed, reduces the danger to the maintenance of that
organization.

These remarks indicate the importance of the fact that the personality is a hierarchical organization of values. It is not, however,
a perfect one, but one in which there are suborganizations which are
capable of functioning more or less autonomously and which,
through the vagaries of selective interest, are capable of usurping
the executive function which belongs to the whole system. Since the
person is always more or less divided, a part always seeks to decide
for the whole, sacrificing all extant espousals for the sake of the
promised satisfaction of imperious cravings. A wrong moral decision is one in which the system of dominant espousals which constitutes the person is shoved aside by the extant interests which a
given alternative promises to satisfy or which they may have suggested. The strength—usually only temporary—of the partial in-

terest prevents the normally dominant system of espoused values from asserting themselves. Normally a right decision is one which strengthens, or at least does not threaten, an organization of values, no matter what partial satisfactions or dissatisfactions of certain interests may also result from it. But there are situations in which the envisaged alternatives have so completely engaged extant interests or elicited new ones that a proposed alternative cannot be foreseen as involving a threat. A choice of such an alternative can seriously disrupt our values, and thus, objectively, we have made a wrong decision. No moral blame can attach to such a decision if the untoward consequences which it brought with it were truly unforeseen. A morally sensitive person, however, recognizes, as involved in a moral activity, the obligation to use fully his reflective intelligence in order to reduce such situations to the least possible number.

No elaborate proof of the fact that the intelligence is centrally involved in moral reflection seems to be required. It is obvious that we are forced to devise alternatives which resolve the moral perplexity, that we must explore what is entailed factually by these alternatives, and that we must make the effort to discover how the entailed facts will affect our acknowledged values. But there are two popular misconceptions of the way in which the intelligence is supposed to function which should be criticized. The first pictures a man making a moral decision by drawing up a list of the values and disvalues which he perceives as involved in the various alternatives, giving them some sort of qualitative rating, and adding and subtracting in order to arrive at the correct decision. This may be the way in which Benthamites arrive at their decisions—but it remains to be seen whether Benthamites can be genuinely moral men. Men endowed with the moral consciences of shopkeepers can be respectable—but between respectability and morality, as Bernard Shaw long ago taught our generation, there sometimes lies an abyss that cannot be bridged. But perhaps I do an injustice to the shopkeeper, since the kind of man I have in mind is the penny-grabbing soul too small to be criminal and too blind to be genuinely good.

The other popular conception, the instrumentalist, pictures the moral intelligence as operating on the model of the scientific intelligence. There is some truth in this conception.[4] But the moral intelligence operates in intimate co-operation with the moral will, which is to say, with the feelings of acceptance and rejection of recognized values as they present themselves when seeking to create interest in themselves or engage interest already existing. Thus in moral inquiry there are factors which are totally lacking in scientific inquiry: in the latter all values but the value of truth are insulated and not allowed to affect the intelligence, whereas in moral inquiry all values are called on to present their claims and moral sensibility consists precisely of the ability to bring forth the claims of relevant values. A moral agent is a man who decides to seek the good and act rightly—a decision which is logically prior to all practical decisions which he makes; whereas a scientist makes a prior decision not to allow any other good to interfere with his search for the truth. Instrumentalism fails to see that the intelligence acts morally because a moral will guides it and that it can act with superb perfection in its own terms, and yet morally abominably in the absence of a moral will which it cannot create but on which it must depend.

The normal moral decision, formulated perhaps in a judgment after it is reached, is the result of the grasp of a total situation and of the feeling of congruity or of fitness between the alternatives that suggest themselves and the inward ethos—the Gestalt quality of one's person, so to speak—as it makes itself felt in the stress of the moral crisis. One decides which of several possible alternatives is the right one, as a painter decides which of the possible ways of arranging a model which occur to him in his search for the right pose will best express what he wants: the moral man wants the morally fitting, the good; the artist wants the aesthetically satisfactory. But, whether one's intelligence happens to be analytically lucid or massively emotional or, what is the same thing, whether one's will is fully intelligent or is somewhat obtuse, the way in which the decision is reached is the same: the attractiveness or repulsiveness of alternatives is grasped by him through his more or less profound reaction (as qualified above) toward their prospective effect on his conception of what ought to be. There is a moral obligation to be intelligent, to use one's full resources; and a complete moral life involves an obligation to develop one's resources and maintain them in full efficiency. But it must always be the whole individual person, in the use of his full endowment, who resolves the moral perplexity. He resolves it through his own imaginative construction of what the alternatives involve. And when a person— which is to say, an organism constituted by a psyche, endowed with powers, and possessing values—functions in this capacity, *he is his conscience*, or he acts conscientiously.[5]

It is some sort of conflict between drives or interests subtending values which constitutes the moral perplexity and elicits the functioning of the conscience. The conflict leads us to seek alternatives which will resolve it, and these tempt us with promises of valuable rewards. A typical case of moral perplexity involves the presence of a desire whose fitness we more or less vaguely suspect and which demands peremptory satisfaction. Reflection reveals that the prospective satisfaction creates resistance or anxiety. But the case is doubtful, since the desire not only possesses strength but is able, so to speak, to bring forward arguments to prove its innocence or at least to mitigate its guilt. Since the person is not a fully integrated system of values, there is no invader or intruder that cannot count upon a fifth column within the citadel of the conscience. Were this not the case, there would be no radical moral problems. But this fifth column is not identified as such, not clearly labeled treacherous; it argues that it represents the true person, the best side of man, and in the heat and dust of the conflict it is soon utterly impossible to tell friend from foe. The decision, when we are confronted with a radical moral perplexity, demands strength to plunge to the depths of the conscience, shrewdness to tell what we truly are, and courage and doggedness to maintain our convictions against the assault of the intruder and his fifth column. What we have to do to arrive at an adequate resolution is to mobilize our total resources, set up a constant watch to discover, as we will if we truly want to, what really are our values. Once discovered, they can usually be counted on to maintain themselves against the invader. For these values, being those we espouse, are themselves not without resources of affective and volitional strength within the person.

We have seen that this total mobilization of our inward resources, this resistance of our threatened values, constitutes what is known as "conscience." The conscience is not a spiritual organ or a psychical mechanism or a special isolated faculty but the activity of an aroused moral personality in the act of defending itself against disruption. We do not have here a mysterious autonomous fourth power on the same plane with the will and the intelligence and our affective capacity, which acts with, but is distinguishable from, these three other powers of the person. The conscience *is* the person in the vital and frequently anguishing and desperate act of defending its integrity. It is true, therefore, as Charner Perry points out, that there is thus something ineradicably "arbitrary" in a moral decision, since it is you, in the fully operative uniqueness of your own personality, after inward search has revealed to you what you are and what you fundamentally desire, that alone can decide what will threaten you or will aid you and may even enable you to grow as a moral person. The voice of conscience is the voice of one's self, the cry of warning against threatening danger or the embittered disapproval of the harm already done; the approval, when the decision is "right," is the gratification of your personality because you have sustained it and, in so doing, have strengthened it against future threats.

Neither the French nor the Spanish have a special name to designate the conscience, and in English the distinction made between "consciousness" and "conscience" has some advantages. It has one disadvantage, however, since it tends to make one think of the person as inherently divided in its moral and in its purely intellectual activities. This tendency and the premium put upon pure verbal intelligence in a technological culture breed philosophic schools whose purpose is to "defend" various views: thus you hear argument to the effect that the conscience is an emotion or a sentiment or that moral judgments issue from the activity of the reason. In truth, the person is constituted by the integrated activity which the body supports, acting intelligently, volitionally, and affectively in the fulfilment of its functions. For certain more or less clear purposes, it is advisable to distinguish these functions, and to some extent, as already noted, it is possible to free some from the co-operation of the others. If we so desire, we can distinguish in a decision of the conscience an intellectual or cognitive component, an orectic one, and an affective tonality. But the person is not to be thought of in terms of the Platonic metaphor of the team driven by a charioteer, since the team can be unhitched and the charioteer, after putting the horses up for the night, goes off to his own home to supper and to rest. The reason employed—it cannot be repeated too often—is desiderative and affective, the will rational and affective, and the feelings not without drive and perhaps sight. In routine perplexities the whole personality is not aroused, and decisions are more or less automatic or involve, at best, only segments of our constitutive values in their response. But let a serious issue come up, and, like a wild animal snarling at the hand that reaches for the feeding young, the conscience, which is to say, our whole person, arouses itself to fight.

Because the term "right" has two legitimate referents which are distinct from each other, it is advisable to discuss them in order to avoid confusion. Let us first distinguish between a relational complex and the relation and the terms in relation that constitute it:

$$(s—R—o)$$

is a relational complex, constituted by the term s and o, which are related by relation R. A moral relational complex consisting of a subject or agent involved in a moral perplexity, s, and an object or possible solution of that perplexity, o, I call a "moral transaction." As we saw, in the usual moral transaction the s term—the subject or agent—is constituted by an operative value system which decides whether the prospective solution, o, will fit or not; and the o term consists of a value whose incorporation into the agent's system is prospectively being considered. Thus o can be spoken of as "good" or "valuable," meaning not only that it is a value but that it is a value which, under the circumstances and as a result of the survey occasioned by the perplexity, is thought to be the best possible. But the term "right" can also be applied to o, and now we say of o that it is the right alternative under the circumstances. Thus "right" and "good" are in this usage—which is allowed by convention—synonymous, and both are used here adjectivally. The term "right," however, unlike the term "good," may also be properly used to refer to the *sui generis* relation of fitness R, which is also part of the moral transaction.

One important point, with which the reader is by now familiar, is that the value of o is an objective character for s, since it appears upon, or has its locus in, a possible alternative considered as independent of the perplexity which led to the survey that discovered it. This kind of objectivity can be called "epistemological," since it reveals itself in the moral inquiry. But from it we cannot argue to the ontic objectivity resident in *o*. *Ontic objectivity can be asserted, however, if we remember that it was shown that the values from which we chose are presupposed in the act of choice and are independent of the choosing agent.* Belief in the objectivity of value gives rise to a very serious metaphysical problem: What is the nature and status of value when not embodied in human experience? I answer that values have the same nature and status as all universals; they are part of the structure that makes spatiotemporal existence possible. Scientific laws are not created by the scientist but are discovered, although it is true that in their formulation there enter, to a greater or lesser extent, idiosyncratic factors and what is called by post-Kantians the "constitutive factor" of the mind in the knowledge process. Similarly, values are discovered by man, not created, although it must be added in the same breath that the degree of modification which the value schemes suffer because of the interests that men have in values is probably greater by far than the modification that the laws of nature suffer in their formulation.

But we are not yet through, for it also follows from the above remarks that decisions are not presumed to be right because they are approved but rather are approved because they are, or are believed to be, right because they fit or are capable of constituting a personality; and we say that they fit if we discern in them the presence of value. Thus what actually makes a choice right, or the best under the circumstances, is that it possesses a value character or quality apprehended as objectively independent of the agent. The choice fits because it possesses this value character. Hence it is necessary to modify our original definition to read as follows: A choice is said to be right because it possesses a value character which fits into the moral system of an agent seeking the solution of a perplexity. Thus the relation "right"—*R*—is not constitutive of the value *o* but is constitutive of the value only as the *o* term in the moral transaction. In other words, it makes no appreciable difference whether in a given context we speak of *o* or of *R*—of the value of the proposed solution or of the relation of value which obtains between the solution and the moral agent, since either involves the other. In cases, however, of total self-condemnation, this is not exactly true, since the beckoning value o, whose superiority is acknowledged and which leads to the reconstruction of the person, cannot be said to fit into a value system and for the simple reason that no system exists, since it has been totally repudiated. This will call for a modification of our definition of "right."

The search for the resolution of a moral perplexity which does not issue forth in total self-condemnation seeks for the right alternative and distinguishes it from what one desires. As Professor Percival puts it: "The rule of right is simply this: Obedience to the will of God; self-surrender, not self-affirmation. 'And if we obey God,' Father Mapple says, 'we must disobey ourselves; and it is in this disobeying ourselves, wherein the hardness of obeying God consists.' "[6] The moral philosopher, trying to develop morality as far as it will go as an autonomous practical discipline, will substitute for the phrase, "the will of God," the phrase "the requiredness of value" or a synonym thereof, though for him it must remain an open question whether the requiredness of value does not ultimately entail teleological assumptions that finally force him to find his way to the portals of theology. Be that as it may, the important point is that the search for the right alternative forces on one a distinction between obedience to something objective and obedience to what one desires, obedience to self. The distinction is vague to the extent that what one desires coincides with what is right. And the ideal, of course, of moral education is that the distinction be totally erased. But only a weak, sentimental, shallow, Pelagian attitude toward human nature would conceive of the ideal as within the reach of men. The City of God is not the City of Man; man cannot hope to rear a perfect city. Normally, therefore, the distinction between what we desire and what is right is very sharp, and the two terms of the distinction are apprehended as more or less exclusive.

If the naturalistic philosopher does not see the difference between desiring a thing and desiring a moral resolution of a perplexity which arose because a thing was desired, all one can say of his failure is that either his eyes are defective or his data limited. Approval serves, at best, as a more or less defective index of the right but can never constitute the essence of what is right. That can be given to us only in the relation of fitness as an objective relation of a contemplated action with our constitutive values. W. D. Ross is, in this, it seems to me, indisputably correct. He is convinced, however, that the discovery of what is fitting is a much easier task than it actually is. The reason for this is that he has not considered seriously the moral problem faced by a man who, for some reason, has been cut off from the respectable ready-made rules of a social group. There are innumerable situations in which we desire earnestly to do what is right but cannot discover which of the alternatives is the fitting one. As he shows in Sermons III and VIII, Bishop Butler is also of the impression that one's conscience can easily decide what its duty is, but, as one of his critics puts it, "The moral genius may indeed sometimes see the path of duty where it is invisible to others; and often he will do so where trained philosophers or moral theologians are at fault. But even he knows times when circumstances are too strong for him. Duty lies somewhere in the thicket of possibilities before him; but thought and prayer are necessary before he can discover it."[7]

The fact that we "discover" the path of duty, as Kirk puts it, expresses only one side, however, of what seems to be the paradox which confronts the moral man when he attempts to resolve his perplexity. The judgment we pronounce refers to an objective situation which possesses its own authority and which we merely record. The good chooses us through the effect of its requiredness upon us, which we merely acknowledge. *We do not create it; we discover it.* Without the impersonal authority of value, we cannot justify the objectivity of our moral decisions. On the other hand, the judgment must be one's own judgment, must represent one, must be fully backed by the unique individual which one is; otherwise, one is not morally responsible. It is the individual who chooses one alternative over the rest. This is a paradox, but it may be removed by considering that, while it is we who choose, what we choose is what we, in our free judgment, conceive to be the good. The choice is our responsibility. But the choosing does not make it good or bad; this is a character utterly independent of our choice. Thus Bishop Butler misleads his reader when he tells him that man is a law to himself. Man freely applies the law to himself but does not make but only discovers the law. This, of course, Bishop Butler clearly knew.[8]

But, while it may be easy to show that there is no genuine paradox in this respect, it is not so easy to show that there is not something seemingly contradictory, or at least confused, in another respect. For the individual who chooses and espouses values does so freely, and through the act of free choices he exercises his freedom and creates his own moral nature. When a man resolves a moral perplexity successfully, he adds a cubit to his stature. But when he thus creates himself freely, he realizes himself as a full human being. And what is not easy to see clearly is that self-realization of one's humanity would indicate a determinate line of development and the achievement of a pre-existing pattern—a concept which seems to be the very contrary of freedom. The puzzle, if it is one, can be solved by due consideration of the fact that man is not God and does not create himself from nothing through the use of his spontaneity. The values which, through his own free decisions, he sought to incorporate and through whose incorporation he grew into a person were not themselves created by him. They found him and exercised on him their requiredness. However, he acted creatively in the decision that it was along this direction and not that, through the choice of this and not that alternative, that the possibility of his growth lay. Again the intuition or grasp of a general, formal notion of what man can and should be is given him through his moral reflection on the content of experience, particularized into schemas supplied by his society and to a great extent determined for him by birth and circumstances. But the actual realization in the concrete is an act achieved, in part at least, through the specific individual decisions through which he grasps the moral matter which constitutes him the specific, unique individual that he is. The act of moral reflection involves a search, as was pointed out above, for what one truly is; and what one truly is remains to be achieved and is thus a creative act. But, while the decision whether to be this or that is a free decision, when one finally decides to be this and not that, one is bound by this decision; and how one goes about achieving one's end is not a question that one can leave to spontaneity or which can be considered an arbitrary affair. I am perfectly free to be a good or an evil man; but, having decided to be a good man, I cannot go about realizing my decision in just any old way. In my station, with its deter-

minate duties, to be good involves the spontaneous giving-up of indeterminate arbitrariness and the autonomous subjection of myself
to the conditions which I must fulfil to be the kind of good man I
can be and want to be.

If I use the word "fitness" instead of "harmony" to denote the
relation to which we have been devoting our attention, the reason is
that in its usual acceptation the term "harmony" is intended to denote a fitness which reduces tension, whereas the rightness of a decision need not eliminate tension, so long as the tension does not produce disruption of previously existing integrations in the value system in which it fits. It might be well, however, to remember that
these are all questions of degree. Here again the analogy with
aesthetics may serve to throw some light on our subject. An aesthetic integration involves tensions among the elements which constitute it which, nevertheless, do not preclude their mutual fitness to
make up a harmonious whole.

If what has been said should prove acceptable, Dewey is at fault
in his insistence that a right resolution always involves a complete
transformation of the values of the personality, and hence a continuous growth by addition. The decision may lead to growth, but
it may also lead to the very opposite, to shrinkage of the values of
the person in the interest of maintaining those essential values which
constitute it. The value system which constitutes it is the agency
and criterion that define the limits of what other values are acceptable, except in those rare cases in which a crisis reveals the need to
repudiate the system. And the idea that every need can call for a
transformation of the mass in terms of a prescription of continuous
progress or growth is monstrous nonsense, which can occur only to
that pathetically disinherited, uprooted animal, the contemporary
liberal. The moral life involves sacrifices, often retrenchments; and
not infrequently it happens that moral reflection reveals that the
growth and enrichment of the person which have taken place previously have led us hopelessly into the wrong and threaten our response to the ideal. Again, the notion put forth by William James,
that "every *de facto* claim creates in so far forth an obligation"; that
every desire, considered by itself, carries with it its own moral
passport; that it is, as he puts it, "imperative to the extent of its

amount; [that] *it makes* itself valid by the fact that it at all exists,"[9] is vicious nonsense. Growth is not a self-evident imperative of morality; rather, one of the many difficult problems which the moral man has to solve is whether and by how much and along what directions he should allow growth in himself. There are times and places when shrinking from growth may well be the only moral decision which we can arrive at. And there are times and places when ceasing not merely to grow but to live is the only moral way out. A man who, in totalitarian countries like Nazi Germany, chooses to grow by the incorporation of Nazi values does not become better through his growth but worse. A good man in that situation naturally makes fewer demands of his environment and resists the incorporation into his personality of the values with which the system tempts him to grow.

A truly serious or radical moral perplexity confronts us when disparity and incommensurability of values or lack of knowledge of possible consequences or the generalized, not individuated, nature of the impulse that sets the problem acts in such a way as to present to reflection choices among which there does not seem to be a decisive difference. Intelligence has gone as far as it can, and it is not possible to discover a basis on which a decision can be reached. Moreover, the very desires whose emergence gave rise to the moral perplexity throw a smoke screen between us and our loyalties and (since, even at best, it is not easy to determine what we really are) successfully conceal from us the values which are truly constitutive of our essential moral selves. Again, pressures from the outside tend frequently to help us to betray ourselves; and forces, resistances, and tendencies lying beyond the reach of introspection confuse us as to our values. The world expects certain things of you, and desire finds no difficulty in convincing you that along those lines lies the correct moral decision. There are also your hidden fears, your subtly disguised aggressive tendencies, against yourself and against others, and the hidden burden of guilt, some of it possibly irrational because infantile, which are as much a part of you as your Sunday-best respectability and your company manners. Some of these forces lie beyond the reach of discovery by reflection and are able to run interference against your self beyond the range of your awareness. They have refined ways of taking revenge if you offend them, deploying their defenses in depth if you threaten them and patting you sweetly until you purr if you keep them content. Psychoanalysts, aware above all other men of these factors, tend to explain away the notion of moral responsibility and to reduce moral failure to disease. This is simply bad thinking, and, as we have seen, their account of the conscience is fallacious. The data they offer cannot be ignored, but they must be reinterpreted, for the problem at issue—whether men are capable of moral choice or not, except, of course, in obviously extreme cases, of distinctive pathological character—is one on which no compromise is admissible.

The process of arriving at a moral decision is not always so easy as the above account may have led us to believe, since the moral perplexity may reveal, by making us reflect about our values, that they cannot pass muster. And the upshot of such an experience is a total condemnation of our extant personality. But first let us ask how this can happen. Not so infrequently as one whose life has run along conventionally respectable channels might tend to believe do disruptive experiences reveal to us values beckoning which are not only genuine but of the greatest importance and for which no place can be found in our present system. And not so infrequently as the conventionally respectable may think do the consequences of our actions force us to look at the unspeakable evil will from which they issued. Any experience that will crack the hard crust of our smugness: a dire calamity or an intense unexpected happiness; illness; the threat of death; a criminal sentence pronounced upon us, with its awful sanction; perhaps only a gentle reproach, like the tap administered by a diamond cutter along the line of cleavage—experiences such as these not infrequently endow us with a sensibility not previously possessed or bring forth latent powers of discrimination until now dormant, which force us to perceive that the values we acknowledge are evil. And the question that the action gives rise to is this: How is it possible to condemn one's self, to say to one's self, "I am evil"? How do we repudiate our constitutive values?

We saw above that, according to the postulational theory, it is not possible to explain how a man can condemn himself. Neither is it possible, according to the interest theory, to explain how a set of defeated interests can recognize freely the validity of the judgment which condemns them. If the interest theory is right, what we have is a constellation of interests in conflict with another constellation, but in terms of the definition each of these sets is as right as the other. As was pointed out earlier in the chapter on Freud, the suppression of one set does not make it wrong, unless all that is meant by "wrong" is "weaker." But the wrong set is not always the weaker and often, although stronger, acknowledges itself to be wrong. "Right" does not mean stronger; sometimes the right is weaker. What "right" means is something else: that we have reached a decision in the light of our apprehension of what a given concrete situation requires to complete itself in an ideal way; and the criterion of ideality is given to the moral agent by the requiredness of the values that he is able to discern. As my friend Professor A. C. Garnett is fond of putting it, man is a creature that "responds to value"; on this fact the moral life is founded. But for the interest theory all that "right" can mean is a successful organization of interests capable of suppressing opposition in favor of its objects. There are times, however, when a right decision is acknowledged as right and accepted because it is right, not merely yielded to, even though it may not have the strength of strong desires to help it impose itself. This is particularly the case when we apprehend that the extant organization of our values, taken collectively, is wrong. All our interests are repudiated, collectively, and, according to the interest theory, it remains a mystery how a powerful organization will yield to the single interest which pronounces the condemnation. Obviously, it is no more possible to explain such a phenomenon by means of the working definition given earlier in this chapter than by the interest and postulational theories criticized in the first part of this essay. If the right decision is one that maintains, or at least does not threaten, the organization of values which constitutes the person, it would not be possible for the system to apprehend that it is itself wrong. Either no such total condemnation ever takes place, or there is more involved in arriving at a right decision than has been broached so far. But how can we deny that there are instances in which men do, in fact, condemn themselves totally and act on the condemnation to change radically the pattern of their lives? Of course, they do not condemn each and every one of their values; they condemn them collectively, condemning their organization or system, and hence the order of rank which wrongfully assigned to some values a pre-eminence which they obviously cannot claim. Our initial definition of right and our initial formulation of the manner in which we arrive at a correct decision must be altered in the face of facts such as these.

What we need to do is to analyze more deeply the phenomenon from which the definition was derived. In choosing normally between prospective alternatives, we choose that which fits; but we do so not because, subjectively, our values decide the choice but because our constitutive values are higher, superior, more valuable, than the values of any of the alternatives which offer themselves as capable of solving our perplexity. The "right," then, is normally the solution that fits, but only because we have chosen one that is the best completion to a value system which we have no reason to challenge. And thus what makes it right is that, having discerned its superior fittingness, we have responded to it. Now what is involved in total self-condemnation is that an ideal "ought-to-be" (as Nicolai Hartmann might put it) has revealed itself by contrast with the actual "is." A value or a constellation of values has been descried, possessing its own requiredness and capable of revealing it because what one acknowledged previously has discredited itself. The situation thus reveals to us that what "right" truly refers to is a relation between a value or a complex of values and a self which has the capacity to respond to the requiredness of values. Normally, as we have already seen, it is not the naked self but one informed by an operative value system that responds preferentially to competing alternatives, and "right" then refers to the relation of fitness; but the critical phenomenon of self-condemnation has left us a naked self, bereft of values and seeking to be informed again. For the self seeks values, requires them for its completion, for its actualization as a moral person. The right is a relation, R, which relates a self, capable of responding to value, to the value whose superior requiredness is apprehended by the responding self. Of course, the response of the self is not totally blind, since, in losing its values, it has not lost its knowledge of value; and, if it has not until now known what the true good is, it has lately learned an awful lesson as to what evil is, and by that experience it has already acquired considerable knowledge.

I have spoken as if the process of self-condemnation and reconstitution of the personality were temporally successive, but this was only a convenient manner of speaking. In fact, the process is complex and takes place all at once. A practical difficulty induces moral reflection which reveals the evil of our constitutive values and, at the same time, searches and discerns alternatives which are likely to consist of precisely the contrasting values which formerly were rejected. A self which past early childhood can remain divested or stripped of values is an abstract figment; the mind gives values up only in the act of exchanging them simultaneously for new ones; and self-condemnation involves, first, the discovery of new values whose apprehension forces the repudiation of the old ones.

If the argument of this chapter is valid, moral perplexities are resolved by all men in the same way, whether they belong to a settled and well-ordered society or one in rapid flux in which governing principles have lost their authority. The difference between situations in which social values are accepted and those in which they are rejected is one of degree—a degree indicated by the amount of uncertainty which precedes decisions in which we lack the support of socially regulative principles. In the case of the rebel who rejects the values of the society (as in the case of individuals who merely doubt them but who, in the resolution of their perplexities, cannot derive help from the rules as they understand them), the decision must "fit." In other words, it must promise to co-operate with and not threaten the values accepted. When a man rebels against a culture and on moral grounds seeks its destruction, he frequently imagines that he repudiates the whole culture, with all its values. But all he manages to repudiate are certain important aspects of it, not all of it; and one thing least of all does he repudiate, and that is the self he is, into whose constitution went the major training energies of the society: his habits, emotional patterns, and trained aptitudes cannot easily be shed. No man, however, is totally a product of his culture. As an individual he has creatively contributed to his own development by the moral decisions which, as he lived, he was called on to make. In seeking to destroy the values he repudiates, the rebel does so on his own responsibility.

The question arises as to how one knows, after the self-condemnation which wrecked one's person, that one is substituting for it a better value system and not another as bad as, or worse than, that which has been repudiated; for the process of conversion, involving traumatic experiences, could easily and radically mislead one. The problem will be taken up in the two following chapters. Here we have been concerned only with a description of the actual process of moral deliberation, not with its validity.

CHAPTER XV

THE GROUND AND THE SOURCE
OF MORAL AUTHORITY

THE preceding account of the manner in which we resolve our moral perplexities may be criticized for leaving the moral judgment entangled in radical subjectivism. To obviate the criticism, we must look into the ground and source of moral authority and into the manner in which we justify our moral decisions.

It is the moral agent who has the authority to make the moral decision. To place the authority elsewhere would be to deprive the agent of his responsibility. But the fact that the conscience must ultimately have the authority to do the choosing and must assume full responsibility for it does not imply that the decision is arbitrary or subjective. The moral decision is not right because *we* choose it but because we choose it *rightly*. The conscience decides upon, but does not constitute, the right. The source of the authority lies in the requiredness of the chosen values which oblige the conscience to acknowledge them. Those theories which give authority to the conscience have usually avoided moral solipsism by claiming some sort of infallibility for its deliverances; but in this essay the conception of the conscience as a special faculty or entity—or even, as Freud would have it, as the judicial function of a special entity—has been precluded by the analysis of it as the whole person engaged in moral deliberation. The conscience has been and is still taken for a faculty which, like the old-fashioned "instinct," is supposed to serve the animal without error. When it is interpreted as the whole person functioning at the special task of resolving moral perplexities, its propensity to error and the ease with which it falls into it cannot be concealed. The human mind has the power to arrive at the truth on questions of morals no less than on other questions, but man's truth is always subject to correction. Apodictic truth is a fruit that man may crave and that he should pursue, for in its search

249

he fulfils himself. The quest for certainty thus defines man's destiny, and to dissuade him from it is to strip him of his armor against despair. But it is the quest and not the result of it that defines his destiny, for certainty is not given to man to possess. Nor is this statement intended to prejudice the question as to whether the term "truth," in the locution "moral truth," is formally or methodologically the same term as is found in the expression "scientific truth." The word "truth" has been used here loosely, and its meaning will not be fixed until we explore the notion of "justification."

The claim that in the realm of morals man enjoys certainty is still made by reputable philosophers, in spite of the destructive attacks to which rationalistic intuitionism in moral philosophy has been subjected since the seventeenth century. Indeed, one of the most vigorous schools of moral philosophy in our day is that which we call "British intuitionism," whose most distinguished representative is W. D. Ross.

According to this author, we are endowed with a special power which enables us to apprehend moral principles: ". . . both in mathematics and in ethics we have certain crystal-clear intuitions from which we build up all that we can know about the nature of numbers and the nature of duty."[1] In his earlier book the same view is maintained; the prima facie rightness of certain types of acts is self-evident. We are warned, however, that "the nature of the self-evident is not to be evident to every mind however undeveloped, but to be apprehended directly by minds which have reached a certain degree of maturity. . . ."[2] A systematic defense of the view is not to be found in the two books of Ross with which I am acquainted, but the reasons for accepting intuitionism seem to be that every system of moral philosophy admits intuition at some point and that the arguments against intuitionism can be disposed of. The objections are that intuitionism admits of too many intuitions and that it admits intuitions which, in practice, contradict one another.[3] The first of these objections is not one which I am disposed to press against Ross's view. The second deserves careful examination; but, before examining it, it seems desirable to indicate that Ross's acceptance of his own intuitions in moral philosophy cannot today derive support from mathematical intuitionism in as cavalier a manner as he thinks it can. Kant could argue that mathematics is a pure product of reason and, moreover, synthetical, and he may have been correct.[4] But today it should be obvious that the validity of mathematical intuitionism is not something which, after 1868, can be taken as self-evident.[5] Moreover, even if intuitionism could be accepted without argument, we would require a rigorous analysis of the criterion by which we can distinguish valid from pseudo-intuitions. No such analysis is to be found in Ross, nor are we told where we can find it.

In any case the claim that there are "crystal-clear" moral intuitions seems to be contradicted successfully by relevant data of which Ross does not take account. For Ross a moral perplexity consists in the difficulty involved in the choice of prima facie obligations; intuition always gives at least to "the best and most enlightened of men an absolutely original and direct insight into moral principles. . . ."[6]

Let us first observe that, *in the manner in which it is stated*, the doctrine is beyond the possibility of impugnment, and Ross is too careful a writer for us to be able to disregard his formulations. Anyone trying to challenge Ross's contention can always be stopped with the answer that those who deny the existence of crystal-clear intuitions do not have them because they are neither the best nor the most enlightened. Should these blind and evil men answer that they are sufficiently good and sufficiently enlightened, it is always possible to point out to them that their failure to have original and direct insights of a crystal-clear nature argues them as lacking the amount of goodness and enlightenment necessary to place them in the class of men of superior enlightenment and goodness who *have* such insights. Ross, however, does not need to allow that his argument is circular or that it is merely a disguised definition; for what he is saying is that the insight into moral principles is self-certifying in somewhat the sense in which Aristotle said that the deliverances of the theoretical reason about first principles were self-certifying or in which the intuition of truth was self-certifying for Spinoza. The good man not only knows truly the principles governing his obligations but knows himself as knowing them. I must confess candidly that the argument as I have stated it here cannot be found in either of the two books by Ross on ethical philosophy with which I am acquainted, but it seems to me to be the only interpretation of his doctrine possible if one is to assume, as I must, that the charge of circularity was too obvious for Ross not to have seen it. Thus interpreted, Ross also avoids the attacks of those who would tend to disqualify the argument because it is alleged to rest on a definition.

But, while Ross's argument cannot be impugned as stated, it rests on an assumption contrary to fact, for he ignores the frequent occasions on which men who are generally acknowledged to be the best and most enlightened are completely balked by a moral perplexity because they cannot discover the principles by means of which they could resolve the situation. Now this frustration happens when, *in respect to a single perplexity*, two good and enlightened men have contradictory intuitions. Ross argues that we never have contradictory intuitions about the same situation but have incompatible intuitions only about different prima facie obligations. It is this argument which is here denied. When the moral intuition of a good and enlightened man tells him that a nation bound by a treaty to defend another nation against unjustified attack should go to war if necessary to keep its obligations, and a pacifist opposes that very intuition because war is always and under any circumstances wrong, we are not in disagreement about two prima facie obligations—that in respect to treaties and that in respect to war—but about the same situation: the question of the morality of taking human life. Two good and enlightened men value life differently; and if one puts treaties above life, it is because the obligation to respect the life of his fellow-beings does not seem to him so important as it seems to the pacifist. Thus the disagreement can indeed be interpreted as Ross interprets it, but it can also be interpreted as disagreement about the intrinsic value of a single situation.

Let us consider another illustration: Abraham may have been perplexed by two prima facie obligations, one toward his God and another toward his son. But he may also have been perplexed by his inability to arrive at a clear intuition as regards his duty toward God; he may have been unable for a time to decide whether one is obliged to obey God conditionally or unconditionally. If this was his initial problem, the conflict between his prima facie obligations to his son and to God still remained after he decided what his duty to God was; but he could not have decided between duty to God and love of son until the true nature of his duty to God was decided. Now, of course, the failure to come to a crystal-clear decision may be formulated either as an inability to obtain such an intuition or as a conflict between two intuitions which contradict each other in regard to the same situation. Thus Abraham, in our hypothetical example, may have been unable to arrive at any clear intuition as to what he should do, or he may have been confronted by two contradictory intuitions in regard to his duty to God, namely, that his duty was conditional or that it was unconditional. Ross's claim is plausible when we artificially isolate values from the system in which they are found hierarchically organized and when we disregard the evidence available against his claim, in the form of a prodigious number of facts accumulated by sociologists and anthropologists about the wide range of differences found in the judgments of the peoples of the earth.

I have no doubt that Ross himself has crystal-clear intuitions. The question can still be asked, however, whether these are valid intuitions, disclosing a moral structure which is universal and prior to what Herskovits, as we saw above, called by the barbaric neologism "enculturation" or whether they are the expression, at the level of judgment, of habituations and trainings exhaustively reducible to mere cultural conditioning of physiological needs. The importance of the question is obscured for Ross by a faith (which obviously, as the reader of his books can see, goes very deep indeed) that there has been moral progress in human history and that he, Ross, stands at the top of it. What Ross takes to be the crystal-clear intuitions of men who are good and enlightened (hence in the forefront of the human trek) could be but the bland prejudices of a well-trained man in the unperturbed enjoyment of his upper-class, hermetically sealed, pre-Buchenwald, pre-Hiroshima, imperial British insularity.

This kind of intuitionism will not save us, I fear, from the fallibility that the flesh is heir to. The rightness of an action does not unqualifiedly consist in its suitability, conceived as a character shining like the flush of youth on its cheek. Suitability or fitness is a relational term, and it defines a relation between (a) a situation, (b) a decision which suits it as capable of resolving (c) a perplexity it gives rise to but (d) that it gives rise to for a specific moral agent.

And the introduction of the last makes it always possible that in the judgment there may be elements of idiosyncrasy and of sheer error.

The ground of moral authority is, nevertheless, the conscience. But its fallibility is obvious to anyone who has considered seriously what is today known about the human psyche with its duplicities, its hidden depths, its strategies of rationalization, and the implacable cunning of its self-hatred and self-love. The problem for us, therefore, is not quite so easy as it is for the intuitionist: we have to examine the claims of the conscience to authority and to decide whether its judgments can be considered objective. Before turning to these problems, however, it is advisable to remind the reader that the ground of obligation, to which we as moral philosophers can point, cannot actually compel a man to act morally who wilfully refuses to do so. If for any reason a man is disposed to suppress his moral responses and to deny the authority of morality over himself, we cannot convince him.[7] Moral philosophy is normative in that it discloses and defines and clarifies the norms operating within the moral conscience of man; one can go to it for help in respect to the perplexities one encounters in one's life. It is not, as Aristotle and Plato clearly knew, a substitute for the existence within the person of the sense of obligation whose principles and objectives moral philosophy defines and helps to clarify. So long as men are free, they can always deny the authority of morality. Freedom is an inalienable possession of man's rational nature; it can be lost only with the loss of one's reason.

On the other hand, the authority of morality cannot be denied without the agent's repudiating, at the same time, his status as person. Thus the acceptance of a single disposition or interest as ultimate and beyond the reach of rational mediation, such as we find in the postulational theory and in Charles Stevenson's doctrine, is not merely the recognition of the limits of morality in cases of radical conflict, but it is also an implicit assertion of the decision of the conflicting parties to abandon their human condition and to descend to the condition of brutes. In the face of such a repudiation we should expect the suasion of moral philosophy to be impotent. But the task of moral reflection is not to invent a system, the publication of which will lead to the conversion of mankind to it, and hence to the abolition of those conditions that the system marks off as evil, but the discovery and elucidation of those principles which, when adequately stated, enable the moral man to understand why actions are right when they are and wrong when, in turn, they are, and thus to choose the truly right action when he possesses the good will to make the choice.

Moral reflection is thus practical, since the clarifications which it achieves can be and are used in practice, but one cannot put them to use unless one first decides to do so. In this respect moral philosophy is no different from logic, another normative discipline. The fictional author of the *Letters from the Underworld* writes: "What have *I* to do with the laws of Nature, or with arithmetic, when all the time those laws and the formula that twice two make four do not meet with my acceptance? Of course, I am not going to beat my head against a wall if I have not the requisite strength to do so; yet I am not going to *accept* that wall merely because I have run up against it, and have no means to knock it down."[8] The writer cannot mean that he rejects logic or mathematics; for anyone who rejects them is crazy. He must mean that he does not accept them in an ethical-religious sense or in a passional-existential or in a "living" sense; for how anyone who was sane could refuse to accept "the stone wall" in a logical or in a natural sense is not easy to conceive. It is impossible to change facts, and no phrase is falser than that which is on our lips today when we boast that we have triumphed over nature, defied the law of gravity, abolished space, and mastered the energy of the atom. This is nonsense, and, if I can be forgiven the platitude, it will be because the truth that it asserts is so frequently lost sight of by modern man in his vanity. He never defied the law of gravity and never can, and, when swishing past faster than sound in his rockets or going down thousands of feet to the cold, black depths of the sea, he is doing nothing that nature forbids; he is obeying her. His true triumph was not over nature but over himself when he taught himself to learn her hidden ways. Santayana has some wise things to say on this point, which, coming from a materialist, should carry weight. Describing the lessons young Oliver learned from his pony, he tells us:

". . . the important point was not to pull the bridle too tight, so as to hurt Dumpy, and yet to pull it hard enough to make him mind. It soon became evident that the secret of control was not so much force as suggestion: and for suggestion to succeed the possibilities of Dumpy must first be consulted. His dumb soul must be solicited and not outraged; and on this sympathetic basis a firm and thoroughly responsible government was soon established by the child over the beast, to the latter's apparent satisfaction, and to the very serious realization on Oliver's part that it was his duty to rule and that he knew how to do it."[9]

If the control of nature that man has gained in the last few centuries were evidence, as pragmatists sometimes contend, of man's freedom, I would be a determinist, for man is never more the slave of nature than when he controls her scientifically. Nature one cannot but accept, nor is one asked whether he will or not. But one need not *resign* one's self to it; one need not exult in one's impotence. Dostoevski saw hidden helplessness behind the vanity of modern man's exultation over his dominion over nature, noticing that in those areas where man could indeed exult, because he enjoyed full freedom, he does not fully use it. Whether there are stone walls—natural conditions—which men ought to accept or not is a moral question; and what Dostoevski was trying to say, if we are allowed to gather it from the sweep of his work, is that there are certain natural conditions to which we ought never to resign ourselves. Moral principles are effective upon the *acceptance* of moral obligation. But a full acceptance of the latter involves a consequent acceptance of the insights and clarifications of moral philosophy, which operates normatively only in a situation within which moral norms are already accepted.

We can now turn to our problem. The account of the moral life elaborated in the preceding chapters is not morally solipsistic or subjectivistic because it does not trace the authority of the moral judgment to the will that chooses between alternatives according to its preferences or dispositions. Of course, normally the moral judgment refers to a suitability or fitness alleged to obtain between a system of values and a practical decision entailing other values which are candidates for incorporation into the system. But, while the latter is a unique entity, since my system is not yours and yours is not Paul's, the suitability of a value to your system is a perfectly objective affair, in regard to which Paul and I, no less than you yourself, can judge and, on occasion, are indeed called on even by you to judge, as we shall see in the next chapter. There is no need to deny what is perfectly obvious and well known, namely, that, when I judge whether a decision is suitable for you, I am likely to fall into error because of my ignorance of your situation and your values. But so am I when I pass judgment on a perplexity by which I myself am confronted; and, whatever practical advantages may exist one way or the other, these do not diminish by the smallest quantity the character of objectivity which may pertain to a judgment about the rightness of a decision.

The judgment may be objective in this sense, however, and yet the authority it possesses may seem to derive from myself, from the values I acknowledge and which constitute me. Since it has been admitted that these are unique, the authority is unique and hence subjective.

This argument is false because it overlooks the fact that the values which one acknowledges, whether as espoused or merely as recognized, one does not acknowledge, as we saw in the last chapter, merely because *one chooses to do so* but also and at the same time because *they choose one* to acknowledge them. It is *in them*, in their requiredness, that the authority has its source. The authority *is* the requiredness, and one's obligation to it is not something which one can accept or reject as one chooses but something which is the necessary result of one's being the kind of man one is, whose endowment enables one to apprehend the requiredness of values and, apprehending it, to respond to it by acknowledging that requiredness, hence owning one's obligation to the value that exhibits it. To the degree to which one is blind to values or insensitive to their requiredness, morality has no authority over one; to that extent one can live like the mere animal which one is. But practical perplexities involve values and hence requiredness and hence the need to choose. A man can refuse to accept the axiological stone wall. Like leviathan, he can dive into the dark depths of his animality. But when he loses his conscience, he loses his humanity, he becomes a mere animal, a brute. When we are forced to choose between values, we claim again our status as persons and thus open ourselves to the demands of obligation toward other persons. A refusal to accept a moral claim, which is to say, a demonstration of insensibility toward proffered values, is indeed frequent among human animals. But such a refusal bespeaks a man as a mere animal.

The moral philosopher is sometimes asked, "Why should we be moral?" Philosophers should have known the answer to this question at least since Socrates' day. If a man possessed the ring of Gyges' ancestor, the Lydian shepherd, he could live unjustly without fear of punishment. Why, then, should he not do so? Before answering the question, let us notice in passing that we are dealing here with the problem of moral obligation. The answer often given is that his conscience will punish him. But need one always fear one's conscience? It would be a great comfort for many an envious coward who does not do evil from fear of punishment or from fear of his conscience if he could be sure that your Goerings and Stalins were men who lost their sleep worrying about the blood that's on their souls. But I rather suspect that neither Goering nor Stalin ever suffered from insomnia. Indeed, from 1932 until at least 1944, Goering seems thoroughly to have enjoyed himself; nor can we argue that a man as passionately fond of Cranach as he was, was a totally coarse man. Shall we then say, as I heard a man who calls himself a Christian not long ago say, that Goering "got his" after his death and so will Stalin? I think we do morality a poor service to put it on the basis of fear. We have to admit that evil men can be happy. Consider, after all, your neighbor Mr. Jones, next door. Is his soul free from the stain of injustice? And does he seem unhappy? Why, then, should I be moral?

The answer I give to this question is not one that I can expect to be generally acceptable to my contemporaries: man ought to be moral because he has two duties from which all his other duties derive, the duty to know God and the duty to make the effort to realize himself as a person. And if he doesn't, what does he lose? Subjectively, if he does not know it, nothing. The Andaman islander, before the nineteenth century, could, in his own terms, be happy and enjoy his life and have his satisfactions and would have refused, on plausible grounds, to exchange his condition for one which was objectively better. But was he a better man than his neighbor, the civilized Indian on the continent? So long as the implicit assumption is that the Indian could be called better only if he enjoyed himself more, the Andaman islander would unquestionably be right in preferring his own condition to the Indian's. This way of thinking is so deeply ingrained in us that we have difficulty in seeing how thoroughly human actions contradict it. Men struggle to remain in their class when, by taking a step down, they could often earn more money and live more easily. Why? Because they believe that economic and social classes define quality. The Englishman who shaves daily and dresses for dinner in the jungle or the clerk who starves in gentility rather than take a highly paid laborer's job acts on the belief that one ought to live up to the highest value that one is capable of. They may be wrong as to what they take to be genuine values, but, as to their obligation to it, they are not. If, instead of trying to maintain their self-respect in terms of superficial values, as they do, men tried to maintain it in terms of the values that are truly worth their loyalty and reverence, the question of why one should be moral would be too obvious to ask.

When a person makes a moral demand of us, we recognize it as *moral* if we recognize the claimant to be a person and the values he is pleading for as values in fact; that is to say, if we recognize *them* to be values.

This double recognition brings the moral claimant, actually or potentially, in respect to the particular claim at least, within the range of the moral interest of the man on whom the claim is pressed. For a person is a human being who possesses intrinsic value and who embodies a system of values, and the man on whom a claim is pressed responds both to the intrinsic value of another and to the values that the other embodies. But he of whom the demand is made does not embody a system of values merely passively. He actively espouses some values and more or less indifferently recognizes others; and, by virtue of those values that he acknowledges, he is open to the effect of the requiredness of the whole range of possible values within his purview. This point could be put more forcefully by saying, in the vernacular, that men are "suckers" for values, which means that in the presence of an external system one cannot help responding to it in at least a minimal way by recognizing its values as such. How we can decide the legitimacy of the specific claim is not here in question; what is in question is how one human being can make a moral demand on another or, rather, how, when one does, the other feels obliged to entertain his demands. For an answer we must fall back on the power that values have over us, once they break into our consciousness, once they brush aside all the commitments and interests and distractions that interfere with our ability to recognize them as values.

This is to say that we recognize another person's moral claim in the same manner in which we recognize any other set of values which presents itself before our consciousness and elicits our espousal, because we respond to its collective requiredness. But this is not all, since we respond chiefly to the requiredness of one value above all, the value of the other person, which we acknowledge as a value by agreeing to consider his demands. Let me illustrate what is here involved. Peter says to Paul, "You ought to grant me this request, *x*." Paul, in acknowledging his obligation to consider its legitimacy (not to grant it), recognizes that Peter is a person and, as such, embodies a value and that to disregard Peter's request is to treat him as a thing. The satisfaction of the demand is thus an addition to the universe of values espoused by Peter and recognized by Paul, an addition which Paul cannot refuse to consider without turning his back on the requiredness of the values in question.

In practice, of course, men do not recognize all human beings as persons. And those whom they do recognize as persons they do not consistently recognize as such. But the reason for the failure is to be traced, in part at least, to *factors which are operative within the moral situation itself and which are susceptible of correction by moral reflection.* One of the factors in a moral situation we might call "centripetal," since it tends to preserve the integration, as already constituted, of the extant values of the moral agent. This force prevents a man from transcending his insularity and leads him to the jealous assertion of his own espoused values as having an exclusive primacy which entails a denial of the claim of any other value on him. This centripetal force usually wins out in cases of radical conflict, and it thus leads to the annihilation of the very moral system which it seeks to preserve. Against this we must set off, however, the requiredness of all values of whatever kind or degree of worth—and that includes the values of the claimant for the agent as well as the values embodied in the claimant's demand.

Exclusive attention to the first of these two conflicting forces, the centripetal, and the total oversight of the other help to account for one of the naturalistic positions which we examined critically in the first part of this essay, the postulational. We have seen how the postulational theory disregards the requiredness of the other's values and insists intransigently on the preservation of the basic commitments of the agent. This argument leads the postulational moralist to a narrow insularity which is the essence of immorality. On the other hand, to argue that the centripetal tendency is, without qualification, undesirable, as is done by the romantic moralist who asserts the primacy of growth, is, in fact, to defend sheer expediency. The romantic moralist overlooks the fact that without a certain concentration, a certain jealousy for one's own values, it is not possible to maintain a system of values.

Thus the moral man has to find an Aristotelian mean between concentration and growth, between openness and closedness. He is torn between these two mutually incompatible tendencies. It is the supreme irony of morality, and one which should not go without comment, that men honestly in the pursuit of the good end up frequently by clutching in their tight fists abominable evil. Frequently, however—or so at least I am inclined to believe—our rejection of the demands of another is to be traced simply to our inability to grant him a status as person, not for immoral reasons, but because of our sheer inability to see the human in the strange featherless biped before us. Let me illustrate with an extreme case.

The discovery of America brought up the problem as to whether the aboriginals were persons. The question was a difficult one to resolve not only because the Europe of the sixteenth century lacked scientific knowledge but, perhaps, also because the Christian integration of values made it difficult for the discoverers to believe that these beings had souls. The Jew and the Mohammedan had forced the Christian European to recognize their status as persons by the exigencies of their practical relationships; but the American Indian, with his alien and repugnant beliefs and customs, could not immediately be recognized as a person. Anyone doubting this assertion has only to read in Bernal Diaz' *La Conquista de la Nueva España* the description of the blood-clotted hair of the priests and the smell of the pyramid of skulls. The conquistadores—themselves not too far above the morality and cultural level of the conquered in such lands as Mexico and Peru—could not fairly be blamed for uncritically rejecting the Indians as persons. It took a genuine Christian like Father Las Casas to transcend the European's insularity through an act of that rarest of qualities, Christian love, to brush aside the barbaric insularism of his age, and to discover the humanity of the Indian. There is deep pathos in the fact that Las Casas' contemporaries, who claimed to be Christians, could not readily follow him. But the pathos is not confined to that age and people; it extends to the whole of our Western culture, which calls itself "Christian" and which is far from being so. Those who blame the deeds of the men of Cortez and of the Pizarros must not forget to blame also the blackbirding expeditions of the English in the islands of the Pacific in the nineteenth century and the unutterable cruelty of the French and Belgians in the Congo. The limitations and shortcomings of our Christianity—what people in history is going to rise and say to another, "You are guilty as we are not"?

In so far as one denies recognition to a moral demand made of him, he denies status as person to the moral claimant and deals with his claim as he deals with all external forces which impinge on him: he either uses it to his ends or overpowers it or circumvents it or yields to it. But, if a person rejects the moral demands made on him by a being whose status as person cannot be denied, the rejection is wrong. It is wrong not only to the other, who makes the claim, but it is also wrong to one's self because, by denying the demand, one repudiates one's own status as person and proclaims one's decision to descend to the level of the mere animal. This we do daily, but we cannot do it without contradicting two truths discovered by Socrates as essential to the moral life: first, that if we deny our own status as persons, we do not know what we are doing, for no man fully cognizant of what he is up to could gratuitously destroy himself; and, second, that the wrongdoer harms himself much more than he harms his victim if he destroys his own personality. It is also possible, but not quite so easy, to destroy the personality of another. Or, rather, since on these questions we must be exact, it was not quite so easy until the nineteen-thirties. Formerly one could kill a man, maim him, but not crush him as a person. It remained for our generation to solve the problem scientifically and to demonstrate that a man's humanity can also be destroyed if we go at the job with the proper experimental objectivity. In the United States we do not yet fully know how to do this, but we know that it can be done. The Germans "solved the problem," and, in their own dialectically refined way, so did the Russians. And anyone who shares the writer's faith in American science believes that we will do it easily when the need arises.

The age of foolish martyrdom is gone. A man can stand up under the most excruciating physical tortures that unscientific men could once devise. But today, in the hands of technicians, he can be "processed" in such a way that he can be made to repudiate himself and accuse himself of any crime his persecutors choose, and he can be made to do so deliberately and without showing any marks of physical torture. Our generation should be proud of its achievements: we conquered the air and the depths of the sea, we conquered the atom, and, finally, we have conquered the soul of man. Prattle about heads "bloody but unbowed" is sheer, unscientific nonsense. Today we can make any man bow his head without a telltale bruise. And those who have followed, however superficially, the literature on the subject know that the glories of scientific sociology which the Germans proudly claimed in Maidenek and Buchenwald have been surpassed by the glories of dialectical materialism. The Germans, in taking a man's dignity, took the appearance of dignity from him. Through dialectical materialism we have learned to take away his dignity and his humanity and yet leave him looking like a man. There is one problem, however, that we do not seem yet to have solved: we have not yet managed to destroy another man's humanity without previously destroying our own. Have we then reached the limits of science?

I destroy that which is most valuable in a person when I force him to fall back on his animality and to have recourse to brute force against me. But, before I can destroy him, I have already destroyed myself because, by denying his moral claim, I have chosen to function in a capacity which I know to be lesser than that in which I do indeed, if I but stop to think, want to function. My obligation, then, to recognize the moral claim of another person springs from my own need: the fact that I recognize him as a person because I cannot deny my own status as a person. Unfortunately, it is only too easy to allow our interests to obfuscate our grasp of what is involved in our recognition of both others and ourselves as persons. But nothing can free us from our primary moral obligation except that which first destroys us as persons; passion is the formal and the final, no less than the efficient, cause of self-destruction. And, thus viewed, we should easily grasp the essentially corrupting immorality of some of the theories which we examined in Part I of this study. The source of moral authority cannot be the will or any other aspect of our psyche. The source is found in the value requiredness to which we respond and to which we must respond in order to remain persons.

Moral behavior may call for the sacrifice of values in favor of a moral system which does not find them assimilable to itself; and in our human relations the values of others may endanger our own integrity. It is one thing, however, to sacrifice a value on stated grounds, whether that value be my own or an alien one, and another thing to deny the status of another as person by rejecting his demands. The former can be done in terms of principles which, since they are not infallible, are open to criticism and are corrigible. The corrigibility is an essential part of our moral activity and one which must be granted by anyone who claims status as person. No moral decision, therefore, is apodictic or absolute. This, of course, means that no person can claim for his judgment, as against the judgment of another, an absolute superiority. So long as such authority is not claimed by either party in a moral conflict, the moral process remains open, at least in theory, and the parties to a moral dispute can carry on. But no moral process can be maintained in the face of the widespread tendency among men to protect their interests at the cost of their personalities. For this reason, whether or not morality is capable of resolving conflicts of interests depends on the values which have been integrated into a system.

In certain human groups the values which are most influential in giving the system its character and in defining its standards, those hierarchically superior, are values which are not hospitable to growth and enrichment and which therefore tend to make short shrift of claims made upon them. But lack of hospitality to alien values bespeaks a morally defective system. And the reason for this is that the essence of the person, as we have seen, is not defined exclusively by its moral commitment to an integrity conceived as static and exclusive but by a tension between the commitment to integrity and the capacity to respond to the requiredness of those values which come within its purview. This requiredness constitutes the basis for the claim made upon a system for the incorporation of new values. And that claim cannot be morally disregarded a priori, although moral reflection may fairly deny it eventually. But the denial of a claim, when made by a person who allows the corrigibility of his judgment, cannot be final but constitutes, rather, the second step in the resolution of a moral perplexity.

Should it be urged that the exigencies of action frequently force us to decide with finality our moral perplexities, the contention cannot, as a fact, be denied; but it is necessary to add that, when we yield to any interest and sacrifice morality to it, we cannot claim at the same time that we are acting morally. If we admit that for any reason we are not able to act morally—and this is what we do when we put our interest ahead of the claims made by a moral situation upon us—no excuse will give our action the character it lacks. It has already been pointed out that the moral life involves sacrifice. A life lived predominantly on the basis of interest also involves sacrifice: the sacrifice we make when we disregard morality, which is to say, when we destroy our personality for the sake of things we want.

The nature of the moral person has not been explained when it is suggested, as it may have been above, that integrity concerns the preservation of a value system against intrusion of unassimilable values. Integrity does indeed involve preservation; but it also involves the preservation of a man's or a people's status as person, as moral agents. A moral agent is concerned with acting morally; and the concern leads him to respond to moral demands made of him in the spirit in which they are made as much as it leads him to wish to protect his moral system from destructive alien values. For this reason among others, philosophers who conceive the moral problem as defined by the need to satisfy desires or co-ordinate interests misunderstand it because they understand it only partially. And one regrettable result of this misunderstanding is that they cannot give an adequate account of human dignity. There can be no dignity unless a person (not a mere animal) is there to have it, and there is no person if a man puts his interests or desires above the moral demands made of him.

It was said above that the claim to satisfaction made of a man by his interests and desires is a claim for *moral* satisfaction. This is obvious, since the interest or desire fastens hungrily on a value and the latter appeals to us not from within outward but from without inward. Desire—considered in the abstract, that is, considered by itself—does not demand that the satisfaction it craves be moral. What desire wants, if it can be said to "want" anything, is simply the thing it wants. However, considered in the abstract, no desire could function, no desire could go toward its object, could, indeed, even have an object. The perception of a need as need is our perception, and so is the perception of the need's object. This means that the need is what it is within the structure of the mind for which it is a need. By itself it is not easy to guess what a need or desire could be, beyond being a physiological event. It may not be quite exact, therefore, to speak of a desire's demand that it be allowed to reach its object and that the reaching be considered moral. But, when this manner of speaking is translated, no error need be involved, and the translation reveals the solution to our difficulty. We want our desires to be satisfied; but, if we stop to reflect a second, we should realize that we cannot want merely to satisfy *them*, for we want the satisfaction to be *ours*, to be part of us, and it cannot be so unless it fits our value organization, unless it is moral. To the extent to which we are not fully integrated but are made up of more or less autonomous subselves, this statement does not apply. But this condition is not one which can obtain without generating conflicts and frustrations which entail the moral problem.

The seat of moral authority, then, is the personality within which the moral perplexity arises, in the sense that our normal decisions are made in terms of the values that we acknowledge. It should be clear, however, from what has been said in this and the preceding chapter that that authority does not have its source in the psyche but in the requiredness that the values acknowledged by the psyche possess, through incorporation of which into the self it becomes a person. The psyche does not decree the law by fiat, nor would such a decree, were it to be made, have any moral authority; the law is made for the psyche by the values that it is able to discover. The appropriation of these values makes one into a person and, at the same time, endows one with responsibility toward the values. In the person we find, therefore, a peculiar ambivalence, for the inwardness of the personality, its uniqueness, and its dignity are the result of the activity of the psyche—which discovers and espouses and recognizes values; but it is no less the result of the fact that these values stand toward their discoverer as something which is distinct and independent of, I would even say *prior* to, himself. While it is I who must make my own moral decisions, I who must assume responsibility for them, and I who possess the freedom without which no decision can be called my own, the authority is mine derivatively; originally it belongs to a collective something which I have appropriated but which I must acknowledge as my superior, namely, the system of values out of which I carved my system.

CHAPTER XVI

THE JUSTIFICATION OF A MORAL DECISION

WHEN a person arrives at a moral decision, he expresses it in a judgment for which he must assume full responsibility. This means that he must justify his judgment by proving that it rests on adequate authority. Justification is the process through which the person accepts his responsibility publicly by testing the adequacy of his decision before the bar of reason. It involves, in its simplest terms, the exhibition of the grounds of the decision: the authority from which it flowed and the perplexing circumstances whose resolution it achieves. When a man exhibits these grounds, he opens them to objective, impersonal scrutiny, he exposes his inwardness, he parades his person nakedly before the eyes of his fellows. In practice this is achieved in several ways, all of which involve the exhibition of the grounds for the decision and the claim—open, of course, to correction—that these are legitimate grounds. A decision is justified when the grounds to which it is referred are adequate because they constitute a value system possessing the authority to arrive at a decision and because the decision is appropriate to the situation. The process thus opens to rational inquiry, so to speak, "the whole record." And in calling the inquiry "rational," what is intended is that the appropriateness or fitness of the decision is acceptable to an "impersonal" judge who is competent, by knowledge of the situation and by sensibility expressed in his acknowledgment of the values involved, to pass on the fitness in question.

Since the impersonality of the judge is itself not operationally testable with accuracy, in the process of justification some techniques and procedures and concepts analogous to legal fictions are introduced which define "impersonality" in a practical way and which are assumed to guarantee at least a minimum of it. We appeal to "the moral sense of the community," to arbitrators, to what people will say, to the pillars of society, to respectable opinion. This is not true of the revolutionist, who repudiates the moral sense of his community. For this reason the revolutionist constitutes a critical case that tests our answer and reveals what is truly intended in the appeal made by men normally to socially acknowledged values. Otherwise we have done no more than go in a roundabout way back to the cultural relativism which has already been criticized.

The revolutionist appeals in the first instance to the values and ideals which the society allegedly espouses but to which it is unfaithful, while at the same time he appeals to a construct of his own making, variously located in the past or in the near future, which he urges that world which he condemns to emulate: democratic Rome with its virile virtues; Canaan, along whose lines the reformer would build the new utopia; a Jerusalem which has no other historical reality than that with which the utopian's fervid thirst for righteousness endows it. If no utopia in the past will do, one in the future is invented: a utopia in which the vices and corruption and iniquity which the reformer resents are absent—a classless society in which each gives according to his capacity and from which each takes according to his need. The *logic* of the appeal in the case of the revolutionist is identical to that of the man who, having no radical quarrel with the values of his society, appeals to a moral sense which he more or less shrewdly imputes to it; he presents an ideal situation which, he hopes, will be responded to by those to whom he appeals. When the ideal is projected into the past, there is probably as little reality to it as there is when the utopia is placed in the future: democratic Rome was never what Rome was taken by revolutionists to be, and a half-naked George Washington dressed as a Roman senator expressed neither past nor present actuality. He embodied a fervid dream, even though later generations find the expression embarrassing and keep him out of sight. All these fictions collapse under the first ray of a logical flashlight, since they represent only rough practical devices to achieve the desired impersonality necessary to the moral judge. The process is vague and, in actuality, is inherently infected with error; but ideally it is not difficult to see that the appeal is made to minds free of immediate interests in the situation (that is, who stand to gain or lose nothing at all in an immediate way by their decision), who, being fully acquainted with the acknowledged values and the circumstances involved, can test the decision in terms of both. The emphasis must be both on "acknowledged values" and on "minds free of immediate interests," for anyone who takes stock of what he is doing when he tries to justify his judgment will see that he is not appealing to social authority because in some unexplained way it is able *morally* to command; what he is appealing to is the authority of the values that society acknowledges, on the more or less obscure notion that society is wiser than the individual and that the values it acknowledges are therefore more likely to be the true and relevant values than those that any individual recognizes or espouses.

A competent "impersonal" judge is one who looks at the total situation, is able to foresee consequences, and is sensitive enough to perceive the values involved in their proper order of rank relative to the situation. But what is the proper order of rank? Is this not precisely what we are trying to determine? Until we define either impersonality independently of the proper order of rank or the latter of the former, we are caught in a rather obvious circle. I beg the reader to allow me to postpone discussion of this problem for a few pages. Here let me suggest, rather, that, if the principles that determine the decision do not both express the value demands of the total situation and fit the value system of the conflicting parties, the decision is not justified. Appropriateness or fitness refers to a relation that obtains between the decision and the total scheme of values constituting the personality. But the process of justification in opening to public view the values of the person brings them, no less than it brings the decision, within the range of criticism, exhibiting the person's excellences and deficiencies and the way in which he is able to cooperate with or endanger the larger world of values on which he depends for his own existence. Ideally this "larger world of values" is the whole realm of values actual and possible, conceived and conceivable, in its relevant aspects to the perplexity and the judgment that resolved it; but practically it is the acknowledged system of values which both the individual and his society share. However, the acknowledged system shared by a man and his society seldom constitutes, as cultural relativists blandly assume, a hermetically closed, neatly organized system. This may be true for a small society of primitives—the Andaman islanders, let us say, up to the end of the eighteenth or the beginning of the nineteenth century, living in relatively effective isolation.[1] It does not apply to a society of primitives that lives in cultural contact with another society, as the process of diffusion which has been so earnestly studied by anthropologists proves. The practical appeal, therefore, to a socially constituted value system is contingent upon the effective closedness and systematic order of rank which actually obtain—a closedness and order which the first challenge by a moral rebel shows up to be but the very absence of all that anyone can claim them to be.

The method by which the examination of the validity of a judgment is carried on is the time-hallowed method which Plato called "dialectics": the interrogation of claims and counterclaims in order to elicit from them the evidence on which they rest. In the give-and-take of the dialectical inquiry the judgments in conflict are corrected by confronting them with the facts to which they pretend to refer; and the principles on which the judgments are based are themselves subject to criticism by reference to objective values, critically apprehended, to which the inquiry is addressed and which remain the ultimate basis of appeal. It is important to notice, however, that what is purely idiosyncratic, whether in the moral agent or in the critic of his decision, is irrelevant to an objective judgment and gradually emerges when the conflicting judgments are put, in Plato's phrase, through the gauntlet of the argument. Criticism seeks to exhibit the values involved in the decision, to test the relation between it and the values in respect to which it is said to be fitting, and at the same time to inquire into the validity of the rating which orders them hierarchically. Thus the judge tries to put himself in a position from which he can evaluate objectively the agent and his decision in relation to the public hierarchy of values which, by membership in a social world, the agent acknowledges. The total process, carried on publicly, results in the gradual crystallization of opinion from which errors of subjectivity have to some degree been eliminated. We may maintain this doctrine and admit freely that the process is not one from which error can be thoroughly removed.

This doctrine would be but a thinly disguised form of cultural relativism were it not for the following radical differences: (1) Cultural relativism assumes that cultural processes are constitutive of value, while in the account here given the opposite is assumed to be the case. Value is constitutive not only of the person but of his culture. (2) Cultural relativism assumes that the authority of the judgment has its source in the rules and values laid down by the culture, whereas it is here claimed that, in so far as any operative system of values has authority, it rests on the capacity that it collectively has of eliciting response, a capacity which the value conflicts within a society prove to transcend any one group or class in the society and even all the members of the society taken collectively. (3) Cultural relativism assumes that moral judgments are valid intra-systemically and denies the possibility of disputation across systems; but, on the view offered here, a cultural value system is effectively connected with values beyond it, since the process of recognizing values is a dynamic one, even in stratified and monolithic societies. It follows that even if, descriptively speaking, a society is effectively isolated, normatively speaking, no society ought to be isolated or it risks destroying the moral status of its members.

The foregoing account will no doubt seem to be infected with circularity to those readers who, not adequately acquainted with the actual complexities of criticism, will think of the problem solely in abstract logical terms and will peremptorily demand logical rigor and elegance above fidelity to the complex facts. But the account is not circular, since it holds that the criticism of the judgment and of the criterion which rules it is always controlled by objectively given values which can be exhibited and to which final appeal can be made. Firsthand acquaintance with the actual procedure of moral inquiry and with the process of justification will reveal them to be characterized by inefficiency and confusion but not by radical circularity. In the give-and-take of criticism, through which the true values embodied in a situation are gradually revealed, the intent of the moral agent and the import of his decision are more or less clarified and his contribution to the moral life of his world assayed. The appeal in the case of conflict is always to objective values, whose "thereness" enables the disputants and the referees before whom the dispute is carried to adjudicate their claims. The referees are the representatives of the fictional objective judges to whom reference was made above—public opinion, the respectable members of the society, or whoever may be ultimately appealed to. It is to them that we turn to decide whether the values in question are or are not what they are claimed to be, and they make their point by exhibiting the values which they discover. I have shown in my criticism of R. B. Perry and of functionalism in anthropology that we do not need to define value in terms of interest. Values are discovered, and men can usually be brought around to apprehend them when they are exhibited to them. Because they make the surface of actuality radiant with their presence or because they tarnish it with their conspicuous absence, usually all we need to do is to turn our eyes upon them, to record their presence in our exclamation of delight. But the "usually" with which I qualified the statement is important, since men intent on something or coarsened by living do not respond readily to the requiredness of value. And the criterion of whether a judge responds to the proper order of rank is whether, in discussion, he can convince those who appeal to him that the order he perceives is indeed the proper order. We see this easily in the field of beauty if we remember that we often meet men of superior sensibility who point out to us aspects of art or nature that we have missed. Of course, a tactless, overbearing individual cannot show us anything. But we frequently learn—and not always from "superior" men. And thus we learn morally also. The judge points to values, and we are forced to acknowledge them. However, since the values to which he points often threaten our vested interests, we are loath to apprehend them, and when we apprehend them we are careful not to give ourselves away. Nevertheless, it is a fact that values can be pointed out to us and that we often recognize them as a result of their being pointed out.

One criticism that has been made of this account must be met. The doctrine has been called "conservative" because, it has been argued, it calls for a criticism which is guided by criteria of publicly accepted values. But this is not a fair interpretation of what the view intends, since established values are not, on this theory, fixed affairs to which the judgment must supinely conform. If, however, it should be insisted that the theory is more likely to give comfort to a conservative than to a revolutionist, since it seems to put so much emphasis on the extant system of social values as a source of criteria of moral adequacy or fitness, it would be well to remember, in justice to it, that the system of values constituting the person is not treated in this doctrine as if it constituted the final criterion, since that system is itself held to be responsive to values presented for espousal.

If this doctrine is open to criticism, it should be so not because it is conservative but because it sounds like Deweyism. But the similarity is specious, and it would be both more fair and more exact to accuse the writer of doing nothing more than explicating the method of Socratic dialectic in contemporary idiom. To this charge he gladly pleads guilty. Unlike Dewey, the writer holds the final criterion to be the objective relationship between a decision and a value system and between this relationship and the larger, open value system of the social world with which the individual's system is continuous. According to this doctrine, values are held to exist prior to their discovery and to be regulative of the judgment. It often happens that the values of an individual lose their vitality; in such cases the loss carries with it its own punishment, since it means the death of the person. If, on the other hand, the growth of the personality takes place at too rapid a pace, as is often the case in our day, the rapidity also carries with it its own punishment, for the person becomes distracted, queer, eccentric, and loses his identity. The romantic ideal of indefinite expansion on which such an exaggerated value is put in our day and which is one of the dogmatic exigencies of pragmatic morals tends to add to the social disorder of which men are victims and thus speeds up the social disintegration that produces it.

The process of justification of our moral decisions completes the moral activity and involves a total repudiation of subjectivism in the moral judgment. The man who refuses to justify his decisions repudiates his place in the moral community and denies the social aspect of his person. Such a man behaves as if his own inner light were the sole and unchallengeable source of authority, as if his decisions were capable of self-validation. But the very conception of self-validation is a contradiction. For this reason, while we must agree with those who insist that private factors do, in fact, enter into valuation and must add that they serve to individuate one's person, we cannot agree with them in so far as they seem to suggest that they ever "justify" it. When a judge falls back on them, he has withdrawn his judgment from all criticism and has asserted that he is interested in the expression of his arbitrary will rather than in the objective justification of his judgment. Note, however, that, if the argument of this essay has been made clear, the phrase "objective justification" should be taken as pleonastic, since the effort to justify a judgment consists precisely in exhibiting the objective and sharable basis on which it rests.

There are, however, two qualifications to be made of this statement. The first is that our formulation of the grounds on which we justify a moral decision does not exhibit all the factors that determined it. There is, indeed, "a private factor" in valuation which enters into our moral decisions and which perhaps could be brought into the public domain only through the effort of deep analysis. After all, our decisions are not arrived at by purely rationalistic calculation. We do not always clearly know why we decide as we do, even though we may be fully convinced of the correctness of our decision. Moral decisions are, in this respect, analogous to the creative activity of the artist: they involve subtle affective factors which one trusts, although one barely makes them out. The mind facing a radical perplexity works below the level of consciousness, in a groping way, and only in the case of shallow decisions of relatively trivial nature is it capable of grasping fully the factors that enter into them. Hence the demand that a decision be justified cannot be met in its entirety. You ask a man who has just arrived at a difficult decision, "Why did you decide as you did?" And he is troubled and somewhat incoherent in his answer. You, who know him and who are well informed about the perplexity which he has faced, suggest, "Perhaps for *this* reason?" At your suggestion his face brightens in gratitude, and he says, "Of course, *that* was the reason; what other reason could I have had?" He is not lying to you or deceiving himself or you by snatching at your suggestion; for your words, lucid and objective, embody the principles that underlie the decision at which he arrived, in so far as these can be reached. When they are made explicit, now, in your formulation, it is easier for him to see that the suggested reason is indeed a fair expression of what he believes and of the values for which he stands.

There are also, it should be remembered, whole areas of conduct in regard to which society does not demand justification—areas to which we may refer as those in which the only social justification required is the exhibition of an idiosyncratic preference. However, the idiosyncrasy is allowed only on the condition that there be no socially pertinent consequences to the individual choice. For instance, in our American society it is assumed that the choice of a wife is a matter of subtle idiosyncratic affinities over which a man has no control. "God knows what he saw in her," his friends say of Paul's bride behind his back, since they do not see anything to commend her for and are puzzled by his choice. Usually it is enough to explain the choice on the basis of some mystic pre-established harmony. But, even in the United States, romantic individualism is sometimes required to give acceptable "public" reasons and to give up its faith in transcendental tropism. Let a man's wife turn out to be an undesirable woman, and catch him at a moment when he needs to talk about his marital troubles. Ask him gently, *why* did he marry the wench? Of course, he may be a very rare person who really believes that "love is all." But even that reason has justificatory validity on the basis of a social appeal to its self-evident truthfulness. Love then becomes a public reason. However, the majority of men will justify their choices by falling back on socially accepted grounds which can be stated more or less clearly and which in our society, for their class and condition, constitute "valid" reasons. Not only, in this case, because our man "fell in love" with the woman (which process is socially structured through and through by axiological determinants) but also because he thought she would make him a good wife—help him in his career, share his interests and tastes, because she came from a good family, would make a good mother for his children, and other plausible reasons. Admitted that one of the reasons he chose her was the quick first shock that went through him on first meeting her and which he quite unconsciously cultivated into an infatuation. The other reasonable reasons, so to speak, are there, too; and, now that our young friend has to justify his choice to himself, he advances them because he is eager to justify his worth as a reasonable, intelligent, sensible man before the bar of his own, no less than his friends', judgment. It is these qualities of his which, in justifying his choice, he must vindicate in the same manner that a man vindicates his "decency" when he justifies a moral action.

The treatment of justification at this length is necessitated by the fact that British moralists since Bentham and American value theorists who have been influenced by Santayana and R. B. Perry have popularized among philosophers a shallow picture of the moral act as if it were carried out on the principles of cost accounting in an industrial enterprise. I have faith that the men who have been responsible for this view are much better than their theory; but in any case their views are shallow and leave out of account one aspect of the moral life which, in my opinion, is of decisive importance and to which we must therefore turn before we can leave our topic. It can be broached by stating that the decision of a moral agent constitutes *a creative act*, expressive of the spontaneity which is central to the psyche and which constitutes the ground of man's heavy burden of freedom.

What a man beset by the need to resolve a moral perplexity is seeking for, we saw, is an alternative that "fits" or is "appropriate to" or is "suitable to" the values that constitute him. But not only is the search involved addressed, as we have noticed, outwardly to an objective practical alternative, but also, to the degree to which it is radical or momentous, it is addressed inwardly to a search for the espoused values that must be elected as determinative of the appropriateness of the decision. However, since these values are not all, like water lilies, on the surface and since even those which are have drooping roots entangled with other roots sunk in the slime of the subconscious, the search for them is, in fact, a search for one's personality. But the search is a *creative* search, since one's formulation of what one truly is influences in *a creative way* what one becomes: the act of expression leads to a clarification of what one is, what one stands for, the values essentially constitutive of one's self. A clarification, then, is not merely an ordering of what is there, a mere verbalizing of what hitherto has remained unexpressed, but an ordering which sets one in motion toward completion of what one is. In achieving a clearer notion of ourselves, we thus create ourselves, and the process has the stamp of spontaneity.

Elsewhere I have argued[2] that the creative activity of the mind must be taken in a literal sense, that the mind is *truly creative*, meaning that the creative mind transforms and transmutes the matter of experience so that what it produces is, in an important sense, utterly unlike what was taken in by experience. In respect to form and content, I have argued, the mind out of its own intrinsic spontaneity makes additions to its experience in the fields of science, art, statesmanship, morality, and religion. The medium through which the addition is made—the language of the scientist or the material of the artist—resists, for it has obdurate ways over which the creative mind must win; but, as the creative idea suddenly illumines consciousness or slowly comes to birth, the matter yields and grows and is informed with something utterly new.

It is not an exaggeration to say that we know nothing about the creative process except that it does occur. The reason for our ignorance is chiefly, perhaps, that the active imagination works unobserved, on its own, after conscious effort gives it its first push. That in some minds the idea seems to pop fully formed and quite unexpectedly into consciousness, while in other no less gifted minds it has to be dragged out painfully, piece by piece, and has to be fitted no less laboriously into completed wholes—these are both easily observable commonplaces. In the latter case, which is probably more common, it is easier to sense the effect of the "not-yet-there" whole controlling the process of creation; but this does not mean that it was absent in the former. For all that, we seem to be utterly in the dark as to how the creative imagination goes about its work. Yet our ignorance is not so abysmal that it will allow us to confuse "the active imagination" with the capacity to solve problems evinced by the merely ingenious, the merely inventive, mind or, as we may call it, the "Hobbesian mind." The difference may be only one of degree, though this is, on the face of it, doubtful; but a few degrees more or less mark an important difference in kind between the quick and the dead in body and *may* mark the difference between the mind of the genius and the merely ingenious mind.

These seemingly paradoxical aspects of moral reflection to which I have referred cannot be ignored in the interests of formal consistency. If there is here a real paradox, honesty to the facts demands of us that we acknowledge it. If it is not real, its resolution should lead to a deeper grasp of the phenomena in which we are interested than we could achieve by making sacrifices to the idols of a misunderstood and shallow logical elegance. The paradox is specious, however, and disappears when we remember that man does not create out of nothing, for he is not God. The mind's activity is creative, since it does not proceed through mechanical determinations; and therefore the results of its decisions are not predictable from a knowledge of the experiential matter that constitutes the content out of which the mind elaborates its decisions. But spontaneity seeks through its activity to complete or realize the mind in whose interests it acts. Otherwise put, the mind seeks to complete itself, to become itself, within the limitations set by the fact that it has a historical locus and a given segment of experiential content to inform it. In the process of creating itself, it comes closer to what a mind is; as men create themselves freely, they become men; and the more they do so, the closer they come to achieving full humanity, the status of complete personalities.

It seems advisable to point out that the reason for speaking of the moral act as if it were divided into two moments—that of resolving and that of justifying—is that it is possible to arrive at a decision by proceeding in what is popularly called an "intuitive" way, which depends on a minimum of that conscious intellection which, when justification is called for, must be put into explicit judgments backed up by arguments. But it is probably true that men differ widely among themselves in the manner in which they think and that some men carry on their mental activity chiefly above the conscious level, whereas others do so below. This is a matter of degree and, I suspect, a question of types. Be that as it may, the moral act involves two distinguishable moments, and both of these, when a man is confronted by a radical perplexity, may call forth the mind's spontaneity.

If the argument of this chapter is acceptable, the final court to which the private moral judgment appeals for justification is, ideally, the world of values which rational minds can descry and to which they can respond, but, practically, it is the conscience of man, of men, "the conscience of the community of mankind." This does not mean, however, that the judgment is, in the last analysis, relative to a social conscience any more than an appeal to the scientific conscience means that the truth of a scientific judgment is decided by counting scientific heads. The conscience of a community is not an entity which has superior authority in some mystic sense and to which appeal can be made as if it were the Supreme Court. It has no rules of procedure; the precedents on which it operates are vague guides for its decisions; but, what is worse, the conscience of the community, even when it can be made articulate, is, for obvious reasons, the lowest moral denominator of a people's moral sensibility. And I imagine that in all cultures, but particularly in civilized societies, this conscience can easily be manipulated by malevolent agencies which are alert to the need to protect their own interests. In an essay entitled "The Great Stereopticon," in his brilliant study of the illness of contemporary society, Richard Weaver examines the most powerful of these agencies, the newspaper, in a manner which those seriously interested in these questions cannot afford to overlook.[3]

It is nevertheless true that the social conscience must not be thought of as always inclined toward evil; for, just as it can be manipulated to serve selfish ends, so it can also, although rarely, be made to rise above its own low level. But, after all that can be said in its favor is on record, it remains true that between the moral individual and the social conscience there is always a tension, and the morally creative insights of individuals are always ahead of the moral sensibility of their society. For this reason the private moral judgment is relative to the public conscience only when that conscience is not challenged to justify itself—which is to say, when there is congruity between the individual's and the publicly acknowledged values. When the public conscience is challenged to justify itself, as is done by the moral prophet, the only manner in which it can do so (simplifying for the sake of the point at issue and assuming that the conscience of the community can be represented by a single voice) is by the same difficult and vague dialectical process that is employed in the resolution of private moral perplexities, now made more vague and more difficult by being carried on amid the din of the market place: by pointing to the fitness of a proposed resolution to the situation which gave rise to the perplexity, as well as by attempting a radical criticism of the values espoused by the society.

The attempt to validate a private judgment when it cannot readily justify itself by an appeal to the social conscience launches the man who makes it into the most arduous and most controversial path he could possibly want to strike out on. At the end of it is usually to be found the martyr's reward: the cross, the stake, social infamy. But the moral life involves precisely the acceptance of just these rewards. However, this is not the whole of its tragedy, for no man can be certain that because he has been selected for the role of martyr he is a true martyr. There is nothing more detrimental to the moral life and more cheapening of the destiny of man than the facile cheerfulness with which it is so often insinuated that the moral life leads to happiness and that in the long run the right always triumphs. No one is forced to be moral—all that we are forced to be is "respectable," which is something easy and rewarding.

PART III
THE ETHICAL LIFE

CHAPTER XVII

THE DISCOVERY OF THE ETHICAL. I

IF WE look critically into the account that we have given of moral activity, it will not be possible to avoid the feeling that it has ignored or overlooked certain manifestations which have been generally recognized as representing the highest expressions of morality of which men are capable. Our account, as already given, would seem to be true of the respectable orthodoxy of any society, whether Dobuan or American, whether in the past or in the present. But there are men who face their moral perplexities in a way that adds to the act a dimension of which our account has not given an inkling. Take, for instance, the Christian; I mean, of course, the true Christian—a very rare person—and not the nominal Christian. At the core of his values we find one toward which he manifests a totally different attitude than he does toward his other values; or, to state it more precisely, we find that he espouses a tightly organized complex of values which is in a class by itself and to which we can inadequately but conveniently refer as the value of "love."

In order to mark the distinction which is to engage our attention in this chapter, I propose the use of the term "moral" to refer to the manner of resolving practical perplexities already discussed, the term "ethical" to designate the processes of valuation and the principles of resolution of practical perplexities with which we shall occupy ourselves in this and succeeding chapters, the archetype of which, for us, will be the Christian ethics. The terminology does not conform to established usage, according to which "morals" and "morality" refer to the actual processes of valuation and "ethics" to the study of these; but I do not know of a more appropriate set of terms to serve us here, and, with regret, I claim the privilege of the student of philosophy—so far studiously and, I hope, more or less successfully avoided—to make arbitrary use of language to serve my own needs.[1]

Now there is an important argument among scholars as to whether in Christian ethics we find an utterly new set of values of which the ancient world had no knowledge or whether it merely represents a higher, perhaps, but a continuous evolution of values more or less clearly prefigured in the world before Jesus. Fortunately, we need not examine the merits of this controversy, for the question we must try to elucidate is not historical or, for that matter, one which concerns the specific nature of Christian ethics, considered from the standpoint of those inherently interested in specifically Christian values. What we seek light on is whether in Christian ethics we find elements not discoverable in those ordinary moral activities of men of which we have tried to give an account and whether, therefore, Christian ethics represents an activity different in kind from the moral. If it could be shown that Christian ethics is absolutely unique, our task would still be what it is, namely, to inquire into those elements which distinguish it from other kinds of moral activity. But if it could be shown, as I tend to believe, that there are other ethical systems that have exhibited those factors which give Christian ethics its moral superiority over other forms of the moral life, we would still be required to analyze the structure of this kind of activity and to isolate its defining constituents.

It is not irrelevant at this point to note, however, that historical controversies about the origin and uniqueness of Christian ethics depend on what exactly Christian ethics is thought to include, and this, in turn, is not a question in respect to which we can show indifference. How, then, can we define Christian ethics?

The first difficulty we encounter when we turn to this question is that it can be fairly claimed that actually there is no such thing as a Christian ethics. There is a utilitarian moral theory, which can be put into practice by a Republican or a Communist, a Chinese or a Peruvian; and there is an Epicurean moral system, which, although entailing a materialistic conception of the world, is—if we look closely—really logically independent of this conception. But a Christian ethics as separate from a Christian religion, however conceived—what sort of thing, quartered and bled white by the operation, could we have in mind when we speak of it? This is not to deny that there are specifically ethical aspects to Christianity, as distinguished from its specifically religious side, but merely to insist that the ethics of Christianity could not be the ethics of any other conception of the world than that of an actively religious Christian, since in the nature of the case his behavior toward his fellows is determined by his attitude toward *his* God. This contention, I believe, is valid. It is nevertheless also true that we can distinguish the ethics from the religion, although we shall not succeed in adequately discussing the former without reference to the latter; that we find that some men who do not partake of the Christian religion's faith do not escape so easily from the ethical influence of Christianity; and, finally, that for our purpose those types of activity prescribed by Christian ethics correspond to similar types of activity imbedded in other visions of the cosmos.

I imagine that one of the most widespread conceptions of Christian ethics is that it consists in the belief in the universal brotherhood of man. Unless I misread him, this is what T. H. Green maintains.[2] But this is a misleading half-truth. Hebrew scholars claim with plausibility that the notion of universal brotherhood is to be found fully developed in the Prophets, and students of ancient philosophy argue similarly about the *Cosmopolis* of the Stoics. If there is a distinction between the Christian and these other systems of moral philosophy, it cannot be what it is usually taken to be, although it is to be found where it is generally sought for.

I would suggest, brushing aside a number of reflections which a historical approach would demand that I submit to the consideration of the reader, that the distinction between Christian ethics and Hebrew and Stoic morality is to be found where it is usually sought for but that, for our purposes at least, the distinction requires a more precise statement than it is possible to give it under the rubric of "universal brotherhood." What Christianity introduces is not merely the universal claim to humanity of all men and hence to their partnership in a universal moral society but something considerably more radical and considerably more obscure. For we must distinguish between a moral attitude which enables us to recognize the moral demands made of us by other human beings whom we acknowledge as persons and one which asks us to treat them as possessing an intrinsic value that it is our duty to espouse and that we ought to recognize as superior to all the other values we espouse.

What the Christian means by this unique and superior value of the person is obscure for two distinct reasons, one practical, the other philosophical. The first consists in our human inability, even on the plane of imagination, to separate ourselves from our malice and antagonisms and divisive fears and hatreds and to conceive what it would be like to feel toward all men—one's hated enemies, odious strangers, those who threaten one's security, and those who are merely different—as we feel toward those who (irrespective of erotic ties) are for us more precious than ourselves. This Christian love is utterly unlike the "fraternity" of the liberal, which is abstract and, so far as my experience goes, is invariably accompanied by an intense hatred of those others who, in the liberal's view, are said to obstruct the spread of the fraternal ideal. Christian love is addressed to the concrete individual and to each and every individual; it is what we today popularly call "existential." The second reason is that, at the moral level at which one habitually lives, the person is constituted by the values he espouses and therefore possesses intrinsic value only derivatively as the composite worth of his espoused and recognized values. At this level, therefore, there are differences of worth between persons, and a hardened criminal is lower on the human plane as defined by morality than a good man. But these differences, so real at this level, are brushed aside as trivial by the Christian, who discovers, beyond the "inherent" values (I am here following C. I. Lewis' terminology) of the person, his "intrinsic" value; and philosophically it is impossible to define this intrinsic value without reference to the religious foundations on which the notion rests.[3]

The philosophical explanation of the Christian belief in the supreme value of the person leads back, of course, to the fact that all men are brothers because they are children of the same Father. And as children of one Father, they are all His creatures, and as such are, as Maritain puts it, "ordained directly to God as to [their] absolute, ultimate end."[4] Their condition as creatures, their brotherhood, and their destiny thus entail one another, and their duty is thus clearly defined. They alone of all creatures have been created for their own sake—have, in the terminology just used, been given intrinsic value—and in them alone is found the image of God. This gives them a capacity no other creature has, the capacity to realize a supreme good. It is at this point that we arrive at something which is of central interest to us: their capacity to realize this good and the nature of the good they can realize, which is not temporal but eternal, give them an intrinsic worth, a status, that no other creature has or can aspire to. It is this intrinsic worth, the presence of which in an animal enables us to call him a person, that defines what I call the "Christian ethic." The essence of this worth is not merely the ground of my obligation to recognize as moral the moral demands made of me by another person and therefore to deal with them when they conflict with mine in a moral way; this insight, T. H. Green is perfectly correct in maintaining, is to be found in the pagans. The essence of Christian ethics is the ground, rather, of my obligation to treat the other as endowed with the intrinsic and ineluctable value which is the person's and which is a supreme and an incomparable value. It is one thing for me to recognize my obligation to acknowledge another's moral demands as standing on the same level as my own; but it is a totally different thing for me to acknowledge that the other embodies an intrinsic and incommensurable value which no other value can claim equality with, much less priority to. T. H. Green is, of course, right in his contention that what makes man ignore the demands made upon him is selfishness and fear and tribalism. But men can overcome these defects thoroughly and be as far as ever from reaching the heights on which the Christian habitually dwells. For what the Christian does is to say to himself, so to speak, the following: "Nothing I want, no value that attracts me, no secular good, whether it be power or wealth or knowledge or happiness, not even the value of life itself, which I espouse so desperately and for the sake of which, if necessary, I would be ready to sacrifice so much—no other value can compare with one special value I ought to espouse. And this is the value that resides intrinsically in each man because he is a person. So that, if I have to choose between injury to all my other values and injury to the person of another, the choice is clear because, no matter what a person may be, I must acknowledge this value above all others."

Whatever the metaphysics of the person—as we may call the analysis of his structure and of the source and nature of his value—the important fact for us as students of moral philosophy is to note clearly that the Christian resolves his practical perplexities with reference to this "absolute value." The problem which the Christian faces when he tries to resolve a practical perplexity is different from that confronting the moral man, because the Christian has a fixed point of reference, in terms of which the integration of his values takes place and which precludes certain patterns of integration that a moral man may find desirable to achieve. If prostitution is legally recognized in a society and is not repudiated by the moral sense of the community, the woman who runs a whorehouse and the interests behind her that profit from it need not feel morally guilty because they profit from that kind of trade. The woman may not be *respectable*, but this need not even be socially inconvenient to a person who does not want to be invited to certain functions by people who live in certain neighborhoods of her city. But if she is kind and honorable in her transactions with her customers and her girls, she is not immoral. A Christian, however, cannot be a whoremaster in any society. Much less could he be a blackbirder. These are activities that destroy the dignity of our fellows and therefore our own dignity. A Christian can be a soldier, but a Christian soldier carries his weapons with a heavy heart. His heart is not heavy because he takes "life" to be sacred. There is nothing sacred about protoplasmic activity. It is heavy because he knows that the person of the other is sacred. And this is quite a different thing.

There is another difference between the Christian and the merely moral man. The values integrated into a moral system give the person which they constitute his dignity for me if I am normally moral. But if I acknowledge the absolute value of personality, I cannot place a man's moral dignity in his successful accomplishment of the integration of the values that constitute him or in the place of those values in the hierarchical scale as I view it, but in something with which he is endowed through no effort of his own: the value of his personality. I have to behave toward him, therefore, in ways that are expressive of my espousal of the absolute and supreme value that he possesses. This value is of his essence; he does nothing to achieve it, and he possesses it no matter what he does or fails to do, no matter how contemptible morally he may be, and no matter how clearly his actions may put him beyond the pale of humanity. But, since I am also a person, I have to behave toward myself in the same way as I behave toward him. Hence toward myself as well as toward him I have duties and concerns which are greater than those that anyone acknowledges at the merely moral plane. It is this factor, the presence of this intrinsic value in the person, that makes the radical difference between the moral and the Christian life. The ethical life, of which the Christian, as I have already said, is the local name, involves a new stage and brings with it a new manner of resolving practical difficulties.

Let us assume, at least provisionally, that the ethical life is indeed "higher" than the moral. This assumption will engage our attention below. Are we not left, if we make this assumption, with the suspicion that, while the ethical life may be possible for a Christian, who on religious grounds believes in the brotherhood of man, it is not possible for anyone who lacks the Christian's religious inspiration to give him direction and to furnish him with the energy required to make the leap? Where does the moral man get his inspiration to deal with his fellows in an ethical way? We therefore want to know whether there is anything in the moral life that could lead one, without distinctly religious aid, to the discovery of the absolute value of the person and which could thus thrust one from the moral onto the ethical plane.

The answer that we must give to this question is a qualified affirmative: It is possible to go from the moral to the ethical without a previously discovered religious reality on which to fall back for aid. But the very process through which one discovers the absolute value of the person and his intrinsic dignity reveals, or rather forces one to notice, that there are factors operative in experience which seem to transcend the process of experience, factors of which it is not possible to give an account which does them justice but which also stays within the restrictions of a naturalistic approach. One can, of course, enlarge the term "natural" and thus give an account of these factors in naturalistic terms. But, after the criticism we have made of such transparent devices as "emergence" and "levels of integration," we ought to disdain such dodges. In a nature ontically value-free the presence of value is a miracle, capable of giving the lie to any naturalism. A much greater miracle is the discovery that man the moral animal respects his fellows in a way that sets them and himself off from the rest of the animals.

It seems desirable, before attempting the analysis of the problems that confront us, to warn the reader that he is in for a trip into the dark and poorly ventilated regions of the human psyche, where the myopic eyes of his present guide will see even less than they have seen in the full daylight we are about to abandon. This is a region where vague moving shapes are hard to identify, where all will be doubt, and where the loud insistence to which we are used in our daylight inquiries—the tenacious "Show me!" or the insistent "How do you know?"—has a tendency to frighten the shadowy quarries and, as they scatter, to create a roiled murkiness. For the descent into these regions a Dostoevski, an Augustine, a Kierkegaard, should be engaged as Virgils. I do not believe that positivists, hard-headed "empiricists," "realistic" moralists, Machiavellians, Hobbesians, Nietzscheans, and the rest of the numerous descendants of Thrasymachus could have read this far; but if any of them have, they are now requested to throw away the book and put their time to better use, since they can get out of the following pages only a dull weariness and irritation.

Our problem, then, is to give an account of the genesis of the ethical attitude when it takes place free from religious aid. Only then can we inquire into the authority of its claims. The ethical life develops from, or out of, the moral; to its source, therefore, we must turn.

Moral activity at best remains ambivalent, torn between two tendencies which the moral agent seeks to satisfy in order to arrive at a satisfactory solution of his perplexity. On the one hand, values urge themselves on him, clamoring for admission into his system, and this clamoring is one toward which the agent responds favorably. On the other, his own integrity tends to reject the values clamoring to be accepted into the system. When an agent is confronted with a moral claim, the jealousy of his integrity prompts him to challenge it. But we live in a rough world, not too publicly concerned with nice moral scruples, and the world's business peremptorily demands our practical attention. Events do not wait for perfect solutions. Decisions must be made which are not always fully or adequately justifiable. Thus life at its best, even when not poisoned by rampant and insurgent evil which normally poisons it, involves an immeasurable amount of ineradicable frustration and downright injustice. To the evil that surrounds us and that wells from within us we tend to "adjust" in innumerable ways. But the most successful adjustment possible, I am convinced, merely serves to save appearances and to cover up our ulcerous sores from the world, and, if we are successful enough, from ourselves. We adjust, we get used to it, well enough at least "to take our minds off our troubles" and do the daily chore. But, for all our successful disregard of it, the noxious seepage does not stop. To the daily bitterness, the friction, the frustration, the coarse disregard of which we are one another's victims, and, not infrequently, the sheer malice are added the futile search for peace, the unslaked thirst for harmony, and the mirage of happiness that seems more perfect as it recedes. Gide tells us somewhere, perhaps in his autobiography, of a moment of unmixed joy which he experienced in Africa and how, ever after, his search for joy was a search for the repetition of the earlier experience. Men hunger for beauty and serenity and humane relations and fill up instead on grief and anxiety and the friction offered by the vicissitudes of the daily round. Morality is an instrument of life through which we seek to achieve our destiny; it is, indeed, life itself in those moments in which we manage to live it at the human level. But behind the façade that respectability builds to shelter us from the public, we live a different life than we appear to live publicly, since our claims are only boasts and, from within our own souls no less than from without, the pollution that constitutes our defeat drains into the consciousness.

Nor is the moral life, could we successfully live it at its best, a mode of living which can be achieved once and for all and which, once achieved, will yield the peace and serenity which we crave. Anxiety is the lot of conscious man, since living consists of an intermittent series of seldom successful efforts by which we attempt, whether we know it or not, to create our humanity. Morality is a hill the top of which we must take, well defended against us, who must charge in open country. Nor do we, when we gain the top, stay there long. In spite of our finest resolutions, we soon find ourselves actively co-operating with the enemy who would dislodge us. Each defeat increases the burden of guilt in our souls and makes the next one easier. No victory is ever clean, complete, decisive. But to the anxiety which thus results and which is the bitter fruit of our human condition as moral beings, we must add that which results from the fact that we can rarely be certain of the values we serve or of our sincerity in serving them.

The picture, of course, is not altogether dark. Men live, or seem normally to live, without awareness of their anxieties. And the reason is that what used to be called "conatus," what at the phenomenal level a Schopenhauerian would call "the will," blindly drives us on, giving us, in spite of the evidence, hope and energy to carry on. Accordingly, when a writer calls attention to the factors on which we have just dwelt, we resent him and dispose of him with facile phrases. The last thing men want is to have anyone call their attention to Thoreau's quiet desperation. Although they experience it, they will not admit that they do so unless compelled by sheer force. But men do not always succeed in ignoring this quiet desperation in which they live. There are ages when the quality of life becomes almost too coarse to bear and when the institutionalized arrangements which hold in leash the brutality to which we are prone break down. And there are societies in which violence and ill-will are potent factors in defining the tone, the affective quality, of daily life. Even in periods of relative stability and social harmony, in societies which call themselves "civilized," the mask that in daily living conceals the naked face of arbitrary force often falls down, letting us see its stark ugliness. The experience of injustice, of wilfulness, outrages the soul and leaves it embittered. The small shock, the daily pinprick, the hurt which is the result of a neighbor's stupidity or indifference or of bureaucratic arbitrariness, the passing pain inflicted by an arrogant elbow that pushes for place—these, too, leave their bitterness behind:

> the whips and scorns of time,
> The oppressor's wrong, the proud man's contumely,
> The pangs of dispriz'd love, the law's delay,

The insolence of office, and the spurns
That patient merit of the unworthy takes . . . .

One need not one's self be the victim of such outrages, nor need these be large and dramatic—they need not involve the systematic exploitation of one class by another or the conquest of a people or the ruthlessness of a totalitarian regime. The sight of injustice may hurt more deeply than its direct experience. I am convinced that it often does. Revolutionary leaders in our day have often been originally members of the oppressor class. The victim of brutality or injustice is compelled by the situation to objectify his attention, to focus it on the untoward circumstances, in order to avoid them. The spectator has more time to consider the total aspect and the formal features; his outrage, to the extent to which he truly grasps the total situation of victim and victimizer, is purer, since it is stimulated not by the felt injury but by the injustice itself. Once when I was discussing with a very intelligent and sensitive student the origin of his awareness of moral evil, the boy told me that his first clear experience of moral outrage dated back to a very early period of his life when he witnessed a policeman beating a drunken man down some basement steps. The poor man's face was bloody and one eye totally closed; nevertheless, with exasperating obstinacy, after the policeman had struck him in the face and knocked him down to the bottom of the steps, the poor fool, mumbling curses, would get up and climb back to be knocked down again. Witnessing the incident without feeling, my student was suddenly overcome by nausea and ran away. For months afterward an almost overwhelming feeling of nausea came over him at the sight of the blue uniform of a policeman. That incident made him a moral man. He brooded over it, brooded over the naked sadistic fist and the dull mumbling of the man crawling back, and the memory of it has never left him. Let one other illustration do. I know a young Venezuelan boy whose awareness of the moral problem, so far as he could remember, became explicit when his father's orderly told him how soldiers were pressed into the army. A recruiting squad went into a district and rounded up all the men whom it could lay its hands on. Without a minute to say goodbye to their families, with the utmost brutality, in the midst of cultivating a row of corn or eating their dinners, the men were pulled out at bayonet's point, lined up, and marched away, and it would be weeks before the desolate family heard from the new soldier. This is the way the orderly had been "caught." This story, of whose truth the boy could not judge, made a deep impression on him and led him to be especially considerate of the orderly, who, acting as he did as a house servant, had a much easier time of it than the other recruits of the regiment. Later, as the boy grew up and came to read of slave ships capturing Africans, the picture of men hunted by their kind became the central symbol in his moral development. As he matured, he felt that his childhood reaction toward the orderly's account, transmuted in a strange way, was at the core of his knowledge of iniquity. But the point I want to make is not that the perception of injustice done to others is the only means of knowledge of good and evil but rather that it is not necessary to suffer injustice one's self in order to come to know it in its full bitterness.[5]

Normally the moral outrages of which men are victims or which they witness can be more or less successfully digested without radical effects or serious impairment of the soul's smugness. If your moral claims are denied, you continue to press them more or less successfully, modifying them as you observe the success or lack of success of your suit. You bargain, you use whatever influence you have at your disposal, state your case more forcefully, insist, and get enough of what in fairness you have coming to you to be relatively satisfied. But what does a man do who becomes the victim of another who for some reason—coarse indifference, ill-will, self-interest—is beyond the reach of the appeal? Let us look into what men, in fact, do in such circumstances. But, before looking, let us thank Mr. Allport and his collaborators for disposing of what he calls the Yale formula of "frustration-aggression" as the kind of scientifically sanctioned oversimplification that, were we to take it seriously, would make us entirely lose our way.[6]

Defeated in his demand for justice, our man may search for other means of satisfying his claim; or he may give it up altogether, shrug his shoulders, and go about his business. This means that the consequences of the breakdown of the normal moral process do not seem to be serious. The injury can somehow be digested. I say "seem,"

because we are too cavalier about what we take to be the trivial consequences of the breakdown of the moral procedures among men.
In any case our victim, defeated in a moral contest, may come out a
better man than he went in, since he may have learned a complex
valuable lesson about the need for prudence and for knowledge of
the ways of the world.

There are times, however, when a moral defeat may become a
serious threat to the defeated. His heart may be deeply set on something which is snatched from him without a show of right. If at this
moment what chiefly hurts is no more than the denial of the desired
object, the situation is of no great interest to us as moral philosophers. But if our victim reacts against the injustice (or perhaps it
would be more exact to say "in so far as" our victim does) rather
than against the loss of the object, the situation is of the greatest
interest. For a man may in such a predicament decide, in the in-
nocent-sounding cliché, to "fight fire with fire." Then the result is
that the victim of injustice, who has a selfish interest in the strengthening and maintenance of the instrumentalities of the moral process,
undertakes to aid his victimizer in their destruction. The psychological reaction is understandable enough, but the logic of it could
not be poorer. Obviously, this is the logic of revenge and of what
we may call "the top-dog argument," according to which in a world
divided into top dogs and underdogs the reasonable choice is to en-
deavor to become a top dog. The argument would hold if men were
truly thus divided in a moral sense. But morally there are no top
dogs and underdogs: there are good and evil dogs only. What the
poor reasoner does not see is that we all—even you, my reader—
are underdogs. The pecking order of hens to which we find so many
references among up-to-date sociologists holds for men only in the
most shallow and trivial way and has no relevance whatever to the
ethical life.

An attempt to make fully explicit the philosophy of the man who
"fights fire with fire" would reveal that the skeleton of the argument commits him to the repudiation of the moral process on the
alleged ground that, since it broke down in one case, it is best dispensed with altogether. What our man says is, "If this is the game,
I, too, can play it." The variations on the theme depend on the in-

genuity of the composer. But the fundamental idea is recognizable throughout: the denial of justice to me releases me of all further obligation toward justice itself.

It would seem that if a man arrives at such a position, not in practice but as a reasoned conclusion, he is rediscovering the philosophy—if something which so radically contradicts wisdom can be called a "philosophy"—of Thrasymachus; and the one redeeming thing we can say about him is that it is difficult to imagine what a man would be like who would effectively practice the doctrine that might makes right. But, while no man may be able to live consistently on Thrasymachus' principles, we all to some extent live according to them. To that extent we are all agents of evil.

Our "Thrasymachus" is an individualist, confident of his own strength, a somewhat coarse, morally shallow, unimaginative man, with whom we need not occupy ourselves, since Plato long ago disposed of him in the *Republic*. But there is another type of man—for whom we shall find a name later—who reacts to the denial of a moral claim in a more complex way and one which comes closer to being the pattern of human action. Outraged by injustice, this man does not simplistically conclude that morality is a fiction but maintains his faith in it as an ideal worth actualizing. But, in view of his experience, he argues, it is clear that it is impossible to make the ideal actual so long as power remains in the hands of men of evil heart who prevent *us*, the victims of *their* injustice, from bringing about the classless and just society. The first step, therefore, toward a moral world must be the extermination of evil men. After that *we* shall have the opportunity to behave toward others according to the dictates of righteousness. We need not ask by what alchemy the victims of social injustice, simply because they are victims, are turned into good and righteous men who seem to be incapable of evil; nor need we inquire into the logic which enables a mere man to decide, without scruples and without diffidence, who among his fellows is good and who is evil, who is just and who unjust. However he does it, the man of whom we speak performs the miracle without any trouble whatever: he decides that the victims of social injustice are good and the exploiters are evil, and the decision proves extremely satisfactory to his needs, since now he can hate and love with a clear heart. The dichotomy satisfies deep Manichaean needs that we all have. Now take a man of this type, capable of deep love and deep hate, give him an outraged conscience for the masses who are the beasts of burden on whose shoulders are carried the refinements of civilization, let him see with his own eyes the consequences of social injustice and of industrial exploitation, give him a powerful intellect and feed that intellect with history and economics, endow him with what Matthew Arnold called a "Hebraic" will, and you have a potential "Karl Marx." He is not necessarily one in respect to accomplishment, for the greatness of the historical Marx is not easily equaled in the pages of history, since men are seldom given the vitality, the intellectual vigor, and the heroic strength which Marx possessed; but he is one in respect to the kind of moral reactions which he will express through his chosen form of activity.

In calling this the "Marx" type, I am not doing it in ignorance of the fierce way in which Karl Marx poured scorn on the moralistic socialists of his day and opposed to the moralistic his "scientific" approach to the social problem.[7] The name is selected because of certain important similarities and for lack of a better, although certainly anyone who denied Marx a strong and insulated moral hatred of the *bourgeoisie* would reveal himself as a man who had never read his writings. Be that as it may, what is pertinent here is that all one can expect from a "Marx" is a steady deterioration of the moral quality of the world over which he has influence and a steady increase in the brutality and stark cruelty of his world. But we need not pursue this matter further, since we are not interested in him and in our "Thrasymachus" for their own sake but only as contrasts to another type, the man whose experiences lead him to the discovery of the ethical process.

Let us call this man, thinking of the goal he seeks, "the ethical man." He may be the direct victim of iniquity, or he may be endowed with an unusual sensibility toward the victims of unrighteousness; in any case he is aware of injustice. But, unlike the majority of men who see it only in their own private spheres, his response, his awareness, are broader, although, of course, they cannot be fully universal in scope. If he is not himself the direct victim of injustice, he identifies himself with its victims so intimately, suffers for them so deeply, lives their experiences so heartily, that for all purposes we can think of him as if *he were* the victim himself; and therefore we can discuss the experiences of both under the same dramatic symbol. The ethical man is not a saint, not even distinctly better than most of us; but he may become a saint. Initially, whatever his actual accomplishments in the path of virtue, his distinction consists of his being endowed with something that we, the mere average, lack: a sensitive and discerning eye for moral phenomena beyond the range of his own immediate concerns. Nor need we stop to inquire from his biography what factors account for the broad range of his sensibility, even though the question is undeniably an interesting one. Unfortunately, the answer to it is not obtainable from what we know of men. A hasty survey of distinctively ethical men would yield an embarrassing wealth of heterogeneous details from which it does not seem possible to pick out causal clues. Thus the greatest representative of the type in our Western history is the son of a lowly old carpenter who with his parents flees the place of his birth while still an infant in arms. We know nothing of his formative years, and the records of his activity which we possess bristle with baffling historical problems. He may have been an illiterate. In any case his obscure life was spent in an unimportant corner of a minor province of the Roman Empire, and there have been numerous well-informed and unprejudiced men who have doubted his historicity. Of another distinguished ethical man we know that he was a gay and dissolute youth, the son of a rich merchant family of turbulent Assisi in a great period of its history. Of the son of the carpenter we have, prior to the period of his activity, nothing but worthless pious legends, and of the man of Assisi nothing, so far as I know, beyond the fact that at the age of twenty-two he suffered a serious illness out of which he came a changed man.

The paucity of knowledge, on the one hand, and the abundance of specimens, on the other, leave us no recourse but to turn to what Santayana has called "literary psychology," not in order to explain why ethical men are endowed with broader and deeper sympathy, but to construct a plausible hypothesis, useful in a heuristic sense, as to how they use their endowment to transcend the plane of the moral and reach the ethical.

CHAPTER XVIII

THE DISCOVERY OF THE ETHICAL. II

EITHER from his own personal experience or with the aid of his imagination, the ethical man feels keenly the sting of iniquity, the weakening, impotent bitterness caused by brutality, the vacuous inward feeling which comes when one's dignity is denied and one is pushed about like a crate. *This kind of experience is indispensable:* unless a man has known injustice, unrighteousness; unless he knows what it is to be a victim of wilful brutality, he cannot be the ethical man of whom we are speaking. The knowledge of injustice may be vicarious or it may be immediate; I suspect that it needs to be only the former. But it is important that he shall have known shame, indignity, defeat, despair. Then only, and not always even then, is he ready to take the step that carries him beyond the moral into the ethical.

In his anguish our ethical man will cry for justice, will denounce evil, and will seek a way out of his predicament. He will ask himself how men can be so brutally devoid of ordinary pity, so blindly arrogant. Since there is no easy answer to this question, our man is in danger of losing his way at this point. The temptation to turn to Thrasymachus or to Marx is great. Our man discovers them and toys with their plausible solutions. But reflection reveals that his acceptance of the answers of both Marx and Thrasymachus would constitute merely a cunning effort on his part to deny the validity of his own moral experience. The effort is natural enough for a man in his plight, but it is ultimately self-contradictory, for both Thrasymachus and Marx effectively increase the amount of evil in the world, the outraged response to which, we have supposed, is the source of his anguish. The clarification of this insight, which for our ethical man may not constitute more than an unconscious, inarticulate response, marks an important moment in our own understanding of the structure of his development and the validity of his conclusions.

In entertaining as plausible hypotheses (which, no doubt, they are) the answers of Thrasymachus and Marx, the ethical man is desperately searching for a conviction which will mitigate the pain caused by the moral outrage of which he is a victim. Active in him is a need, not necessarily clear or even conscious, for the katharsis which a stoic attitude can produce: "If I know the truth about the world and about my real relations to it, I am beyond the reach of the disappointment and the grief which come from mendacious faith in justice." In other words, if our ethical man can deny the reality of moral evil by denying objective criteria and thus reduce evil to mere catastrophe, which it is senseless to condemn morally, he does not deny the reality of the practical results of the injustice; what he does is deny his sense of indignation and of outrage. Thus the practical results can now be dealt with like any practical calamity, which we try to control or to which we resign ourselves without the inward laceration which injustice produces. Or, put still more simply, in so far as the denial of justice as such is the source of anguish, in order to get rid of the anguish all we need to do is to get rid of our faith in justice.

But, for the strategy to succeed, our ethical man must stop where we have just left him; and that is not easy to do, since it involves denying the stubborn and deep conviction that an injustice has been committed. This denying has two aspects, the subjective, existential aspect and the objective. Let us look into the objective aspect first: When a man grasps clearly that a situation which is now actual ought not to be and that another that does not now exist ought to exist, he does not mean to assert that he desires or does not desire something in a subjective sense or that he subjectively or idiosyncratically approves or disapproves of something. Sometimes this is all he means; but in that case he does not refer to a clearly perceivable relation; and we are talking only of those cases in which he does mean such a relation. That it is possible to distinguish between things that ought to be or ought not to be and things that we desire or toward which we have an aversion may be easily seen by considering that we do not desire all that we know ought to be and we often desire things that we know ought not to be. To deny that an injustice has been committed is therefore no different from denying that a fact which is perceived as such is not a fact. We may not recognize that an act is an injustice, just as we often do not recognize facts for what they are, but we cannot deny the objectivity of injustice when we do recognize it for what it is. It should, of course, be remembered that the factuality of a fact does not depend on our perception of it, or there would be no truth possible beyond the subjectivistic relativism that Protagoras chose to call "truth." The existential aspect of the denial of justice or injustice cannot easily be separated from the objective, since it consists in the felt outrage, in our reaction to the objective situation; we feel that it is unwarranted and cannot dismiss as groundless the appeal whose denial brought about the outrage.

The victim's need to posit a moral scheme is no proof, of course, that what he posits actually exists outside the need itself. From the subjective point of view, all we can establish is that the denial of the moral scheme ends up by producing the opposite effect from what it was intended to have. This is clearly seen in a moral catastrophe. Tell an inmate of Maidenek on the way to the gas chamber that he has not been condemned to die by an iniquitous monster and that what he takes to be evil is not really evil but a meaningless catastrophe, an accident, like suddenly discovering in one a malignant tumor or like dying in an accidental fire. Do you think you have lightened his misery? You have wantonly increased it. The moral scheme preserved the victim's dignity and gave him a superiority over the victimizer. You have taken that and more from the poor wretch; you have said to him, in fact, "You are not a man. You are not even as lucky as a steer led to slaughter. You will not be used for an end which will justify your death. True, out of the little fat that sticks to your ribs soap will be made, and the gold of your teeth will contribute to the treasury, and the rest of you will fertilize the cabbages, and the skin of your back will make an odd lamp shade. But don't get the impression that the reason why you are being killed is that you are useful. You are not being killed for any reason whatever. Those who will kill you just don't like you, and merely that is the cause of your death. Make no mistake, there is no sense to your death. Killing you involves no crime, no violation, no good or evil. You are being slaughtered only to satisfy the irresponsibly senseless whim of those in power."

This is not reasoning that the victim of injustice clearly rehearses in his mind. But what one can, it seems to me, legitimately claim is that the victim of injustice can discover in his crisis the reality of justice, the objective validity of the moral scheme, at the phenomenological level, as an ideal requirement which would turn an immoral actuality into a moral one. The victim is not saying, "There is justice," but, on the contrary, "There is no justice and there ought to be." But he does not mean that there ought to be merely to satisfy his own subjective demands. That would not be justice, and the victim would clearly know it. He means that there ought to be, in order to satisfy the demands of a situation which, as it exists at present, is awry, which inherently and intrinsically lacks something it ought to have to be a fit human situation.[1] And what it lacks, it lacks in the same manner in which a painting or sonnet lacks something which the artist or the critic discerns not as existing but precisely as lacking, which is to say, as needed to complete the object. The ought-to-be thus apprehended as subsisting and as demanding actualization through human effort may not satisfy the demands of the victim; it satisfies the demands of what under the circumstances he *ought* to desire; and what he ought to desire is what is fitting. It satisfies the demands of the situation as a human situation. The lack is discovered through certain conditions mentioned above—namely, by a man either sympathetically or actually in an extreme situation—and is apprehended as objective, as independent of the conditions which led to its discovery. The objective validity of proof in any cognitive discipline is discovered by means of a certain subjective condition in the knower, namely, intelligence, but does not depend upon this for its status as valid. We are not concerned here, of course, with establishing that the phenomenal grasp of values as objective is a fair basis on which to claim their ontic reality. As we have already seen, only on a metaphysical assumption that the reductionistic world of physics defines the real can we impugn the ontic reality of values.[2] An individual, then, who normally is blind to values or who habitually reduces value experiences to the gratification which their actualization yields can discover their objectivity in what we can call (borrowing an expression for our purposes) "an extreme situation."[3]

If we stop to consider this objective character of the moral scheme to which appeal is made, as it reveals itself in extreme situations, we shall notice that the ground of our conviction of objectivity is found not only in the epistemic deliverance whose import we have earlier sought to establish by denying the cogency of the interest theory of value and by calling attention to the way in which values are discovered; the ground is also found in a complex factor which does not cognitively warrant the objectivity but which reinforces the conviction gained through the epistemic deliverance. We have just referred to this factor as "subjective" or "existential"; I propose to look into its role in greater detail. Note, however, in passing, that the fact that an extreme situation enables us to observe the subjective factor with ease does not mean that it is only through such a situation that we find this component of the moral life.

The existential factor is a condition of all moral experience, since it is constitutive of the person. The denial of the objectivity of evil and the acceptance of a reductive account of it which traces it to subjective dispositions deny the veracity of the deliverances of perception and thus threaten the foundations of all possible knowledge—namely, the perceived objective malformation of an evil situation. They deny also the validity of the ground for the demand that certain values be realized, the actualization of which is urgently craved in order to reduce the malformation and to restore the personality to normal functioning. But this denial of the right to make moral demands based on objective grounds involves a serious threat to the total personality. Let us consider why.

A denial of justice involves a denial of values which are actualized through espousal or are in prospect of actualization. As we have already seen, under the stress of living, but particularly under the pressures generated by a moral crisis, the organization of psychic values which constitutes the personality undergoes shifts, so to speak, in its center of gravity. As fluid situations change, the values directly involved are the ones which represent the personal organization in its transaction with the world. In an extreme situation the shift of values is more radical, and those (whether actual or prospective) involved in the response to the external threat become representative of the whole self, while values which, under normal conditions, were considered basal lose their pre-eminence. These threatened values suddenly appear as essential to the maintenance of the personality, and the threat to them becomes a threat to the whole person: they are seen as constituting the keystone of the arch and their removal as involving its collapse. In blunt terms this is to say that it is either they or madness. If, however, the threat to them can be felt as the product of an evil will, the loss of values is not complete, since it is merely the failure to actualize them and not a denial of the possibility of doing so, or at least of the possibility of establishing that there is a malformation in respect to which an objective scheme points the need for their actualization. So long as there is an ideal possibility of improvement of the malformation, even if, actually, no probability of improvement exists, one is not totally crushed. For all that one can demand is not the acknowledgment of the validity of the claim but that the means of testing it be not denied. If we are making a *moral* claim, we are implying that we will abide by the results of the moral process. A valid moral denial of our claim is no loss to us but a gain. But the denial of the objectivity of values denies the right to make the appeal and reduces the issue to a conflict of brute force which has already been lost by the victim of evil. Hence the anguish and the humiliation which one feels in the extreme situation are merely a matter of the perspective from which the situation is viewed. This amounts to telling one that the evil he is undergoing, which causes this grief, is pure illusion and the grief baseless. And this is the one thing that the victim of evil knows his grief is not. And he knows that it is not, because it is defined by the objective situation, whose objectivity is intrusively present before his eyes. Therefore, neither can the justice to which the victim appeals be an illusion, since on that assumption his appeal has no ground and his grief is an illusion. One does not condemn evil and appeal against it to an untoward superior force on the ground that one does not like it or finds it unpleasant. Ultimately it can be condemned only on an objective ground—if only on the utterly unconvincing principle that the unpleasant *ought* not to be imposed on men. This is, then, what the existential factor amounts to: that there is a *vital* necessity (as distinct from an epistemic one) for asserting the objectivity of value which extreme situations force us to take cognizance of.

But this vital necessity is the satisfaction of a condition of our rationality, and hence it not only reinforces our epistemic deliverance of axiological objectivity but is presupposed by all epistemic activity and constitutes the necessary axiological condition of all knowledge, as well as of moral experience. The reason for this is that rationality—whether in its purely intellectual or in its distinctively moral sense—involves the capacity to make axiological judgments. In its intellectual aspect we make judgments of truth; in its moral, of goodness. The absence of the capacity to make judgments is what we mean by "madness." Thus the maintenance of a personality—of a structure of acknowledged values—is the maintenance of the condition of rationality.

The reference here is to something analogous to what Kant called the "postulates of the practical reason." In practical life we accept the objectivity of value, for which we have independent epistemic evidence, because the vital need to maintain the rational structure of our personality also compels us to believe in it under a severe penalty. The objectivity of value is a *practical* postulate. But, while the word "practical" should not be a source of trouble, the word "postulate" can be. It is not intended to designate an arbitrary fiat or a merely logically primitive proposition functioning as the basis of an implicative system and hence valid only in that context; it is intended to designate a condition of rationality. Rationality can be rejected, but then, of course, no argument for or against it can be examined; argument can merely be ignored. Nor does the reference to vital needs mean that we must lie to ourselves in order to make life bearable or pleasant. Nor is it a question of a pragmatic "will to believe." It is a question of recognizing that the rationality by means of which we make distinctions essential to epistemic, no less than to moral, activity (of reality and illusion, valid and nonvalid, true and false, and the like, as well as of right and wrong) is grounded on certain conditions which we must accept but which cannot be proved, since they are presupposed by all proof.

We thus see that in an extreme situation we are able to discover with relative ease something which in normal moral perplexities can be grasped only accidentally or only by an extremely sensitive person, namely, that rational activity at the moral level (but it is also true of the epistemic), while autonomous, involves the acceptance of metarational conditions, to threaten which is to endanger all normal living, for normal living is defined by the rationality which governs it. An abstract intellectualism seeks to deny the existential source of rationality, to ignore it, or to challenge its authority and position as the condition of all reason. The effect in any case is to cut the line which attaches theory to its source in the total experience of man, in order that, by a denial of the latter's reality, theory may be assigned to a single segment of man's experience. The judgment of theoretical validity, of objective truth, even when it refers to objective relations which constitute the world of physics, expresses a vital decision of the scientist no less than it expresses certain relations which can be apprehended by a pure disembodied intellect. These relations are objective, and their objectivity is warranted by certain tests. No objection can be made to them when warranted, and certainly none to the scientist's interest in them (unless it be a moral objection that the interest may not be in place under given circumstances) so long as they are not passed off for more than what they are: namely, selections from complex data. If the term "real" is reserved for them, it becomes necessary to remind the user that reality is not a predicate; but, even if it were, the arbitrary use of a term does not create similarities or erase distinctions which the subject to which the predicate applies may have within itself or with other things.

It is also important, in view of the fact that some positivists deny that "truth" is a value, to remember that the relations expressed in scientific judgments could not be glimpsed by a pure scientific intellect unless, by a prior nonscientific decision, the pure scientific intellect decides to restrict its interest to these relations and to take only those warranted by the tests agreed on. This decision is not itself a scientific, but an existential, condition which makes scientific activity possible. Of course, the decision calls for accepting the deliverances of the pure intellect only if they abide by certain specifiable conditions which warrant their validity. But, for all that, the logic of the decision is identical with the logic of the decision of a practical man to accept the moral problem and the conditions necessary to resolve it. These conditions are inquired into by the moral man and are decided upon by his moral consciousness in the same way as the conditions which resolve the scientific problem are decided by the scientist; the former are autonomous in the same sense in which the latter are. The scientific intellect qua scientific can no more pass on the moral validity of a judgment than the moral qua moral can on scientific validity. There is no point, of course, in denying that the judgments of the pure scientific intellect have a clarity and freedom from ambiguity which the inherently obscure and irreducibly ambiguous data of the moral conscience could never equal. Nevertheless, since the aim of the moral conscience is not the selection of material in order to express it in clear propositions which have predictive function but rather to make choices among values, no matter how perplexingly vague and obscure these values may be, the inherent defects of its judgments as compared with the judgments of science cannot be a basis for rejecting them, although their vagueness may constitute a basis for seeking to clarify them as far as possible.

At this point it is desirable to gather the results of our discussion. Observe then, first, that the argument led to the conclusion that a victim of injustice who reflects on what he experiences discovers that the evil of which he is a victim is objective, in the epistemic sense that it appears before his mind as constituted by the lack of certain relations required to complete the situation in a fitting manner, and in the existential sense that the objectivity of the injustice is demanded as one of the conditions of rationality. Observe, next, that the perception of evil involves, at the same time, the grasp of the order of ideal relations whose actualization would complete the situation and would obviate the adverse judgment passed on the situation. But nowhere throughout the argument has the claim been made that the objectivity of either good or evil, justice or injustice, has ontological, a priori status. That argument was made at an earlier time when the distinction between espoused and recognized value was discussed during the examination of the interest theory of R. B. Perry.[4] And it was completed through the argued denial that the abstractions of the positive scientist are the only objects which are ontically real.

Our discussion has prepared us to answer the question which was posited immediately after the discussion of Christianity, and to this question we must at last turn. The question—it will be remembered—is whether a man can discover the ethical life without the aid of religious conviction. I suggested that the answer would be a qualified affirmative. Let us see, then, how the discovery can be made. We saw that the practical predicament into which our ethical man has fallen cannot be solved by the usual moral appeal to the victimizer and that the strategies of escape offered by Thrasymachus and Marx are seen to be self-defeating. Practically, then, barring suicide, the only way out is resignation. But resignation is never totally passive; it never completely stills one's mind. One asks in a silent voice, now in rancor, now in despair: "What is this justice whose authentic reality one cannot deny and whose impotence is so patent?" Or one asks: "What offense has one committed, what wrong done, to what can the plight in which one now finds one's self be traced?" An honest examination of conscience cannot let one off free, as if one were innocent. But does the discovery of one's faults bring with it the conviction that one's plight is deserved, that the victimizer was justified? If it does, there is no further problem in personal terms. If it does not, the problem remains in its entirety, for the excess of undeserved punishment in the indubitably objective moral scheme is a puzzle, and one must dig again in search for the root of evil. The perplexed, searching conscience now asks: "Why evil, why iniquity?" And the answer it gives itself is: "You know what the root of evil is; look inside yourself and you will find it. Perhaps not the root of *this* evil but of others for which *you* are responsible. For, certainly, you, too, even you, who now appeal to justice, have you not also denied to others that for which you now appeal, even as it is now being denied you? Well, in precisely that disregard of another person or, rather, in the practical assertion of the primacy of your own values over the value of the other as person is to be found the root of evil. And have you never brushed off in arrogance another's moral claim? Come now, never?"

"I am myself indifferent honest; but yet I could accuse me of such things that it were better my mother had not borne me. I am very proud, revengeful, ambitious; with more offences at my beck than I have thoughts to put them in, imagination to give them shape, or time to act them in. What should such fellows as I do crawling between heaven and earth? We are arrant knaves, all . . . ."

At this point it is advisable to interrupt the ethical man's soliloquy in order to call attention to what has happened: The victim, concerned with his own plight, has translated the problem from its original singular, first-person terms into universal terms. To this translation he was led by the examination of conscience which he started when he inquired into the reason for his present plight and answered its inquiry by pointing to his own faults. It is no longer possible to ask, "What is the source of the evil he now suffers?" There has taken place a broadening of the query: "What is the source of evil in general?" But the query does not obliterate, of course, the personal interest, for the self answers not only in terms of his own experience but in awareness that the answer applies to himself. It is disregard of another's claims that constitutes evil, and at the same time, as counterpoint, it is my disregard of the status of another as person that constitutes the evil I am so abundantly guilty of. But why does one—no, why do I—disregard the person of another? Why, indeed, if not because I fear that his plea will threaten my cherished espousals? Why, if not because one prefers one's own values to anything that may happen to the other?

From here on, our path is considerably easier. For, if what one wants is to abolish the possibility of situations such as that of which one is the victim, the means of doing so have already been discovered. And this is what one has come to desire, through the discovery that one is as much an agent of injustice as one is its victim. The evil does not consist in the denial of the concrete claims in their material specificity, after they have been fairly heard, but in the denial of the right of another person to institute a moral claim—a denial which usually springs out of an unconscious fear that the other's claim may force me to give up valued objects as the result of the moral inquiry. My recognition of the right of another to submit a moral claim keeps the moral process open. And the evil in which originally I was exclusively interested is one by which not only now, but always, and not only I, but everyone else, is threatened so long as we do not keep the moral process open.

CHAPTER XIX

THE DISCOVERY OF THE ETHICAL. III

S O MUCH, then, seems reasonably clear: If we want to avoid the possibility of evil, we must find some means of keeping the moral process open. But how can we keep it open when to do so is to threaten our cherished espoused values? How can I admit another's claim when that claim threatens to destroy the organization of my values and hence my personality? A man who has no values to espouse, hence no personality to threaten, and whose integrity means nothing to him can give up anything that is asked of him. Such a man would be a perfect pragmatist; and, if he is possible at all, he is very rare indeed. But does not such an attitude mean the abandonment of morality?

I can keep the moral process open, without giving up my integrity, when I effectively and actually put as the keystone of my value arch one value to which I give absolute primacy: the espoused value of the other as person.

When this condition is lacking, evil does not necessarily follow, because conflicts between persons are not always radical; but it always hovers ready at hand, since one never knows when a conflict will reveal itself as radical. When I have grasped this insight, I have arrived, theoretically, at the ethical plane. But whether or no that purely theoretical accomplishment leads to my espousal of the ethical as an effective operative value whose absolute primacy becomes the basis of the resolution of my moral problems is an empirical question which can be answered by each man who has discovered the ethical. Let him who institutes successfully as his primary value the primacy of the other, in spite of his own passions and prejudices, his own malice and selfishness, come forward to claim the prize.

At this point the empiricist is clamoring to be heard. He has a criticism to record. Let us hear him.

He says that, so far as he can see, the pretty picture I have painted does not prove that the espousal of the primacy of the other as person, assuming, for the sake of the argument, that it is practical counsel, will in fact achieve the desirable results I have claimed for it. Christianity's failure proves the utter impracticality of the ethical life. Furthermore, while he may grant that I have put my finger on the source of one kind of evil, it has not been shown to be the source of all moral evil whatsoever. For what I did was to equate, without giving my reasons for doing so, the term "injustice" with the term "evil."

The fact which is the basis of the last objection, I reply, is justified. I did take for granted that the terms are equivalent; but let me adduce, in justification, the following considerations: First, the evil in which we have been interested is that which is the result of the breakdown of the moral process. We must distinguish this evil from catastrophe, which is the harm that comes as the result of causes beyond human control—illness and death not caused by negligence and any other harm which is the result of uncontrollable accident. Within the scope of our inquiry we do not call these events "evil," for we save the term for the untoward consequences visited on a person through the decisions explicit or involved in another's actions. But the relationship from which these decisions arise can be referred to under the generic term of "justice," in the sense that they refer to the use of power to accept or deny a moral claim. The objection is thus a purely verbal one.

As regards the first criticism of the empiricist, it should be borne in mind that a perfectly ethical life does not seem possible, and I have myself suggested so in the last line of the preceding section—it by "perfect" we mean a life which is not marred by failure. The perfect ethical life is an ideal which, in so far as it is approached, succeeds to some extent in sweetening and humanizing the beast in man. In a recent poll conducted by the *Ladies' Home Journal*[1] a number of Americans were asked, among other questions, whether they loved their fellow-man when he was an enemy of the country and when he was a member of a political party thought to be dangerous. To the first of these two questions 63 per cent replied "No," and to the second, 57 per cent; but to the first, 12 per cent replied "No opinion" and to the second, 16 per cent. On this criterion, this means—if the poll is assumed to meet statistical demands, and the *Ladies' Home Journal* did not give data from which to check on this important point—that only between 25 and 27 per cent of the American population is Christian. (On other criteria one could propose, I dare say that the number is much less.) I suggest that the quality of contemporary life in industrial countries would be found to correlate rather closely with the effective practice of the Christian ideals of love. A perfect ethical life is impossible for men as at present constituted; but love and hatred can be increased or diminished as dynamic forces in human living, and within the scanty knowledge of history I possess I see no reason to assume that there is more love (agape) in this scientifically enlightened and humanitarian age of ours than there was in those ages which partisanship and historical ignorance dismiss as the days of the Inquisition. All the evidence points with some clarity the other way. Let us remember that it was left to our generation to invent the fact, no less than the term, "genocide."

The first criticism of the empiricist also involves a rather difficult methodological problem, already touched on in the discussion of Dewey's philosophy. In so far as an ideal is accepted because of the good consequences it promises to realize, its test is made by means which, broadly speaking, we can call "empirical." Thus, if a social ideal, let us say "socialism," promises a certain kind of life, whether the ideal is valid or false depends on the kind of life which, when put into practice, socialism does, in fact, make possible. This is, of course, utterly obvious. But the question as to whether the kind of life to which socialism leads is better than the kind of life that feudalism makes possible cannot be tested by the simple comparison of the one kind with the other but can be tested only by means of a criterion which is broader than each and capable of criticizing both; and such a criterion is itself not testable empirically, since it defines what the good life is. Suppose that you told a Nazi that the kind of life his ideals lead to is inferior to the democratic because it excludes a good deal of talent from contributing what it can to the social good. True, he would say, but that kind of contribution we do not find "good," and the evil our exclusion of undesirables brings is infinitesimal compared with the evil involved in having to co-operate with them. Now add: But your ideals involve war, destruction, and conflict. True again, he will retort, but the quality of life involved in war, the virtues it makes possible, are, for us, the highest and worth the price we are forced to pay for them. There is no need to pursue the point any further. The Nazi cannot be condemned according to a criterion which merely accuses him of traducing *my* concrete ideals; he can be condemned only according to a criterion which can criticize both the Nazi and all other competing systems in order to show how near each comes to a general notion of human perfection. That this can be done we have already attempted to show. But this ideal of human perfection, since it is normative, defines what is the desirable as human and, if what it thus defines is not acceptable, it cannot be rejected on empirical grounds but only in terms of a dialectical analysis of the ideal itself, through the process of criticism already outlined. Suppose that the Puritan was correct and that human perfection was to be found by means of his rejections and denials; surely, it would be no argument against the ideal to urge that it narrowed the scope of man's gratifications, for precisely that narrowing is demanded as the price of perfection. I labor this point because today one constantly hears even from philosophers, who ought to know better, irresponsible appeals to "empiricism" as if the "validation" of normative criteria could be achieved by reference to the facts of human life as these appear to the objectively descriptive historian or social scientist, whose method forbids his making normative choices among the data. Dobuan life is bad because it is instinct with paranoid traits and paranoid traits are bad, and this judgment transcends Dobu and its values and takes us to the criteria of perfection (unfortunately vague and dangerous to use) by which not only Dobu but all other societies can be criticized. If this is nonsense, we would do well to quit fooling ourselves with unstable attempts to look at the truth, for the other firm alternative is the frankly "might-makes-right" morality of the positivist, which Stevenson clarified for us in our day and which we can trace back through William James, through Hobbes, to Thrasymachus.

At this point, the postulational moralist, who has sat impatiently while I tried to answer the empiricist, interrupts me. "Isn't this ideal or criterion," he says, "to which you have referred, this absolute primacy of the person, *a postulate?* For you do not pretend that you *intuit* it. And, since you do not claim that it is the result of an induction, what other alternative is there?"

We can reply that, if we view the moral process as "a logical system," the primacy of the person does indeed function as a postulate, but that thus to view it is erroneous. It does function as a postulate, since it is a primitive premise, itself not provable in the same way in which judgments dependent on it are provable by it. But ethical activity is not susceptible of formulation into a logical system, since it involves the creative activity of the moral imagination and the analogy between symbolic or logical systems and value systems, as already pointed out, is false. Indeed, it is high time that a correction was introduced. I have been speaking of "a value system" acknowledged by a man and constituting his personality. I have said that the system was organized hierarchically and that, on given occasions, some values in it functioned as basic. Actually, this is only approximately true, since the degree of systematic organization that we are likely to find in any man's or people's values is not very high. The principles of order which govern our value systems are precisely what are in question when a man faces a serious moral decision. Therefore, the comparison between the concrete existential value complex and a symbolic system is inadmissible, since the former is dynamic, more or less inchoate, never fully finished, and hence the principles of order that govern it are never fully or clearly known.

The primacy of the person, however, is a "postulate" in a totally different sense: in the sense that Kant meant when he spoke of the "postulates of the practical reason." The ethical man in the situation in which he discovered the necessity for "postulating" the primacy of the person was not picking out arbitrarily one sentence or proposition among many to lay at the base of a deductive, purely symbolic system. He was completing the moral process by discovering the necessary conditions required to resolve the problem of evil.

We could argue, on the other hand, that the ethical decision remains conditional, since it really involves the assertion that *if* one wants to be ethical, one needs to assert unconditionally the primacy of the person. And hence the categorical character of the ethical demand has disappeared, giving way to a mere hypothetical situa-

tion. This is true, but it is further true that the moral man is confronted all along with this alternative: either morality or chaos.
The question as to whether he will accept one choice or the other is
practically nonsensical, since one alternative must be rejected. The
question for him, therefore, is not whether morality is possible but
how it is—what its necessary conditions are. And this is the question because he has already made the initial choice by accepting
morality. The other alternative, chaos, is not theoretically impossible, since it does not involve an internal incoherence. Indeed, on
one reading of human experience it seems probable. This reading
cannot be dismissed: Callicles, Thrasymachus, the Athenian ambassadors to the Island of Melos, Hobbes, and Nietzsche are not
men whose interpretation of human experience can be lightly dismissed. The moral man, nevertheless, knows it is not the correct
one. The content of human experience presents factors that these
men seem to have been blind to. Thus it seems to be a fact, ignored
by the prophets of force, that men universally want to be persons.
What makes the difference between men is not that some want to
be persons and others wilfully and deliberately choose consistently
not to be, but that some choose rightly and others wrongly how to
become and maintain themselves as persons. We may say of a
criminal: "He is not a human being," meaning that he is not a person. And we may go so far as to assume that he chooses the wrong
values because he has no regard for himself as person. But, strictly
speaking, we are wrong, since we forget that in some vague and
confused way criminals choose what to them seem to be values
which they maintain and for the maintenance of which they are
capable of sacrifice, of courage, of stubborn effort. Their values are
hopelessly wrong, but a kind of self-respect and a conception of
excellence, nevertheless, they do have. They do not want merely to
live. No man wants merely to live—to live protoplasmically, purely
biologically, to live at any cost. Men want to live as men, or as
what they in their darkened minds take men to be. There is honor
in thieves, although perhaps not always among them; and they are
no less punctilious in its defense than the good man is in the defense
of his honor. This is the reason why the totally abject man, utterly
without self-respect, is inconceivable and why we say that even the
worm will turn. Dostoevski was specially fascinated by the utterly

shameless man, but he found that the shamelessness was deceptive, that it constituted a means by which the shameless man sought to maintain some corner of self-respect by lacerating himself publicly. The man who loses his self-respect regains it in his own eyes by exposing his own shame, thus saying, "I am capable of shame, and, to prove that I am, I expose my shame."

There is another reason why it seems inadvisable to call the criteria which govern ethical judgments "postulates" or "commitments." In both Williams' and Charner Perry's presentation, the moral act subserves the will which, through the practical realization of the decision, expresses itself by enforcing its dictates. But a will thus served represents what we can call the "despotic conscience," a pathological manifestation of the moral conscience. In fact, the ethical will or, more precisely, the will deciding to abide by the criterion of the ethical life is a will which abrogates itself. If it should be insisted that it is despotic, it should be added that its despotism is turned inward upon itself, since it is addressed against the tendency—seemingly inherent in all wills—to become despotic. Thus the ethical decision is an act of the will that makes the will renounce what gives it its ethically objectionable character—the assertion of its primacy and the refusal to reconsider its primacy. The will thus, rather than using value for its ends, submits to the requiredness of value and freely becomes the instrument of that requiredness. We can thus see the radical distinction that exists between the moral and the ethical. In the moral, ideally, there is no radical conflict between the will and the value system which constitutes the person, since the whole system is espoused, which means incorporated into the person through a volitional act. If there is conflict, it expresses a divided will, whereas, in the ethical, the espousal of a single value absolutely—the primacy of the person— involves our loosening our hold on all our other values. There is no conflict because the other values, either viewed from our standpoint or viewed from their end, exercise in vain their requiredness on us. This fact is of the utmost importance, since it is at the root of the ethical man's tendency toward otherworldliness.

It might be suggested that the ethical, as here conceived, is in conflict with moral activity, for it is distinctive of the moral activity that no given organization of values, no matter how deeply espoused, can be instituted as an absolute to which moral claims must conform. But in the ethical, the primacy of the value of the other is just such a fixed absolute, one which becomes the criterion for all values, whether of the ethical agent or of others. However, it is not true that in the moral life there is no fixed value, for the value to entertain all moral claims and judge them from an impersonal point of view, which is the essence of the moral life, is a fixed value, definitive of the moral life. Again, the positing of the primacy of the person as the keystone of the ethical organization of values does not mean that the individual thereby ceases to be receptive of moral claims made against him, but, quite the contrary, it means that he becomes much more receptive than the moral man, who frequently fails in his moral activity by disregarding the value of the personality of the other. Moreover, the readiness involved in the moral life to accept all claims does not mean a duty to accept the values that are involved in the claims, but only a duty to consider them. The duty to accept all claims would condemn the individual to the moral fluidity recommended by instrumentalism. In the latter, however, there is a valuable truth of which we must not lose sight, namely, that the person who, like the postulational moralist, insists on the primacy of his commitments is a man who is rationalizing the demands of his despotic conscience. The belief in the primacy of the person is a moral belief as well as an ethical one, since it is the key to the organization of values of the moral agent, and the specific organization is threatened only by a moral perplexity in those rare cases of total and radical self-condemnation.

But, although the criterion in terms of which decisions (whether at the moral or at the ethical level) are resolved is not, for all its similarities to them, either a postulate or a commitment; it is, again in its formal aspect, the principle by which we arrive at a real definition, for it functions in distinguishing the moral and the ethical from their contradictories and both pairs of terms from the amoral and ethically neutral. However, the definition is a real definition in the sense that what it does is to point to real distinctions in a given subject matter: the subject matter which constitutes the range of experiences of concern to a man who is practically perplexed. Such a man distinguishes one type of conduct from another. He *calls* one type the "moral" and the other, which obstructs its realization, the "immoral"; "moral" and "immoral" are contradictories because moral conduct precludes immoral and vice versa. He *calls*, at another level, one type of conduct "ethical" and the other "unethical" for the same reasons. The terms do not matter so long as it is borne in mind that the distinctions which they point to are distinctions in the subject matter.

The conviction was expressed in the last chapter that it was possible to discover the ethical without the help of religious commitments. I have shown, I hope, that intellectually it is possible to arrive at the conclusion that the root of evil among men is to be found in their mutual disregard of the primacy of one another's personalities; but this cannot satisfy those who read sympathetically the first chapter of this essay in which it was laid down that moral philosophy was a practical science whose end was enlightened action and not theoretical knowledge. There is no indication in what has been said so far about the discovery of the ethical that it involves more than a theoretical grasp of certain relations in a subject matter. A practical science involves not merely the possession of a given range of knowledge but also the possession of a will docile to the insights of that knowledge—and the discovery of the ethical does not entail the docility of the will. The religious man could therefore argue that, if we dispense with religion, we divorce the ethical practice from the theory, for only religion can bring about that second birth which enables the will to subject itself to the ends of the ethical insight.

To this criticism I cannot reply altogether satisfactorily. In so far as a reply is at all possible, it consists of reviewing the steps by which the ethical man was led to his insight, in order to show that more was involved than was recorded above, namely, a total volitional-affective, as well as intellectual, experience, which constituted a second birth. In fashionable language the insight was the result of a trauma which reorganized the personality by shaking it loose from its old values. The critic may object that it was not the trauma that loosed the ethical man from his values but the denial involved in the injustice. This is a nice point. My opinion is that the injustice caused the trauma, which consisted in the realignment of one's espousal and the introduction of a new value—that of the person—having more authority than all the others. But this does not exhaust the experience. The reflective man, undergoing the anguish of his second birth, discovering the primacy of the person and the evil to which our moral espousals, when unregulated by an absolute value, so readily lead, may go beyond the moral-ethical sphere and ask questions which fall within the range of the religious. Let us, in a sketchy manner, without attempting proofs and articulate arguments, which would turn this essay into a work on theology, look into these questions and their possible answers.

The discovery of the ethical entailed the discovery of a moral order proper to human beings: a system of objective relationships involving them in their activity as humans and thus defining their destiny as consisting in the actualization of ideal values in a certain hierarchical manner controlled by one absolute value. But this whole structure points—as all structure does, but moral structure does much more clearly—to an axiological order which is prior to its discovery and has ontic status, although, like all structure, it does not exist but can be said only to subsist. This is to say that the discovered order exhibits the objective traits of rationality. It does not exhibit the subjective traits, since in the order the presence of consciousness or mind is not directly disclosed, as it is in human intercourse through existential communication. At the purely human level the presence of such objective traits furnishes warranted ground for inferring a mind and a purpose (agent and end). At the cosmic level the inference is challenged by the critical philosopher, the skeptic, and the positivist. The critical and the skeptical philosophers both argue, by different routes, to the conclusion that the alleged objective, ontic order is a human projection. The positivist denies the possibility of making meaningful statements about the ontic status of order and claims that after Darwin any teleological argument involves the use of gratuitous assumptions which obfuscate rather than clarify issues. The structure of the world—if structure there be—can be explained, either conceptualistically or nominalistically, as generated by the very procedures through which we grasp our world. As Nagel has argued, logic does not need an ontology.[2] In short, the order found in the universe is the order which we happen to find; but we must not believe that it is independent of the means employed in finding it, since it is strictly relative to these means. Or he may argue, as does Dennes,[3] that the order which the universe exhibits is an empirically discovered order and necessitates no assumption as to agency or end, since it is an arrangement that is not intrinsic to the ordered elements but extrinsic to them. Any arrangement, for any purpose, is an order, and the arranger is the human knower who arranges for the purposes of knowing. Thus the cosmic reference is utterly gratuitous. Dennes, however, has not denied order but has merely said that the specific arrangement discovered by a knowing mind is no more intrinsic than any other that it may wish to institute. However, that a knowing mind exists, that in terms of a variety of arrangements it knows, and that therefore some sort of harmony exists between it and its objects are factors which the philosopher cannot neglect. No single discovered order may be more intrinsic than another from the standpoint of objective knowledge, but all orders are intrinsic to the mind that knows, and, since the naturalist says that mind is part of nature, we still find order as intrinsic to nature.

The ethical man who is, axiologically, a realist is convinced not merely that the order found by him is a projection which is only a descriptive correlate of his mental deficiency in his capacity for apprehending utter chaos but that it has ontic status and that that order entails some sort of agent, somehow analogous to the human agent, and therefore also an end. You can, for the purposes of prediction, merely record such order as is discovered, so long as the objective of your search is to find it for the end in view of predicting future events, considering your job done when the recorded order is verified by the more or less happy outcome of your prediction. In order to discover objectively its intrinsic nature, the best thing to do is to limit your assumptions and procedures rigorously to the ends of your inquiry—prediction. But, such as they are, the orders which men find—physical, aesthetic, or moral—stimulate in the philosopher questions as to their ontic status and origins; and these questions clearly go beyond the objectives of the positive scientist. It is a commonplace today that the order discovered in the physical world is not the simple, elegant order which was assumed by men like Galileo, Huygens, and Leibniz. If God is a geometrician and if his alphabet is number, he is not limited to using the geometry of

Euclid, and the numbers he employs are not only those we studied in the grades. The order discovered by the conscience is so vague, so weakly fluttering and unsteady, so deeply instinct with incoherence, so essentially baffling, and so cruelly mocking that it is capable of throwing the minds of men who, like Dostoevski, look at it boldly, into serious fits of skeptical doubt. And, in spite of the fact that in its defense have been employed the most strenuous efforts of the deepest and most energetic minds produced by Western civilization in two and a half millenniums, it has not yet been established lucidly as incontestably and unqualifiedly "there," and it does not seem likely ever to be so established.

But after we have said that the moral order is ambiguous and mockingly cruel, I believe that an earnest examination of the texture of human experience will reveal that there is some sort of order and that it appears to be "there" as more than the result of an axiological projection. Such as it is, order demands rationality, and rationality demands a rational agent. The teleological proof is not admissible at the biological level simply because biology is a science and science is not interested in ends but in processes, but it is admissible at the cosmological. Here the order to which it refers is not the organization achievable through mechanical processes of adaptation, whose structure and origin can be posited as given, but is an order whose origin and end constitute a genuine problem. Assuming a structure of invariant relations, positive science can engage in the discovery of specific subsystems of such relations within restricted areas of reality. What is in question for the philosopher, however, is what the scientist posits as given—the structure. If it should be argued that the question as to its origin and nature or ontic status is not intelligible, the answer is that it is not intelligible in terms of an analysis of meaning derived from the limited data furnished by the scientists; but such a conception is based on the assumption of the univocal character of the term "truth," an assumption which is not established by the methods of the positive sciences.

Our difficulties, however, are not over, for, if we assert (as Augustine did) the existence of an agent and an end beyond the spatiotemporal world as essential in the account of cosmic order, we will soon be stopped by the request for a theodicy. Here again all we can do is barely to sketch the lines along which an answer could be given.

The simple assertion of the omnipotence of the causal agent to whom we have traced the cosmic structure runs us into a contradiction if we simply assert its goodness also. Hume made this adequately clear. A proper understanding, as one can find it in Augustine, of the freedom of the will resolves, I am convinced, the problem of evil as we used the term above (as distinguished from mere catastrophe) from the standpoint of the agent of evil. But what about the victim of that evil, in so far as he is innocent, and what about the victim of catastrophe? Is it not possible that Captain Ahab was right? Remember what Ishmael reported:

" 'Vengeance on a dumb brute!' cried Starbuck, 'that simply smote thee from blindest instinct! Madness! To be enraged with a dumb thing, Captain Ahab, seems blasphemous.'

" 'Hark ye yet again,—the little lower layer. All visible objects, man, are but as pasteboard masks. But in each event—in the living act, the undoubted deed—there, some unknown but still reasoning thing puts forth the mouldings of its features from behind the unreasoning mask. If man will strike, strike through the mask! How can the prisoner reach outside except by thrusting through the wall? To me, the white whale is that wall, shoved near to me. Sometimes I think there's naught beyond. But 'tis enough. He tasks me; he heaps me; I see him in outrageous strength, with an inscrutable malice sinewing it. That inscrutable thing is chiefly what I hate.' "[4]

The questions to which these words of Ahab give rise are altogether beyond the scope of an essay on moral philosophy, but they are not unrelated to it. To Ahab's suggestion that the agent, the unknown but still seemingly reasoning thing behind the unreasoning masks, may be a malignant will endowed with an outrageous strength, how can one reply but with an *ad hominem?* "Poor man, poor, poor man, you are mad. Or do you think you are the only creature of the agent who ever felt the sting of its whip? Do you think you are the only one who was ever humiliated with the curse? Or are you going to say that you, because you are Captain Ahab, do not deserve it? You have never sinned? You are a righteous man? You never humiliated another? You were always kind and decent and just? Why, old man, in your heart there never was love, never. And your very excellence, your strength, and your unquestioned primacy were insults to those around you, all the more since they could not contest it. Did you ever notice that? Have you ever pitied or loved? Obviously, it is not good for a man to feel, as you have too long felt, that he is the absolute master of the lives of his crew. It makes him feel, as you feel, that you are God. Your power or your pride or the devil that has you in his hands and makes you dance your pathetic dance like a marionette has made you forget, old man, if you ever learned it, that you are a creature and the agent that struck at you through the whale is not. You will harpoon it, tie it to the ship, and carve it? Poor mad man, it is hard to tell whether you are comical or pathetic. It was egregious pride that led to the first fall of all, the fall before the Fall in the Garden. The only way in which one can reconcile one's self to the evil of which one is the victim is not rationally—to seek for such a reconciliation is the first irrationality—but irrationally, as Dostoevski counseled, through love."[5]

But this opens vast horizons toward which the moral philosopher cannot march with his limited equipment.

CHAPTER XX

THE PRIMACY OF THE PERSON

IN THE mind of the reader who has followed our account of the ethical life, there must have arisen some questions with which it is necessary to come to grips. The first refers to our analysis of the category of "person." In chapter xii it was said that a person consists of a system of values integrated hierarchically by the psychic powers and abilities of the human animal into a moral agent. The "dignity" of the person has its ground in the capacity of the person to acknowledge, through espousal and through recognition, the requiredness of value. But when a man transcends the moral life and reaches "the ethical stage," he asserts the value of the other's personality without qualification. This assertion means that the ethical man espouses the value of "personality" as over and above all other values which he espouses and even above the values espoused and recognized by others.

The question that has probably arisen in the reader's mind refers to the fact that it has not been shown in anything that has been said why the person comes to acquire the indefeasible value given him by the ethical man. On the contrary, it would seem that a consideration of what has been said about the person would lead us to believe that the imputation to him of an indefeasible and supreme value is not justified. For that imputation presupposes distinctions which the foregoing analysis of "person" leaves no room for: it calls for a distinction between the person and the values he acknowledges; and it gives the former a value which is independent of these and superior to them. Experience indicates that the person who presses a moral claim does not allow the validity of these distinctions but rather argues that, so far as he himself is concerned, *he is each and every one of those values which he espouses* and without which he is nothing but an animal. This was, moreover, what was insisted on above. But if a person is his values, it is not easy to see in what sense one can ascribe to him a value distinct from and independent of the total worth of the values he espouses. One can argue on this basis that the ethical man is merely a moral man, the principles of whose value organization are no different from those of anyone else, even if the values he organizes do differ in one respect, since one of the values of his system is particularly precious to him. Still this does not give us a foundation on which to ground the intrinsically indefeasible value of the person. Nothing has been said that establishes the dignity of man in any other but a relative manner: relative to him who grants it. Man's dignity can be said to arise from the values he acknowledges, but it must also be compared with the dignity which arises from the values acknowledged by other men. Therefore, the saint, the hero, and the genius are distinctly better, worthier persons, deserving more of the respect that dignity elicits than the average run of men.

In order to meet this difficulty, we shall have to amplify and extend the analysis of the person put forth in chapter xii. There only those aspects of the person were presented which were directly relevant to moral activity. This was suggested at the beginning of the section, and the reason for this manner of treatment was that a more complete analysis of the notion of personality would have deflected us from the exposition of the moral life which was at the time the task in hand.

Now it is true that a person is constituted by his values and that we cannot arbitrarily disregard his value claims without disregarding him as a person; but the emphasis should be put upon "arbitrarily," for we could not have rightly asserted that the specific value claims of another man are, as presented, indefeasible simply because he is a person and he makes them. He can be mistaken. The person's claims can be challenged and require justification. Whatever the moral claimant may argue about the identity between himself and his values, when we recognize him as person it is not his specific values that we acknowledge—for these constitute a fortuitous organization from among the indefinitely large number from which he could have selected; what we acknowledge is *his right to espouse a value system and the importance for him as person of such an espousal*. Whether the specific values he espouses are morally valid or not depends on whether they stand the test of justification, and this is another and an independent question, to be decided on its own merits. If a philosophy asserts that a man has the unchallengeable right to what he claims, that philosophy is but a superficial variant of the postulational moral theory, and it leads to the same consequences. Such a philosophy has one absolute, the will that constitutes or chooses values. The essence of a man's moral personality is not constituted by his will. This is precisely what a man discovers in the moral experience, particularly when he is forced to make a transition from the moral to the ethical. The source of injustice and of those calamities of which men are the victims and which have their origin in their fellows can generally be traced to the erection of the will into a discretionary arbiter. Postulational moral philosophers misconceive the nature of morality, and the root reason is probably that they do not really believe that there resides in the person an intrinsic worth distinct from the total worth of the values he espouses. The value of the person as person is distinct from the total worth of the values he espouses and recognizes. And our question remains: Wherein does that value reside?

It has been argued that the person is endowed with an inherent value because "a person" means "a carrier of moral values and disvalues," as Nicolai Hartmann puts it.[1] Because an individual is an agent whose function is to actualize and maintain a system of values, value inheres in the activity which defines his function, and it is the possession of this value which constitutes his dignity, claimed by himself and acknowledged by others. It could be argued further that the claim of such worth in one's self involves one necessarily in the acknowledgment of it in others, even though the acknowledgment need not be made explicitly but may be only implicitly involved in one's practical treatment of the other. This argument is valid, so far as it goes, but it does not satisfy the demands for a ground for the ethical regard for the person, which must depend (using C. I. Lewis' important distinction) on an *intrinsic* value of the person as person and not on an *inherent* value derived from his function.[2] The ethical consciousness would answer that, if the value is derived, it is relative and comparative; and this answer could not advance us beyond the mere moral level, according to which a person has the value his status and role in society give him. On this view a person's dignity is acquired from the functions he performs and his success in performing them and hence is defeasible. Such an inherent value, again, requires for recognition no special insight beyond that possessed by a normal moral man. Men quite naturally tend to respect one another because of the values they serve or the functions they perform, as determined by the cultural hierarchy of values they recognize. The moral philosopher could say that they tend to do so all too readily and that fawning deference before social values is of the very structure of social man. If this social dignity serves as a basis for respect, it also serves as a basis for disrespect, since the value inhering in the person through his function is comparative. Morally it is not possible to respect a coward as much as a hero, nor is it possible to respect a brothel-keeper as much as a sister of charity; but the ethical man respects the other person and treats him in such a way as to avoid violating his dignity, no matter how unworthy morally he may be known to be. For him, beyond moral distinctions lies the intrinsic worth of a man which neither vice nor weakness nor accident can annihilate. The keeper of the brothel has intrinsic worth, no less than the self-sacrificing nurse serving in the leper colony, and the ratcatcher or garbage man no less than the king. The insight on which such an attitude toward one's fellow-beings is based may not have any objective validity. If it has, the person has an intrinsic value whose ground must be exhibited.

It is not an adequate answer to this question to argue that the primacy of the person is discovered through an act of love. It is undoubtedly true that without love the person's primacy is not *discovered*; but love cannot create the value of the person, it merely discovers it. Wherein, then, does the primacy of the person reside? Why does the person have the indefeasible value he has? I shall consider two possible answers to the question, logically independent of each other. Because it is convenient to have them labeled, I shall refer to the first, although apologetically, since the label does not seem adequate, as the "cosmological argument" and to the second as the "argument from the nature of man."

The cosmological argument establishes the primacy of the person either through his relation to God, conceived as the immanent rationality of the universe, as the Stoics did, or to a personal, transcendent God, as the Christians do. In this respect, Stoic doctrine is formally identical with the Christian doctrine, even though their metaphysical differences are radical. Epictetus speaks, at least in my translation, almost like a Christian when he tells us "that we are all, before anything else, children of God, and that God is the Father of Gods and men."[3] From this belief follows the equality of men, and their mutual citizenship in Cosmopolis or in the City of God. But for the Christian the relation is more intimate, since he holds that it is a genuine brotherhood.

The second is the argument from the spiritual nature of man. For its adequate development this argument would demand a book, for it takes us into obscure problems of metaphysics. The argument, succinctly put, is this: The person deserves unqualified respect because he is not merely psyche but also spirit, and spirit is, so far as we know, the highest possible form of being. I shall offer here a more or less summary statement of the grounds on which we can establish our belief that the ethical insight is valid. Let us go back to the account given of the person in chapter xii. There it was said that a psyche endowed with powers and aptitudes capable of integrating a hierarchical system of values from among those which press upon man for acknowledgment constitutes the person. In this account, which I have said was far from complete, no notice was taken of the fact that the psyche that creates the person is a finite being but that it is endowed with powers the presence of which define it as spirit. *The intrinsic value of the person is constituted by the value he possesses as spirit.*

Merely as the kind of finite being that it is, the psyche is intrinsically valuable, for being is valuable through and through, and hierarchically valuable. The value possessed by the psyche is higher than that possessed by many other types of finite beings—inorganic or merely living or organic beings. But spirit is highest, and what makes it highest is that, in it and through it only, is the world able to achieve cognizance of its status as creature, to perceive its character as valuable, and through man's efforts to fulfil a destiny which it freely accepts. This is a metaphysical fact, which I must assume without further proof, accepting as sufficient validation here the intuitive deliverance of my rational consciousness that mere matter in me is lower than my vegetative process and that these are lower than the will and this, in turn, lower than my intelligence, such as it is, and this, finally, than my objective spirit, on which I depend for my grasp of the world of value which constitutes me and without which I would be an incomplete man. Were I pressed for further proof, I would be forced to fall back on the consensus of mankind and point out that men, in fact, find spirit the most valuable of all forms of being; and in their practical life, in their cultural evaluations, in their myths, and in their religions and philosophies they eloquently assert or imply that the value it possesses inheres in it and is the highest value known to man. Even in the philosophy of a distracted age and culture, antihuman and barbaric, such as pragmatism, spirit is given primacy, not for what it is but for what use it can be put to—but still it is given primacy.

But it could still be argued that the primacy of spirit is not inherent but imputed. This essay can be taken as an extended polemic against such a position. Paraphrasing Nicolai Hartmann loosely, one can say that an extended inquiry into the phenomena of the moral life of men, which seeks to do justice to it without reducing it in order to fit it into a physicalist metaphysic, reveals the apriority of value and that the deeper one analyzes, the clearer does it become that the Hobbesian theory of value fails to do justice to the phenomena. This fact is ignored or denied by naturalism, whose conception of being, borrowed from positive science, has been, for the purpose of scientific elaboration, stripped naked of the value which existentially resides in it. But the "being" of positive science is not true existential being, but an abstraction or isolate for the purpose of discovering the kind of invariant relations which it is the business of the scientist to capture in his predictive formulas. True being—or reality or existential nature—is not "value-free." It is intrinsically valuable. An obvious, if well-nigh universally current, confusion holds that the world of the physicist is the physical world and blandly assumes that the physical world is the real world. But, as Heidegger, I believe, has suggested, the world of the physicist is a "deformed abstraction" of the physical world, which itself is but a part of being or reality or the existential world. But, while the value which resides in the psyche is enough to place man above organic life and physical being, it is not enough to give him a place above the animal level, for that value is intrinsic generally to all animals or, at least, to the highest. In man it is the possession of *spirit*—as, following Scheler, I shall call it—which gives him his intrinsically supreme value, absolutely above all the values that he as man can actualize. It is not merely a matter of arbitrary terminology that makes me follow Scheler's use of the term "spirit" in preference to the classical "reason" to designate that capacity the possession of which distinguishes men from animals and endows them with their intrinsic primacy. The term "reason"—with its predominantly noetic referent—has been compromised by the limited meaning which technological man has come to give it through his interest in positive knowledge. When we say that the faculty of reason is the agency of knowledge or that the function of reason is knowledge and truth, using these terms in their classical acceptations, they include much more than contemporary naturalistic philosophy assigns to them. It is therefore best to avoid the term "reason," which has been narrowed in its intension by modern positivistic naturalists.

What is this spirit whose presence in the animal gives him primacy? In developing an answer to this question, I shall follow Scheler; but the source of the doctrine is not particularly relevant to my purposes, since the doctrine is here offered on its own validity and not on the basis of authority.[4] Scheler points out that what distinguishes man from the animals below him is not the former's possession of intelligence, for it has been demonstrated that animal activity at times exhibits authentic acts of intelligence, acts which are not merely instinctive. What the animal below man gives no sign of possessing and what constitutes a difference *of kind*, not of degree, is the principle which the Greeks called "reason," but which Scheler prefers to designate under the broader term "spirit." The marks of "spirit" are *freedom, objectivity*, and *self-consciousness*. By "freedom" is here meant "existential autonomy," which is conceived as freedom from all that belongs to mere "life" and to the impulsive intelligence which is proper to life. A spiritual man is thus not tied to his impulses or to his organism's ambient world but is "open" to the world by which the organism is circumscribed and which consists of centers of resistance for the organism without spirit. Man transforms these centers of resistance that he encounters into "objects." As centers of resistance, ambient things are dealt with under the determination of animal, vital impulse and of organic reaction. To transform ambient resisting things into objects is to consider them as what they are in themselves. More simply put, spirit responds to the object seen, not through the modification of vital impulse, of organic need, but objectively because it is independent of organic need. An animal endowed with spirit responds *theoretically* to the things that come within the range of its experience, responds as a spectator, and thus grasps the relation of these "objects" to other objects and beyond to still further ones. Thus the spirit lives in an open world, whereas an animal not endowed with spirit lives closed in by the unbreakable wall of his limited organic demands. But spirit is also able to choose whether to suppress or to yield to its own impulses, to inhibit or to release them, on grounds not of impulse itself but of the ideal values that spirit either may want to actualize or may decide that other spirits ought to actualize. And, finally, spirit is reflexive: it is consciousness conscious of itself. Through its reflexiveness, spirit converts itself and the body in which it dwells into an object and is able not only to transform the ambient world—as all animals do—but to transform itself in terms of ideal values free of organic need. Man is the only animal, it seems, that molds itself.

I see no need to make any radical qualifications of this conception of spirit, although some additions will have to be made; but certain observations seem to be called for in order to avoid possible misunderstanding as to the sense in which and the extent to which I accept this view of spirit. Not that on this question one can say anything that is beyond misunderstanding. The secularistic ethos of our culture, the illegitimate metaphysical claims made by positive scientists superbly ignorant of the difficult philosophical problems over which they march roughshod, and the formidable impetus of naturalistic propaganda today shut most ears tightly against any claims which do not coincide with popular materialistic psychology. To make a distinction between psyche and organism is retrograde enough; to make a distinction between spirit and psyche puts one on an intellectual level with the Australian aboriginals or, what is perhaps worse, with "metaphysicians." And to discuss the problem and not once mention the central nervous system and the cortex or the thalamus or whatever other organs the fashion happens at the moment to use as shibboleths guarantees one nothing but obloquy and derision.

Now Scheler seems convinced that the principle through or by means of which man objectifies the world (spirit) cannot be part of the world, nor can it be localized in a determinate time or place. It can reside only in the ground of being itself. But, certainly, the assertion cannot be intended to deny that the spirit which is now seeking to elucidate these problems by writing this essay and the other spirit which follows this attempt were not in the world a few years ago and somehow in some sense are now here and in a few years more will be, so far as we can positively tell, nowhere to be found. The spirit, wherever it may have come from, seems somehow to dwell in a body in a legitimate sense of "in." It is not *in* the body in the obvious sense that, for instance, the brain is *in* the skull and that my body is now *in* a room. While the writer's body remains in his study, in his home, in Columbus, Ohio, U.S.A., there is a sense in which, at the same time, his spirit can now be back in Caracas in 1910 or in New York in 1920. Nevertheless, a spirit is *in* a body in the no less legitimate sense that it seems closely related to the body and seems to be able to make itself manifest to other spirits only through the means which their bodies provide. The spirit may be said to own a body—even though only temporarily. Nor can we know, with the same kind of positive knowledge that we know of its sojourn in the body, what its fate is when it abandons its fleshly abode. But if the statement means (as we suspect from other sources that it must) that the principle is not *created* by physical factors, themselves devoid of spirit, then we must comment as follows: For certain, all we positively know is that spirit is different from psyche. We do not positively know what makes its appearance possible. We do positively know a few minimal physical conditions of its sojourn. We know, for instance, that the disturbances of certain glands can make a man into a mere psychophysical organism almost utterly devoid of the lucid flame of spirit; but, while we learn more and more about how to make the flame retain a bright and lambent blue cone, we can neither kindle the flame nor hope to do more than merely delay for a brief instant the moment in which it will be extinguished. For certain, we know very little about the brief candle and how it comes by its flame. But we do know, in the same positive way in which we know some of its conditions, that the spirit is something real, although immaterial and different from the body, just as the lambent flame of a wax candle, with its blue cone, is different from the candle and the physical processes which constitute the necessary conditions of its appearance. We also know that spirit is superior to the psyche in which it appears and the physical organism in which it dwells, since spirit is free and in its freedom inheres intrinsically a higher value than in any other form of being with which men are empirically acquainted. If it be claimed, however, that spirit is of an utterly different stuff from that which constitutes the physical world or the psyche, this is a claim on which I find it impossible to be dogmatic, since I am not clear as to its intention. It would seem to be so, but the speculations which back up the conviction do not constitute positive knowledge.

The metaphysical perspectives that open at this point are limitless, and the difficulty of mapping the country ahead from our own vantage point and without actually surveying it is prohibitive. If spirit is a different kind of "stuff" or substance or process from that which constitutes the physical and organic world, as it seems to be, the question cannot be settled by the positive sciences, since they are restricted by methods and objectives to the formulation of invariant relations among phenomena of sensible nature. For their purposes the sciences can operate fairly adequately, it seems, on several mutually incompatible metaphysical foundations. To say that spirit is a different "principle" or "stuff" or "process" raises questions but does not solve any; for one would naturally ask what is meant by any such statement, and the question leads straight into overwhelming problems of metaphysics and ontology. At the plane at which spirit comes within the purview of our analysis (through an examination of man and a comparison of his powers and faculties with those of the other animals), it seems to me that it is legitimate to assert that nothing we know from a study of physiology enables us to reduce without residue the psyche to the physiological basis in which it somehow resides and that nothing that we know of animal psychology enables us to reduce man's distinctive powers and aptitudes—his spirit—to those which naturalistic psychology studies by means of analysis of animal behavior and its sign-using powers.[5]

This does not deny that the study of correlations between physical and mental processes is advancing rapidly and will continue to advance as long as scientific research pushes on, but it takes a special philosophic structure to identify the physical and the mental terms thus correlated. The argument back of such identification is valid if one disregards the special objectives of the scientist which the moral philosopher does not share. For the latter it is legitimate to assert that spirit is something distinct from organic activity and that, as yet, the extent to which and the manner in which the spirit is controlled in its sojourn by organic processes are something in regard to which we are pathetically in the dark.

I do not see what can be gained or lost by denying or asserting that spirit is positively known only as somehow embodied in an organism and that the speculations as to whether it can exist independently of the organism to which it is anchored are vague, obscure, and far from decisive. One can have *faith* in immortality, but I do not see what *positive knowledge* of it one can have. To repudiate these speculations, however, because they do not have the clarity and distinctness that we find in mathematical analysis or in the positive sciences is possible only to positivists, to whom subject matter is of no intrinsic importance and only the way in which it is manipulated counts. But to deny that they are inconclusive is unworthy of a student of philosophy. To this writer, at any rate, it is the subject matter which is of chief importance, and, if vagueness and obscurity are all that he can achieve, he sees in such inadequate results a reason not for abandoning the problem but for doing his best with it. Much could be gained if we could convince the men who in the field of moral philosophy will accept nothing but positive knowledge that they are playing a trivial game—but that is another question. In any case it is neither desirable nor possible successfully to contradict anyone who chooses to formulate the difference and relation between spirit and psyche and psyche and body as a difference which can be correlated with hypothetical differences in the organic structures of men and the other animals, in regard to which information is not yet at hand. If this information is offered in good faith, if the correlation does not turn out to mean the denial of one of the correlates, as it does with the idealists and materialists, and if the "perhaps" and the "hypothetical" are not lost while turning the page, as they all too frequently are, and are thus not intended ultimately to serve as a basis for the denial of the actual difference, there can be no objection to the inquiry or to its results.

Nothing that has been said here can possibly give comfort to contemporary American naturalists, who are intent on denying, through semiotic analysis behavioristically oriented, the specific difference in kind between psyche and organism and hence would deny also the difference between spirit and the animal psyche. For what is at issue is not the means employed by spirit or by psyche for the expression of its activity—which is all that the behavioristic semiotician can legitimately study within the purview of his discipline and the limitations of his method; no one would deny, it seems to me, that the means in both cases are clearly physical. Even idealists—Bosanquet, for instance—readily grant this. But, if the means are physical, they are open to positive science for investigation. What is at issue is whether the positive scientist *exhausts* the problem while staying within the confines of his methods and maintaining his orientation. By "exhausting" it is meant that he answers all the questions we may legitimately ask. I would argue that he does not exhaust it and that, if he supposes that he does, he makes two mistakes: the first is that of confusing the power or aptitude which constitutes spirit (whose discernible marks, as was said, are freedom, objectivity, and self-consciousness) with the means that it employs to manifest itself (which consist of symbolic structures); and the other is that of reducing the meanings and values of these structures to the physical means through which the meanings and values are expressed. These differences are such that for his purposes the behavioristic psychologist and the semiotician can legitimately disregard and ignore them; however, these men are seldom content to disregard them. On the basis of a doubtful metaphysics, according to which what does not interest them does not exist, they deny them, if not always explicitly, at least always in an effective, tacit manner. Stating the same thing in other words, we can say that the objectives of "behavioristics" legitimately enable the behavioristic semiotician to dispense with the notion of mind and therefore of spirit. Lest the reader be puzzled by the term, I should inform him that "behavioristics" is a science recently invented by Neurath, which, with many other useful inventions of recent times, is the subject of great a priori speculation as to its method and of very little empirical research. Therefore, for the purposes of the "behavioristician," as I imagine we must call him, a man is only an animal whose behavior includes the use of signs. Besides the interest in semiotics, there are, however, many other interests, and these rest on the same plane of legitimacy as that which leads to the development of semiotics. The semiotician argues that he alone possesses "scientific knowledge" and that the "mentalist"—as he calls those who posit "mind" seriously as a term of discourse—do not. As he defines "scientific knowledge," it need not be argued that he possesses it and that the mentalist does not. But, of course, it should be remembered that there is a number of problems which the semiotician cannot solve with his methods while keeping faithful to his objectives. What he calls "scientific knowledge" is not the only kind of knowledge, since other quests besides the scientific can be carried on by intelligent men and these quests have generic traits in common with what he calls "scientific knowledge." These other quests are as important as, if not more so than, are the inquiries of the scientist to a broad human economy. It is not impertinent to add, however, that, if what Charles Morris has to offer about art is a fair sample of the light that the behavioristic semiotician claims he throws on the activities of the humanist, we have been given enough evidence to judge the results of the new science as trivial.[6]

But does not the anguish which is the heavy burden of spirit and which Kierkegaard and his disciples have forced on our attention give spirit a disvalue, it may be asked, or at least force us to discount heavily the inherent value that it has? Because its freedom is not complete, since spirit is finite and hence not omnipotent, and because it apprehends infinity—and for other reasons which one does not quite clearly know—spirit, it is true, is always heavily burdened with anguish. Let us remember Kierkegaard.[7] There is no man who is not somehow burdened with a sense of despair. Thoreau glimpsed the fact, which was also known by Paul and perhaps by the Stoics and by the Orphics and by Plato. There is no man at the bottom of whose consciousness there is not to be found a certain disquietude, a perturbation, a disharmony, a fear of the unknown or of something he does not dare face or of himself. This is a disease that, on occasion, fear reveals to him. Kierkegaard believes that only the true Christian is free of this disease. And he is probably right, since the only true Christian who ever lived is now found in heaven, sitting at the right hand of His Father. But whether more than one Christian has ever lived or not, because spirit is so burdened, as Santayana tells us, "it longs first for happiness and at last for salvation."[8] It maintains its search for happiness as long as it can, against all odds and in the face of the most difficult obstacles. But the search (and this is what worldlings are too myopic to see and too insensitive to care about when it is pointed out to them) merely increases the unhappiness of the world and, in the end, the weight of the burden which the spirit must carry. One reason for this is that the pursuit of happiness is the pursuit of a mirage, a chase after a travesty of what spirit really wants—that completion in the Infinite which alone can slake its thirst. This we could have learned from Augustine if we had not spoiled our taste for wisdom: *Thou hast made us for Thyself, and our heart is restless until it finds rest in Thee.* Another reason is that the pursuit of happiness, as the worldling conceives of it, is a flight from authenticity; but this is not a topic which we should stop to elucidate here, since the existentialists have written fully on it and with a penetration I could not match. So long, therefore, as men keep up the futile effort to abolish the anguish of spirit, they will end up by merely increasing it. This is why a life merely moral; a life not leavened by the ethical insight, not touched by love, a life indifferent to the primacy of personality, is a life essentially brutal and unjust and, at the core, a lie, since it prefers the lesser to the greater good. The true destiny of man is not reached by the path of happiness but by the path of salvation, and it includes (although it is not fully defined by it) the ethical life. But what, someone may ask, is salvation? At the moral level salvation is surcease from the anguish that the burden of our guilt creates in us, which is too heavy for anyone to carry. The burden cannot be thrown off, but it can be lightened by love.

The question, however, is now only the more insistent: Does not the anguish which is the heavy burden of spirit detract from the primacy of its worth, or at least force us to discount its inherent value heavily? This question reveals inadequate knowledge of what anguish is and of what role it plays in the activity of the spirit. The anguish points to the road of liberation, and the tension of which it consists is an earnest of what the fully actualized goodness of the liberated spirit can be. Anguish is the burden of spirit, and it cannot be dropped; we must pull it after us like a riveted iron ball. But, although anguish is the eternal companion of finite spirit, it never succeeds, except in moments of overwhelming catastrophe, in destroying altogether the joy that is the essence of spirit. The joy of finite spirit, however, is never pure joy. How can it be when it must forever contend for supremacy with the anguish which is our lot? But to assert that life is only anguish is as erroneous as to affirm that it is only joy. The error, I believe, of the existentialists who are pessimists, is that they have not done justice—as the main tradition of European philosophy has—to the fact that *existence is valuable*, is never utterly devoid of value, and that the perfect actualized mode of self-realization of spirit—as we can see by extrapolating from our own imperfections—is joy. They have not read experience correctly, since they have overlooked a factor of it which is no less important than the anguish of which they make so much. The burden of anguish cannot be dropped; but the very tension which constitutes the anguish, the oscillation between the extremes of nothingness and being in which its movement consists, is a search for the goodness of existence that a finite creature never fully possesses. This is true for Kierkegaard, who, as a Christian, believed in the possibility of salvation. And if it is not true of German and French atheistic existentialism, the reason is obvious: that philosophy has lost God. Sartre said in a speech in Canada on his first trip to America after the war, unless my memory deceives me, that the fact that God does not exist does not amuse the existentialist. We can complete the statement for him and add that it is the cause of his despair. If there were no greater goodness than that which I now possess, if the disvalue of my finitude did not point to the full value which could complete it, I would be forced to accept the conclusions drawn by these men. But the distance between actuality and the ideal which anguish reveals marks the curve of the dialectic of existence from the finite to the infinite, from that which we are to that which we could be, from incompletion to fulness, from the creature to its cause, from partial to total value. The sputtering, feeble joy which actuality contains reveals the full, steady amplitude of the joy with which that complete actuality, could we but reach it, would flood spirit. Anguish does not indicate total disvalue; that would be utter nothingness, the unthinkable void. Nor does it indicate that we possess all the amplitude of joy that we could possess. It indicates that to a more complete reality, a less finite finitude, belongs a greater joy, and to the infinite the greatest joy. Anguish is our burden, since we are placed between nonbeing and Real Being.

We need not doubt, then, that the possession of spirit marks a difference in kind between man and the other animals. But is it so obvious that spirit is free? In the chapter on "Indeterminacy and Indeterminism" in his *Foundations of Ethics*, W. D. Ross concluded his discussion with the following remarks: "A philosophical genius may some day arise who will succeed in reconciling our natural thought about freedom and responsibility with the acceptance of the law of causality; but I must admit that no existing discussion seems to be very successful in doing so."[9] Whether Ross's problem can be solved or not, one thing would seem obvious—that the solution cannot be arrived at by the mere asseveration of a point of view which is all that we have done so far. But what, first, is meant by the freedom which has been claimed for the spirit? For Scheler the freedom of spirit means its autonomy, which is to say, its independence from organic factors, manifest in the capacity we have of surveying our organic impulses and, in the light of our apprehension of ideal values, of deciding whether we will yield to them or not or which among them we will satisfy. The determinist will say that this is *subjective* freedom but that, *objectively*, the choices are determined by factors unknown to the chooser but operative nevertheless in the selection of alternatives. What evidence is offered for this claim? Since the factors are admittedly unknown, the evidence is not empirical but a deductive inference drawn from the so-called "law of causality," which holds that all events whatsoever must have a cause. However, when we ask how the believer in this socalled "universal law" came by it, we see that, as regards the freedom of the spirit, he begs the issue until he shows one of two things:

either that spirit, although a phenomenon different in kind from organic phenomena, is determined in the same way that organic phenomena are or that spirit is not a different kind of phenomenon, as it has here been claimed to be. In other words, the law of causality cannot be applied deductively to spirit until it is inductively verified for it. For those who claim the freedom of spirit need not deny the validity of causality in the physical realm; they need only hold that it does not apply to phenomena of a different kind, namely, the spiritual.

Of course, the freedom of the spirit in no way abrogates the bondage to which man—who is more than spirit, who is also flesh—is subject. Man is a creature of habit, of impulse, of passion, driven here and there by forces of nature which are beyond his control and, as we shall see, ineluctably determined at both terminal points of his trajectory. His freedom is limited, episodical, far from omnipotent. But, in so far as he is spirit, he is free. And the law of causality cannot be said to apply to him until it is shown in detail that his spiritual activities are controlled either at the physical or at the psychical level or both by specific determinants verified in terms of predictions.

So long as the creative activity of the spirit remains the mystery that it is, we have a right to reject the distinction between subjective and objective determinism with which Schopenhauer and determinists since his day have tried to fasten their dogma on philosophy. I am free because the "I" which claims the freedom is the spirit in me, a thing which I have reason to believe is distinct from the organism that sustains it, a body on which my spirit may, for all I know, depend for its existence but which does not seem to control me entirely. I am free because I can use the organism for my spiritual purposes, which are ideal and which transcend my body's impulses and needs and not infrequently frustrate them, and I am free when I decide that I will not allow my body to use me for *its* purposes. There is no denying that the organism imposes conditions on my spirit; charges it, so to speak, for its room and board. And to that extent my spirit is in bondage. I have to take care of my body, my health; I have to sleep, to play, or the body will not let me do my work and may dislodge me altogether before my work is done. The body distracts me, too, with importunate demands and encases me in a hard shell of habits; so that I am never utterly free, nor is the freedom I possess a gift. To maintain it is not easy, and I am never utterly free, nor could I ever be, since I am not God. The freedom I possess is always qualified and incomplete. But, if spirit wants to assert its freedom, it can always and in all circumstances do so, since it can at any time decide to break the moorings that attach it to its body. If the body becomes arrogantly importune and bondage to it unendurable, spirit can decide on flight. I think Socrates and the Christians are probably right, as opposed to Epictetus, when they tell us that we do not have a right to take our own lives. But death is seldom difficult, and, if spirit decides on flight, there is nothing the beggarly body can do, for all its cunning and sullen, insufferable tricks but resign itself to turn back to the condition of mere thinghood, to become a carcass. If this is not freedom, what is it?

Heidegger argues that man's only freedom consists in his capacity to see the world in its real meaning and that therefore all that freedom can do is engender detachment, submission, renunciation.[10] Nor are men capable of rising above their fate. The reason is that man's life is determined by two ineluctable facts over which he has no control: he is thrust into life without his consent and snatched from it without his leave. These are undeniable, although Heidegger's conviction that beyond death lies nothing is not quite so certain as he seems to believe. But between the poles of birth and death there is an area over which we have some mastery, since between them we can exercise in spontaneity the creativity of our spirit, can play with beauty, create truth, and mold even our own character. If the bondage gets too heavy, we can will nothingness—if that is all there is beyond life. We are not God, which is perhaps what a demoniac spirit like Heidegger would want to be before he would be content with his freedom. Since we are only finite creatures, our freedom is qualified and partial, but it does seem to consist of more than a Spinozistic apprehension of the order of determined things; for one of the things it seems clearly to apprehend is that the order of things is not fully and through-and-through structured.

Once the primacy of the person has been established, it is not difficult to see why the formula of the ethical can be expressed practically in the Golden Rule and, from another point of view, in Kant's "kingdom of ends." But it is not superfluous to point out that an ethical life is a practical—not a theoretical—task, something to be lived whether one philosophy or another does justice to the factors which constitute it. This is said to introduce a remark which will, no doubt, seem obvious to the reader but without which I could not consider my exposition complete. The ethical life is a matter of existential attitudes involving the feelings and impulses with which men regard themselves, their fellows, their ambitions, their children, and their goods and which define the turn they would like to see things actually take. It is not possible without Christian love and charity and respect for the other man. But in calling it "Christian" love, we should remember that this love is often manifested by men who never heard of Christianity and that it is only rarely manifested by those who call themselves "Christians." Christian love is something which no theoretical activity—the reading of this book or of any other on ethical philosophy, however superior to this one—can create in a man. Intellectual activity is effective in practice in a complex and roundabout, indirect way; but it cannot be a substitute—as Aristotle saw—for the growth and development which the moral man undergoes and the second birth which, I have argued, the ethical man achieves. The ethical life, in particular, is not a matter of philosophy, however much the student may concern himself with its structure and sources, but of the way in which we treat our fellows at the humble level of humdrum existence and of the concern, the gentle, unyielding vigilance lest our interests and passions make us forget what our function as human beings is. Nor does it seem to correlate in any way whatever with a man's literate culture of belletristic achievements. There is no evidence on which to base the belief that we find it realized more frequently among the learned or the aesthetically sensitive or the worldly respectable than among the lowly or the disinherited.

But if the ethical life consists in the way in which we regard the person and value his intrinsic worth as above all other values, in what sense does it transcend the moral life? Or could we not interpret the phenomenon which defines it as an aspect of moral experience? The answer is that we would not do it justice if we interpreted it in this way, because the moral life involves the manner in which claims can be satisfied by integration into a fortuitously organized system of values, none of which singly, or all together, can claim a priori justification as opposed to any claim that could be made against them. The ethical life involves the recognition of one value which, in regard to the moral system acknowledged by the ethical man, functions with a priori validity and which is therefore, in respect to that moral system, "absolute." However, the ethical does not demand in an a priori way a given system of values of an a priori nature as a moral context within which it functions. This in practice means that one could live an ethical life in Dobu no less than in the Roman Empire of Diocletian's day or in the Spain of Philip or in the America of the Robber Barons or in the Mexico of Cortez. What a man's dignity is at the ethical level does not depend on the artificialities of the world and what it chooses to consider his dignity in an institutional sense. The dignity of the President of the United States and the respect we owe him are one thing, his inherent dignity as man quite another. When the king enters, a subject uncovers himself, bows, and addresses him as "Majesty" or "Sire." A Spanish grandee you address as "Alteza," and a naval officer as "Sir." You give these men signs of your respect. But these actions have nothing to do with their primacy in an ethical sense. You can, if you are strong enough, dethrone the king; you can tie him to your chariot and drag him along the crowded streets. As a man, you cannot dethrone another man or drag him without dethroning and dragging yourself first. To kill a king may be a *political* necessity which a Lenin can argue about with a Suarez. It can never be an *ethical* necessity, since the only necessity that the ethical man would recognize is that of living according to his primary insight. When the two necessities—the political and the ethical—clash, you may be facing a tragic conflict in the sense that whichever way you choose to resolve it involves irreparable loss. But your ethical insight will tell you that the greatest loss of all is that which is involved in repudiating your destiny.

For this reason the ethical man is a hopelessly burdened man, set in the midst of a fierce conflict; he functions within a system of moral values, and, if he gives these up or repudiates them, he gives up the matter which the ethical life informs. His ethical insight has led him to see beyond the values of his moral system, and he knows deep in his heart that the effort and concern with which men espouse their values are never justified, for in their fierce espousals and with the best intentions, for the sake of their moralities they willingly sacrifice their most precious value, their dignity as men. If the possible pathological developments of the moral man are found in the despotic and the overanxious conscience, as they are, that of the ethical man is an exaggerated asceticism which denies all values except the value of love, since the espousal of any other value than love may imperil love—as it indeed does. But when a man loves men and despises what they love in general and without discrimination, what he loves is an abstraction. Nevertheless, the ethical is otherworldly. The ethical insight detaches us from our moral espousals, from our worldly loyalties, and turns us toward the source of our freedom and the goal of our salvation. But this—which points the way in which the ethical transcends itself and becomes the religious—is a subject for another essay.

NOTES

NOTES

INTRODUCTION

Moral Philosophy Is a "Practical Science"

1. In an article that came to my attention when I was correcting the typescript of this essay I find that Dewey makes it a point to emphasize the intellectual task of philosophy clearly and explicitly. Dewey writes: "To *philosophers*, however, it is a vital matter that they have an active share in developing points of view and outlooks which will further recognition. . . ." And: "For the work that needs to be done *is* at the present juncture primarily intellectual . . ." ("Philosophy's Future in Our Scientific Age," *Commentary*, VIII, No. 4 [October, 1949], 393 and 394, respectively). (Italics in text.)

2. John Dewey, *Theory of Valuation* (Chicago: University of Chicago Press, 1939), p. 28.

3. *Ethica Nicomachea* vi. 2. 1139ᵃ. 31. See also Richard P. McKeon, *The Philosophy of Aristotle* (a mimeographed study obtainable in the University of Chicago library), pp. 60–68.

4. Moritz Schlick, *Problems of Ethics* (New York: Prentice-Hall Book Co., Inc., 1939), p. 1.

5. "Value and Fact," *Philosophy of Science*, VI, No. 4 (October, 1939), 439.

6. See his article, "Individual Differences and Cultural Patterns," in *Personality in Nature, Society, and Culture*, ed. Clyde Kluckhohn and Henry A. Murray (New York: Alfred A. Knopf, 1948), chap. xi, pp. 131–43.

7. Bernhard Groethuysen, *La Formación de la consciencia burguesa en Francia durante el siglo xviii* (Mexico: Fondo de Cultura Economica, 1943), *passim*.

8. For my purposes any edition of Hume will do. The Open Court edition of *An Enquiry concerning the Principles of Morals* is easily available, as is the "Everyman's" edition of *A Treatise of Human Nature*.

9. George Santayana, *The Life of Reason* (New York: Charles Scribner's Sons, 1928), V, 213.

10. *An Enquiry Concerning the Principles of Morals*, Sec. IX, Part I.

11. Schlick, *op. cit.*, p. 17.

12. *Naturalism and the Human Spirit*, ed. Yervant H. Krikorian (New York: Columbia University Press, 1944), p. 45. Hereafter cited as "*Naturalism*."

13. *Ibid.*, p. 2; see also pp. 18, 65, 242.

14. *Philosophy for the Future*, ed. Roy Wood Sellars, V. J. McGill, and

Marvin Farber (New York: Macmillan Co., 1949); *Readings in Philosophical Analysis*, selected and edited by Herbert Feigl and Wilfrid Sellars (New York: Appleton-Century-Crofts, Inc., 1949).

15. *Naturalism*, pp. 44–45. (Italics in text.)

16. Victor Brochard, *Les Sceptiques grecs* ("Librairie philosophique" [Paris: J. Vrin, 1923]), pp. 293 ff. The evidence for these generalizations will be found in an article entitled "Two Notes on the New Naturalism," *Sewanee Review*, LVI, No. 3 (summer, 1948), 477–95. The preceding paragraphs come from this article. After this chapter was written, I had the opportunity to read Joseph J. Schwab's article, "The Nature of Scientific Knowledge as Related to Liberal Education," *Journal of General Education*, III, No. 4 (July, 1949), 1–22. With specific evidence, I am happy to see, Schwab confirms my contention by pointing out that even among scientists themselves there is no agreement concerning the nature of science.

17. George Edward Moore, *Principia Ethica* (Cambridge: At the University Press, 1903), p. 40.

CHAPTER I

MORES AND MORALS

1. Thus conceived, the term "morality" includes all kinds of regulations, from regulations that apply to activity involving serious threat or promise to human life to those that apply to conventions designed to facilitate intercourse, which are usually classified as outside "morality" and under the term "manners." The reason for stretching the term to include manners is that questions of manners are always threatening to become moral problems, while in a refined society moral questions tend to become questions of manners.

2. Melville J. Herskovits, *Man and His Works* (New York: Alfred A. Knopf, 1948), chap. v, sec. 2. This quotation is from p. 66. See also the devastating review by Arthur Child in *Ethics*, LIX, No. 3 (April, 1949), 222–25.

3. *Op. cit.*, p. 63.

4. *Ibid.*, p. 77.

5. *Ibid.*

6. Sir Alexander Grant, *The Ethics of Aristotle* (London: Longmans, Green & Co., 1874), I, 183.

7. "Value and Fact," *Philosophy of Science*, VI, No. 4 (October, 1939), 437.

8. Herskovits, *op. cit.*, pp. 63 and 69–70, respectively. (Italics in text.)

9. R. F. Fortune, *Sorcerers of Dobu* (London: George Routledge & Sons, Ltd., 1932), *passim*.

10. George C. Vaillant, *La Civilización azteca: Versión española de Samuel Vasconcelos* (Mexico: Fondo de Cultura Economica, 1944), *passim*.

CHAPTER II

The Interest Theory. I

1. George Santayana, *The Sense of Beauty* (New York: Charles Scribner's Sons, 1896), pp. 14–31; *The Life of Reason* (2d ed.; New York: Charles Scribner's Sons, 1929), Vol. I, chaps. viii–xii, Vol. V, chaps. viii–x; *Winds of Doctrine* (New York: Charles Scribner's Sons, 1912), pp. 138–54.

2. Ralph Barton Perry, *General Theory of Value* (New York: Longmans, Green & Co., 1926). Hereafter referred to as "*General Theory*."

3. Thomas Hobbes, *Leviathan* (London: J. M. Dent & Sons, 1914), Part I, chap. vi, p. 24. "But whatsoever is the object of any man's Appetite or Desire; that is it, which he for his part calleth Good . . ." (Richard McKeon [ed.], *The Basic Works of Aristotle* [New York: Random House, 1941], p. 1343) (*Rhetorica* i. 5. 1362a. 22).

4. William James, *The Will To Believe* (New York: Longmans, Green & Co., 1927), pp. 184–216.

5. *Ibid.*, p. 206.

6. "Henry and William: Two Notes," *Kenyon Review*, V, No. 4 (1943), 581–87.

7. George Santayana, *The Life of Reason* (2d ed.; New York: Charles Scribner's Sons, 1929), II, 125 and 127.

8. Henry James, *The American Scene* (New York: Charles Scribner's Sons, 1946), pp. 425–26. For William James's comments on Santayana see Henry James (ed.), *The Letters of William James* (Boston: Atlantic Monthly Press, 1920), II, 122–24, 234–35.

9. *The Letters of William James*, II, 123: "Moreover, when you come down to the facts, what do your harmonious and integral ideal systems prove to be? in the concrete? Always things burst by the growing content of experience. Dramatic unities; laws of versification; ecclesiastical systems; scholastic doctrines. Bah!"

10. Ralph Barton Perry, *The Moral Economy* (New York: Charles Scribner's Sons, 1909), *passim*; *General Theory*, p. 686 and from chap. xx to end.

11. *General Theory*, chap. xiii, Sec. V, p. 383.

12. *Ibid.*, p. 385. (Italics in text.)

13. *Ibid.*, pp. 383 ff.

14. *The Moral Economy*, pp. 3–15.

15. *The Will To Believe*, p. 205.

16. Paul Arthur Schilpp (ed.), *The Philosophy of George Santayana* (Evanston, Ill.: Northwestern University, 1940), pp. 328–38.

17. F. H. Bradley, *Appearance and Reality* (Oxford: Clarendon Press, 1946), chap. x.

18. A. E. Taylor, *Elements of Metaphysics* (London: Methuen & Co., Ltd., 1912), Book IV, chap. iii.

19. William James, *The Principles of Psychology* (London: Macmillan &

Co., Ltd., 1901), Vol. I, chap. x; Bradley, *op. cit.*; B. Bosanquet, *Psychology of the Moral Self* (London: Macmillan & Co., Ltd., 1897), pp. 51 ff.; Taylor, *op. cit.*

20. George W. Howgate, *George Santayana* (Philadelphia: University of Pennsylvania Press, 1938); Milton Karl Munitz, *The Moral Philosophy of Santayana* (New York: Columbia University Press, 1939); Schilpp, *op. cit.*

21. *General Theory*, p. 433.

22. *Ibid.*, p. 435.

23. *Ibid.*, chap. xv, subsecs. 176, 177, 178.

24. *Ibid.*, p. 611.

25. *Ibid.*, pp. 433 ff.

26. *Ibid.*, p. 302.

27. *Ibid.*, p. 524.

28. *Ibid.*, pp. 525–26.

29. Sigmund Freud, *New Introductory Lectures on Psycho-analysis* (New York: W. W. Norton & Co., Inc., 1933), p. 103. The reader is begged to believe, in spite of the impression that my use of Freud may have given up to this point, that I am not a Freudian, for I do not accept Freud's Weltanschauung (see the last chapter of *The New Introductory Lectures*) and I am convinced that the insights of psychoanalysis that can be accepted today as *theoretically* valid, as distinct from those acceptable because of their therapeutic utility, are those that disclose the structure of the self, not those that account for the genesis of the neuroses. In other words, Freud's naturalistic philosophy and the inchoate moral theory he so uncritically built upon it are rejected by the writer. On the question as to whether sex and the pleasure principle play the role that Freud assigns to them in the self's genetic process, sufficient evidence seems to be lacking. The practical success of the technique of deep analysis in therapy is no proof of its *truth*. However, Freud's observation of the self, particularly his effort to give an account of what lies under the range of direct inspection, his dive into the depths of the soul, I believe must, on the whole, be accepted. Acceptance, of course, should be only provisional, and we must be prepared to have to change our notions of what lies beyond the conscious with the enlargement and correction of the account which are the inevitable result of progressive inquiry. The attitude of the Freudian analysts and literary critics toward the master and their insistence on literalistic orthodoxy reveal their unscientific attitude and retard progress.

30. *General Theory*, p. 584.

31. *Ibid.*, p. 588.

32. Otto Fenichel, *The Psychoanalytic Theory of Neurosis* (New York: W. W. Norton & Co., Inc., 1945), p. 464.

33. *Ibid.*, p. 463.

34. *Ibid.*, p. 466.

35. *General Theory*, p. 660.

CHAPTER III

THE INTEREST THEORY. II

1. *General Theory*, p. 33.
2. *Ibid.*, p. 29.
3. *Ibid.*, p. 30.
4. The term "subtend" has been criticized by a reader of the manuscript and, I fear, with good grounds, since it is strange and is likely to give unnecessary shock to the reader. I apologize for its use and beg my reader's indulgence, on the ground that its employment will save me wasteful circumlocutions. I mean by it that the physical aspects of an object serve as basis for the value, that the value rests upon them, that they somehow entangle it, give it anchorage.
5. *General Theory*, pp. 33–34.
6. Clarence Irving Lewis, *An Analysis of Knowledge and Valuation* (LaSalle, Ill.: Open Court Pub. Co., 1946), p. 413.
7. *Ibid.*, pp. 390–96.
8. *Ibid.*, p. 458.
9. See below, chap. xii, for a criticism of functionalism, which is relevant to this discussion.
10. A discussion of the Freudian theory of "identification" will be found in chap. ix.
11. After this chapter was written, I had opportunity to read an article entitled "Naturalism and the Concept of Obligation" by my friend Arthur C. Garnett (*Review of Metaphysics*, Vol. II, No. 8 [June, 1949], particularly pp. 20 ff.). Garnett argues against G. H. Mead, but in the pages referred to he discusses the problem created for Mead by the fact that sometimes individuals will spread universalistic ethical doctrines in a society which does not yet recognize these doctrines. How did these individuals discover such ideas? An explanation probably can be devised, but it becomes cumbersome and its *ad hoc* nature is painted all over its face.
12. *General Theory*, pp. 31–32.
13. *Ibid.*, p. 124.
14. *Ibid.*, p. 30.
15. *Ibid.*, p. 34.

CHAPTER IV

THE INTEREST THEORY. III

1. *The Life of Reason* (2d ed.; New York: Charles Scribner's Sons, 1929), I, 237 and 257, respectively. For the basis of Santayana's conception of the life of reason, see Vol. I, *passim*, and Vol. V, chaps. viii–x.
2. *Ibid.*, Vol. V, chaps. viii, ix, x; and *Interpretations of Poetry and Religion* (New York: Charles Scribner's Sons, 1922), chap. vii.
3. In *General Theory*, see sec. 157, p. 385; sec. 241, p. 595; sec. 248, p. 615; and the whole of chap. xxi. In *The Moral Economy* (New York:

Charles Scribner's Sons, 1909): "I count it to be important thus to trace morality back to the original love of life, since only so is it possible to understand its urgency . . ." (p. 27; see also pp. 13, 14, and 56).

4. For instance, I. A. Richards, *Principles of Literary Criticism* (New York: Harcourt, Brace & Co., 1928), pp. 47 and 52 (italics in text); Herbert J. Muller, *Science and Criticism* (New Haven: Yale University Press, 1943), p. 27; R. W. Gerard, "A Biological Basis for Ethics," *Philosophy of Science*, IX, No. 1 (1942), 92–120; T. H. Huxley and Julian Huxley, *Touchstone for Ethics 1893–1943* (New York: Harper & Bros., 1947), pp. 130–44.

5. Muller, *op. cit.*, chap. ii, secs. 2 and 3; Gerard, *op. cit.*, pp. 103 ff.

6. See, e.g., Tom Harrison, *Savage Civilization* (New York: Alfred A. Knopf, 1937), chap. i.

7. Ralph Linton, *The Study of Man* (New York: D. Appleton–Century Co., 1936), p. 331; but chaps. xviii, xix, and xx should be read as a whole; Melville J. Herskovits, *Man and His Works* (New York: Alfred A. Knopf, 1948), pp. 86 ff. and chaps. vi, vii.

8. *The Moral Economy*, p. 123.

9. *Ibid.*, p. 134.

10. *Ibid.*, p. 132.

11. Paul A. Schilpp (ed.), *The Philosophy of George Santayana* (Evanston, Ill.: Northwestern University, 1940), pp. 328 ff.

12. *Ibid.*, pp. 337–78.

13. Sigmund Freud, *On War, Sex, and Neuroses* (New York: Arts and Science Press, 1947), pp. 215–17.

14. Sigm. Freud, *Beyond the Pleasure Principle* (London: Hogarth Press, 1942), p. 47, and *New Introductory Lectures on Psycho-analysis* (New York: W. W. Norton & Co., Inc., 1933), p. 146.

15. *Beyond the Pleasure Principle*, p. 70. The notions of the inhibition of instincts and of the death instinct are basic to Freud and are frequently found in his pages. For instance: *The Future of an Illusion* (New York: Liveright Pub. Corp., 1949), p. 11; also the important "The Economic Problem in Masochism," in *Collected Papers*, II (London: Hogarth Press, 1949), 255–68, and "Repression," *ibid.*, V, 84–97. The universality of dread is basic to Kierkegaard. The quotation was taken from *Stages on Life's Way* (Princeton: Princeton University Press, 1945), p. 109; see also *The Sickness unto Death* (Princeton: Princeton University Press, 1946), p. 32.

CHAPTER V

The Postulational Theory

1. The first of Charner Perry's articles, accompanied by a number of criticisms, appeared in the *International Journal of Ethics*, XLIII, No. 2 (1933), 127–66; the second in *Revue internationale de philosophie*, I, No. 4

(1939), 666–83. I refer to them hereafter as "Arbitrary" and "Principles." The Perry referred to throughout this chapter is Charner Perry, not R. B. Perry. Williams' essay appeared in the *Philosophical Review*, XLII (1933), 399–411.

2. *Naturalism*, p. 57: "A moral ideal is a prescription to act in a certain situation or class of situations in determinate ways that will organize the human needs and wants involved so as to fulfill a set of other values which are postulated as binding in relation to the problem in hand." Hook goes on to warn that these ideals are *"not arbitrarily postulated"* (his italics), but they are "arbitrary" in Perry's and Morris Cohen's sense of the term. Edel varies the expression. He tells us: Ethical statements "are normative to the person or group adopting them as rules of choice. This adoption may be implicit in conduct or it may be explicit in reflection on conduct." But later he adds: "Ultimate values are simply intense or pervasive attitudes of men in a natural and social world functioning in a special way in relation to their other values" (*ibid.*, pp. 72 and 85, respectively). I can make sense of Edel's views only by interpreting him to mean that ethical statements are attitudes of varying degrees of pervasiveness and intensity which are adopted—or postulated.

If this were a historical essay, it would be imperative to cite and analyze other instances of the postulational point of view besides those of Perry and Williams and to establish carefully the similarities and differences. One might cite, for instance, Morris R. Cohen's concise statement of this view in *Reason and Nature* (New York: Harcourt, Brace & Co., 1931), p. 434: Skepticism "is justified in insisting that there is an arbitrary (in the sense of volitional) and indemonstrable assumption in every moral system, since we cannot have an *ought* in our conclusion unless there is an *ought* in one of our initial assumptions or premises."

Another manner of introducing value into premises that are themselves value-free, scientific facts, which is used by contemporary naturalists and which has very much the same result as the postulational, is "to define" value. The view examined in chapter x and referred to as "hedonistic subjectivism" employs this technique, for the hedonistic subjectivist knows that we cannot deduce value from the value-free facts of psychology. He therefore selects certain facts and defines these as the basic values in terms of which he claims he will be able to organize the facts of value comprehensibly. In chapter x, I reject his theory on other grounds and from another point of view. Here all I believe necessary is to call attention to these techniques of creating value by definitional fiat, which, no doubt, have this advantage, that they avoid or seem to avoid the difficulties into which the postulational theory gets. But if the ontological proof for the existence of God is not valid, why should the creation of value by definition be?

3. "Principles," p. 666.

4. Charner Perry, "Proposed Sources of Practical Wisdom," *Ethics* LVIII, No. 4 (1948), 262–74.

5. Charner Perry, "Sound Ethics and Confused Language," *ibid.*, LV, No. 3 (1945), 209–15.

6. "Arbitrary," p. 133. (Italics in the text.)

7. *Ibid.*, p. 140.

8. "Principles," p. 669.

9. *Ibid.*, pp. 671 and 680, respectively; but see also pp. 668 and 678, respectively.

10. *Ibid.*, p. 680. For quotation in preceding sentence, p. 679.

11. *Ibid.*, p. 680.

12. "Arbitrary," p. 143; also "Principles," p. 682.

13. "Arbitrary," p. 143.

14. "Principles," p. 668.

15. "Arbitrary," p. 135.

16. *Ibid.*, p. 136.

17. "Ethics as Pure Postulate," pp. 399 and 404, respectively. (Italics in text.)

18. "Arbitrary," p. 135.

19. E. B. McGilvary, "The Warfare of Moral Ideals," *Hibbert Journal*, XIV (1915–16), 45–64.

CHAPTER VI

The Instrumentalist Moral Theory. I

1. John Dewey and James H. Tufts, *Ethics* (New York: Henry Holt & Co., 1925), p. 38; (rev. ed., 1932), p. 43, and chaps. iv and v.

2. *Ibid.* (1925 ed.), p. 73. Hereafter this edition will be referred to as "*Ethics*"; the 1932 rev. ed. as "*Ethics rev.*"

3. *Ethics*, p. 181.

4. Bronislaw Malinowski, *Crime and Custom in Savage Society* (New York: Harcourt, Brace & Co., 1932), chap. i.

5. John Dewey, *Theory of Valuation* (Chicago: University of Chicago Press, 1939), p. 4. Hereafter referred to as "*Valuation*."

6. *Ibid.*, p. 21.

7. *Ibid.*, p. 29.

8. *Ibid.*, pp. 31–32.

9. *Ibid.*, p. 15.

10. *Ibid.*, p. 19.

11. *Ethics*, pp. 75–76.

12. Charles Morris, "Individual Differences and Cultural Patterns," in *Personality in Nature, Society, and Culture*, ed. Clyde Kluckhohn and Henry A. Murray (New York: Alfred A. Knopf, 1948), pp. 131 ff.; Erich Fromm, *Escape from Freedom* (New York: Rinehart & Co., Inc., 1941), *passim*.

CHAPTER VII

The Instrumentalist Moral Theory. II

1. John Dewey, *Logic: The Theory of Inquiry* (New York: Henry Holt & Co., 1938), p. 159. (Italics in text.) Hereafter referred to as "*Logic*."
2. *Valuation*, Sec. VI, p. 40; *Logic*, chap. ix, particularly pp. 159–68; *Essays in Experimental Logic* (Chicago: University of Chicago Press, 1916), chap. xiv.
3. Charner Perry, "Arbitrary," pp. 136 and 138, respectively. My italics.
4. *Ibid.*, p. 135.
5. *Human Nature and Conduct* ("Modern Library" ed. [1930]), Part III, Sec. VII; *Ethics rev.*, chaps. xii, xiii, sec. 2, and xiv, sec. 5.
6. *Ethics rev.*, chap. xiv, sec. 5, p. 307.
7. See, e.g., his criticism of asceticism (*ibid.*, chap. xi, sec. 6, pp. 219–24). For experimental morality see *ibid.*, chap. xvi, sec. 5, pp. 364–67. Dewey's secularism will be discussed in the next chapter.
8. *Ibid.*, p. 365.
9. *The Philosophy of John Dewey*, ed. Paul Arthur Schilpp (Evanston: Northwestern University, 1939), p. 276. See also the essay of Gertrude Jaeger, "The Philosophy of the Once-born" (*Enquiry*, Vol. II, No. 1), for an incisive criticism of Dewey's doctrine of human nature from a point of view not irrelevant to my remarks on the subject.
10. *Human Nature and Conduct*, p. 4.
11. *Ethics rev.*, p. 367.
12. Wolfgang Köhler, *The Place of Values in a World of Facts* (New York: Liveright Pub. Corp., 1938), chaps. ii and iii, and "Value and Fact," *Journal of Philosophy*, XLI, No. 8 (April 13, 1944), 197–212.
13. *Human Nature and Conduct*, p. 239.
14. *Ethics rev.*, p. 367.
15. John Dewey, *Liberalism and Social Action* (New York: G. P. Putnam's Sons, 1935), p. 79.

CHAPTER VIII

The Instrumentalist Moral Theory. III

1. *Naturalism*, pp. 1–16.
2. The Hegelian roots of Dewey's instrumentalism have been studied by Morton G. White in *The Origin of Dewey's Instrumentalism* (New York: Columbia University Press, 1943). White shows that Dewey has not abandoned certain basic Hegelian elements.
3. Sidney Hook, *Education for Modern Man* (New York: Dial Press, 1946), *passim*.
4. After this manuscript was finished, an article came to my attention in which Dewey expresses ideas that seem to indicate a small but significant

358   NOTES TO PAGE 131

change in his opinion as to the relation between philosophy and science and between both and moral reflection. Dewey writes: "What is most to be feared is a continuation of the policy of indifference to the extension, to the development of *methods* of inquiry into *human* conditions—*methods* so basic that their results (and only these) merit the name *moral*. The fact that the professed and professional guardians of morals continue to assert the adequacy of moral standards and points of view that were framed in a society upon which competent understanding of the physical and physiological conditions of human life had not dawned, is one of the obstacles in the way of what needs to be done." In a footnote attached to the italicized words he explains further: "The word 'methods' is italicized as a precaution against a possible misunderstanding which would be contrary to what is intended. What is needed is not the carrying over of procedures that have approved themselves in physical science, but *new* methods as adapted to *human* issues and problems, as methods already in scientific use have shown themselves to be in physical subject matter." What seems to be new here, so far as my acquaintance with Dewey's writings goes, is a clearer and a more explicit expression of a point that until now was, if at all, only implicit in his thought, namely, that the methods of the exact or positive sciences, whose application to moral problems he had advocated even as far back as "Logical Conditions of a Scientific Treatment of Morality" (1903), need to be modified to be applied to morality. The change, put briefly, is from "method" to "methods." One could maintain that the distinction between the methods of the physical and those of the human sciences was always made by Dewey, who never argued for the application of the method of physical science in its present state to our moral problems but always advocated the need to develop it further. Such argument would be plausible. The article on "Qualitative Thought," in *Philosophy and Civilization* (New York: G. P. Putnam's Sons, 1931), pp. 93–116, might be offered in evidence of this. In any case in the present article the point is again clearly and explicitly stated with reference to contemporary issues: the sciences of man require the development of new methods.

There are several comments I would make about these quotations. The first is that I am highly skeptical of the possibility suggested by Dewey in this article of developing "methods" by themselves. Methodolatry here leads him to betray his empiricism. Science develops methods and laboratory techniques in the day-to-day task of carrying on its research, and methods developed outside its research have never played an important role in its progress. The second point is this: If all that Dewey is advocating is the need for developing new methods to study the human situation, there could be no objection whatever to his advice. It is hard to see how any man or organization could seriously make the claim that he or it has already in his or its possession the knowledge needed to control the human situation. There are those, of course, and some seemingly intelligent men, who say— and they seem to be serious—that what we need is to apply this or that religious doctrine, this or that code of morals, and the world will be saved. If it is this class of men that Dewey is so stubbornly fighting, I disparage his manner but have no desire to disagree with the point. But Dewey's statements are moored to the same assumptions that I am discussing in this chapter; and in several places in the article from which the quotations were taken these assumptions become fully explicit. Note these lines: "What is said is said in behalf of a future for philosophy as broad and as penetrating as that claimed by metaphysical and theological systems in their days of utmost vigor; but a philosophy that is to be fully relevant to a new age in which issues flow from natural science, and not from a supra-natural world or from a philosophy purporting to deal with what is supra-mundane and super-human." The question that I asked in the text is this: Is science fit for man? It is here, by implication, clearly answered. We are to adapt ourselves, our convictions, our philosophy—and these, of course, make up the body of what we call our "truths"—to the one fixed unalterable fact: to the "implications" of science. It turns out that the interactive modification of ideas and the world runs into one hard, unyielding fact—the truths of science. Again, notice that the assumption seems to be that, while knowledge is probable and open to modification from moment to moment as inquiry proceeds, one thing is not probable but certain: convictions about a supra-natural dimension are false. One more comment seems desirable. Dewey is fighting those who already have knowledge of the truth. But both those whom he so bitterly fights and he himself share one assumption, namely, that the universal adoption of one philosophy will indeed succeed in solving for us our human and tragic problems. This is not consistent with Dewey's relativism or with his pluralism. The quotations come from "Philosophy's Future in Our Scientific Age," which appeared in *Commentary*, VIII, No. 4 (October, 1949), 388–94. The italics are in the text.

5. P. 56.

6. *Ibid.*, p. 81. How many readers still remember what Hook means by "the tragedy of Warsaw"? And how can we blame anyone for forgetting it since there was no Herodotus to record it?

CHAPTER IX

THE FREUDIAN THEORY

1. Edwin B. Holt, *The Freudian Wish and Its Place in Ethics* (New York: Henry Holt & Co., 1915); John R. Reid, *A Theory of Value* (New York: Charles Scribner's Sons, 1938), chap. v; J. C. Flugel, *Man, Morals, and Society: A Psycho-analytical Study* (New York: International Universities Press, 1945); Erich Fromm, *Man for Himself: An Inquiry into the Psychology of Ethics* (New York: Rinehart & Co., Inc., 1947). In an essay which I read after this chapter was finished and ready for the printer, entitled "Reflections on Dewey's Questions about Value," Henry David Aiken points out that "insufficient use has been made in most previous theories of

value of the important and often revolutionary discoveries of psycho-analysis and dynamic psychiatry." It is possible that the youngest genera-tion of philosophers will be more hospitable than their elders have been to what in the twenties used to be called the "new" psychology. I do not be-lieve, however, that psychoanalysis can be assimilated by naturalistic value theories now current in this country, as Professor Aiken advises. The psychological presuppositions of current naturalistic value theories allow no room for Freud's revolutionary concepts (*Value: A Cooperative In-quiry*, ed. Ray Lepley [New York: Columbia University Press, 1949], n. 36, p. 42).

2. The claim is sometimes made that psychology, particularly abnormal psychology, does away with what writers long in hope and short in philosophic sophistication call "metaphysics," meaning, of course, by the term something below contempt. A less naïve claim is found in writers like Flugel, who speaks of the "substitution of the psychological for the moral point of view" and who claims that "with the development of psychology, this restriction of moral judgment and the substitution of judgment in terms of psychological insight is rapidly increasing. . . ." The latter statement, only half-true, represents developments now taking place, truly enough, but does not tell the whole truth, and that is that "psychological insight" includes not only psychological knowledge but uncritical implicit accept-ance of vitalistic values. There is also the problem of the change in attitude toward moral responsibility which results from the deterministic habits of thought acquired by psychologists. Wertham would not punish criminals but would cure them, since they are sick men who cannot help themselves. These are only two sets of problems which require attention and are not getting it. See Flugel, *op. cit.*, pp. 14, 15, for the quotations, although, of course, the whole chapter is relevant.

3. Freud's Weltanschauung is made explicit in the last chapter of *The New Introductory Lectures on Psycho-analysis* (New York: W. W. Norton & Co., Inc., 1933).

4. See also *Beyond the Pleasure Principle* and *The Ego and the Id* (London: Hogarth Press, 1947).

5. *New Introductory Lectures*, p. 85. Hereafter referred to as "*New Lec-tures*."

6. *Ibid.*, p. 86.
7. *Ibid.*, p. 89.
8. *Ibid.*, p. 92.
9. *Ibid.*, p. 89.
10. *Ibid.*, pp. 90–92.
11. *A General Introduction to Psychoanalysis* (New York: Garden City Pub. Co., Inc., 1938), p. 314.
12. *New Lectures*, p. 95.
13. *Ibid.*
14. T. H. Huxley and Julian Huxley, *Touchstone for Ethics 1893–1943*

(New York: Harper & Bros., 1947), p. 117. Hereafter referred to as *"Touchstone."*

15. *Ibid.*, p. 118.

16. *Ibid.*, p. 120.

17. Paul Henle, "The Status of Emergence," *Journal of Philosophy*, XXXIX, No. 18 (1942), 486–93. D. W. Gotshalk, "Causality and Emergence," *Philosophical Review*, LI, No. 4 (July, 1942), 397–405. Henle's paper was commented on and along certain lines amplified by Gustav Bergman in a study entitled "Holism, Historicism, and Emergence," in *Philosophy of Science*, II, No. 4 (October, 1944), 209–21. The consideration of the subject to be found in "Studies in the Logic of Explanation," by Carl G. Hempel and Paul Oppenheim, *Philosophy of Science*, XV, No. 2 (April, 1948), 146–52, further elucidates the subject. The theory of levels was recently suggested in succinct terms in *Philosophy for the Future*, ed. Roy Wood Sellars, V. J. McGill, Marvin Farber (New York: Macmillan Co., 1949), p. vi.

18. *Philosophy for the Future*, p. vi.

19. Gotshalk, *op. cit.*, p. 399.

20. *Ibid.*

21. Paul Weiss, *Nature and Man* (New York: Henry Holt & Co., 1947), Part I, and particularly the brilliant chaps. i and ii.

CHAPTER X

A POSTSCRIPT

1. Charles L. Stevenson, *Ethics and Language* (New Haven: Yale University Press, 1944). Hereafter cited as "Stevenson."

2. Charner Perry, "Sound Ethics and Confused Language," *Ethics*, LV, No. 3 (April, 1945), 209–15. Quotation from p. 209.

3. Stevenson, p. 21. But see also chaps. iv and x.

4. W. H. Hay, "C. L. Stevenson and Ethical Analysis," *Philosophical Review*, LVI, No. 4 (July, 1947,) 422–30.

5. Stevenson, p. 90. There is a typographical error in the first printing of this book; the first line of the quotation should read "suppose that a man morally disapproves . . . ," etc.

6. *Ibid.*, p. 11.

7. *Ibid.*, p. 131.

8. Charles L. Stevenson, "The Nature of Ethical Disagreement," in *Readings in Philosophical Analysis*, selected and edited by Herbert Feigl and Wilfrid Sellars (New York: Appleton-Century-Crofts, Inc., 1949), p. 591. (Italics in text.)

9. Clarence Irving Lewis, *An Analysis of Knowledge and Valuation* (LaSalle, Ill.: Open Court Pub. Co., 1946).

10. *Ibid.*, pp. 390 and 381, respectively. See also pp. 380, 387, 391, 393, 406, 407, 413.

11. *Ibid.*, p. 369.

12. A programmatic and avowedly incomplete sketch of this view has been presented by Philip Blair Rice in "Science, Humanism, and the Good," in *Value: A Cooperative Inquiry*, ed. Ray Lepley (New York: Columbia University Press, 1949), pp. 261–90. My presentation of the position has been drawn from this essay.

13. What we need for a sociological theory of value has already been discussed in the Introduction. On the present dismal state of the so-called "science of personality" see the brilliant paper of Melvin Seeman, "An Evaluation of Current Approaches to Personality Differences in Folk and Urban Societies," *Social Forces*, XXV, No. 2 (December, 1946), 160–65.

14. I am not speaking here of theory but of practice, for, were I saying that there is no consistent hedonistic theory to be found, there would be no difficulty in disposing of the ignorant assertion: Epicureans, sybarites, and hedonists at the practical level cannot consistently act as their interest in pleasure counsels. It is impossible to do so. It is possible, however, to construct a theory which prescribes acting for the sake of pleasure. But what kind of life such a theory would lead to is precisely the final question as regards its acceptability.

Again my remarks hold only for temporal existence. Supernaturalists who believe in immortality sometimes hold that it is desirable and possible to live in happiness in eternity and that, in fact, so to live is the soul's destiny. But this is not a question into which we need to enter here.

15. *Kant's Critique of Aesthetic Judgment*, trans. James Creed Meredith (Oxford: Clarendon Press, 1911), pp. 47–48.

CHAPTER XI

Summary

1. I hope that I do not abuse the reader's patience when I warn him again that I do not hold that the discrimination of the objects of science can be made by minds that are empty tablets without mastered knowledge which has been assimilated and is operative in the act of intuition. What I claim is that, for common-sense discriminations of value, all that is necessary is that men be endowed with the faculties with which they are normally born and be in possession of the kind of knowledge that they normally gather in the world in a more or less unsystematic way. As Schopenhauer said somewhere, if science or philosophy were necessary for salvation, hell would be full of the saints.

2. In a book that came to my attention after this manuscript was already in the printer's hands I find a naturalist confirming, as fully as I could desire, my point. He writes:

"The great wars did not in any obvious way constitute turning points in American philosophy; nothing happened in either case which could be said to have produced the death or the birth of a movement, or to have given philosophical ideas a significant change in direction. The effect was rather on the philosophers than on the philosophies. Students disappeared from classrooms, and money disappeared from budgets; and, as a consequence, many teachers of philosophy, either voluntarily or by pressure of circumstances, changed their activity to government service in one form or another. This produced in their philosophical outlooks nothing more striking than an increased sense of insecurity, enforced, perhaps, by a clearer recognition of the importance of the problem of evil in an adequate philosophy of life. But rarely was there a fundamental change in metaphysical outlook or in the conception of the task of philosophy. Even pragmatism, which may properly be said to have its roots in the social situation, was little affected by the war. . . ."

The writer states the fact only and does not point out that he is thus making a devastating criticism of his colleagues (A. Cornelius Benjamin, "Philosophy in America between Two Wars," in *Philosophic Thought in France and the United States*, ed. Marvin Farber ["University of Buffalo Publications in Philosophy" (Buffalo, 1950)], p. 365).

CHAPTER XII

The Resolution of a Moral Perplexity. I

1. The term "requiredness" was introduced, as students of theory of value know, by Wolfgang Köhler in *The Place of Value in a World of Facts* (New York: Liveright Pub. Corp., 1938), chap. iii. Although, unfortunately, it seems to grate on the sensitive ear, I shall, after apologizing, keep it because I cannot think of another that so exactly expresses the idea Köhler wanted to convey.

2. E.g., John Dewey, *Human Nature and Conduct* (New York: Modern Library, 1930), pp. 34, 133, 153, 252.

3. Gordon W. Allport, *Personality* (New York: Henry Holt & Co., 1937), chap. ii.

4. Joseph Conrad, *Lord Jim* (Garden City: Doubleday, Doran & Co., Inc., 1934), pp. 79–80.

5. Felix Krueger, *La Totalidad psiquica* (Buenos Aires: Universidad de Buenos Aires, Facultad de Filosofia y Letras, 1945), *passim*.

6. Max Scheler, *Die Stellung des Menschen im Kosmos* (Munich: Nymphenburger Verlagshandlung, 1949), *passim*.

7. Bronislaw Malinowski, *A Scientific Theory of Culture and Other Essays* (Chapel Hill: University of North Carolina Press, 1944), p. 171; see also pp. 41, 55–66, 72, 75–84, and chaps. ix, x, xi. See also the article by Dorothy Gregg and Elgin Williams, "The Dismal Science of Functionalism," *American Anthropologist*, L, No. 4 (October–December, 1948), 594–611.

8. Malinowski, *op. cit.*, p. 174.

9. See his remarks in *Naturalism*, p. 228.

10. Susanne K. Langer, *Philosophy in a New Key* (Cambridge: Harvard University Press, 1942), p. 40.

11. Moral philosophy seems singularly silent about the facts which can be bracketed within the term "multiple personality." For Dostoevski "the double" created a serious problem. We can no longer disregard these data— to which no serious attention has been paid by all but one of the naturalistic moral philosophies examined in Part I of this essay. For a recent and comprehensive treatment of the problem of multiple personality at the psychological level see Gardner Murphy, *Personality* (New York: Harper & Bros., 1947), Part III, chap. xviii, and Part V.

12. Benbow Ritchie, "The Formal Structure of the Aesthetic Object," *Journal of Aesthetics and Art Criticism*, III, Nos. 11–12 (n.d.), 5–14; *Naturalism*, pp. 257 f.; and my criticism, "Two Notes on the New Naturalism," *Sewanee Review*, LVI, No. 3 (summer, 1948), 495–509.

13. *Personality in Nature, Society, and Culture*, ed. Clyde Kluckhohn and Henry A. Murray (New York: Alfred A. Knopf, 1948), p. 14.

14. Stephen C. Pepper, *A Digest of Purposive Values* (Berkeley: University of California Press, 1947); Albert Hofstadter, "Objective Teleology," *Journal of Philosophy*, XXXVIII, No. 2 (1941), 29–39; see also the companion study, "Subjective Teleology," *Philosophy and Phenomenological Research*, II (September, 1941), 88–97.

15. *Philosophy for the Future: The Quest of Modern Materialism*, ed. Roy Wood Sellars, V. J. McGill, and Marvin Farber (New York: Macmillan Co., 1949), p. vii.

CHAPTER XIII

The Resolution of a Moral Perplexity. II

1. For an up-to-date summary of work in this field see S. G. Soal, *The Experimental Situation in Psychical Research, Being the Ninth Frederic W. H. Myers Memorial Lecture, 1947* (London: Society for Psychical Research, n.d.), *passim*; see also H. H. Price's review of J. B. Rhine, *The Reach of the Mind*, in *Mind*, LVIII, No. 231 (July, 1949), 390–95.

2. It is desirable to state what position the writer takes toward the power that distinguishes man from the other animals and which I refer to here as "intelligence." Contemporary behavioristic psychology seeks to erase the line that separates human from merely animal intelligence, and the behavioristic semioticians undertake to give a behavioristic account of all the activities of the mind. This book is not the place to consider these claims. It is enough to observe that, as Mrs. Langer has pointed out (see n. 10 in chap. xii), the power of symbolizing indicates a break in the evolutionary development which naturalists have not yet been able to bridge. Human intelligence is distinguished from mere animal intelligence because the human animal is able to use symbols, while the lower animals are able only to use signs; because the human is capable of objectivity, while the lower animals give no indication of capacity for objectivity; and because the

human is creative, while the problem-solving of the merely animal intelligence seems incapable of creative expressiveness. Symbolic power, objectivity, and creativeness have not been shown to be common along the whole range of biological forms in the natural world. "Intelligence," therefore, as I employ the term, is more than what the psychologists study in the animal laboratory under the heading of "learning" or "problem-solving." It includes what below I shall call "spirit."

3. There was, of course, a strong development of natural science in the ancient world, and one could with as much propriety speak of Aristarchus or Archimedes as of Copernicus or Galileo. Those who trace the origins of exact science to the ancient world are quite correct in doing so. I hope that I am not totally ignorant of this fact. Again a man engaged in writing a philosophic essay cannot deny objectivity to his activity without stultifying himself. It is a question of degree. Exact natural science approaches objectivity to a degree that philosophy and common-sense knowledge do not.

CHAPTER XIV

The Resolution of a Moral Perplexity. III

1. Gardner Murphy, *Personality* (New York: Harper & Bros., 1947), p. 443.

2. Morton Prince, *The Dissociation of a Personality* (2d ed.; New York: Longmans, Green & Co., 1913), *passim*.

3. Murphy, *op. cit.*, p. 449.

4. John R. Reid, "The Apotheosis of Intelligence," *Journal of Philosophy*, XXXII, No. 14 (July 4, 1935), 375–85.

5. Compare Kenneth E. Kirk, *Conscience and Its Problems* (London: Longmans, Green & Co., 1948), chap. i.

6. M. O. Percival, *A Reading of Moby-Dick* (Chicago: University of Chicago Press, 1950). The quotation from Father Mapple comes from Herman Melville, *Moby-Dick* (New York: Oxford University Press, 1947), chap. ix, p. 40.

7. Kirk, *op. cit.*, p. 37.

8. Joseph Butler, *The Analogy of Religion* (London: Henry G. Bohn, 1856), Sermon II, p. 403.

9. William James, *The Will To Believe* (New York: Longmans, Green & Co., 1927), p. 195. (Italics in text.)

CHAPTER XV

The Ground and the Source of Moral Authority

1. W. D. Ross, *Foundations of Ethics* (Oxford: Clarendon Press, 1939), p. 144. Hereafter referred to as *"Foundations."*

2. *The Right and the Good* (Oxford: Clarendon Press, 1930), p. 12.

3. *Foundations*, p. 82.

4. *Kant's Prolegomena*, ed. Paul Carus (Chicago: Open Court Pub. Co., 1933), p. 32.

5. It was in 1868 that Riemann's work on the hypotheses that serve as the basis of geometry was published.

6. *Foundations*, p. 172.

7. But this does not mean that I agree with Stevenson (whose theory was discussed in the Postscript, chap. x), since he argues that two men, both clear about their respective intentions to be moral, cannot mediate their differences, and I argue that this holds only as between a moral and an *amoral*, not an immoral, man. But are there any genuinely amoral human beings? And, if there are, are they human?

8. Feodor Dostoevski, *Letters from the Underworld* (London: J. M. Dent & Sons, Ltd., n.d.), p. 17.

9. George Santayana, *The Last Puritan* (New York: Charles Scribner's Sons, 1936), p. 99.

CHAPTER XVI

THE JUSTIFICATION OF A MORAL DECISION

1. A. R. Radcliffe-Brown, *The Andaman Islanders* (Glencoe, Ill.: Free Press, 1948), Introd., esp. pp. 6–9.

2. "Two Notes on the New Naturalism," *Sewanee Review*, LVI, No. 3 (summer, 1948), 501 ff. All too kindly commenting on this article, Professor Brand Blanshard noted the similarity between it and his own argument in *The Nature of Thought* (London: Allen & Unwin, Ltd., 1939), chaps. xxi and xxii. It is quite possible that there is more than a coincidental similarity between these two arguments, although when I wrote the *Sewanee* article I did not have consciously in mind the Blanshard book. But I had read it sometime in 1940 or 1941, at a time when I was desperately looking for light to help me out of the dark forest of naturalism in which I suddenly found myself utterly lost. I am glad of the opportunity to acknowledge my deep debt to Professor Blanshard, and I wish I could find the opportunity to acknowledge my debt to the many other writers who helped me in my spiritual and intellectual distress.

3. Richard M. Weaver, *Ideas Have Consequences* (Chicago: University of Chicago Press, 1948), chap. v.

CHAPTER XVII

THE DISCOVERY OF THE ETHICAL. I

1. I introduced this terminology in a review published in *Kenyon Review*, IV, No. 3 (autumn, 1942), 419–22, as a result of the study of Kant and Bergson which I undertook when I was trying to free myself from the errors of naturalism. At the time that I was struggling with this problem, a paper of Paul Weiss, "Morality and Ethics," published in the *Journal of*

Philosophy, Vol. XXXIX, No. 14 (July 2, 1942), helped me both terminologically and materially to see the need for drawing the distinction.

2. Thomas Hill Green, *Prolegomena to Ethics* (4th ed.; Oxford: Clarendon Press, 1899), Book III, chaps. iii and v.

3. Clarence Irving Lewis, *An Analysis of Knowledge and Valuation* (LaSalle, Ill.: Open Court Pub. Co., 1946), p. 392.

4. Jacques Maritain, *The Person and the Common Good* (New York: Charles Scribner's Sons, 1947), p. 5.

5. Ignazio Silone makes this point, out of a fund of experience that deserves the deepest respect, in his recent account (which came into the hands of the writer after this chapter was written) of his road to Moscow and back *(The God That Failed,* ed. Richard Crissman [New York: Harper & Bros., 1949], pp. 82 ff.).

6. G. W. Allport, J. S. Bruner, and E. M. Jandorf, "Personality under Social Catastrophe," in *Personality in Nature, Society, and Culture,* ed. Clyde Kluckhohn and Henry A. Murray (New York: Alfred A. Knopf, 1948), pp. 347–66.

7. Karl Marx, "Moralising Criticism and Critical Morality: A Polemic against Karl Heinzen," in *Selected Essays* (New York: International Publishers, 1926), pp. 134–70.

CHAPTER XVIII

THE DISCOVERY OF THE ETHICAL. II

1. Note that the needs of human beings are involved in the situation, since the fitness is the fitness of a situation to a human being. But it is not the idiosyncratic needs, the subjective needs, the passing needs, of human beings, or the needs of this person, the individual involved in the situation. It is the needs of any human being in such situations. Or, better, the needs of a person in a situation, but considered not in his and its unique specificity but in his and its universal aspects. This is where naturalists and positivists go wrong. A situation is not right because desired—it is right because desired in a certain way, desired impersonally; and it is desired in such a way because it is what, under the circumstances, ought to be desired. We say, "it shouldn't happen to a dog," and thus express our conviction that there is an order fitting to human beings and an order fitting to living beings that are not human and that human beings often are the victims of events which fall below the latter order.

2. See chap. iii, pp. 77–79 and chap. xiii, pp. 221–23.

3. I do not use the expression in the way in which Bruno Bettelheim employed it in his well-known article. I refer to situations that force the person to face the moral crisis (Bruno Bettelheim, "Behavior in Extreme Situations," *politics,* I, No. 7 [August, 1944], 199–209).

4. See n. 2.

CHAPTER XIX

The Discovery of the Ethical. III

1. November, 1948.
2. Ernest Nagel, "Logic without Ontology," in *Naturalism*, pp. 210–41.
3. William R. Dennes, "The Categories of Naturalism," in *Naturalism*, p. 290.
4. Herman Melville, *Moby-Dick, or The Whale*, ed. Willard Thorp (New York: Oxford University Press, 1947), chap. xxxvi, p. 153.
5. The reader has a right to complain that I do not treat the problem of evil with adequate seriousness, and I am afraid that he is perfectly correct. These remarks do not pretend to solve a problem which has baffled the best minds of Europe since Plato's days. In this essay, in which I have struggled against centrifugal tendencies to keep within the confines of moral philosophy, the discussion of this problem would take us too far afield. Succinctly stated, my opinion is that, while viewed psychologically, there is nothing more real than evil, viewed metaphysically, we must follow Augustine's *De natura boni*. A few scattered and, no doubt, muddled thoughts that have occurred to me on this awful problem are to be found in my forthcoming article, "The Two Dimensions of Reality in *The Brothers Karamazov*," to be published in *Sewanee Review* in 1951.

CHAPTER XX

The Primacy of the Person

1. Nicolai Hartmann, "Moral Phenomena," in *Ethics* (New York: Macmillan Co., 1932), I, 316.
2. Clarence Irving Lewis, *An Analysis of Knowledge and Valuation* (LaSalle, Ill.: Open Court Pub. Co., 1946), p. 392.
3. *The Stoics and Epicurean Philosophers*, ed. with an Introduction by Whitney J. Oates (New York: Random House, 1940), p. 229; see also Paul Barth, *Los Estoicos* (Madrid: Revista de Occidente, 1930), p. 176.
4. Max Scheler, *Die Stellung des Menschen im Kosmos* (Munich: Nymphenburger Verlagshandlung, 1949), *passim*.
5. J. R. Jones, review of E. D. Adrian, *The Physical Background of Perception*, in *Mind*, LVII, No. 226 (April, 1948), 244–49.
6. See my criticism of Morris' aesthetics in "Two Notes on the New Naturalism," *Sewanee Review*, LVI, No. 3 (summer, 1948), 479 ff.
7. Søren Kierkegaard, *The Sickness unto Death* (Princeton: Princeton University Press, 1941), Book II, p. 32.
8. George Santayana, *The Realm of Spirit* (New York: Charles Scribner's Sons, 1940), p. ix.
9. W. David Ross, *Foundations*, p. 251.
10. A. de Waehlens, *La Filosofia de Martin Heidegger* (Madrid: Consejo Superior de Investigaciones Científicas, 1945), p. 270.

INDEX

INDEX

on logic and ontology, 321
cited, 368
Naturalism
meanings of, 16–22
cosmological, 19–20
methodological, 19–20
and teleology, 85
and philosophy of history, 85–86
of C. Perry, 91
and secularism, 124–25
and methodolatry, 130
and emergence, 150–55
and principle of continuity, 198–99
and being, 331
and reason, 332
and the analysis of person, 337–38
Naturalism and the Human Spirit
(Krikorian), cited, 349, 350,
355, 357, 363, 364, 368
Naturalistic value theory
vitalistic, 22
and value realism, 61
cannot assume pre-existing interests, 73
logical fallacies of, 81–82
material fallacies of, 81–85
and culture, 82–85
and individual, 86–89
and reductionism, 143, 199
Stevenson's, 164
viewed panoramically, 175–81
conception of man in, 199
and desire, 239–40
and discovery of ethical, 291–92
and psychoanalysis, 359–60
and multiple personality, 364
and the right, 367
Nature
Moore on, 19–20
bifurcation of, 63–64
control of, 256
and cosmic order, 321–23
Nature and Man (Weiss), 361
Nature of Thought, The (Blanshard),
366
Need (*see also* Desire; Impulse)
and moral vitalism, 22
hidden, 58
in functionalism, 195–97
and teleology, 203–5, 211
and espoused values, 212–13

and moral growth, 242
and its object, 266
and spirit, 333
and the right, 367
Neurath, O., 337–38
*New Introductory Lectures on Psycho-
analysis, The* (Freud)
origin of conscience, 140, 142
cited, 352, 354, 360
Nietzsche
on antivitalist tendency, 87
on keeping one's word, 147
psychological insight of, 189
cannot be dismissed, 317
Nominalism
of Stevenson, 159, 162
empirical, 203–4
and cosmic order, 321–22
Normative
valuation is, 114
theory of man needed, 118, 315
ethics and Stevenson, 156
criteria and psychology, 177
moral philosophy is, 254, 256
Notions which organize interests, 51
Novelty, 154, 201

Oates, W. J., 368
Object
of science, 63
of experience, 66
epistemic, 67
of moral transaction, 237
Object-cathexes, 141–42
Objective relativism, 166
Objectivity (*see also* Value, objectivity of)
and reality, 308
of spirit, 332–33
in science and philosophy, 365
Oppenheim, P., 361
Order of rank; *see* Value hierarchy
Order of universe, 207, 321–23
Organism
and crypto-emergence, 152
and causal inquiry, 201–2, 208
used by spirit, 342
Organization
of interests, 58
of constitutive values, 191

Suppression (repression)
  and genesis of conscience, 143–44
  and guilt, 146

Taboo, 83, 88
Taylor, A. E., 49, 95, 351, 352
Teacher, task of, 131–37
Teleology
  in cultures, 84
  "potentiality" and, 167–68
  and personality, 200–211
  and its cause, 321–23
Theism, 210
Theodicy, 323
Theology, 126–27
Theory of Valuation (Dewey), 106, 110, 131, 349, 356
Theory of Value, A (Reid), 359
Thorp, W., 368
Thrasymachus
  lucid advocate, 29
  as type, 297–99, 301–2, 310
  ancestor of Hobbes, James, and Stevenson, 315
  cannot be easily dismissed, 317
Thucydides, 98, 133, 136
Totalidad psiquica, La (Krueger), 363
Touchstone for Ethics (Huxley), 354, 360–61
Treatise of Human Nature, A (Hume), 14, 349
Truth
  relativistic theory of, 34–36
  is a value, 177
  feeling involved in discovery of, 222
  apodictic, not given to men, 249–50
  existential factor as condition of, 306–7
  not a univocal term, 323
Tufts, J. H., 103–6, 110, 112, 356

"Unconscious," 200
Unity, of science, 153
Universals, 238

Vaillant, G. C., 41, 350
Value
  absolute, 290, 321, 345
  acknowledged
    and of life, 59

  and obligation, 149
  includes "espoused" and "recognized," 190
  constitutes moral agent, 199
  and resolution of moral perplexity, 212–18, 266
  as basis of justification of decision, 269–70, 273
  aesthetic
    objectivity of, 68–70, 78–79
    Malinowski on origin of, 195
  basic, 166, 168
  carrier, 328
  constitutive
    not clearly known, 188–89
    discovered in crises, 190–92, 230, 240
    hierarchically organized, 199–200, 214–17
    how added to, 204, 227
    not well integrated, 235, 316
    and self-condemnation, 244
  criterion of
    lack of, in our age, 12
    for Hume, 15
    for Herskovits, 34
    acceptance not required of, 37
    in objective order, 273
    not consequence of espousal, 314
  espoused
    defined, 71
    relation of, to interest, 72–74
    and personality, 190
    and institutions, 213
    and recognized, 217–18
    and "deep-level" self, 228
    and wrongness, 232–33
    and self-creation, 241, 257, 267
  extrinsic, 69
  hierarchy of
    never perfect, 199–200
    appealed to, by social protestant, 215–19
    in question in moral perplexity, 316
    and its cause, 321–23
  inherent
    defined by Lewis, 69
    as potential, 168–69
    in person, 328
  instrumental, 69, 165